TEXTBOOK ON

CIVIL LIBERTIES

TEXTBOOK ON

CIVIL LIBERTIES

Professor Richard Stone, LLB, LLM

BLACKSTONE
PRESS LIMITED

First published in Great Britain 1994 by Blackstone Press Limited,
9-15 Aldine Street, London W12 8AW. Telephone: 081-740 1173

© R. Stone, 1994

ISBN: 1 85431 278 2

British Library Cataloguing in Publication Data
A CIP catalogue record for this book is available from the British Library

Typeset by Style Photosetting Limited, Mayfield, East Sussex
Printed by Ashford Colour Press, Gosport, Hampshire

Contents

1   Introduction   1

1.1 The political context   1.2 Human rights and civil liberties   1.3 Meaning of rights   1.4 Protection of liberties within the British Constitution   1.5 European Convention on Human Rights

2   Freedom of the Person I: Stop, Search and Arrest   29

2.1 Introduction   2.2 PACE and its codes   2.3 Stop and search   2.4 Arrest 2.5 Challenging the police   2.6 The European position

3   Freedom of the Person II: Detention and Questioning   55

3.1 Introduction   3.2 Preliminary procedures at the police station   3.3 Time for detention   3.4 Conditions during detention   3.5 Obtaining evidence during detention   3.6 Challenging the police   3.7 The European position

4   Property Rights: Entry, Search and Seizure   95

4.1 Introduction   4.2 Land and premises: rights of entry   4.3 Personal property: seizure powers   4.4 Personal property: production orders   4.5 Forfeiture and confiscation powers   4.6 Remedies   4.7 European Convention and property rights

5   Freedom of Expression I: Official Secrets and Freedom   130
of Information

5.1   The meaning of 'freedom of expression'   5.2 Arguments for the protection of freedom of expression   5.3 Arguments for and against official

6   Freedom of Expression II: Contempt of Court   168

7   Freedom of Expression III: Obscenity and Indecency   193

8   Freedom of Assembly   229

9   Freedom of Movement: The Right of Residence   256

10   Protection of Reputation and Privacy   282

11   Freedom from Discrimination   311

12   A Bill of Rights?   343

Preface

This is a law book, not a book on political or moral philosophy. Its aim is to provide an introduction to the legal rules which, in England and Wales, impinge on the area of civil liberties. This approach is one which I adopted when I first began to teach a course in civil liberties to law students, some 17 years ago. I thought then, and still think now, that the right starting point for the law student is to learn what the current legal rules are, before moving on to discuss the broader issues of policy, morality and politics. It is all very well to have strong views on, for example, the rights and wrongs of imposing restrictions on pornography; for the lawyer, however, it is important to know what the law actually does, and to appreciate the problems of turning policy into practice. This does not mean, of course, that the wider implications should be ignored altogether. Chapter 1, in particular, tries to place the subject in a broader context, and attempts are made throughout to point the directions in which a debate on such matters might proceed. The main focus, however, is on the law itself.

The approach in a book such as this is inevitably selective. There are areas which I might have dealt with, but have omitted, such as freedom of religion, prisoners' rights, or the right to life. Some may be surprised at some of the matters which are included. My aim, however, has been to cover a range of topics which will illustrate the variety of approaches which are taken within the English legal system to the protection and restriction of civil liberties. The influence of European Community law and the European Convention on Human Rights has generally been dealt with in separate sections towards the end of each chapter. It may well be that in time such an approach will have to be abandoned, and the European aspects incorporated into the main discussion. At the moment, however, my view is that separate treatment gives a more accurate impression of the practical impact of these areas. It is still the case that reference to European Community law or the European Convention is the exception: the vast majority of cases involving civil liberties issues are decided on the basis of domestic law alone.

It is hoped that this book will be of use to the law undergraduate, studying civil liberties as part of constitutional law, or as a course in its own right. This is the audience to whom it is primarily directed. I also hope that it may be of interest to anyone who seeks to discover the law that lies behind the headlines on such matters as police powers, official secrecy, public order and privacy.

The law is, as far as possible, stated as it stood on 1 August 1993, though one or two later developments have been noted.

I must take this opportunity to acknowledge the influence of two colleagues from Leicester University. First and foremost there is David Bonner, with whom I devised a civil liberties course in 1976, and with whom I have had the pleasure of teaching it from then until 1993. Our discussions and debates over the years, which I have greatly valued, have inevitably left their mark on my own thinking. Secondly, I have had the pleasure over the past two years of working with Noel Whitty. His fresh approach to a number of areas, and in particular that of freedom of speech, has encouraged me to think through my own position more thoroughly. However, while acknowledging the benefits that I have gained from working with both David and Noel, I must stress that neither of them has had any direct input into this book, and that any inadequacies in it must be laid squarely at my door.

The book was produced to a relatively tight schedule. As a result my wife, Maggie, and my children, have had to put up with more weekends than they should when I have disappeared into my study to worship at the twin gods of Macintosh and Microsoft. My heartfelt thanks go to them for their tolerance and support.

Richard Stone
Oadby
November 1993

Table of Cases

Table of Statutes

Table of EC Legislation

Table of International Conventions

ONE

Introduction

1.1   THE POLITICAL CONTEXT

The subject matter of this book is the extent to which civil liberties are protected, or more frequently, infringed, by the law of England and Wales. Later in this chapter it will be necessary to look at what is meant by the phrase 'civil liberties'. Before embarking upon that, however, the political context in which the discussion of the law is to take place must be considered.

As indicated in the Preface, this is a book about law, and legal rules, and not about political philosophy. All writing about law, however, involves the writer in making some assumptions about the political, economic and social context in which the law operates. Often these assumptions are implicit, as it is taken that the reader will share roughly the same viewpoint on such matters as the writer. In the context of a book on civil liberties, however, it is very important that these assumptions should as far as possible become explicit. The borderline between law and politics in this area is so narrow that the influence of one on the other cannot be ignored, and it is particularly important that the reader should know where the writer stands, and from which political viewpoint the subject is being approached.

Let me start, then, by placing my cards on the table. I write as a white, Anglo-Saxon male, brought up in the Christian tradition, but currently espousing no religious belief. What many would regard as some of the most influential years in the development of a person's ideas, those between the ages of 15 to 21, were for me largely spent in the 1960s, a time when in many parts of the Western world there was particularly strong youthful rebellion against authority, and advocacy of individual freedom. No doubt aspects of that background will subconsciously affect my approach to some of the civil liberties issues discussed in the following chapters. On the conscious level, my political adherence is to the broad framework of the modern Western liberal democracy, under which the people are ruled by an elected government, and laws are applied by independent courts. On the economic front, central government needs to exercise overall control, but private enterprise should generally be regarded as a beneficial aspect of society. The 'mixed' economy is the desirable model, though the most appropriate balance between the various elements in the mixture may be hard to determine.

Turning specifically to the issue of 'civil liberties', my starting point is the value of the individual human being, and the diversity between individuals. This leads to the demand that any interference with any aspect of an individual's life requires the strongest justification. To use the terminology of the legal process, the burden of proof lies on those who would restrict the freedom of the individual to show that such restriction is necessary. On this issue, and indeed on many other issues relating to civil liberties, I make no apology for the fact that, despite all that has been written on these topics over the past hundred years, I still find that many of my own feelings find their clearest expression in John Stuart Mill's *Essay on Liberty* (1859). In particular, the following much quoted passage is my starting point on a wide range of civil liberties issues:

> [T]he only purpose for which power can be rightfully exercised over any member of a civilised community against his will, is to prevent harm to others. His own good, either physical or moral, is not a sufficient warrant. He cannot rightfully be compelled to do or forbear because it will be better for him to do so, because it will make him happier, because, in the opinions of others to do so would be wise, or even right. These are good reasons for remonstrating with him, or reasoning with him, or persuading him, or entreating him, but not for compelling him, or visiting him with evil in case he do otherwise.

This focus on the individual, and individual freedom, means that I do not feel particularly sympathetic towards what for many people is becoming an increasingly important area of debate, that is, the issue of 'group rights' or 'collective rights'. Those who espouse this idea take the view that in some situations the need to promote the interests of a particular group which has suffered in the past in some way, means that the rights of the individual must be subordinated to the needs of the group. A particularly clear example of the difficulties that this can cause for those concerned with the protection of civil liberties arose from an inquiry by the National Council of Civil Liberties ('NCCL') into the the policing of the miners' strike of 1984. The conflict which this caused within the NCCL, and its place in the debate about collective and individual rights, is well summarised by Gostin in 'Towards resolving the conflict' (ch. 1 in *Civil Liberties in Conflict*, ed. L. Gostin, Routledge, 1988). The inquiry was established primarily to investigate the 'civil liberties implications of the role of the police' in relation to the strike. The interim report of the inquiry (*NCCL Independent Inquiry in to the Policing of the Miners' Strike*, Interim Report (1984), London: NCCL), however, made comments on such issues as whether:

> In the absence of policing, would mass pickets have physically prevented miners from going to work rather than peacefully trying to dissuade them? What were the nature and extent of violence or threats in mining

communities? Does picketing of the private home of a working miner infringe upon the civil liberties of his family? (*Civil Liberties in Conflict*, pp. 15–16.)

This led to the inquiry being criticised by both the NCCL Executive Committee and an NCCL Annual General Meeting, for exceeding its terms of reference, and because the recognition of an individual's right not to take part in an industrial dispute 'undermines the collective rights of others, and cannot be supported as a fundamental freedom'.

In this dispute my sympathies lie entirely with the members of the inquiry rather than the executive and AGM of the NCCL. The freedom of the individual is for me the highest good, and the tyranny of the majority is still tyranny even if exercised by a trade union rather than the organs of the State. It is not surprising, therefore, that the closest that this book comes to discussing 'group rights' is in chapter 11 which deals with discrimination on grounds of race or sex. Even here, however, it is the individual's right to equal treatment which is for me the fundamental issue, rather than the rights of women, blacks, etc, *as a group* to challenge oppression.

The emphasis on individual freedoms does not, of course, mean that they can never be challenged, nor that the needs of 'society' as a whole have to be ignored. When the behaviour of one individual causes harmful effects, and in particular, harmful effects to another individual, restraints on freedom may well be justified. The issue then becomes that of identifying precisely what kinds of harm will justify intervention. In chapters 3 and 4, police powers to restrict individual freedom are justified on the basis of the need to apprehend those involved with criminal activities (which society has by definition designated 'harmful'). The main problems here relate to the *extent* to which freedom should be able to be limited in relation to those who have not been convicted of any offence, and the *safeguards* which should be put in place to prevent abuse of the powers. In chapter 6, similar issues surround the discussion of publications which may prejudice a fair trial. In chapter 5, however, which is concerned with publications which may harm the 'State', and chapter 7, which is concerned with the control of obscene publications and related issues, the question of what exactly is 'harmful' in this context is a much more central matter of debate.

As will be seen, a range of harms is accepted by English law as justifying interference with freedoms in different contexts. Part of the issue under consideration in this book is the extent to which the definitions of 'harm' which are used are defensible, and acceptable, from a civil libertarian perspective.

1.2 HUMAN RIGHTS AND CIVIL LIBERTIES

The areas of individual freedoms which are discussed in this book are often discussed in terms of 'human rights'. This is particularly so in the international context, with documents such as the United Nations' Universal Declaration of Human Rights, and the European Convention on Human Rights. On the municipal level, however, the discussion is often in terms of civil liberties, and it is this phrase which has been used as the title of this book. Does it matter? In other words, are 'civil liberties' and 'human rights' interchangeable concepts? Or do the two phrases have differences in meaning which it may be important to identify?

There is no doubt that there is a large area of overlap. Three chapters of this book, for example, are concerned with issues related to freedom of expression, which is recognised as a 'human right' by both the Universal Declaration (Art. 19), and the European Convention (Art. 10). There are, however, two ways in which it may be important to distinguish between the two concepts. First, there is the question of the difference between a 'right' and a 'liberty'. This is discussed in the next section (1.3). Secondly, civil liberties can operate at a much more specific and detailed level than human rights. For example, Art. 6 of the European Convention on Human Rights recognises the right to a fair trial. It states the presumption of innocence (Art. 6(2)), and various other rights, such as the right to be informed of the charge, and the right to have time to prepare a defence. English law, however, recognises other rights or liberties in the criminal process which are not part of the Convention. For example, the right to silence, under which a person suspected of an offence is not obliged to answer questions, and no adverse inference may be drawn by a court from such refusal is not specifically recognised (though it should be noted that in *Funke* v *France* (1993) 16 EHRR 297 the Court assumed that Art. 6 protected the privilege against self-incrimination, and therefore a right of silence in this context: para. 44). This is regarded as a very important (though not uncontroversial) aspect of civil liberties within the English legal system. It cannot, however, be called a fundamental human right. It would be quite possible to protect the basic right to a fair trial without having a right to silence. A possible distinction is, therefore, to say that the human right is the right to a fair trial, whereas the means by which that right is protected within a particular domestic legal system comprise the individual's civil liberties. On this basis, therefore, civil liberties are subsidiary to human rights, and may legitimately be changed, provided that the human rights objectives which the particular liberties are intended to further are protected in some other way. The distinction cannot, however, be said to operate neatly and cleanly in all situations. The line between human rights and civil liberties, if indeed there is one, is blurred, and there is probably no particular benefit in spending much time in trying to make it more distinct.

1.3 MEANING OF RIGHTS

An issue which was raised in the previous section was the distinction, if any, between 'rights' and 'liberties'. It is important to consider the issue of what is meant by a 'right' for several reasons. First, because the concept of a 'right' is a strong one, it is at times used to give rhetorical force to an argument where its use may be questionable. For example in statements such as 'Everyone has a *right* to a house, or a job, or a decent standard of living', it is necessary to be careful to analyse what exactly is meant by a 'right'. Does it mean the same thing as when we assert a '*right* to life', or a '*right* to enforce a contract'? The distinction between positive and natural law approaches to rights should also be noted. This concerns the issue of the derivation of rights: are they purely creatures of a legal system of some kind, and therefore only exist when created by human beings (the positivist viewpoint), or can they be said to be based on some external source, such as a deity, or the nature of being human (the natural law approach)? Some argue, like the eighteenth/nineteenth century political philosopher, Jeremy Bentham, that the only proper use of the word rights is in relation to legal rights. In his 'Anarchical Fallacies' (reproduced in J. Waldron, ed., *Nonsense upon stilts*, London: Methuen, 1987) discussing Art. 2 of the *Declaration of the Rights of Man* of 1789, he commented scathingly (at p. 53):

Natural rights is simple nonsense: natural and imprescriptable rights, rhetorical nonsense — nonsense upon stilts.

Others (J. M. Finnis, in *Natural Law and Natural Rights*, Oxford: Clarendon Press, 1980 provides a good recent example) suggest that natural rights can be identified outside the confines of a positive legal system. This debate need not detain us long, however, since the rights which are dealt with in this book are all ones which are given recognition within municipal or international legal systems. As a matter of practice, therefore, we are dealing with positive rights, and need not concern ourselves with whether they have any other provenance.

The distinction of rights from liberties may also be important, if it helps us to resolve other difficult issues. If, for example, we decide that a 'right' is stronger than a 'liberty', then we may be able to resolve some situations where the interests of two individuals appear to be in conflict. If one individual has a 'right' and the other simply a 'liberty', then we can say that the right-holder should win, and the other party will have to accept a restriction of liberty.

The following sections look at some suggested analyses of the concepts of rights and liberties, starting with that of W.N. Hohfeld, who in his article 'Some Fundamental Legal Conceptions as Applied in Judicial Reasoning' (1913) 23 *Yale Law Journal* 16, made explicit the variety of meanings which lawyers (and others) often attempt to convey by use of the single word 'right'. Before looking at this, however, it is worth noting as a final introductory point, that although there is a tendency to talk about a right as if it were a 'thing' (and indeed in some situations 'rights' can be bought and sold in the same way as corporeal property), they are perhaps better regarded as a description of a *relationship* between two people, or perhaps between a person and property.

1.3.1   The Hohfeldian analysis of rights

Hohfeld argued that the relationships generally referred to when we are discussing legal rights can be analysed into eight distinct concepts. The four main ones, any of which might be meant when a person talks generally of 'rights', are 'right', 'privilege', 'power', and 'immunity'. There are four other concepts which are 'correlatives' to these, namely, and respectively, 'duty', 'no-right', 'liability' and 'disability'. What are the characteristics of these concepts?

1.3.1.1 Right or claim The characteristic of the 'right' or 'claim' is that it places a duty on others. Hohfeld's example relates to the ownership of land, and the right to exclude others:

> [I]f X has a right against Y that he shall stay off the former's land, the correlative (and equivalent) is that Y is under a duty toward X to stay off the place.

It could also apply to a contractual right, such as, for example, the right of a buyer in a sale of goods contract to demand delivery, or the seller to demand payment. In both situations the other party is under a duty to comply, and it is this which identifies the relationship as one of 'rights' in the strict sense. Hohfeld regarded the use of the word right in relation to such situations as its only 'proper' use.

1.3.1.2 Privilege Again, in defining a privilege Hohfeld uses an example taken from the ownership of land. The owner of a piece of land has the privilege of entering on the land. We might well say that he has a 'right' to do so; but, as Hohfeld points out, this is not a 'right' in the sense used above, because there is no correlative duty imposed on anyone. It is therefore better regarded as a privilege, to which the correlative is an absence of a right in anyone else to stop the person from entering. This absence he labels (for want of a better existing word) as a 'no-right'. As Hohfeld himself puts it, in trying to explain the distinction between the right properly so called and a privilege:

> the correlative of X's [the landowner's] right that Y shall not enter on the land is Y's duty not to enter; but the correlative of X's privilege of entering himself is manifestly Y's 'no-right' that X shall not enter.

A privilege has a lot of similarities to, and may even be a synonym for, what we should more usually call a freedom, or liberty. Thus freedom of speech is almost certainly a Hohfeldian 'privilege' rather than a 'claim-right'. There is no correlative duty to the freedom, simply no right in others to stop its exercise. As regards personal freedom, however, an individual has a right not to be interfered with (just as a landowner has a right to prevent trespass), and others are under a duty not to breach that right by assaults, etc.

1.3.1.3 Powers An example of a 'power' is the 'right' of the owner of goods to sell them. This is not a claim-right, because it involves no correlative duty. It is not a privilege either however, because it has the effect of creating liabilities in others, such as, for example, the person to whom the goods are sold. The correlative of a power is thus the existence of a liability on the part of another. The contractual situation of an offer which has not been accepted is in Hohfeldian terms a power on the part of the offeree (that is, to create a contract by accepting the offer) and a liability on the part of the offeror.

1.3.1.4 Immunity Hohfeld's example of an immunity is again drawn from land ownership. The owner of a piece of land has immunity from the exercise of powers by others over the land, and those others are consequently under a correlative 'disability'. Another example might be the power of a bailiff to seize goods in order to satisfy a debt. Under English law certain goods, such as the essentials of life or the tools of the debtor's trade, may not be seized. Here we might say that the debtor has a right that the articles should not be seized. In Hohfeldian terms it might also be said that the debtor has an immunity in relation to the exempted articles, and that the bailiff is likewise under a disability.

1.3.1.5 Conclusions on Hohfeld The analysis outlined above should not be taken as being by any means the last word on legal 'rights'. It has been the subject of criticism, particularly in relation to the concept of duty, which is not analysed (see, for example, J. Waldron, ed., *Theories of Rights*, Oxford University Press, 1984, p. 8). The most helpful aspects of the approach for our purposes are that, first, it reminds us to be careful in the use of the terminology of 'rights', to be sure that we know exactly what type of relationship we are discussing, and if we find that 'rights' appear to be in conflict, to make sure that we are comparing like with like. Secondly, the distinction between a 'claim-right' and a 'privilege' may well be helpful in the analysis of civil liberties, many of which may appear to be better categorised as privileges, or freedoms, rather than rights. This may be particularly so within a constitution like the British Constitution, which contains no document giving positive rights to particular freedoms, and imposing duties on others to uphold them, but leaves it to the courts to resolve specific cases on an *ad hoc* basis. Civil liberties may well then take on the status of privileges rather than rights, and as a result be less well protected than they should be.

1.3.2 Other analyses of rights
There have been many other attempts to analyse the nature of rights and liberties. In the area of moral philosophy discussion of the concept of the 'right' has developed an extensive literature. (For an introduction to a range of different approaches see, for example, J. Waldron, ed., *Theories of Rights*, Oxford University Press, 1984). It is beyond the scope of this book to venture into this debate. One writer, Ronald Dworkin, will be briefly considered, however, because he has centred his discussion of rights very much in the legal context. Like Hohfeld, Dworkin emphasises the need to take care in using the word 'right' and to be clear about what is meant by it. In 'Taking Rights Seriously' (ch. 7 in *Taking Rights Seriously*, Duckworth, 1977) he points out (at p. 188) that the word 'right' has a different force in different contexts:

> In most cases when we say that someone has a 'right' to do something, we imply that it would be wrong to interfere with his doing it, or at least that some special grounds are needed for justifying any interference.

This use of the word 'right' (which Dworkin refers to as the 'strong' sense) must be distinguished from the situation where it is said that a particular course of action is the 'right' thing for a person to do, or at least that the person would do no 'wrong' in pursuing it. As Dworkin points out (at pp. 188–189):

> Someone may have the right to do something that is the wrong thing for him to do, as might be the case with gambling. Conversely, something may be the right thing for him to do and yet he may have no right to do it . . . If our army captures an enemy soldier, we might say that the right thing for him to do is to try to escape, but it would not follow that it was wrong for us to try to stop him.

Applying this distinction to the civil liberties context, the claim that there is a right to freedom of speech, for example, is, Dworkin contends, using 'right' in the strong sense. As a result, governments may be criticised as doing wrong if they restrict this freedom, at least on something other than clearly defined, and exceptional grounds. It is inconsistent with the claim of a 'right' of free speech that a government could be justified in overriding it 'on the minimal grounds that would be sufficient if no such right existed' (see pp. 191–192).

Perhaps more importantly for our purposes, Dworkin aims to show, by his analysis of individual rights in the strong sense, the way in which they may be used to challenge utilitarian arguments (promoting the welfare of the majority) which would restrict individual freedom. See, for example, *Taking Rights Seriously*, at p. xi:

> Individual rights are political trumps held by individuals. Individuals have rights when, for some reason, a collective goal is not a sufficient justification for denying them what they wish, as individuals, to have or to do, or not a sufficient justification for imposing some loss or injury upon them.

This approach is very much in line with the view of individual rights which is taken in this book.

Finally, it may be worth drawing attention to the distinctions that it is possible to draw between 'political' rights, and 'social' or 'economic' rights. By political rights are meant such things as the right to life, freedom of the person, freedom of speech, freedom from discrimination. Economic and social rights are concerned with such things as the right to work, housing, education, etc. A distinction may be drawn on the basis that political rights do not in general call for any resources to be provided for people to be able to enjoy them. Economic and social rights, on the other hand, will generally require some allocation or redistribution of resources. For this reason, although in practical terms they may contribute far more directly than political rights to the welfare and happiness of individuals, there may well be a reluctance to enshrine them in a constitutional document. Governments may be happy enough to allow people to say what they want, but much less happy at a commitment to providing them with the means to earn a living. This difference may well encourage attempts to argue that economic and social rights are *essentially* different from political rights, and that political rights may be regarded as superior. This may lead on to the argument that it matters less if economic and social rights are infringed. This debate leads into difficult philosophical waters, which are again beyond the scope of this book; but it is nevertheless important to look carefully at attempts to categorise rights. What are the motives of the person doing the categorisation? Are the distinctions which are drawn valid? Are 'rights' which are given a lesser classification in fact any less important to the individual than those which are given the higher status?

From these broad issues, we now move to a consideration of the specific ways in which civil liberties are currently protected within the British Constitution.

1.4 PROTECTION OF LIBERTIES WITHIN THE BRITISH CONSTITUTION

There is no one constitutional document which provides the rules for the operation of the British Constitution, and the relationship between its various elements (sovereign, government, parliament, courts, etc). Whether this means that the British Constitution is 'unwritten', or simply 'uncodified' (see, for example, Pollard and Hughes, *Constitutional and Administrative Law*, Butterworths, 1990, p. 2), need not concern us. What is certainly true is that we have no equivalent to the United States' Bill of Rights, or the Canadian Charter of Rights: that is, a document which sets out a range of fundamental freedoms, and to which the government, legislature, and courts, must have regard in deciding what laws to enact and enforce, or how such laws should be interpreted. The nearest we get to it is the European Convention on Human Rights; but this is an international treaty, rather than an integral part of the English legal system, and thus only operates in a rather tangential way in relation to proceedings within our domestic institutions. Its role as a guide to the courts is considered in a later section (1.4.2); its availability as a source of redress for individuals who claim that their freedoms have been infringed is considered separately (1.5). Thus, although we have a number of important constitutional documents, such as Magna Carta (1215) and the Bill of Rights 1688 which deal with such matters as the limits of power of the monarch and parliament, they do not tell us what are the freedoms of the individual citizen of England or Wales. As regards freedom of speech, for example, the Bill of Rights 1688 simply states:

That the freedome of speech and debates or proceedings in Parlyament ought not to be impeached or questioned in any court or place out of Parlyament.

Members of parliament must be allowed to speak their minds, but this says nothing about any more general freedom of expression.

Protection of civil liberties in the 1990s in England and Wales therefore largely rests in the hands of parliament and the courts. Parliament should ensure that legislation is not passed which will unduly impinge on individual freedom; the courts should interpret the law so as to allow the greatest freedom possible, consonant with the clear dictates of the common law, or the wishes of parliament expressed through legislation. The next two sections of this chapter consider the way in which this role is played.

1.4.1 The role of parliament

There is no doubt that a government which tried to introduce legislation to remove all political rights from people who are left-handed would not succeed in getting it through parliament. Such a blatant and arbitrary attack on personal freedom would not be accepted. To that extent, parliament does act as a guardian of civil liberties. There are, however, several important limitations to the extent to which parliament can fulfil this role.

First, there is the danger of incremental infringement. Parliament may accept that one type of control is necessary. Its existence in one area may then justify its application to another, in a way that may in fact involve a more significant infringement of liberty. An example in recent years might be taken from the powers of the police to obtain access to confidential material. The Police and Criminal Evidence Act 1984 gave the police powers in certain situations to obtain a court order compelling people who hold personal or confidential information which is relevant evidence in relation to a serious criminal offence to hand it over. Subsequently, similar powers were included in the Drug Trafficking Offences Act 1986, and the Prevention of Terrorism (Temporary Provisions) Act 1989. In both cases the powers given look at first sight to be the same as those contained in the Police and Criminal Evidence Act. In fact, however, there are significant differences. In neither case under the later Acts does the material have to be 'evidence': it must simply be likely to be useful to police investigations. Moreover, whereas the procedure under the Police and Criminal Evidence Act involves an *inter partes* hearing, where the person from whom the information is sought can challenge the application by the police, in relation to both the other powers the hearing is *ex parte*. Thus the later powers involve a clear further encroachment on civil liberties, but one that was probably made easier by the fact that the first step in that direction had already been taken in the 1984 Act. (All of these powers are discussed in more detail in chapter 4, 4.4).

Another limitation on parliament's control is the fact that it may easily be 'panicked' into reacting with undue disregard for individual liberty by a situation of perceived emergency. The 1911 Official Secrets Act, which contained the notorious s. 2, making it an offence to reveal any information concerned with any government department, however innocuous, passed all its parliamentary stages in a day. Section 2 was not debated at all. The speed was justified on the basis of alleged dangers from German espionage activity. Whatever the justification for that fear, the fact remains that parliament played no role as a guardian of civil liberties, and allowed the enactment of a provision which acted as a serious restraint on freedom of expression for nearly 80 years. (For further discussion of this area, see chapter 5).

This limitation does not arise solely from the situation where a government has a large majority and can therefore by and large legislate as it pleases. In the mid-1980s a private members' Bill was introduced to establish a comprehensive scheme of pre-censorship for videocassettes. Because of a fear, which had been fanned by some sensational press reporting, of some very dubious research which purported to show massive viewing among children of so-called 'video-nasties', the civil liberties implications of the Bill received little or no attention. To suggest that it might be unnecessary, or too restrictive, would have been to be labelled as being in favour of polluting the minds of young people with sex and violence. MPs with an eye on the reaction of their constituency if they were identified with the opposition to this Bill, were unlikely to speak against it. It was much safer to support it, and turn a blind eye to the fact that it was introducing the most restrictive control over the home viewing of videos to be applied anywhere in Europe. (This case is discussed further in chapter 7, 7.5.2).

A similar problem arises with any attempt to raise civil liberties issues in relation to measures designed to attack terrorist activities. The problem is not so much that it is decided that the rights of the individual must give way to the desire to prevent moral pollution, or to control terrorists, but that this issue is never even raised.

For all the above reasons it is impossible to take parliament seriously as an effective guardian of individual liberty, other than at the most general level.

1.4.2   The role of the courts

If parliament cannot fulfil this role effectively, can the courts do so? There is no doubt that our judges do at times take seriously the need to protect individual freedom. There are two limitations on their effectiveness, however, one constitutional and one practical. The constitutional limitation is that the courts are subordinate to parliament, and cannot decide to ignore the clear provisions of legislation which has been properly passed (*British Railways Board* v *Pickin* [1974] AC 765), unless, perhaps, it is in conflict with the United Kingdom's legal obligations under European Community law (*Factortame Ltd* v *Secretary of State for Transport* [1990] 2 AC 85). The practical limitation is that, even where there is ambiguous statute law, or none at all, the judges have no guidelines as to the weight to be given to arguments of individual liberty, and how these are to be measured against the needs or demands of society as a whole. We will, for example, see in chapter 8 that Lord Denning in one case expressed strong support for the individual's freedom to participate in public protest on matters of concern, but made this subject to there being no 'disruption to the traffic'. This might be thought to be giving undue weight to the maintenance of uninterrupted progress on the highway, as opposed to the right to demonstrate public support for a cause, but there is no easy way for a judge to draw the line between such issues. The approach of the courts to this difficulty in relation to claims for freedom of expression has been carefully examined by Alan Boyle ('Freedom of Expression as a Public Interest in English Law', [1982] *PL* 574). His conclusion (pp. 609–610) is that freedom of expression has been recognised by the English courts as an important public interest, but that it is not treated as an 'absolute value'. As a result, where there has been a conflict with opposing public interests, the weighing of those interests, and the exercise of judicial judgment necessarily involved, has in many cases led to a decision which is 'unfavourable to the precise claims made in the name of freedom of expression'. The problem is 'not that judges do not recognise the value or relevance of freedom of expression, but rather when they do, they fail to give enough importance to it' (see p. 610).

A good example of the courts' approach to civil liberties issues is to be found in two recent cases concerned with the privilege against self-incrimination. In *Lam Chi Ming* v *R* [1991] 3 All ER 172, the Privy Council was considering an appeal from Hong Kong as to the admissibility of certain video recordings as evidence against the accused in a murder trial. The recordings, which were produced by the police and showed the accused indicating where the murder weapon had been disposed of, were admitted by the judge, although he refused to admit confessions which the accused had made prior to the recordings, on the basis that these had been extracted by police brutality, and were not voluntary. In holding that the video evidence should not have been admitted, Lord Griffiths, giving the opinion of the Privy Council, said (at p. 179):

> The privilege against self-incrimination is deep rooted in English law, and it would make a grave inroad upon it if the police were to believe that if they improperly extracted admissions from the accused which were subsequently shown to be true they could use those admissions against the accused for the purpose of obtaining a conviction.

Applying this approach to the video recordings, he felt that:

> it is surely just as reprehensible to use improper means to force a man to give information that will reveal he has knowledge that will ensure his conviction as it is to force him to make a full confession.

Thus, in this case, the court not only recognises the strength of the individual's privilege against self-incrimination, but allows it to be applied in a broad way to achieve its overall purpose, even where it is concerned with incriminating actions (that is, the indication of the whereabouts of the murder weapon) as opposed to statements. This approach may then be contrasted with that of Lord Mustill, speaking on behalf of a unanimous House of Lords, in *Smith* v *Director of Serious Fraud Office* [1992] 3 All ER 456. The House was considering whether the power to question a person under investigation given to the Serious Fraud Office by s. 2 of the Criminal Justice Act 1987, was limited by the general prohibition on questioning after charge, revealed by the caution required to be administered on charging with an offence (that is, 'You do not have to say anything unless you wish to do so, but what you say may be given in evidence', see Police and Criminal Evidence Act 1984, Code of Practice C, para. 16.5). The matter was further complicated in that s. 2 of the 1987 Act, where applicable, *requires* the person under investigation to answer questions. Lord Mustill referred (at p. 471) to the opinion of Lord Griffiths in *Lam Chi Ming* v *R* regarding the importance of the privilege against self-incrimination, and confirmed that he himself would not wish 'to minimise its importance in any way.' He then went on to note, however, that there had been many occasions where there had been statutory interference with the privilege. After a careful analysis of the nature of the privilege, and the general reasons for the prohibition on questioning after charge, he came to the conclusion (at p. 474) that the provisions of s. 2 must take precedence:

> . . . the principle of common sense, expressed in the maxim *generalia specialibus non derogant*, entails that the general provisions of Code C yield to the particular provisions of the 1987 Act in cases to which that Act applies; and that neither history nor logic demands that any qualification of what parliament has so clearly enacted ought to be implied.

In other words, the courts are bound to apply the clear words of a particular statute, even where this appears to conflict with generally accepted civil libertarian principles. The criticism here is not that the judges fail to take civil liberties issues seriously: Lord Griffiths's approach in *Lam Chi-Ming*, and Lord Mustill's thorough analysis in *Smith*, both indicate otherwise. Whereas, however, in a situation governed primarily by common law (as in *Lam Chi-Ming*), those liberties can be given full effect, once parliament has intervened (as in *Smith*), the courts may be insufficiently willing to use their powers of interpretation to allow the language of a statute to be limited by general principles. For these reasons it cannot be said that the courts provide a mechanism for more than a partial protection of our liberties.

This is not to deny that the *mechanisms* for control of the executive branch of government have not been developed. The remedies available by means of the application for judicial review will be referred to at numerous points during the rest of the book. And in *M* v *Home Office* [1993] 3 All ER 537 the House of Lords confirmed that even Ministers of the Crown are bound to obey court orders (in this case, not to deport an individual pending a further hearing of his case). The problem is that these mechanisms can only be effective where parliament allows them to be so. If the executive can prevail upon parliament to enact laws in specific and unambiguous terms which allow government Ministers, or others, to act in ways which impinge on civil liberties, the courts will not intervene. The only possibility of their doing so is where the law is for some reason unclear. If this is the case, the courts may rely on 'general principles' to try to determine the issue, or may now in some cases turn to the European Convention on Human Rights for guidance.

1.4.2.1 European Convention on Human Rights ('ECHR') As will be explained in the next section (1.5), the Convention is an international treaty to which the United Kingdom has subscribed, and which sets out a range of human rights which should be protected within the domestic legal systems of States which are signatories. In some countries the ECHR has been made a directly enforceable part of the domestic legal system; that approach has not been adopted in the United Kingdom. The starting point for the current significance of the Convention in deciding cases is to be found in Lord Denning's statement in *R* v *Chief Immigration Officer, Heathrow Airport, ex parte Salamat Bibi* [1976] 3 All ER 843 (at p. 847):

The position as I understand it is that if there is any ambiguity in our statutes, or uncertainty in our law, then these courts can look to the convention as an aid to clear up any ambiguity or uncertainty, seeking always to bring them into harmony with it . . . But I would dispute altogether that the convention is part of our law. Treaties and declarations do not become part of our law until they are made law by parliament.

This amounted to a retreat from a rather stronger statement made by Lord Denning in the earlier case of *R* v *Secretary of State for the Home Department, ex parte Bhajan Singh* [1976] QB 198, where he had suggested that the provisions of the ECHR might be directly applicable to immigration officers in their operation of the Immigration Act 1971. Later cases have confirmed that the ECHR should only be used to clarify ambiguities and fill gaps.

What if the gap is total? In other words, there is no statute or common law authority governing a particular situation, but it is one that appears to be covered by one of the rights contained in the ECHR? This issue had to be confronted by Sir Robert Megarry VC, in *Malone* v *Metropolitan Police Commissioner* [1979] Ch 344, where it was argued that phone tapping constituted an infringement of a general right of privacy, as guaranteed by Art. 8 of the ECHR. While accepting that the ECHR could be used as an aid to interpretation, Sir Robert concluded (at p. 379) that this could not assist the plaintiff in the present case:

I readily accept that if the question before me were one of construing a statute enacted with the purpose of giving effect to obligations imposed by the Convention, the court would readily seek to construe the legislation in a way that would effectuate the Convention rather than frustrate it. However, no relevant legislation of that sort is in existence. It seems to me that where parliament has abstained from legislating on a point that is plainly suitable for legislation, it is indeed difficult for the court to lay down new rules of common law or equity that will carry out the Crown's treaty obligations, or to discover for the first time that such rules have always existed.

The ECHR cannot therefore be used to create new rights (in this case a general right of privacy), but only to give effect (by interpretation of the law) to those which have already been recognised.

Even within this agreed approach to the use of the ECHR as an aid to interpretation, there have been divergences in the enthusiasm with which different judges have looked to its provisions. Compare, for example, the approach of Lord Diplock with that of Lord Scarman, in *Harman* v *Secretary of State for the Home Department* [1983] AC 280. Lord Diplock took the view (at p. 299) that the case was '*not* about freedom of speech'. Futhermore, it did not:

call for consideration of any of those human rights and fundamental freedoms which in the European Convention of Human Rights are contained in separate articles each starting with a statement in absolute terms but followed immediately by very broadly stated exceptions.

Lord Scarman, on the other hand, thought it appropriate to give detailed consideration to various Articles of the ECHR, and concluded (at p. 317) that to interpret the law against the plaintiff 'might well be inconsistent with the requirements of the European Convention'. A similar conflict between the same two judges occurred in *Secretary of State for Defence* v *Guardian Newspapers* [1985] AC 339, in relation to the proper interpretation of s. 10 of the Contempt of Court Act 1981 (see 6.2.7).

The most recent consideration of the relevance of the ECHR to the interpretation of statutory powers occurred in *R* v *Secretary of State for the Home Department, ex parte Brind* [1991] 1 All ER 720. This concerned the exercise by the Home Secretary of the power under s. 29(3) of the Broadcasting Act 1981 to issue a 'notice' requiring the Independent Broadcasting Authority 'to refrain from broadcasting any matter or classes of matter specified in the notice'. In 1988, with the aim of depriving those connected, directly or indirectly, with terrorist activity related to Northern Ireland of the 'oxygen of publicity', the Home Secretary issued a notice (which is still in force) prohibiting the broadcasting on television or radio of the voices of any person speaking on behalf of a 'proscribed organisation' (for which, see the Prevention of Terrorism (Temporary Provisions) Act 1989, s. 1), or one of the political groups thought to have links with terrorists, namely Sinn Fein, Republican Sinn Fein, and the Ulster Defence Association. The words used could be reported, provided that the voice of the spokesperson was not broadcast. The challenge to this prohibition was, in the House of Lords, based primarily on the argument that it was contrary to the United Kingdom's obligations under Art. 10 of the ECHR, guaranteeing freedom of expression. It was said that the Home Secretary should have had regard to the ECHR in exercising the discretion under s. 29(3). The House of Lords was quite prepared to accept that there was a presumption that parliament would enact laws that were in conformity with the ECHR. Thus, where a statute permits of two interpretations, one in line with the ECHR, the other contrary to it, the interpretation which fits with the ECHR should be preferred. The House of Lords was not prepared to accept, however, that where a discretion was to be exercised, it must be presumed that parliament intended that it should be exercised having regard to the ECHR. As Lord Bridge pointed out (at p. 723), that would go beyond the resolution of ambiguity, and would in effect compel the courts to enforce conformity with the ECHR:

> by the importation into domestic administrative law of the text of the Convention and the jurisprudence of the European Court of Human Rights in the interpretation and application of it.

Applying this approach to the case before it, the House could find no ambiguity in s. 29(3). The only basis for challenge was therefore that the Home Secretary's decision was unreasonable in the *Wednesbury* sense. In assessing the reasonableness there was no need to take account of the ECHR. (For '*Wednesbury* unreasonableness', which means essentially that the exercise of discretion must not be irrational, see, for example, D. W. Pollard and D. J.

Hughes, *Constitutional and Administrative Law*, Butterworths, 1990, pp. 405–408).

The scope for using the ECHR in the interpretation of statutes is thus accepted, but severely limited. The situation is much the same when we turn to the common law.

The most recent discussion of this issue appears in *Derbyshire County Council* v *Times Newspapers Ltd* [1993] 1 All ER 1011, which was concerned with the question of whether a local council could bring an action for libel (see 10.2). In deciding that it could not, the Court of Appeal ([1992] 3 All ER 65) placed strong reliance on the ECHR. Balcombe LJ held that, on the basis of earlier authorities, Art. 10 of the ECHR could be used in three situations:

(a)   to resolve ambiguities in legislation (as has been noted above);
(b)   in considering the principles on which the court should exercise a discretion (for example, whether or not to grant an interlocutory injunction (*Attorney General* v *Guardian Newspapers Ltd* [1987] 3 All ER 316; *Re W (A Minor) (Wardship: Restriction on Publication)* [1992] 1 All ER 794));
(c)   when the common law is uncertain.

All three members of the Court of Appeal agreed that the common law was uncertain on the relevant issue, and that the court was therefore entitled to take account of the ECHR in deciding the case. The plaintiffs appealed, and the House of Lords, while agreeing with the result arrived at in the Court of Appeal, did so without relying on Art. 10 of the ECHR. Lord Keith said (at p. 1021):

I have reached my conclusion upon the common law of England without finding any need to rely upon the European Convention. Lord Goff in *Attorney-General* v *Guardian Newspapers Ltd (No 2)* [1990] 1 AC 109 expressed the opinion that in the field of freedom of speech there was no difference in principle between the English law on the subject and article 10 of the Convention. I agree, and can only add that I find it satisfactory to be able to conclude that the common law of England is consistent with the obligations assumed by the Crown under the Treaty in this particular field.

While it may be a little disappointing to see Lord Keith downplaying the importance of the ECHR in this way, it is important to note that he did not dissent from Balcombe LJ's approach, either. It seems clear, then, that in resolving uncertainties in the common law the ECHR *may* be considered (cf *Rantzen* v *Mirror Group Newspapers, The Times*, 6 April 1993). It does not appear, however, that there is any *obligation* on the courts to resolve issues in this way. Other sources, as for instance in the *Derbyshire* case, the jurisprudence of the United States Supreme Court, may be looked at in reaching a conclusion.

It is probably to be expected that consideration of the ECHR in relation to the interpretation of both statutes and common law will increase, now that the English courts have opened the door to its consideration, and that the judges seem happy to take it into account, although with varying levels of enthusiasm. An example of the kind of approach that may well be expected to occur in the future is to be found in *R v Advertising Standards Authority, ex parte Vernons Organisation* [1993] 2 All ER 202. Laws J was considering an application for an order prohibiting the publication of a report by the Advertising Standards Authority, pending an action for judicial review in relation to the report. In refusing the application, Laws J said that such restraint on publication should only be allowed 'on pressing grounds'. Referring specifically to 'the language of Strasbourg' (that is, of the European Court of Human Rights, which sits in Strasbourg), he indicated that there would have to be a 'pressing social need' in order to restrain the authority form carrying out its functions in the ordinary way. We may perhaps expect that 'the language of Strasbourg', and therefore the principles of the European Court, will gradually, but ever more frequently, become accepted as part of English jurisprudence, and that the ECHR and the common law will continue to converge, even without the formal adoption of the Convention into English law.

1.5   EUROPEAN CONVENTION ON HUMAN RIGHTS

As we have seen in the previous section, the ECHR is an increasingly important source for the interpretation of English law. It also contains, however, a procedure whereby individuals and States may challenge the actions of other States as being contrary to the Convention. This procedure is available to UK citizens, and is thus a method by which English law may be challenged on the basis that it infringes one of the rights guaranteed by the ECHR. Before looking at the detail of this procedure, however, and the specific rights which are protected under the Convention, it is desirable to consider first the background to it, since this provides some explanation of its style and content.

1.5.1   Background
The ECHR was signed in Rome on 4 November 1950, and came into force on 3 September 1953. Its immediate background was the Second World War (1939–1945) and the subsequent Nuremberg Trials, which had involved the investigation of many atrocities and abuses of human rights. It was produced by the Council of Europe, which was then a group of ten (currently twenty-five) European nations formed in May 1949 with a view to promoting international action and collaboration to protect human rights. The Convention was inevitably to some extent a compromise, as regards both content and procedures, given that it was the result of negotiation between countries with varied histories and constitutional systems. This needs to be kept in mind when looking at the provisions of the Convention, and is an issue to which we shall return in chapter 12, in considering the ECHR as a model for a possible British 'Bill of Rights'.

The other point which it is important to remember, as it is often a source of confusion, is that there is no direct connection (though there is a considerable overlap of membership) between the Council of Europe and the European

Community. Both the ECHR and the EC have a Commission and a Court, but these are entirely separate pairs of institutions. Both of the ECHR institutions are based in Strasbourg, whereas the EC Commission is in Brussels, and the European Court of Justice sits in Luxembourg. The European Court of Justice has at times looked to the ECHR as a source for fundamental rights, but the Convention has no formal role within the law of the European Communities.

1.5.2 Procedure

There are two ways in which the provisions of the ECHR can be enforced. First, there is a procedure under Art. 24 whereby any *State* which is a party to the Convention can bring an application alleging breach of its provisions against another State which is a party. There has been relatively little use of this procedure, though one notable case, which involved the United Kingdom, was *Ireland* v *United Kingdom* (Series A, vol 25, 18 January 1978). This resulted in a finding by the Court that certain interrogation practices used by the British Army in Northern Ireland amounted to 'inhuman and degrading treatment' contrary to Art. 3 of the ECHR.

Secondly, Art. 25 provides for applications by individuals, groups of individuals, or non-governmental organisations. In each case the applicant must be an alleged victim of a violation by one of the State parties to the Convention. This is not an automatic right: it only arises where it has been accepted by the State against which the complaint has been lodged. The United Kingdom has accepted such claims since 1966, but not on a permanent basis. The current acceptance was renewed in 1991 and runs until 1996. Most of the claims against the United Kingdom have been the result of applications by individuals.

It will be noted that in relation to both types of claim, the proceedings must be taken against a State. The ECHR is not concerned with infringements of human rights which are the responsibility of other individuals, or non-governmental organisations. It would not be possible to use Art. 8, for example, which recognises a right of privacy, directly against press intrusions. A challenge might, however, be possible on the basis that the State had failed in its duty under Art. 1 to 'secure to everyone within [its] jurisdiction the rights and freedoms defined' in the Convention. The Court accepted this approach in *Young, James and Webster* (1982) 4 EHRR 38 (which was concerned with trade union exclusive membership agreements, commonly known as the 'closed shop'), holding (at para. 49) that:

> if a violation of one of those rights and freedoms is the result of a non-observance of the obligation in the enactment of domestic legislation, the responsibility of the State is engaged.

The failure of English law to recognise, either under the common law, or statute, a right of privacy, might therefore, in an appropriate case, justify an application under the ECHR against the United Kingdom.

A claim under either Art. 24 or 25 is initially considered by the Commission. It may subsequently come before the Court or the Committee of Ministers.

The respective roles, and the relationship between these three bodies, must now be considered.

1.5.2.1 The role of the Commission The constitution of the Commission is governed by Arts 20–23. It consists of one member for each State party to the Convention. The members serve as individuals, however, rather than as representatives of a particular State (Art. 23). On receiving an application the Commission will first consider whether it is 'admissible'. This is governed by the provisions of Art. 26 (in respect of all applications), and Art. 27 (in respect of applications other than by States).

Article 26 requires that all 'domestic remedies' have been exhausted before a claim will be considered. The ECHR does not therefore operate as a parallel jurisdiction to the domestic one, but as a court of 'last resort'. This does not necessarily mean, however, that only those cases which in the United Kingdom have been heard by the House of Lords can result in an admissible application. Where an appeal would undoubtedly be rejected, because there is, for example, clear binding authority which goes against the applicant, the application may be accepted. On the other hand, it appears that if there are *administrative* as opposed to legal remedies which might be pursued, it will nevertheless be expected that these should be pursued before petitioning the Commission (see *Golder* v *United Kingdom* (Series A, vol 18, 21 February 1975: appeal to the Home Secretary by a prisoner). Art. 26 also requires that the claim must be made within six months of the final decision in relation to the domestic remedies.

Under Art. 27 there are several grounds for declaring an application inadmissible. First, the Commission may not deal with a claim which is anonymous, or which is substantially the same as one which has already been examined by the Commission or been submitted to 'another procedure of international investigation or settlement' (for example, in connection with the United Nations' human rights activities) (Article 27(1)). Secondly, any application which the Commission considers 'incompatible with the provisions' of the ECHR (that is, not within its scope), or 'manifestly ill-founded' (within its scope, but showing no *prima facie* case of a breach), or 'an abuse of the right of petition', will be ruled inadmissible (Article 27(2)). The Commission normally decides issues by a majority vote (Article 34), but where an application has been accepted, and during the course of investigation it appears that one of the grounds of inadmissibility applies, a decision to reject the application at that stage must be unanimous (Article 29).

Only a small percentage (under 10 per cent: see Bailey, Harris and Jones, *Civil Liberties Cases and Materials*, 3rd edn, Butterworths, 1991, p. 757) of applications are declared admissible. This may well suggest that there is a considerable unfilled need in relation to human rights grievances.

Once the Commission has found an application admissible, it will investigate it (Art. 28). This will involve ascertaining the facts through representations (including oral representations) by the parties. The Commission may conduct its own investigation, if necessary. The object at this stage is to try to secure a 'friendly settlement' of the dispute. For example, in one case involving the United Kingdom, challenging an aspect of English contempt law, a settlement was reached on the basis of an agreement that the law would be amended, and the costs of the applicant paid by the government (*Harman* v *UK*, Report of 15 May 1986, 46 DR 57). As we shall see, in two of the corporal punishment cases, the settlement took the form of the payment of compensation, plus costs (see 1.5.4).

If a friendly settlement is not possible, the Commission must draw up a report on the facts, and give its opinion (which may be by a majority vote) as to whether the facts disclose a breach by the State concerned of any of its obligations under the Convention (Art. 31). The Report is sent to the Committee of Ministers, and to the State or States concerned (who are *not* entitled to publish it), but not, at this stage, to an individual applicant. It does not in itself have any legal status, but may form the basis for a ruling by the Court.

1.5.2.2 The role of the Court The European Court of Human Rights consists of a number of judges equal to the number of member States of the Council of Europe. The judges are elected by the Consultative Assembly of the Council of Europe from candidates nominated by the member States. Judges are usually, but not necessarily, nationals of the State which nominates them (Liechtenstein is currently represented by a Canadian judge). The procedure for the election is set out in Art. 39.

Cases can only come before the Court after they have been considered and reported on by the Commission. Thereafter the case can be referred to the Court by the Commission itself, a member State whose national is alleged to be a victim, a member State which referred the case to the Commission, or a member State against which the complaint was lodged (Art. 48). Note that the individual applicant has no power to refer the case to the Court. The Ninth Protocol to the ECHR 1990, ETS 140, provides for such a power, but it seems unlikely that this will come into force in the foreseeable future, and in any case the UK government has apparently no intention of accepting this Protocol (Bailey, Harris, and Jones, *Civil Liberties Cases and Materials*, Butterworths, 3rd edn, p. 759).

Under the current rules of procedure adopted by the Court, an individual applicant will be notified when a case has been referred to Court, and given the opportunity (while not strictly being a party to the case) to present arguments in person, or through a lawyer.

Once it has heard the arguments of the Commission, the State parties and, if applicable, the individual applicant, the Court will issue a judgment, declaring whether or not there has been a breach of the Convention. The judgment need not be unanimous, and indeed dissenting judgments are common. The issue of a judgment finding that a State's laws are in breach of the Convention, will impose an obligation under international law on that State to bring itself into line. The decision of the Court in the *Sunday Times* case (1979) 2 EHRR 245 (below, 6.4), for example, led to amendments in the English law of contempt of court (Contempt of Court Act 1981, see 6.2.2). The Court also has the power to order an infringing State to make 'just satisfaction' to an injured party. This may take the form of financial compensation, as for example in *Young, James and Webster* (1982) 4 EHRR 38, where it related to loss of earnings and injury to feelings. It may also simply amount to a contribution towards the applicant's costs, as in the *Spycatcher* cases (*The Observer and The Guardian* v *The United Kingdom* (1992) 14 EHRR 153; *The Sunday Times* v *The United Kingdom* (1992) 14 EHRR 229; see 5.8).

1.5.2.3 The role of the Committee of Ministers If a case is not referred to the Court within three months of the Commission's Report, the case falls to be dealt with by the Committee of Ministers (Art. 32). This consists of the Foreign Ministers of the member States of the Council of Europe. The Committee, without any further hearing, decides whether there has been a violation of the Convention. The decision must be by at least a two-thirds majority of those entitled to sit. If it is decided that there has been a violation, the Committee will indicate the measures which must be taken by the State which is in breach, and give a time limit for compliance (Art. 32(2)). If there is a failure to comply, the Committee, again by a two-thirds majority, must decide 'what effect shall be given to its original decision', and will also publish the Commission's Report (Art. 32(3)). The remedies available to the Committee are not very clear. In particular, it must be assumed, since there is no mention of it, that the Committee does not have the power to order the payment of compensation to an individual victim of a breach of the Convention. The sanction on a State which fails to comply must be primarily one of international pressure, with the threat of expulsion from the Council of Europe as the ultimate penalty. In 1970 Greece temporarily withdrew from the Council of Europe in the face of a finding by the Committee of Ministers that it had committed breaches of various Articles of the ECHR, including torture under Art. 3.

1.5.3 Content of the ECHR
The rights protected by the ECHR are broadly stated, and primarily 'political'. A number of the articles deal with basic personal freedoms. These include the right to life (Art. 2), freedom from torture, etc (Art. 3), freedom from slavery (Art. 4), the right to liberty and security of the person (Art. 5), and the right to marry and have children (Art. 12). Articles 6 and 7 are concerned with fair treatment within the legal process, and Art. 8 with privacy. Articles 9 and 10 deal with freedom of conscience, religion, and expression, and Art. 11 with freedom of assembly and association. Article 14 provides that the enjoyment of the other rights provided for in the Convention must be secured without discrimination on grounds of 'sex, race, colour, language, religion, political or other opinion, national or social origin, association with a national minority, property, birth, or other status'.

Two points may be made about this list. First, despite the fact that the preamble recognises the importance of 'effective political democracy', none of the rights given relate specifically to this. Thus, there is no right to elect a government, or otherwise to participate in the institutions of democracy. This may well be a reflection of the diverse constitutional backgrounds of the original contracting parties. Secondly, not all the rights are given in an unqualified form. Articles 5, 8, 9, 10 and 11 are all subject to significant limitations that may be considered 'necessary in a democratic society'. A striking contrast may be drawn, for example, between the First Amendment to the United States Constitution, which states, without qualification, 'Congress shall make no law . . . abridging the freedom of speech, or of the press'. Article 10 of the ECHR starts equally strongly: 'Everyone has the right to freedom of expression'. Even before the end of the first paragraph, however, the limitations start: 'This Article shall not prevent States from requiring the licensing of broadcasting, television or cinema enterprises'. Then, in Art. 10(2), further restrictions are permitted (on the basis that freedom of expression carries with it duties and responsibilities), in the interests of:

> national security, territorial integrity or public safety, for the prevention of disorder or crime, for the protection of health or morals, for the protection of the reputation or rights of others, for preventing the disclosure of information received in confidence, or for maintaining the authority and impartiality of the judiciary.

This lengthy list of exceptions detracts considerably from the force of the opening statement of the right. It is perhaps another reflection of the origins of the ECHR in a political compromise between a group of nations, and is indicative of a rather pragmatic, rather than evangelistic, approach to the promotion of human rights and civil liberties.

The ECHR, perhaps for similar reasons, does not venture into 'social rights', relating to housing, employment, etc. The closest that it comes to this is in Art. 2 of the First Protocol to the Convention (Cmd 9221, 1952), which states that 'no person shall be denied the right to education'. It continues:

> In the exercise of any functions which it assumes in relation to education and to teaching, the State shall respect the right of parents to ensure such education and teaching in conformity with their own religious and philo- sophical convictions.

Although the UK government is a party to the Protocol, it has made a reservation that it accepts the principle as to parents' rights only in so far as 'it is compatible with the provision of efficient instruction and training, and the avoidance of unreasonable public expenditure'. Social rights are always liable to face difficulties in relation to resources, and it is not perhaps surprising to find the UK government avoiding what might be, particularly in an increasing- ly multi-cultural, and multi-religious, society, a very expensive commitment.

1.5.4 The ECHR in practice: the corporal punishment cases
At various points in the rest of this book, generally in the final section of each chapter, the specific provisions of the ECHR relevant to a particular area will be considered, and any case law discussed. The opportunity is taken here, however, to discuss a group of cases which are not discussed elsewhere, but

which may be used as examples of the way in which the ECHR operates in practice. These are the cases concerned with corporal punishment.

The first case to come before the Court was *Tyrer* v *United Kindgom* (1978) 2 EHRR 1. The applicant, when 15, had been convicted of an assault occasioning actual bodily harm, and had been sentenced by a juvenile court in the Isle of Man to three strokes of the birch. Sentence was passed on 7 March 1972. Following an unsuccessful appeal, it was carried out on 28 April 1972. The applicant was examined by a doctor, and then (2 EHRR 4):

> He was made to take down his trousers and underpants and bend over a table; two policemen held him while a third administered the punishment . . . The applicant's skin was raised but not cut and he was sore for about a week and a half afterwards.

The applicant then applied to the Commission, alleging that the United Kingdom, being responsible for the Isle of Man's international relations, was in breach of Art. 3 of the ECHR, which prohibits torture and inhuman or degrading treatment or punishment. The Commission found that there was a breach of Art. 3, and also that there was an admissible issue relating to Art. 14 (which prohibits discrimination on the grounds of, *inter alia*, sex) in that the punishment was only available in relation to young males. Despite the fact that the applicant had indicated a wish to withdraw the application, the Commission then referred it to the Court. This indicates that the procedures under the ECHR are not solely concerned with individual rights in particular cases, but with the more general maintenance of respect for rights.

The Court (with the British judge dissenting) held that there had been a breach of Art. 3. The suffering that the applicant underwent was not sufficient to reach the level of 'torture' or 'inhuman treatment'. The birching did, however, constitute 'degrading punishment'. The view of the local population was not relevant to this issue, nor was the fact that birching might there be regarded as deterring crime (para. 31):

> [A] punishment does not lose its degrading character just because it is believed to be, or actually is, an effective deterrent or aid to crime control.

The factors which were relevant to the finding that it was degrading were that it constituted institutionalised violence, carried out by total strangers; that it constituted an assault on 'precisely what it is one of the main purposes of Article 3 to protect, namely a person's dignity and physical integrity'; and that there was a considerable delay between the passing of sentence and its being carried out, which meant that the applicant 'was subjected to the mental anguish of anticipating the violence he was to have inflicted on him' (para. 33). The Court felt that (para. 35):

> The indignity of having the punishment administered over the bare posterior aggravated to some extent the degrading character of the applicant's punishment but it was not the only or determining factor.

As a result of its decision on Art. 3, the Court had no need to consider the discrimination issue under Art. 14.

The outcome of the *Tyrer* case was that the practice of corporal punishment as a penalty for criminal offenders in the Isle of Man was abandoned. The Convention thus produced an increase in the respect for civil liberties. It produced no direct benefit for the applicant, however. His indication of a wish to withdraw the case, while not preventing it from proceeding, meant that the Court felt that there was no need to consider 'just satisfaction' under Art. 50 (para. 44).

The next case to be initiated was that of *Campbell and Cosans v United Kingdom* (1982) 4 EHRR 293. Although it was again concerned with corporal punishment, the context was rather different. The action was brought by the mothers of two schoolboys. Both of the boys attended schools in Scotland where corporal punishment, in the form of the tawse administered across the pupil's hand, was in use. In Mrs Campbell's case her ground for complaint was that the local authority which was responsible for the school refused to guarantee that her son would not be punished in this way. Mrs Cosan's son was ordered to receive corporal punishment, for taking a prohibited short cut, but refused. He was suspended from the school, until he was willing to receive the punishment. After some months, the school agreed to reinstate him, the length of the suspension being regarded as sufficient punishment. His parents, however, refused to send him back to school unless it guaranteed that their son would not be subject to corporal punishment while he remained at the school.

There were two main grounds of complaint in both cases. First, that the use of corporal punishment as a disciplinary measure constituted treatment contrary to Art. 3. Secondly, that there was a breach of Art. 2 of the First Protocol, which requires the State to:

> respect the right of parents to ensure . . . education and teaching in conformity with their own . . . philosophical convictions.

The Commission found no breach of Art. 3, but a breach of Art. 2 of the First Protocol, and referred the cases to the Court.

The Court referred to the criteria which it had established in the *Tyrer* case concerning the notion of 'degrading punishment'. Neither of the boys had actually received the tawse, so the Court did not have to consider whether its application would have fallen foul of Art. 3. It accepted, however, that in certain circumstances the threat of conduct prohibited by Art. 3 might in itself conflict with that provision (para. 26). In applying this approach to the case before it, the Court noted that corporal punishment was traditional in Scottish schools, and appeared 'to be favoured by a large majority of parents' (para. 28). This in itself did not, as had been established in *Tyrer*, prevent its being degrading. However, in this case the Court took the view (para. 29), that in the light of the circumstances obtaining in Scotland, it had not been established:

> that pupils at a school where such punishment is used are, solely by reason of the risk of being subjected thereto, humiliated or debased in the eyes of others to the requisite degree at all.

Nor was there any evidence that either of the boys had been humiliated or debased in their own eyes. Cosans might well have felt apprehensive when ordered to be punished, but this was not the same as degrading treatment. Still less could Campbell, who had never been directly threatened, be said to have suffered in this way.

The conclusion was that the Court, without actually deciding whether the *use* of the tawse would contravene Art. 3, held that the *threat* of its use did not do so. This shows one of the limitations of the Court, in that the real purpose of these cases was to challenge the system of corporal punishment in Scottish schools. The Court, however, refused to deal with this issue directly, because it was not precisely raised by the applicants' cases.

As to Art. 2 of the First Protocol, here the Court considered (para. 36) that the parents' views related to:

a weighty and substantial aspect of human life and behaviour, namely the integrity of the person, the propriety or otherwise of the infliction of corporal punishment and the exclusion of the distress which the risk of such punishment entails.

They fell, therefore, within the scope of 'philosophical convictions', and were not simply concerned, as the United Kingdom government had suggested, with matters of internal school administration. The Court was, furthermore, not convinced that a system of schooling which took account of these matters could not be achieved without prejudicing 'the provision of efficient instruction and training' or giving rise to 'unreasonable public expenditure', which, as we have seen (see 1.5.3) were the United Kingdom's reasons for partial derogation from this Article. The failure to respect the parents' wishes on this matter therefore amounted to a violation of Art. 2 of the First Protocol.

The possibility of compensation for the applicants was accepted in this case, though not quantified at the time of the judgment. More generally, the decision added impetus to the process which was already underway of banning the use of corporal punishment in State schools throughout the United Kingdom. That the government had accepted that this was inevitable is perhaps shown by the case of *X* v *United Kingdom*, Application No. 7907/77, (1981) 24 YBECHR 402; *The Times*, 27 February 1982. The applicant in this case was the mother of a schoolgirl, who, when 14, had been caned by her headmistress. The caning was found to have produced weals (one over a foot long) on the girl's buttocks, and hand. She was 'in discomfort for several days and traces of the caning remained for a considerably longer period' (para. 5). As with *Campbell and Cosans* the application complained of a violation of Art. 3, and Art. 2 of the First Protocol. The Commission declared the application admissible. As we have seen, this indicates the view that there is a *prima facie* case (see 1.5.2.1). In this case, however, rather than proceeding to a hearing of the merits, the 'friendly settlement' procedure produced a result. The settlement proposed by the Commission, and accepted by the parties, was for:

(a) an *ex gratia* payment to the applicant of £1,200;

(b)   a contribution of £1,016.19 towards the applicant's legal costs; and
(c)   the dispatch of a circular letter by the government to local education authorities stating that the use of corporal punishment may in certain circumstances amount to treatment contrary to Art. 3 of the ECHR.

This case shows that the friendly settlement procedure can be not only a relatively speedy way for an applicant to receive compensation, but can also involve a broader response to the infringement of rights involved, as indicated by the requirement of the circular letter in this case. That went beyond any remedy to deal with loss or injury suffered by the applicant, but addressed the wider problem lying behind the application, that is, the continued use of corporal punishment in schools. The only cautionary note which must be sounded is that the mother in this case was reported to have accepted the settlement simply because of a desire to avoid publicity. She was afraid that if she went ahead to a hearing, anonymity would be lost for her and her daughter.

Two other cases on this issue have raised the issue of the effectiveness of local remedies. In both, a civil action had been brought against a teacher who had administered corporal punishment. In *Maxine and Karen Warwick v United Kingdom* (1986) (Commission's Decisions and Reports 60), a 16 year old girl had received one stroke of the cane across her hand, administered by her headmaster in the presence of the deputy headmaster and another girl. In *Y v UK* (1992) (Series A no. 247-A) a 15 year old schoolboy had received four strokes of the cane across his clothed buttocks from his headmaster. In both cases the county court judge found that the punishment was reasonable, and did not constitute an assault. In *Warwick* the Commission found (by 12 votes to 5) that there had been a breach of Art. 3, in that the punishment caused the applicant humiliation and attained a sufficient level of seriousness to be 'degrading'. In reaching this decision it took into account in particular the fact that the punishment had been administered by a man, in the presence of another man, and that the girl was, under English law, a woman of marriageable age. The punishment caused bruising which remained visible for more than a week, and could not be said to have been 'of a merely trivial nature' (para. 87). There was also the possibility of adverse psychological effects. The Commission also found that there had been a breach of the girl's mother's rights under Art. 2 of the First Protocol. In relation to both these infringements, there was also a breach of Art. 13, in that no effective remedy was provided under English law. This case was not referred to the Court. The reason for this is not clear, but as a result it fell to be considered by the Committee of Ministers. The Committee, which does not give reasons for its decisions, failed to reach the required two-thirds majority in relation to the Art. 3 claim, and so did not uphold the Commission's decision on this issue, or the related Art. 13 claim. It did, however, agree that there had been a breach of Art. 2 of the First Protocol, and of Art. 13 in relation to this claim. It recommended that the United Kingdom government should pay £16,950 costs to the applicants, but in the light of the changes being brought into effect in English law, recommended that no further action was necessary.

In *Y v United Kingdom*, the injuries to the boy were more severe, involving heavy bruising and swelling, and he received some medical treatment. The

Commission found the claim admissible, and found that there had been a violation of Arts 3 and 13. However, the applicant then reached a friendly settlement, under which he was paid £8,000 (without any admission of liability on the part of the government), plus costs. Although the Commission was clearly unhappy with Y's acceptance of 'a mere financial settlement' (*Report*, para. 16) at such a late stage in the proceedings, it did not object, and the Court, noting the settlement, struck the case from its list.

The cases looked at so far in this section have all fitted into a general trend against the use of corporal punishment. Partly as a result of these actions, such punishment is now banned from all State schools in England, Wales and Scotland. In independent schools it may only be used in relation to pupils who are not State-funded. The final case, however, indicates that applying to the Commission will not always lead to a favourable decision. In *Costello-Roberts* v *United Kingdom* (1993) (Series A, no. 247-C), the applicant was a boy who at the age of seven had attended a private boarding school where (in 1985) corporal punishment was still in use. It was used, for example, when a pupil had received five demerit marks. The applicant received five such marks. Five days later the headmaster, having discussed the matter with colleagues, informed the applicant that he would be punished by receiving 'three "whacks" on the bottom through his shorts with a rubber-soled gym shoe'. The punishment was administered three days later. There was a disagreement between the boy's parents and the school as to its effect, the parents alleging that their son was very upset, the school reporting an improvement in behaviour. The boy's mother eventually lodged a claim with the Commission. Breaches of Arts 3, 8 (respect for private and family life) and 13, were alleged. The Commission declared the mother's complaints inadmissible, but accepted the claim by the boy himself. It found that there had been no violation of Art. 3, but that there had been a violation of Arts 8 and 13. The case was referred to the Court by the Commission. The Court agreed with the Commission that there was no violation of Art. 3 in this case. There was no evidence that the punishment in this case had produced any severe or long-lasting effects. These were not essential for a breach of Art. 3, but the punishment must have reached a 'minimum level of severity' (*Report*, para. 32). Although the Court had 'certain misgivings about the automatic nature of the punishment, and the three-day wait before its imposition', it did not think that this minimum level had been reached. Furthermore the Court, disagreeing with the Commission, did not feel that the treatment complained of involved sufficient adverse effects for the applicant's physical or moral integrity to amount to a breach of Art. 8. Finally, as regards Art. 13, the fact that an action for assault in the county court would have been unlikely to succeed did not mean that there was no procedure under which infringement of the rights under Arts 3 or 8 could in appropriate circumstances be compensated. There was therefore no breach of Art. 13, either.

This sequence of cases on the area of corporal punishment show both the good and the bad sides to the Convention's procedures for enforcement. On the one hand, the cases undoubtedly helped in the move to reduce, and even abolish in most cases, the use of physical punishments against children. The willingness of the government to accept friendly settlements in two of the cases, indicates its unhappiness at being brought before the Court, and being found to be in breach of its obligations. On the other hand, there are problems for the individual applicant. The procedures are very slow, with the cases taking five to seven years to be decided. Moreover, it is only in the two cases that were settled that the applicant received any compensation for the breach that had occurred. The verdict must be that the ECHR is a beneficial force in the development of civil liberties in England and Wales, but that it does not provide an ideal solution to individual problems. There are those who argue that the procedural deficiencies would be remedied by incorporating it into English law. That is an issue to which we shall return in chapter 12, in considering the ECHR as a candidate for a Bill of Rights.

TWO

Freedom of the Person I: Stop, Search and Arrest

2.1 INTRODUCTION

One of the hallmarks of a free society is the ability of its citizens to go about their business without the need to explain to anyone in authority what they are doing, and without the fear that they may be subject to arbitrary challenge or arrest. It is recognised in the United States Bill of Rights, in the 4th Amendment, in the Canadian Charter, ss. 7–10, and in the European Convention on Human Rights, Art. 5 (this is discussed in 2.6). This aspect of personal freedom is of great importance. It is sometimes treated as an element of a more general right of privacy, which covers also the freedom to enjoy property, and the freedom from the disclosure of personal secrets. To categorise it in this way, however, runs the risk of downgrading its importance. A person's physical freedom is surely more important than the quiet possession of their home, or the maintenance of their domestic secrets. To interfere bodily with a person strikes at the heart of their individuality. Invasion of bodily integrity is regarded as a most serious offence when committed by one citizen against another. Assaults and related offences are treated as serious crimes, which attract substantial penalties. This may be said to reflect the importance that society attaches to this aspect of the individual's existence. It is therefore reasonable to expect that when similar invasions are authorised on behalf of the State, by, for example, giving its police force the power to stop people, to search them, or to compel them physically (by arrest) to attend a police station, this should only be on the clearest grounds, and in situations of necessity.

This chapter is primarily concerned with the laws which justify such invasions of personal freedom. The majority of the powers discussed are available to police officers only, though in some cases they may be exercised by other officials, or even by private citizens. Virtually all the powers discussed in this chapter are based in statutes, many of them being contained in the Police and Criminal Evidence Act 1984 ('PACE'). This statutory framework needs to be considered, before moving on to the details of the powers.

2.2   PACE AND ITS CODES

The enactment of PACE did not constitute a full codification of police powers,
though it was a substantial step towards it. The Act provides the framework
for the exercise of powers of stop and search, arrest, and detention (which is
discussed in chapter 3). It derived largely from the recommendations of the
Royal Commission on Criminal Procedure which reported in 1981 (Cmnd
8092), though it did not follow them precisely. Of almost equal importance in
practical terms to the provisions of the Act itself, are the Codes of Practice
associated with it. There are currently five of these Codes, covering stop and
search (Code A), entry to premises (Code B), detention and questioning (Code
C), identification (Code D), and tape recording of interviews (Code E). They
provide detailed regulations which in many cases fill out the broad powers
contained in the Act, and explain how they should operate in practice. The
legal status of the Codes is set out in ss. 60, 66 and 67 of PACE. Sections 60
and 66 simply impose on the Home Secretary the responsibility for issuing the
Codes. Section 67(8) to (11) deal with their legal status. First, s. 67(11)
confirms that the Codes are admissible in evidence in any legal proceedings
(criminal or civil) to which they are relevant. In practice, the most common
reference to the Codes has been in criminal proceedings, where the defendant
is arguing that evidence is inadmissible because of a breach of one of the Codes
(see 3.6.3). Secondly, a failure by a police officer to comply with the provisions
of a Code will not in itself render the officer liable to any criminal or civil
proceedings: s. 67(10). Thus, breach of the Codes is neither a criminal offence,
nor a statutory tort. A police officer who breaks the Codes will, however, be
liable to disciplinary proceedings on that basis: s. 67(8). Finally, any person,
even if not a police officer, who has the duty of investigating criminal offences
or charging offenders, must have regard to the relevant provisions of the
Codes: s. 67(9).

The Codes thus have a legal status, but not such a strong one as the
provisions of PACE itself. If, for example, a police officer steps outside the
provisions of the Act in carrying out a search, this may well lead to a charge of
assault. If a provision of the Code on stop and search is not followed, however,
there is no automatic consequence, other than that the officer will be liable for
a disciplinary offence. Breach of the Code will, however, be relevant, for
example, in deciding whether to admit any evidence obtained as a result of the
search.

2.3   STOP AND SEARCH

2.3.1   Common law
The position at common law is that neither a police officer, nor anyone else, has
any right to stop a person, unless they are going to arrest them; nor is there any
general obligation to answer questions put by a police officer. The rule is
illustrated by *Rice* v *Connolly* [1966] 2 QB 414. Rice had been observed for
some time by two police officers in the early hours of the morning, walking the
streets of Grimsby. A number of burglaries had been committed that night,

and the officers were on the look-out for suspects. They eventually challenged Rice, and asked where he was going. He refused to answer, and gave generally unhelpful replies. When asked to go with the officers he refused, and was arrested and charged with obstructing a police officer in the execution of his duty. The Divisional Court allowed his appeal against conviction. Lord Parker (at p. 419) stated the legal position in the following terms:

It seems to me quite clear that though every citizen has a moral duty . . . to assist the police, there is no legal duty to that effect, and indeed the whole basis of the common law is the right of the individual to refuse to answer questions put to him by persons in authority, and to refuse to accompany those in authority to any particular place; short, of course, of arrest.

All that is allowed to the police is to attract a person's attention in order to address a question to them. This may include touching (*Donnelly* v *Jackman* [1970] 1 All ER 987), provided that this does not 'transcend the norms of acceptable behaviour' (*Collins* v *Wilcock* [1984] 3 All ER 374). Physically preventing a person from going away from the officer will clearly be impermissible. In *Collins* v *Wilcock* the officer grabbed the arm of a woman she wished to talk to, in order to stop her from walking off. This was held to exceed that officer's lawful powers.

Unless, therefore, there is available a specific statutory power to stop, a police officer cannot lawfully detain a citizen other than by an arrest. Arrest is discussed at 2.4.

2.3.2 General statutory provisions

A number of statutes contain powers of stop and search. Some general provisions applying to all such powers are now contained in PACE, s. 2, and Code A.

The notes of guidance in the Code emphasise the fact that stops and searches should be used sparingly (note 1A), but also state that police officers are entitled to speak to or question people. It is also stated (note 1B) that the citizens have a 'duty' (presumably a moral or social duty is meant) to help police officers to prevent crime and discover offenders.

2.3.2.1 Reasonable suspicion

The reasonable grounds for suspicion which will be required for most powers of stop and search must exist before a person is stopped. There is no power to stop in order to find grounds for carrying out a search (Code A, para. 2.1). On the other hand, once a person is lawfully stopped, the officer is encouraged to question the person, since this may reveal information which will render a search unnecessary (para. 2.2).

The Royal Commission regarded 'reasonable suspicion' as a concept which could not be defined. Some attempt is made, however, in Code A to try to indicate what it does and does not mean. Paragraph 1.6 starts by making it clear that there must be an 'objective' basis to it. The police officer's 'hunch' or 'feeling' about a person is never going to be enough; nor may it be based on 'personal factors alone' (para. 1.7). Thus, colour, age, hairstyle and clothing, or previous convictions cannot be used in isolation, or in combination with each other as the sole basis for a reasonable suspicion justifying a search. 'Stereotyped images' that certain persons or groups are more likely to commit offences may also not be used. The Code does, however, give some examples of factors which may ground reasonable suspicion. Information received (the source does not apparently matter) describing an article or a person may be enough. The way in which a person is behaving can form the basis of a reasonable suspicion, if, for example, the person is 'acting covertly or warily' or is attempting to hide something. A person's being 'out of place' is frequently mentioned by police officers as a basis for suspicion. This is recognised in the Code as potentially reasonable, so that it may justify a stop and search where 'a person is carrying a certain type of article at an unusual time, or in a place where a number of burglaries or thefts have been known to have taken place recently'.

All of this allows the police officer a fair degree of discretion. Provided that some objective basis can be shown for the suspicion, the courts are unlikely to reject it as unreasonable. It is only where the decision is clearly random, or based on a 'hunch' or prejudice, that the officer's action is likely to be regarded as unreasonable.

The original version of the Code stated that reasonable grounds for suspicion justifying a search were the same as reasonable grounds for an arrest. The police disliked this statement, and it does not appear in the current version of the Code. It is not clear whether this means that a lesser level of suspicion is now required in relation to searches. It is difficult to see that where there is a power to search for a certain type of article, for example, drugs, and at the same time a power of arrest for the offence of possession of such an article, that the grounds for reasonable suspicion of possession can be different according to whether a search or an arrest is being undertaken.

The concept of 'reasonable suspicion' is central to the operation of discretionary police powers, and therefore crucial to the freedoms of the citizen. It is disappointing that it remains such a nebulous concept which has never been adequately explained either by definition or example, in case law, statute, or Code of Practice.

2.3.2.2 Notification provisions   Section 2 of PACE requires certain information to be given to a person who is stopped, if a search is to follow. If the officer stops with a view to searching, but decides, quite properly (s. 2(1)), not to proceed because such a search is unnecessary or impractical, no information has to be given, and no record need be made (see 2.3.2.4).

Where there is to be a search, the constable must, before starting, take reasonable steps to bring to the suspect's attention:

(a)   if the constable is not in uniform, the constable's warrant card (s. 2(2), Code A, para. 2.5);

(b)   the constable's name, and the police station to which the constable is attached;

(c)   the object of the proposed search: that is, what is being searched for;

(d)   the constable's grounds for proposing to make it; and

(e)   the fact that if a record is made of the search (see 2.3.2.4), the suspect is entitled to a copy.

These procedural requirements have two effects. They require the constable to address explicitly the issue of why the search is being carried out, and whether it is necessary. They also provide the suspect with information which may help to explain what is going on, and therefore make it less intimidating, and which may also provide the basis for action if there is a subsequent wish to challenge the legality of what has been done.

2.3.2.3 The conduct of the search   The Act itself says little about how the search should be conducted. The only relevant provision is s. 2(9), which states that a constable conducting a search without arrest, may not require a person to remove any clothing in public, other than an outer coat, jacket or gloves. Paragraph 3 of Code A goes into more detail, operating within the general principle that every reasonable effort should be made to minimise the embarrassment of the person being searched (para. 3.1). Cooperation should be sought in every case, even if the suspect initially objects. Reasonable force may, however, be used as a last resort (para. 3.2; see also s. 117). Where the basis of the suspicion justifying the search is that an article has been seen to be slipped into a pocket, the search should be confined to that pocket. Searches for small, easily concealable, articles, may justifiably be more extensive. Searches going beyond what is permitted by s. 2(9) should be done out of public view, in a police van, for example, unless the person searched is willing to remove more (Notes for Guidance, para. 3A). Note for Guidance, para. 3A also indicates that an empty street should still be regarded as being 'in public'. If the search involves the removal of more than outer coat, jacket, gloves, headgear or footwear it must not take place in the presence of a person of the opposite sex, unless the person being searched specifically requests this (para. 3.5).

The duration of the detention for the purpose of the search should be limited to what is necessary to carry out the search at the place where the person was stopped or nearby (s. 2(8)). As the Notes for Guidance state (para. 3B), searches in public 'should be completed as soon as possible.'

These controls over the conduct of the search are basically satisfactory, except to the extent that they allow the person being searched to 'opt out' of the restrictions. In the absence of any method for ensuring that consent was genuinely given, the 'consent' exceptions leave wide open the possibility of people being too timid, or unsure of their rights, to object to what the police want to do, and for this to be subsequently interpreted as 'consent'.

2.3.2.4 Procedures following a search   Once a search has been carried out (but not if there has been a stop without a search), there is an obligation on the constable to make a record of it in writing, unless it is not practicable to do so (s. 3(1)). The wording of s. 3(1) (referring to a search 'in the exercise of any such power') suggests the possibility that there is no obligation to record a

voluntary search. Code A, para. 4.1, however, states that there is such an
obligation whenever 'an officer has carried out a search', whatever the basis for
it. The limitation of 'impracticability' will apply, for example, in a situation of
public disorder, where the number of searches to be conducted, or the general
situation, will effectively preclude the keeping of records.

The record must be made on the spot if at all possible, or if not, for example
because of the weather conditions (Code A, para. 4.2), as soon as practicable
thereafter (s. 3(2)).

The police have a standard form for the recording of searches, the 'national
search record', which Code A, para. 4.3 says *must* be used. If, for some reason,
this is not available, however, there is no reason why the record should not be
made on any piece of paper.

The content of the record is spelt out in s. 3(3) to (6), and Code A, paras
4.4–4.5. It must include the name, or a description of, the person searched; the
identity of the constable; the object of, and grounds for, the search; the date,
time and location; and the consequences. These include whether or not
anything was found, and whether any injury to a person, or damage to
property, resulted from the search. Code A additionally requires the constable
to seek, if possible, the person's address and date of birth, and to make a note
of the person's ethnic origin. The person searched is entitled to a copy of this
record, on request, at any time within 12 months of the search (s. 3(7), (9)).

These requirements follow the recommendations of the Royal Commission,
and are an attempt to provide safeguards against the improper use of police
powers of stop and search. Whether they do so to any great effect is open to
question. In particular, research on the operation of PACE (K. Bottomley, *et
al.*, *The Impact of PACE*, University of Hull, 1992), has found that there was
limited awareness of the role of the forms, and 'no universal expectation that
they would be completed meticulously and scrutinised thoroughly afterwards'
(at p. 47). It is hard not to agree with the researchers' conclusion that as a result
'the role of the records and the monitoring of them as safeguards must be open
to some scepticism'.

There are also provisions of a similar kind relating to searches of vehicles.
These are discussed in chapter 4.

2.3.3 The PACE powers
The procedures outlined above apply to virtually all powers to stop and search.
PACE itself introduced new powers, and these are to be found in ss. 1 and 4.
Only the powers to stop vehicles, and to stop and search individuals are
discussed here. The Act also gives powers to search vehicles, but these are
discussed in chapter 4, in the context of freedom of property.

2.3.3.1 Stolen or prohibited articles The main stop and search power is
contained in s. 1(2). The Act does not, in fact, generally use the word 'stop'.
The relevant provision in s. 1 states that a constable may 'detain' a person or
vehicle for the purpose of a search to which the section applies. This is
consistent with the procedures outlined above, which make it clear that a 'stop'
or 'detention' can only take place where there are reasonable grounds for

suspicion justifying a search. In relation to vehicles, s. 3(9) provides that only a constable in uniform has the power to stop vehicles. The general power of a constable to stop vehicles is discussed further at 2.3.4.3.

Section 1(2) gives a constable the power to search any person for stolen or 'prohibited' articles, or 'any article to which subsection 8(A)' of s. 1 applies. Stolen articles are not further defined, so anything which constitutes stolen goods for the purpose of the Theft Act 1968 is presumably covered (Theft Act 1968, s. 24: this includes goods obtained by blackmail, or criminal deception, for example). 'Prohibited articles' are defined in s. 1(7) of PACE. There are two main categories. The first is 'offensive weapons'. The second is various articles which may be used in relation to offences under the Theft Act 1968.

'Offensive weapon' is defined in s. 1(9) of PACE, to mean any article made or adapted for use for causing injury to persons, or intended by the person in possession of it for such use by that person or another. This is based on the similar definition of offensive weapon used in the Prevention of Crime Act 1953. It is clear that it covers articles which are in themselves 'offensive', such as guns, and flick-knives. It also covers innocent items which have been adapted for causing personal injury, such as a bicycle chain attached to a handle (creating a flail), or a screwdriver sharpened to a spike. Finally, and most controversially, it covers everyday, unadapted items, which are capable of being used to cause injury. Most of the contents of the kitchen drawer, or the tool-box, will come into this category. Such items become prohibited articles when they are in the possession of a person whose intention is that the article should be used for causing injury. Thus a constable, in order lawfully to stop and search for such an item, must have reasonable suspicion not only of the fact that the person to be searched has possession of the article, but also of that person's state of mind in relation to the use of the article. It is difficult to see that this could ever be the case, unless the article has *already* been used for such a purpose. Section 1(8A) brings within the stop and search power a specific type of potentially offensive weapon, that is any article which has a blade or is sharply pointed, other than a folding pocket knife with a blade of three inches or less. A folding knife which can be locked open comes within the scope of s. 1(8A): *Harris v DPP, Fehmi v DPP* [1993] 1 All ER 562. It is an offence under s. 139 of the Criminal Justice Act 1988 to be in possession of such an article in a public place, unless the person in possession can prove that there was a good reason or lawful authority for this. The burden of proof is thus on the possessor to prove an innocent reason for having it in a public place. Section 1(8A) of PACE applies to 'any article in relation to which a person has committed, or is committing, or is going to commit an offence under s. 139 of the Criminal Justice Act 1988'.

The second category of prohibited article is defined in s. 1(7)(b) and (8) of PACE. It covers articles made or adapted for use, or intended by the possessor for use, in connection with the commission of the following Theft Act offences: burglary (1968 Act, s. 9), theft (s. 1), taking a motor vehicle without authority (s. 12), or obtaining property by deception (s. 15). It could cover, therefore, a crow-bar, skeleton keys, car keys, credit cards, or again, virtually any item from a standard domestic tool-box, provided the relevant purpose can be established.

In order to exercise the power under s. 1 of PACE, a constable must have reasonable grounds for suspecting that the person to be searched has possession of one of the articles outlined above (s. 1(3)). The 'reasonable suspicion' will have to be determined as explained in 2.3.1.1. The power may be exercised in any public place. This means any place to which the public, or a section of the public, has access, on payment or otherwise, as of right or by virtue of express or implied permission (s. 1(1)). It includes, therefore, not only the street, but shops, football or other sports stadia, theatres, cinemas, or clubs. It would also presumably cover public libraries, museums and art galleries. In relation to places other than the street, the constable must have a right to be on the premises. The power under s. 1 gives a constable no general right to enter premises without the permission of the occupier. There appears, however, to be an exception to this in that s. 1(1) also states that the power may be exercised in any other place, not being a dwelling, to which 'people have ready access'. There are two situations which this will cover. First, it will allow a search to be carried out on premises which are sometimes open to the public, but are not open at the relevant time. An obvious example would be a car park, which is only open when adjacent shops are open (see, for example, *Marsh* v *Arscott* (1982) 75 Cr App R 211). Secondly, it would seem to apply in a situation where, in order to attempt to avoid an anticipated search, a suspect steps off the street into a nearby garden. In order to give any effect to this provision, it must be assumed that the constable will be regarded as having an implied licence to go on to the premises to carry out the search. (Powers of entry to premises are discussed fully in chapter 4.)

The possibility of a search taking place in a garden is dealt with further in s. 1(4). If the constable wishes to search a person who is in a garden or yard, or on other land, which in either case is attached to a dwelling, a search is only permissible if the constable has reasonable grounds for suspecting that the person does not live in the dwelling, and is not on the land with the express or implied permission of someone who lives in the dwelling. Thus a person approached on the street by a constable can escape the possibility of a search by moving to their own front garden, or that of a friend or relation who would consent to their being there. This confirms that the extension of the power to areas to which the public has 'ready access' is designed primarily to deal with the situation of the person trespassing in order to escape the attentions of the police.

Finally, if a search carried out under the s. 1 powers leads to the discovery of an article which a constable has reasonable grounds to believe to be an article of a kind which may be searched for *under the section*, that article may be seized (s. 1(6)). If drugs, for example, are found, this section gives no power to seize them. Strictly speaking, it seems that another search should be undertaken, and the suspect notified accordingly. In practice, however, it seems highly unlikely that any court would exclude evidence which has been obtained in this way. (For the power to exclude evidence, see 3.6.3). The situation can also probably be regularised by an arrest, and the use of the consequent general power of seizure under s. 32 (see 2.4.5.1), or possibly by the use of the general power under s. 19 (see 4.3.2). This assumes that the reference in s. 19 to things found 'on premises' can include things found in the possession of a person who is on the premises ('premises' being defined to include 'any place': s. 23).

2.3.3.2 Road checks The general police powers to stop vehicles are discussed below (see 2.3.4.3). Section 4 of PACE gives a specific, though rather limited power to the police to establish road checks. This will allow the police to stop either all vehicles, or vehicles selected by any criterion (s. 4(2)), in order to check on who is travelling in the vehicle (not to search for property). Essentially, therefore, this a power to stop vehicles randomly, without the need for any reasonable grounds in relation to any particular vehicle in relation to which the power is exercised. This is a serious inroad into the freedom of individuals to go about their business without arbitrary interference. The Royal Commission thought, however, that this might be justified in situations of emergency (Cmnd 8092 para. 3.32).

Generally, the decision to establish a road check must be taken by a police officer of at least the rank of superintendent (s. 4(3)), though a more junior officer may do so 'if it appears to him that it is required as a matter of urgency' (s. 4(5)). In this case a written record of the time it was authorised must be made, and a superintendent or above informed, as soon as is reasonably practicable (s. 4(6), (7)). The officer receiving the report must decide whether or not to authorise the continuance of the road check (s. 4(8), (9)).

There are four purposes for which a road check may be authorised. These are to check whether a vehicle is carrying:

(a) a person who has committed an offence. The authorising officer must have reasonable grounds for believing that it is a serious arrestable offence, and reasonable grounds for suspecting that the person who committed it is, or is about to be, in the locality of the proposed check; or

(b) a person who is a witness to an offence which the authorising officer has reasonable grounds for believing to be a serious arrestable offence; or

(c) a person intending to commit an offence. The authorising officer must have reasonable grounds for believing that it would be a serious arrestable offence, and reasonable grounds for suspecting that the person is, or is about to be, in the locality of the proposed check; or

(d) a person who is unlawfully at large (that is, having escaped from custody), and whom the authorising officer has reasonable grounds for suspecting to be, or to be about to be, in the locality of the proposed check.

The concept of the 'serious arrestable offence' is discussed in more detail below, see 3.3.3.1. Suffice it to say that the use here indicates the exceptional nature of the power.

Authorisations of road checks should be in writing, and specify the name of the officer giving it, the purpose of the check (which should include an indication of the relevant serious arrestable offence), and the locality in which vehicles are to be stopped (s. 4(13)). The period for which the check is to last, which may not be more than seven days, should be specified at the time that it is authorised by a superintendent, or above. This officer should also decide whether the checks should be continuous, or only take place at specified times (s. 4(11)). An officer of the rank of superintendent or above (not necessarily the officer who issued the initial authorisation) may, in writing, extend the check for a further period of up to seven days (s. 4(12)). The wording of the section, referring to this power being exercised 'from time to time', suggests that more than one such extension may be granted.

The Act contains no regulations as to the procedures to be adopted during a road check, and there is no relevant Code of Practice. Such matters are therefore entirely at the discretion of the police. Given that the power is exclusively for the purpose of identifying the occupants of the vehicle, a visual inspection of the interior, including the goods section of a van or lorry and possibly the boot of a car, is all that will be justified. The officers may, of course, ask questions about the identity of the occupants, or where they are travelling from or to, but there is no obligation to answer, and no power to detain in order to put such questions.

The person in charge of any vehicle which has been stopped is entitled to obtain, within 12 months of the day on which the vehicle was stopped, a written statement of the purpose of the road check (s. 4(16)). It is not specified to whom such a request should be addressed, but presumably it may be made to any police station in the area in which the road check took place. The police are not obliged to inform people who are stopped of this right.

There is also a power to stop vehicles under the Road Traffic Act 1988, s. 163 (see 2.3.4.3).

2.3.4   Other statutory powers
Powers of stop and search arise under a variety of statutes. A list of the powers is given in an Annex to Code of Practice A. There is only space to consider two of these here, namely the powers under the Misuse of Drugs Act 1971, and the Sporting Events (Control of Alcohol etc) Act 1985. In addition, police powers in relation to road traffic offences are considered.

2.3.4.1 Misuse of Drugs Act 1971, s. 23 This is one of the most commonly used powers of stop and search. In 1991, for example, 36 per cent of all stops and searches (i.e. 109,600) were for drugs (Home Office Statistical Bulletin, 15/92). Only searches for stolen goods (37 per cent) were more frequent. Section 23 empowers any constable to carry out a search of a person whom the constable has reasonable grounds to suspect is in possession of a controlled drug. The person may be detained for the purpose of carrying out the search (s. 23(2)(a)). A 'controlled drug' is one defined as such in s. 2, and Schedule 2 to the Act. It will currently include, among many other substances, cannabis, heroin, cocaine, crack, LSD, and ecstasy.

The power can be exercised anywhere: it does not have to be in a public place. Thus, police officers who have entered private premises in the execution of a search warrant relating to stolen goods, for example, will be entitled to search a person found on those premises who is reasonably suspected to be in possession of a controlled drug.

Nothing is said in the section about the way in which the search should be carried out, but the general provisions outlined above will apply. Paragraph 3 of Code of Practice A, in noting that where there is a search for a particular article it may only be reasonable to search the pocket into which it has been seen to be slipped, goes on to say that:

> In the case of a small article which can be easily concealed, *such as a drug*, and which might be concealed anywhere on the person, a more extensive search may be necessary. [*emphasis added*]

There is nothing in the section to prevent the search, if taking place in private, from being a strip search (i.e. involving the removal of more than outer clothing). An 'intimate search' is, however, prohibited by PACE, s. 53(1) (see 3.5.3.2).

There is also power to stop and search a vehicle, on reasonable suspicion that controlled drugs may be found in it (s. 23(2)(b)). This presumably is also available where the drugs are suspected to be on a person in the vehicle.

Anything found in the course of a search under s. 23 which appears to the constable to be evidence of an offence *under the Act* may be seized. If offensive weapons, or stolen goods are found, this section gives no power to seize them. As noted above (2.3.3.1), however, there are other powers which may justify seizure, and it is in any case unlikely that any court will refuse to admit evidence which has been obtained in this way.

Intentional obstruction of a constable exercising powers under this section is an offence (s. 23(4)).

2.3.4.2 Sporting Events (Control of Alcohol etc) Act 1985 This Act is unusual in that it makes unlawful in certain circumstances the possession of articles which may normally be carried quite legally in a public place. It was directed primarily at the problems of football violence, which were seen as being fuelled by alcohol. As a result it is made an offence to be in possession of alcoholic drinks while in certain types of vehicle travelling to certain sporting events (s. 1). A power to stop and search relevant vehicles travelling to or from a designated sporting event is given to constables by s. 7(3), and is exercisable on reasonable grounds for suspicion that an offence under s. 1 is being or has been committed.

In addition, it is an offence to be in possession of alcoholic drinks, or any drink container (full or empty) which is capable of causing injury to a person struck by it, while present at a designated sporting event, or while entering or trying to enter a designated sports ground (s. 2(1)). A constable who has reasonable grounds to suspect that a person is committing or has committed an offence under the Act may search that person.

Somewhat surprisingly, no specific power to seize items is given in connection with either of these search powers. If an arrest follows the search, however, a power of seizure will arise under PACE, s. 32 (see 2.4.5.1). It may also be possible to rely on the general seizure power under PACE, s. 19 (4.3.2).

As noted above, these provisions represent an unusual infringement on personal freedom. The possession of alcohol is not normally illicit. The powers are presumably thought justifiable because of (a) their limited scope as regards times and place; and (b) the magnitude of the problem they were passed to address.

2.3.4.3   Road Traffic Act 1988, s. 163   The widest power which is given to any police officer to stop citizens is contained in s. 163 of the Road Traffic Act 1988. Section 163(1) simply states:

A person driving a motor vehicle on a road must stop the vehicle on being required to do so by a constable in uniform.

Section 163(2) contains a similar provision applying to bicycles, and s. 163(3) makes it an offence to fail to comply with a direction to stop.

Note that the power under s. 163 is not in itself dependent on any reasonable suspicion on the part of the constable. The stop may apparently be entirely at random. The question may be asked as to why, if this is the case, is there the need for the provision as to road checks in PACE, s. 4? Could the police not simply use s. 163 of the Road Traffic Act 1988? Part of the answer to this lies in s. 4(2) of PACE. This refers to a road check under s. 4 as being a specific use of the power under s. 163. The effect is that if the police want to set up a road check for one of the purposes covered by s. 4(1), they must use the procedures there set out. If they wish to carry out a road check for other purposes, for example to check on compliance with the regulations concerning safety belts, they may simply rely on s. 163, and the limitations and procedures contained in s. 4 are inapplicable. The power to stop in s. 163 is complemented by the powers in ss. 164 and 165, to require the driver of a vehicle to produce certain documentation, such as a driving licence, certificate of insurance, and 'MOT' test certificate of roadworthiness. There is no power, however, to require the driver of a vehicle to take part in a 'census' of cars travelling on a particular road: *Hoffman* v *Thomas* [1974] 2 All ER 277.

The most recent consideration of this power (in its incarnation as s. 159 of the Road Traffic Act 1972) is in *Lodwick* v *Sanders* [1985] 1 All ER 577. The two members of the Divisional Court agreed that the section gives a constable a *power* to require the driver of a vehicle to stop (as was stated in *R* v *Waterfield* [1963] 3 All ER 659), and does not simply impose a *duty* on the motorist to stop (as was suggested in *Steel* v *Goacher* [1983] RTR 98). Once stopped the driver is under a duty to remain at a standstill at least until the constable has had the opportunity to exercise the powers under ss. 164 and 165. The constable will, however, only have the power physically to detain the vehicle, for example by seizing the ignition key, where there are reasonable grounds (which may have arisen after the vehicle has been stopped) to believe the vehicle to be stolen. This will in effect amount to an arrest of the driver, and the procedures relevant to arrest (below, 2.4) should be followed.

There is a surprising amount of uncertainty concerning the exact scope of this power, which comes as close as any under English law to being one of random stop and search. Given this, one would have thought that parliament would at some stage have taken the opportunity to clarify exactly to what situations it was intended to apply.

2.3.4.4 Breath tests It is in this context that there have been the most frequent calls in recent years for the police to have the power to stop motorists at random. Concern over the level of deaths and injuries on the roads attributable to alcohol has for some reached a stage where it outweighs the rights of the individual to be free from arbitrary detention. The current powers to require breath tests do not go this far, however, and are contained in the Road Traffic Act 1988. There is no power to require a vehicle to be stoppped in order for a breath test to be carried out. If the power under s. 163 is used, however, grounds for carrying out a breath test may quickly arise (see, for example, *Steel* v *Goacher* [1983] RTR 98, where the smell of alcohol on the driver's breath after he had stopped gave rise to a reasonable suspicion justifying a test).

Section 6 of the Road Traffic Act 1988 sets out the situations where a constable has the power to require a person to provide a specimen of breath, and thus to be detained for this purpose. All the grounds require reasonable suspicion on the part of a constable. First, a constable in uniform may require a breath test on the basis of reasonable suspicion that a person is, or has been, driving or attempting to drive a motor vehicle on a road or other public place, and that the person either has alcohol in their body, or has committed a moving traffic offence (s. 6(1)(a) and (b)). These provisions also apply to a person reasonably suspected of being, or having been in charge of a motor vehicle, in the same way as to a suspected driver. Secondly, if a road accident has occurred, any constable may require any person who there are reasonable grounds to believe was driving, or attempting to drive, or in charge of a vehicle at the relevant time, to provide a specimen of breath. In relation to this power, the person may, if the constable thinks fit, be required to give the specimen at a police station specified by the constable.

A person who has been required to provide a specimen of breath may be detained at a police station, in order to stop them driving whilst still intoxicated, and thus committing an offence under s. 4 or 5 of the Act (s. 10). The power will continue until a constable decides that the person would no longer be committing such an offence by driving.

There are further powers in relation to the taking of samples of breath, blood, or urine, under s. 7 of the Act. These powers will generally follow an arrest, and be exercised at a police station. They are not considered further here.

2.4 ARREST

The powers that have been considered so far only authorise a very limited period of detention; that is, sufficient to carry out a search, to ask questions with a view to deciding whether or not a search is necessary, or to carry out a breath test. If the police wish to detain people in order to question them about their suspected involvement in a criminal offence, or in order to remove them from a scene of a disturbance, for example, this can only be done by using a power of arrest.

PACE contains no definition of what amounts to an arrest, so this remains a matter to be determined largely by the common law. No particular words or procedures are necessary. PACE, s. 28 assumes that an arrest can take place simply by a constable informing a person that they are under arrest. There are cases prior to the Act which suggest that this may not be enough in itself to constitute an arrest. In *Genner* v *Sparks* (1705) 6 Mod Rep 173, 1 Salk 79, for example, it was held that a statement that a person was under arrest, which was followed by the immediate departure of the proposed arrestee, would be ineffective. Some physical contact, albeit simply a touch, was needed. Thus, a police officer who shouts at a suspect who is on the other side of the street 'You are under arrest', does not effect an arrest. If, on the other hand, the person to whom the words are spoken acquiesces in the arrest, and goes with the officer, it would seem that no physical contact is necessary: *Russen* v *Lucas* (1824) 1 C&P 153. It is not clear whether these decisions should still be regarded as good law on this point, but although the issue of when an arrest occurs has been discussed in later cases (for example, *R* v *Inwood* [1973] 1 WLR 647; *R* v *Brown* [1976] 64 Cr App R 231; *Pedro* v *Diss* [1981] 2 All ER 59; *Murray* v *Ministry of Defence* [1988] 2 All ER 521), none of them has contradicted the principles stated above. If the arrest is constituted by physical detention, any physical restraint going beyond what is necessary to attract a person's attention, and any involuntary detention beyond the period justified by the exercise of the powers in the previous section, will constitute an arrest. If the procedures outlined below are not followed, it will be unlawful.

Where a person has initially been questioned with consent, it may be more difficult to decide when an arrest has taken place. A person may, either on the street, or at a police station, voluntarily 'help the police with their inquiries' without being arrested. It may be difficult in such situations to identify the point in time when an arrest occurs. What is clear from PACE, s. 29, and Code C, para. 3.15, however, is that as soon as a constable has decided that there are lawful grounds for arresting a person, and that the constable would not allow that person to leave police custody, then the person should immediately be told that they are under arrest.

Although there is no Code of Practice dealing specifically with arrest, some provisions of Code A and Code C (as noted above) are relevant, and ss. 28–31 of PACE deal with some procedural issues.

No particular formality is required in order to place somebody under arrest. As we have seen, the mere fact of physical detention, or the use of words indicating that an arrest has taken place, is sufficient. Where the arrest is by physical detention, the person must immediately be told that they are under arrest: s. 28(1). This is so even where the fact of arrest is obvious (s. 28(2)). The constable placing handcuffs on a suspect who has been caught robbing a bank is still obliged to say 'You are under arrest'. This particular form of words does not need to be used. In *R* v *Brosch* [1988] Crim LR 743, the Court of Appeal approved the statement of Stephenson LJ in the pre-PACE case of *R* v *Inwood* [1973] 1 WLR 647 that 'There is no magic formula; only the obligation to make it plain to the suspect by what is said and done that he is no longer a free man'. In *Brosch* in was held to be enough that the person effecting the arrest (in this case the manager of a restaurant) grabbed the suspect's shoulder and said 'Stay there'.

Whatever the manner of the arrest, there is also an obligation to tell the person arrested the grounds for the arrest (s. 28(3)). This must be done at the time of the arrest, or as soon as practicable thereafter. Again, the requirement remains even if the grounds for arrest are obvious (s. 28(4)). Thus, in the example of the bank robber the constable must not simply say 'You are under arrest', but 'You are under arrest for robbery'. The only exception to either of these requirements recognised by the Act is where the person escaped from custody before it was reasonably practicable to fulfil them. The obligation to give reasons for the arrest, has, however, been considered in two cases since the Act came into force. In *Brosch, supra*, it was held that the statement 'You're on drugs, aren't you' made immediately prior to the arrest was sufficient to indicate the grounds. This was presumably treated as being made 'at the time of' the arrest. In *DPP* v *Hawkins* (1988) 88 Cr App R 166, the court had to consider the situation where the giving of reasons was impracticable at the time of the arrest. Hawkins had violently resisted arrest, and this clearly brought the case within the 'impracticability' exception. He was taken to a police station, but even then was not told of the grounds for his arrest. It was held that this rendered the arrest unlawful, but that this did *not* mean that the police officers were not acting in the execution of their duty when they apprehended Hawkins and took him to the police station. In effect, the arrest appears to remain lawful until a point has been reached where it is practicable to give reasons. The failure to do so at that stage is not retrospective. This does not correspond to the most obvious reading of the wording of s. 28, which states:

[N]o arrest *is lawful* unless the person arrested is informed of the ground for the arrest at the time of, or as soon as is practicable after, the arrest. [*emphasis added*]

It may well be argued, however, that the literal reading would make things too difficult for the police in dealing with those who violently resist arrest (see D. Birch, [1988] Crim LR 742). Hawkins' only remedy would thus appear to be to sue the police for false imprisonment in relation to any detention *subsequent* to the point where it was practicable to give reasons.

A person who is arrested should be cautioned as to the right to remain silent (Code C, para. 10.3, see 3.5.1), unless such a caution has been issued immediately prior to the arrest, or it is impracticable because of the person's condition or behaviour.

2.4.1 Power of arrest at common law

The only power of arrest under the common law relates to 'breaches of the peace'. A constable may arrest a person who is causing a breach of the peace, or who is behaving in such a way as to lead the constable reasonably to apprehend an imminent breach of the peace, or who, where a breach has occurred, behaves in a way which leads the constable reasonably to believe that a breach will recur (*R* v *Howell* [1982] QB 416). What is a 'breach of the peace'?

For such an ancient concept, with case law going back to at least the eighteenth century, it is surprising that there is no absolutely certain answer. The definition which appears to be most widely accepted currently is that given by Watkins LJ in *R* v *Howell* [1982] QB 416 at 427:

> We are emboldened to say that there is a breach of the peace whenever harm is actually done or is likely to be done to a person or in his presence his property or a person is in fear of being so harmed through an assault, an affray, a riot, unlawful assembly or other disturbance.

Mere rowdiness, then, does not constitute a breach of the peace. (It may constitute an offence under the Public Order Act 1986: see 8.4.6). Something in the way of actual or potential harm to a person or property is needed. A much broader definition was used by Lord Denning in *R* v *Chief Constable of the Devon and Cornwall Constabulary, ex parte Central Electricity Generating Board* [1982] QB 458. He claimed (at p. 471) that there is a breach of the peace 'whenever a person who is lawfully carrying out his work is unlawfully and physically prevented by another from doing it'. The other members of the Court of Appeal, however, did not follow this definition, finding on the facts that violence was likely, and that the police could intervene on this basis. The *Howell* approach thus seems to be the one to follow.

A breach of the peace can take place on private premises to which the public are admitted (*Thomas* v *Sawkins* [1935] 2 KB 249), or even in a residence (*R* v *Lamb* [1990] Crim LR 58).

The imminence of an apprehended breach of the peace will be a question of fact in each case. In *Moss* v *McClachlan* [1985] IRLR 77, Skinner J referred to the need for a 'close proximity both in place and time'. In that case a distance of one-and-a-half miles, which could have been covered in less than five minutes by car, was held to be sufficiently proximate to allow powers to prevent a breach of the peace to be used.

The cases and issues arising relating to breach of the peace are discussed further in chapter 8 at 8.5.

2.4.2 Arrest under warrant

The police may obtain, from a justice of the peace, a warrant for arrest in relation to any person who has, or is suspected of having, committed an indictable offence: Magistrates' Courts Act 1980, s. 1(1), (4). In practice, however, the powers available to arrrest without warrant under PACE and other statutes are so extensive that the police have little need to use this power, and it is not discussed further.

2.4.3 Powers of arrest under PACE

There are two powers of arrest under PACE. One applies to 'arrestable offences', the other to any offences, provided that certain other conditions (the 'general arrest conditions') are satisfied.

2.4.3.1 Arrestable offence, PACE, s. 24 A constable may arrest without warrant anyone:

(a) who is, or is reasonably suspected to be, about to commit an arrestable offence (s. 24(7)); or

(b) who is, or is reasonably suspected to be, in the act of committing an arrestable offence (s. 24(4)); or

(c) who is guilty of committing an arrestable offence (s. 24(5)); or

(d) who is reasonably suspected to be guilty of having committed an arrestable offence (s. 24(5), (6)).

The constable's powers are wider than those of the private citizen. Only a constable has the power under (a). In relation to (d), the private citizen only has such a power where an arrestable offence has actually been committed: s. 24 (5) (confirmed in *R* v *Self* [1992] 3 All ER 476); the constable on the other hand may arrest where there are reasonable grounds to suspect that such an offence has been committed. It was held, however, by the Court of Appeal in *Plange* v *Chief Constable of South Humberside Police, The Times*, 23 March 1992, that meeting the requirements of s. 24 may not be sufficient, even for a constable. In the highly unusual situation where a constable has reasonable grounds to suspect a person, but knows that there is no possibility that a charge will be brought, an arrest would be unlawful, because the arresting officer would be acting on 'some irrelevant consideration or for an improper purpose'.

What, then, is an 'arrestable offence'? The definition is contained in s. 24(1). It covers murder (an offence 'for which the sentence is fixed by law': s. 24(1)(a)), and any other offence which carries a maximum penalty of at least five years' imprisonment (s. 24(1)(b)). This will include all offences that are generally regarded as 'serious', for example, manslaughter, serious assaults (i.e. ss 18, 20 and 47 of the Offences Against the Person Act 1861), rape, theft, robbery, and arson. In addition, certain offences which carry a lesser penalty, are specifically designated as 'arrestable' by s. 24(2) of PACE. These include various offences relating to customs and excise, official secrets, causing prostitution, taking vehicles without authority, and disorderly behaviour at football matches. There is no obvious link between these various offences which would indicate why, despite the relatively low penalties attached, a power of arrest without warrant is thought to be necessary. In relation to offences of disorder, for example, the Public Order Act 1986 provides for a number of specific powers of arrest (see 8.4) but does not make the offences 'arrestable' for the purposes of PACE. The offences under the Football Offences Act 1991 which are included in s. 24 of PACE are of a very similar kind, but are made arrestable. So far as any policy is indicated by PACE itself, it appears to be that individual powers of arrest under particular statutes should as far as possible be avoided. Section 26 repealed most of those which existed at the time that PACE came into force (while preserving some in sch. 2). This policy has not been consistently followed subsequently, however. As has already been noted, the Public Order Act 1986, for example, includes specific powers of arrest. The conclusion must be that the categorisation of

offences seems haphazard, and the result is that the law on this issue is
confused, and lacking in any clear policy.

The consequences of an offence being 'arrestable' under PACE, as opposed
to having a power of arrest attached to it under another statute, are as follows.
First, the various arrest provisions under s. 24(4) to (7) noted above will be
available, thus giving powers of arrest to the private citizen as well as the
police. Other statutory powers will normally limit the power of arrest to a
constable. Secondly, there are increased powers of search where a person is
arrested for an arrestable offence (s. 18, see 4.2.3.2). Thirdly, the offence has
the potential to be a 'serious arrestable offence', which gives the police wider
powers to obtain access to property (see 4.2.5.1), and the possibility of
extended powers of detention before charge (see 3.3.3). There is therefore
considerable scope for the actions of the police to impinge on personal
freedoms where an offence is arrestable, and parliament should as a result be
careful about granting this status to new offences.

2.4.3.2 General arrest conditions, s. 25 Where a constable witnesses the
commission of an offence which is not arrestable, and to which no other
statutory power of arrest attaches, the normal procedure should be for the
person to be proceeded against by way of summons. In other words, for these
less serious offences, it should not be necessary to take suspects into police
custody; they can simply be required to answer a charge before the courts. It
is recognised in PACE, however, that in some circumstances this may not be
practicable, and that there may be reasons for allowing the constable to arrest.
This is provided for by s. 25, which sets out what are referred to as 'general
arrest conditions'.

Section 25 applies to any offence which is not 'arrestable'. In theory,
therefore, it also applies to those offences which have a separate statutory
power of arrest under a statute other than PACE, though in practice there
would not seem to be any reason why s. 25 should need to be relied on in
relation to such offences. The section says that a constable who has reasonable
grounds to suspect that any non-arrestable offence has been, or is being,
committed or attempted, may arrest a person reasonably suspected to be
responsible, if it appears to the constable that service of a summons is
inappropriate or impracticable because any of the general arrest conditions is
satisfied. Note that as far the commission of the offence, or the identity of the
suspect, are concerned, the constable has to have reasonable suspicion; in
relation to the general arrest conditions, an honest belief in the existence of one
or more of them is apparently sufficient. The constable therefore has
considerable, and to a large extent unchallangeable, discretion in deciding
whether or not to use the power of arrest under s. 25.

The conditions themselves are set out in s. 25(3). They fall into two main
categories, relating to the identity of the suspect, and the behaviour of the
suspect. Looking at the first category, the constable will be entitled to arrest if,
for example, the suspect's name cannot be readily ascertained, or no
satisfactory address (needed for service of a summons) has been given.
Equally, if the constable has reasonable grounds to doubt that a name given is

correct, or that an address is satisfactory for service, he may arrest. Mr and Mrs Duck who decide to name their son 'Donald' should be aware that this may make him more likely to be arrested; those tempted to rename their cottage 'Windsor Castle' should also be aware of the problems which this may create in this respect.

Turning to the second category, the constable will have power to arrest on the basis of a reasonable belief that this is necessary to prevent the person arrested 'causing physical injury to himself or any other person'; or causing loss or damage to property; or committing an offence against public decency in a situation where members of the public cannot reasonably be expected to avoid the person (s. 25(3)(d)(iv), (5)); or causing an unlawful obstruction of the highway (s. 25(3)(d)). The constable also has a power to arrest on the basis of a reasonable belief that this is necessary to protect a child or 'other vulnerable' person from the person arrested (s. 25(3)(e)). This cannot be simply because the suspect may assault the vulnerable person, since this is already covered by s. 25(3)(d)(i). What other reasons for protection there might be, however, is not clear, but may perhaps arise where the arrested person is a man suspected of committing a non-arrestable sexual offence in relation to a member of his family, who may suffer psychological harm unless the suspect is removed (see V. Bevan & K. Lidstone, *The Investigation of Crime*, Butterworths, 1991, p. 242).

Finally, the arrest conditions will be satisfied where the constable has reasonable grounds to believe that the suspect will otherwise suffer physical injury (s. 25(3)(d)(ii)). This type of 'protective' arrest is unusual in that, unlike all the other powers under s. 25 it does not depend on what the suspect says or does, but on what might be done to the suspect. Presumably the power is there to deal with the situation where the commission of an offence leads to a hostile reaction from other members of the public who have witnessed what happened. The driver, for example, who as a result of careless driving (a non-arrestable offence under s. 3 of the Road Traffic Act 1988) has knocked down and injured a child, may need to be removed from the scene rather than being left to the mercies of the passers-by.

It is important to remember that in all cases under s. 25 the person arrested must have been a suspect *before* the general arrest conditions arise. In *G* v *DPP* [1989] Crim LR 150, G was at a police station for the purpose of making a complaint. He was asked for, and gave, his name and address, but the officer did not believe that this was correct. G became abusive and was arrested for disorderly behaviour under s. 29 of the Town Police Clauses Act 1847 (not an arrestable offence). The arrest was held to be unlawful, because G was not a suspect at the time he was asked to give his name and address. The actions which might have constituted the offence took place subsequently.

2.4.4 Other statutory powers
As has already been noted, PACE repealed the majority of statutory powers of arrest existing at the time. Certain powers were, however, preserved by s. 26, and are listed in sch. 2. There is no general principle governing the preserved powers. They are available, for example, to recapture people unlawfully at

large; to stop people driving while under the influence of alcohol; for
protection of the person arrested (for example, a mentally disordered person);
or to deal with squatters. These powers are not examined in detail here. No
special matters of principle apply to them, and they are primarily concerned
with those who are reasonably suspected of having committed, or who have in
fact committed, offences. Similarly the powers of arrest which have been
enacted subsequent to PACE, under the Public Order Act 1986 and the
Sporting Events (Control of Alcohol etc) Act 1985, for example, are generally
based on the standard requirement of 'reasonable suspicion' of having
committed an offence. One power which is rather different in form, however,
is that under s. 14(1)(b) of the Prevention of Terrorism Act 1989, and that is
now considered in a little more detail.

2.4.4.1 Prevention of Terrorism Act 1989 This Act, most of the
provisions of which can be traced back to its precursor, the Prevention of
Terrorism (Temporary Provisions) Act 1974, constitutes an important part of
the government's response to the problems of (principally) Irish terrorism as
it affects the British mainland. Because of its aims, it includes a number of
exceptional powers, which tend to give rise to civil liberties' problems. Aspects
of the Act will need to be considered in each of the next two chapters. Here the
focus is simply on the power of arrest under s. 14(1)(b).

Section 14(1)(a) gives a power of arrest in relation to a person whom a
constable has reasonable grounds to suspect has committed an offence under
certain provisions of the Act. This is a standard form of arrest power. Section
14(1)(b), however, is different. The reasonable suspicion required in this case
is simply that the person arrested 'is or has been concerned in the commission,
preparation or instigation of acts of terrorism'. Although acts of terrorism will
almost certainly involve the commission of an offence, what is unusual here is
that the police need have no particular offence in mind; nor need they worry
overmuch about the level of involvement of the person arrested. The person
does not need to be a principal, an accessory, a conspirator, or an attemptor.
'Being concerned in' is certainly wider than any of these. In particular, it
allows police to arrest on the basis of intelligence information that a person has
a links with terrorist organisations, or with other individuals who are
themselves suspected of being involved in terrorism. It is also important to
remember that this may be the first stage of up to seven days' detention
without charge (see 3.3.4), during which time the police may question the
person arrested with a view to obtaining valuable information about terrorist
activities, and activists, rather than acquiring the evidence necessary for a
charge to be brought. That this is the way the power is used seems to be
confirmed by figures showing that over 80 per cent of those detained under this
power, or one of its predecessors, between 1980 and 1990 in connection with
Northern Ireland terrorism, were released without charge (see S. Bailey, D.
Harris & B. Jones, *Civil Liberties Cases and Materials*, 3rd edn, pp. 293–294).
In 1991 and 1992 the pattern continued, with 313 people being detained under
the Act, but only 29 (i.e. 9.3 per cent) being charged, and other nine excluded
or deported (Home Office Statistical Bulletin, 5/93).

Consideration of whether this exceptional power of arrest is justifiable will depend to some extent on its scope, and the problems against which it is directed. 'Terrrorism' is defined in the 1989 Act, s. 20 as meaning 'the use of violence for political ends'. It also 'includes any use of violence for the purpose of putting the public, or any section of the public in fear'. This definition, and in particular the first part of it, is very wide. Are members of a left-wing organisation, who use force to break up a fascist rally terrorists? What about pickets on strike against the policies of the government, who forcibly prevent workers from entering their work place, or intimidate them by gathering outside their houses and chanting? Their behaviour may well be unlawful, but is it terrorism? Some limitation on the scope of the definition operates in relation to s. 14(1)(b), in that s. 14(2) says that it only applies to acts of terrorism which are either connected with Northern Ireland, or which are not connected solely with the affairs of the United Kingdom, apart from Northern Ireland. In other words, 'international' terrorism (relating to the Middle East, for example) is covered, but not the activities of political extremists seeking independence for Scotland, for example, or some other part of Great Britain.

Apart from this limitation, however, the use of the vague words 'concerned with', and the nebulous concept of 'terrorism', combine to leave the police with very wide discretion. Lord Jellicoe in his 1983 *Review of the Operation of the Prevention of Terrorism (Temporary Provisions) Act 1976* (Cmnd 8803), stated that this arrest power 'should be exercised only where the use of no other power is appropriate to the end sought' (p. 23). The figures given above as to the level of use must raise doubts as to whether this is being followed.

Apart from the grounds for its exercise, the power of arrest under s. 14(1)(b) is like any other arrest power. The procedures to be followed at the time it is used (see 2.4) and subsequently (2.4.5) are the same (see also, at 2.6, *Fox, Campbell and Hartley* v *United Kingdom* (1990) 13 EHRR 157).

2.4.5 Powers and procedures following arrest
The powers and procedures to be followed after an arrest are set out in PACE, ss. 30–32.

2.4.5.1 Power of search
When any person has been arrested other than at a police station, a constable may carry out a search of the person on three grounds. First, there is a power of search where the constable has reasonable grounds for believing 'that the person arrested may present a danger to himself or others' (s. 32(1)). The power is not further explained, but presumably is intended primarily to enable the police to discover any weapon which the person might have in their possession. It would also presumably cover harmful drugs, if there is thought to be a danger of the arrested person attempting suicide. Section 32(8) allows the seizure and retention of anything which the constable has reasonable grounds to believe the arrested person might use to cause physical injury 'to himself or any other person'.

Secondly, a constable may search for anything which might be used by the arrested person to escape, on the basis of reasonable grounds for believing that some such thing is concealed on the person (s. 32(2)(a)(i)).

Thirdly, a constable may search for evidence of *any* offence, not just the offence for which the arrest took place, on the basis of reasonable grounds for believing that such evidence is concealed on the person arrested (s. 32(2)(a)(ii)).

In relation to the last two powers, they are limited to what is reasonably required in order to discover what is suspected to be concealed (s. 32(3)). In relation to either power the constable may seize and retain anything discovered (other than an item subject to legal privilege (for which see 4.4.1.1)) which the constable has reasonable grounds for believing might be used to assist the arrested person to escape, or is evidence of, or has been obtained in consequence of, the commission of any offence (s. 32(9)).

None of the powers under s. 32, however, authorises the constable to require the removal in public of more than an outer coat, jacket or gloves (s. 32(4): compare the powers in relation to stop and search, see 2.3.2.3).

Certain powers to enter and search premises also arise as a consequence of arrest, under ss. 18 and 32. These powers are discussed in chapter 4, at 4.2.3.2.

2.4.5.2 Procedure following arrest The basic procedure following arrest, and any search that may have taken place as a result, is for the arrested person to be taken to a police station (assuming that the arrest has taken place elsewhere) (s. 30(1)). This should happen 'as soon as practicable'. Generally the police station should be a 'designated police station' (s. 30(2)), which in practice will mean one of the larger police stations in the area (see s. 35). There is an exception, however, if the period of custody is likely to be relatively short (less than six hours), and the constable is working in an area covered by a station which is not designated (s. 30(3) and (4)). The constable may also take the person to a non-designated station in two other situations: first, where an individual constable has carried out the arrest, or taken charge of the arrested person (for example, following a citizen's arrest), and has no assistance from other officers available (s. 30(5)(a)); and, secondly, where the constable thinks that there is a risk of injury to the arrested person, the constable, or someone else, if the person has to be taken to a designated station (s. 30(5)(b)). These are exceptional cases, however, and in any case, a person who is first taken to a non-designated station should be moved to a designated station, or released, within six hours. This is to ensure that the proper procedures relating to detention, which require the supervision of a custody officer (see 3.2.1), are carried out, where any extended period of detention occurs.

A final situation in which the arrested person need not be taken to a designated station is where the constable decides before arrival that it is no longer necessary to keep the person under arrest (s. 30(7)). This might occur, for example, where a person arrested under s. 25 (see 2.4.3.2) decides to give a satisfactory name or address, or no longer appears to be a danger to anybody. Release in this way should be recorded by the constable (s. 30(8)). Thus all arrests should be recorded, either upon arrival at a police station (see 3.2), or upon prior release.

It was noted above that, under the normal procedures, the arrested person should be taken to a designated station as soon as practicable. Section 30(10) recognises one particular situation where delay may be justified. This is where the presence of the arrested person is required elsewhere, in order to carry out investigations which it is reasonable should take place immediately. This would be the case, for example, where the police wish to search premises immediately after the arrest, and wish to have the arrested person present. The reasons for any such delay must be recorded as soon as the arrested person arrives at a police station (s. 30(11)).

The purpose of s. 30 is to ensure that the arrested person is received as soon as possible into the system of detention, and its associated safeguards, which is set out in Part IV of the Act (and discussed in chapter 3). The fact that some exceptions are allowed, however, may encourage the police to try to find reasons for delay so that they can question the person, or obtain other information, before entering the realm of compulsory access to legal advice, and tape-recorded interviews. As will be seen at 3.5.2.1, amendments to the Codes of Practice have been introduced to counter this by extending the notion of what constitutes an 'interview', and to reduce the advantages to the police of using the 'mobile interview room' (that is, a police car), to take the 'scenic route' to the police station. Some of the problems which still exist for the arrested person, however, are shown by *R* v *Kerawalla* [1991] Crim LR 451. The arrest took place in a hotel room, and Kerawalla was questioned there for some time. It was held that he had not been wrongly deprived of his right to legal advice under s. 58 of PACE, because this right only applied to people in custody at a police station. Moreover, although the police were in breach of their duty under s. 30 to bring Kerawalla to a police station as soon as practicable, this breach was not such as should render the evidence obtained from the questioning at the hotel inadmissible. Although the Court of Appeal emphasised the point that in this case they did not think there was any bad faith involved on the part of the police, and that they were not delaying taking the suspect to the police station simply to avoid his having access to legal advice, the decision can only act as an encouragement to the police to stretch the limits of s. 30 as far as possible.

2.5 CHALLENGING THE POLICE

There are various ways in which an allegation that the police have exceeded or abused their powers as regards stop and search, or arrest, can be pursued. Civil actions, official complaints, and attempts to have evidence excluded, may all be appropriate in particular cases. The most frequent complaints of this kind, however, arise out of procedures during detention. Discussion of these issues is therefore left until the next chapter at 3.6.

2.6 THE EUROPEAN POSITION

Article 5 of the European Convention on Human Rights sets out the standards to be applied in relation to infringements of personal freedom. After stating the general right to 'liberty and security of person', the Article goes on to recognise various exceptions. The one that is relevant to this chapter is

Art. 5(1)(c), which allows deprivation of liberty 'in accordance with a procedure prescribed by law', where it takes the form of:

> the lawful arrest or detention of a person effected for the purpose of bringing him before the competent legal authority on reasonable suspicion of having committed an offence or when it is reasonably considered necessary to prevent his committing an offence or fleeing after having done so.

Further, a person who is arrested must be told promptly, and in a language which the person can understand, of the reasons for the arrest (Art. 5(2)). Various of the other provisions of Art. 5 are more relevant to the procedures at the police station, and so will be discussed in chapter 3.

The interpretation of Art. 5 has arisen in a number of cases before the European Court. One of the most recent is the 1990 case, *Fox, Campbell and Hartley* v *UK* (1990) 13 EHRR 157. This concerned arrests under s. 11 of the Northern Ireland (Emergency Provisions) Act 1978, which allowed an arrest without warrant of 'any person suspected of being a terrorist'. The Court made it clear that the mere fact that an arrest took place under this power, which contained no requirement of *reasonable* suspicion, did not make it unlawful. It was necessary to decide in each case whether there was in fact reasonable suspicion. Thus the provision itself cannot be struck down; only particular actions taken under it (para. 31). The Article requires 'reasonable suspicion of having committed an offence', but the court seemed quite prepared to accept that this would be satisfied by 'reasonable suspicion of being a terrorist'.

The Court also considered the application of Art. 5(2) which requires that the arrested person be informed of the grounds for the arrest. The Court accepted that the purpose of this requirement was to enable the person to be in a position to challenge the arrest. Telling the applicants that they were being arrested because they were suspected of being terrorists was not sufficient for this purpose; but subsequent questioning over the next seven to eight hours in relation to specific criminal acts, and membership of proscribed organisations, was sufficient to indicate the reason for the arrest, and met the requirements of Art. 5(2) (paras 41–43). What is required in terms of content and promptness must be assessed in each case 'according to its special features' (para. 40).

Two other points from the cases are worth noting. First, in *Lawless* v *Ireland* (1961) 1 EHRR 1, it was emphasised that the *purpose* of arrest under Art. 5(1)(c) must be to bring the arrested person before a competent judicial authority. This was confirmed more recently in *Brogan* v *United Kingdom* (1989) 11 EHRR 117, which was concerned with the exercise of the powers under s. 12 of the Prevention of Terrorism (Temporary Provisions) Act 1984, which was the equivalent of the current s. 14 of the Prevention of Terrorism (Temporary Provisions) Act 1989 (see 2.4.4.1). In *Brogan*, however, the Court stated that the fact that those arrested are not charged, nor brought before a court, does not necessarily mean that the purpose of the arrest was out of line with Art. 5(1)(c). There was no need for the police to have, at the time of arrest, sufficient evidence to bring charges (para. 53). As the Court then commented:

There is no reason to believe that the police investigation in this case was not in good faith or that the detention of the applicants was not intended to further that investigation by way of confirming, or dispelling, the concrete suspicions which, as the Court has found, grounded their arrest.

This approach by the Court makes it harder for a person arrested under s. 14 of the Prevention of Terrorism (Temporary Provisions) Act 1989 to argue that the arrest falls outside the scope of what is permitted under Art. 5(1) because it is being used to gather intelligence. As it has been suggested above, the figures indicate this is the most common way in which this particular power of arrest is used (see 2.3.4.1). The *Brogan* interpretation of the *Lawless* 'purpose' requirement, also appears to give legitmacy to use of arrest powers generally for the purpose of questioning prior to charge. This is obviously of great practical importance to the police, but it is not the most obvious reading of the wording of Art. 5(1)(c).

Secondly, in *Guzzardi* v *Italy* (1980) 3 EHRR 333, the Court ruled that the reference in Art. 5(1)(c) to the use of arrest to prevent a person committing an offence, only applied in relation to a 'concrete and specified offence' (para. 102). It could not be used to justify a policy of general prevention directed against an individual, or category of individuals, who, like members of the Mafia, for example, are dangerous because of a continuing propensity to commit crimes. Thus, what in effect this part of Art. 5(1)(c) is primarily intended to cover, is the situation recognised, for example, in s. 24 of PACE, where a power of arrest is given in relation to a person reasonably suspected of being about to commit a specific arrestable offence (see 2.4.3.1).

What of the other powers which have been looked at in this chapter? Are they justifiable under Art. 5(1)(c)? Powers of stop and search will probably be regarded as acceptable, either because they do not involve sufficient deprivation of liberty to fall within Art. 5 at all (see, for example, *Engel* (1976) 1 EHRR 647), or under the *Brogan* approach of allowing the use of arrest to question with a view to allaying or confirming suspicions. The statutory powers of arrest such as those under PACE, ss. 24 and 25, are generally sufficiently directed towards court proceedings also to be legitimated. And, as we have just seen, the wider powers under the terrorism legislation also appear, on the basis of *Brogan*, to be acceptable.

Finally, the requirement to give reasons for the arrest in PACE, s. 28, corresponds to the similar requirement in Art. 5(2). Indeed, s. 28 is probably stricter, since *Fox, Campbell and Hartley* v *UK* regards it as acceptable that the information should be given over a period of time, and indirectly. Whether what happened in *Hawkins* (see 2.4) would also be acceptable is more doubtful. If, as seems quite possible, the failure ever to give the reasons for arrest in this case amounted to a breach of Art. 5(2), then Hawkins should have had a right to compensation, by virtue of Art. 5(5). That he had no effective remedy might well amount to a breach of the Convention.

Overall, however, it seems that in this area, the powers and procedures under English law, relating to stop and search and arrest, are within the scope of what is allowable under Art. 5 of the European Convention, as interpreted in the cases. It is important to remember, however, that the Court looks at individual cases, not particular rules and procedures. Thus, in the same way that the Court may decide that the way in which a power which is perhaps too widely framed in domestic law has been applied in the case before it means that there is no breach of the Convention, the contrary must also be true. If a power which is framed in a way which meets the requirement of Art. 5, is applied oppressively in a particular case, there is then the possibility of a challenge under the Convention.

THREE

Freedom of the Person II: Detention and Questioning

3.1 INTRODUCTION

This chapter continues the consideration of issues raised in chapter 2. While that chapter was concerned, however, with the initial decision to stop a person, and prevent them from departing, this chapter looks at the issues arising from more extended detention, generally at a police station. The focus here is on the grounds for such extended detention prior to charge, and the procedures which must be adopted in relation to it. The chapter does *not* deal with the procedures after a charge has been made, or after a person has been convicted. Both may involve deprivation of liberty, but the civil liberties issues are different where someone is either facing a specific charge, or has been convicted of an offence. They are not discussed further in this book. What we are concerned with are the rights of the citizen who is simply 'under suspicion', and against whom the police do not have sufficient evidence to charge with an offence.

A number of the issues and procedures dealt with in this chapter have been the subject of recommendations by the Royal Commission on Criminal Justice ('RCCJ') which reported in July 1993 (*Report*, Cm 2263). The Commission was set up under the chairmanship of Lord Runciman, largely as a response to concerns about the operation of the criminal justice system in the wake of the acquittals of the 'Guildford Four' and the 'Birmingham Six', but with far-reaching terms of reference. Its report deals with the whole of the criminal process from questioning by the police prior to charge, through to the mechanisms for appeal, and review of convictions. The relevant recommendations of the Commission, which are drawn from chapters 2 and 3 of the *Report*, are noted at the relevant points in this chapter. At the time of writing, however, it is unclear whether, and if so when, the government intends to act on any of these recommendations.

3.1.1 Reasons for extending detention prior to charge
Why should the police have the power to detain prior to charge? The main purpose of such detention is to enable the suspect to be questioned, with a view

to deciding whether there is sufficient evidence to bring a charge, or to obtaining such evidence, for example, in the form of a confession. The need to obtain evidence cannot, however, in itself justify the deprivation of liberty involved. It is not thought right to give the police compulsory powers of detention in relation to witnesses to criminal offences. Such people are perfectly entitled to refuse to cooperate with the police. Of course, if the matter goes to trial, the witness can be compelled to attend to give evidence, and may be in contempt of court for failing to do so. At the stage of acquiring evidence in the course of an investigation, however, the fact that such people may be in possession of vital information is not thought sufficient to entitle the police to force them to submit to questioning. In a limited range of situations it may be an *offence* to fail to give information. For example, under s. 18 of the Prevention of Terrorism Act 1989 it is an offence not to provide information about terrorism related to Northern Ireland; but even here, there is no power to arrest and detain unless there is a suspicion of direct involvement with terrorism.

The special powers of detention given in relation to suspects must therefore be justified by the suspicion itself. As we have seen in chapter 2, for an arrest the police must have reasonable grounds for believing that the person was in some way involved in criminal activities. Because there is such a belief, and therefore the reasonable possibility that the person has committed a criminal offence for which they will have to stand trial, it is acceptable that, in certain circumstances, the police should be able to detain the person with a view to obtaining the evidence they need to proceed. Such detention will only be for a restricted period of time, however, and is subject to a variety of procedural safeguards.

3.1.2 The PACE framework
The powers and responsibilities of the police, and the rights of the suspect, as regards those detained prior to charge, are now primarily governed by Parts IV and V of PACE, and Code of Practice C. For the relationship between the statute and the Code, see chapter 2 at 2.2. PACE places much of the responsibility for ensuring that the provisions of the Act and the Code are complied with on to the shoulders of the 'custody officer' (see 3.2.1), who is in charge of the 'custody record' which should provide documentary evidence as to what was done in relation to each suspect in detention. Here, as in other parts of the Act, the main method of trying to achieve a balance between police powers and the freedoms of the citizen, is by the use of record keeping, to attempt to ensure that the limits are not overstepped. There are, however, in this part of the Act some positive rights given to those detained, most importantly the right of access to legal advice, under s. 58 (see 3.4.2).

The Code of Practice, as will be seen at 3.4.4, goes into considerable detail on the conditions of detention, spelling out, for example, the details of the type of meals to be provided. The problem here, however, is that there are no very effective methods of enforcement (see 3.6).

The procedures that follow are described as they apply to an adult, of sound mind, who understands English. Special rules operate in relation to various category of particularly vulnerable suspects, but for reasons of space these are not dealt with here.

3.2 PRELIMINARY PROCEDURES AT THE POLICE STATION

As we have seen, people arrested away from a police station, must normally be taken to a designated police station without delay (see 2.4.5.2). Some people may be arrested at the police station. For example, if the police have been interviewing somebody who has been attending the police station voluntarily, and a constable decides that if the person wanted to leave, that would no longer be allowed, the person must be arrested (s. 29). There must, of course, also be grounds for an arrest. As soon as the arrested person arrives at the police station, or the person at the station is arrested, they become the responsibility of the custody officer.

3.2.1 The custody officer, and the custody record

Appointment of custody officers is the responsibility of the chief officer of police for the area (that is, normally, the chief constable) though the power may be delegated (s. 36). The custody officer will almost always be a sergeant. No officer of lower rank may be appointed as a custody officer (s. 36(3)), though in some circumstances a constable may temporarily act as a custody officer (s. 36(4), (7)). Officers of the rank of sergeant or above who are not custody officers may also act as such in the same circumstances. Each designated police station will generally have a number of custody officers, so that there will always be one on duty. There is no legal obligation on a chief constable, however, to appoint more than one per station: *Vince* v *Chief Constable of the Dorset Police* [1993] 2 All ER 321. The RCCJ has recommended that the use of acting sergeants as custody officers should be kept to an absolute minimum (*Report*, chapter 3, para. 26).

It is the responsibility of the custody officer to open a custody record in relation to any person brought to the police station under arrest, or arrested at the police station (Code C, 2.1). This will act as a 'log book' of the person's time at the police station. All entries must be timed and signed by the maker (Code C, 2.6). The detainee, and the detainee's legal representative have a right to a copy of the custody record for 12 months from release (Code C, 2.4), and there is also right, on giving notice, to inspect the original (Code C, 2.5).

3.2.2 Information to be given at the start of detention

When an arrested person comes under the supervision of a custody officer, certain information must be given immediately (Code C, 3.1). This information is, first, the right to have someone informed of the arrest (see 3.4.1); secondly, the right to legal advice (see 3.4.2); and thirdly, the right to consult the Codes of Practice (which must be available at every police station). It should be made clear that these are continuing rights, which may be exercised at at any time during custody.

The custody officer must also provide the person with a written notice. This should set out the above three rights, and in addition draw attention to the right to a copy of the custody record (see 3.2.1) and arrangements for obtaining legal advice (Code C, 3.2). A further written 'notice of entitlements' should be given, dealing with such matters as visits during custody, provision of meals and other facilities, and the conduct of interviews (Code C, 3.2, Note 3A). Just to make sure that all this is done, the person must be asked to sign the custody record acknowledging receipt of the various notices. A refusal to sign must be noted on the custody record.

These procedures are obviously better than nothing, but they are no guarantee that the person actually understands the entitlements, let alone is put in a position to enforce them. For many people who have just arrived at a police station under arrest, reading documents containing lists of rights is likely to be a low priority, and a request to sign, issued by a confident custody officer, is likely to be construed as an order to be obeyed, without necessarily much attention being paid to what is being signed. All this may well happen without any attempt to manipulate the procedures on the part of the police; they are no safeguard at all against an officer or officers who decide to act in bad faith.

3.2.3   The decision to detain
The first obligation of the custody officer, having issued the above information, is to decide whether the person is to be detained. This is governed by s. 37 of PACE. The custody officer must first decide whether there is sufficient evidence to charge the person with the offence for which the arrest was made (s. 37(1)). If there is, then the person should be charged. The presumption is that release from custody (with or without bail) will follow a charge, unless there are particular reasons for continued detention, as specified in s. 38. This aspect of police procedures is not considered further here. If the custody officer decides that there is insufficient evidence for a charge, then, again, the starting point is release with or without bail. In two circumstances, however, the custody officer may authorise continued detention. The first is where there are reasonable grounds for believing that this is necessary to secure or preserve evidence relating to an offence for which the person is under arrest. There may be a risk, for example, that the suspected thief, if released, will dispose, or arrange for the disposal, of the stolen goods. The second, and most frequently used, ground for continued detention before charge is where the custody officer has reasonable grounds to believe that this is necessary in order to obtain evidence by questioning the person. The reasonable grounds in this case are likely to come largely from the investigating officer, who will no doubt seek to convince the custody officer that a period of questioning will result in a confession, or the obtaining of other evidence which will link the suspect sufficiently to the crime to justify a charge. The RCCJ has recommended that the Code should be amended to clarify whether the custody officer is entitled to invite the suspect to comment on the arresting officer's account of the arrest, or as to whether there should be further detention. The RCCJ found that there were divergent practices on this, and that custody officers were not sure whether any such exchange should be treated as an 'interview'. This point also needed clarification (*Report*, chapter 3, para. 16).

If the decision is to detain, the custody officer must make a written record of the grounds (s. 37(4)). This should normally be done in the presence of the detainee, who should also be told of the grounds of the detention (s. 37(5)). This need not be done, however, if the detainee is at the time incapable of understanding what is said, or is violent or likely to become violent, or is in urgent need of medical attention (s. 37(6)). A detainee who is not in such a state must then be asked to sign the custody record to indicate whether legal advice is wanted or not. If it is, then it is the duty of the custody officer to try to arrange the provision of advice (Code C, 3.5), unless grounds exist for refusing access to it (see 3.4.2).

3.2.4 Search of detainees

Section 54(1) places an obligation on the custody officer to make an inventory, which will be included in the custody record and should be signed by the detainee (Code C, Note 4A), of everything in the possession of a detained person, including items taken from the person on arrest. A search may be carried out (by a constable of the same sex as the detainee) in order to facilitate this, though an intimate search or a search requiring the removal of more than outer clothing must follow the procedures in Annex A to Code C (which is discussed at 3.5.3.2). Paragraph 4A of Code C states that the inventory need not be made if the person is clearly only to be detained for a short period, and is not to be placed in a cell. In that case the custody record should be endorsed 'not searched', and the detainee asked to sign. If the detainee refuses to sign, the custody officer will be obliged to compile an inventory in the normal way.

The custody officer may normally seize and retain any item in the possession of the detainee (s. 54(3)). Clothes and personal effects (which does not include cash or other items of value (Code C, para 4.3)), however, may only be seized where there are reasonable grounds to believe that the detainee may use them to cause physical injury, to damage property, to interfere with evidence, or to assist escape (s. 54(4)(a)). Any clothes or personal effects which the custody officer has reasonable grounds to believe may be evidence relating to an offence (not necessarily that for which the person is detained) may also be seized (s. 54(4)(b)). The detainee, unless violent or likely to become violent, or incapable of understanding what is said, should be told the reasons for any seizure of property (s. 54(5)).

3.3 TIME FOR DETENTION

The period for which a person may be detained without charge is never without limit. The maximum period differs, however, according to whether the person is being held under the terrorism provisions (see 3.3.4), on suspicion of a 'serious arrestable offence' (see 3.3.3), or for any other offence (see 3.3.2).

3.3.1 The 'relevant time'

In calculating the permitted period of detention without charge, it is obviously important to identify the point when time starts to run. This is referred to in the Act as 'the relevant time', and is defined in s. 41. The standard situation is where a person is arrested and then taken to a police station. The relevant time is arrival at the police station (s. 41(2)(d)). Note that if the person is taken to a station other than a designated station (see 2.4.5.2), time still starts to run from arrival at that station. If arrival at the police station has been delayed, either legitimately, for example, to enable a search of premises to be carried out in the presence of the suspect, or illegitimately, as in *R* v *Kerawalla* [1991] Crim LR 451 (see 2.4.5.2), the time prior to arrival will not count towards the period of detention.

In relation to a person arrested at a police station, the time of arrest is the relevant time (s. 41(2)(c)).

Special provisions apply where a person is arrested outside the police area in which their arrest is sought. If the arrest takes place in another police area in England and Wales, and the person is not questioned about the offence in that police area, the relevant time is normally the time at which the person first arrives at a police station in the area where the arrest was sought (s. 41(2)(a), (3)), subject to a 'safety-net' provision, whereby if the person is not taken to such a police station within 24 hours of the arrest, time will start to run anyway. If the person *is* questioned in the other police area, then the standard rule will apply, that is, the relevant time will be the time of first arrival at a police station, wherever situated. Thus is if a suspect sought in Area A is arrested in Area B, and questioned in a police car which takes the suspect to a police station in Area C, before being moved to Area A, the relevant time will the time of arrival at the station in Area C.

Where the arrest takes place outside England and Wales (for example, in Scotland) the relevant time will be either the time at which the arrested person arrives at a police station in the area where arrest was sought, or 24 hours after the person's arrival in England or Wales, whichever is the earlier (s. 41(2)(b)).

Finally, there is the situation where a person is being detained by the police in police Area A, and arrest of the person for another offence is sought in police Area B, so that the person is taken from A to B for the purpose of being questioned about that offence, not having been questioned about it in Area A. The relevant time is then either 24 hours after leaving the place of detention in A, or the time of arrival at a police station in B, whichever is the earlier (s. 41(5)).

As is clear from the above, rather complicated, provisions it is quite possible for a person to be in police detention for up to 24 hours before time starts to run against the police. Although there will be limitations on the power to question the detainee in this preliminary period, the additional time must be borne in mind when considering the statutory periods of permissible detention prior to charge.

3.3.2 The standard period of detention

Section 41(7) states that in general a person who is in police detention 24 hours after the relevant time, must be charged or released. The exceptions to this are noted at 3.3.3–3.3.4. The police may not obtain another 24 hours by releasing and re-arresting. Section 41(9) prohibits a person released under s. 41(7) from ever being re-arrested without warrant for the same offence, unless new evidence has come to light. Arrest for a slightly different offence may well be permissible, however. For example, a person released after being detained in relation to suspected importation of cannabis might be re-arrested for possession with intent to supply. This would be likely not to be regarded as an abuse, unless the police were clearly acting in bad faith (see, for example, *R v Great Yarmouth Magistrates, ex parte Thomas* [1992] Crim LR 117, dealing with custody limits after charge). It should also be noted that the wording of s. 41(9) does not apply to a person released before the expiry of the 24 hour period. In theory, therefore, a person might be detained for 18 hours, released, and then re-arrested for the same offence, with the prospect of a further 24 hours detention. If no new evidence is available, however, the custody officer, in exercising the power to decide whether to detain under s. 37 (see 3.2.3), should surely refuse to agree to a further period of detention in relation to the same offence.

3.3.2.1 Reviews of detention Just because the custody officer has decided that detention is justified does not mean that the investigating officers automatically have 24 hours to question the suspect. Regular reviews of the need for continued detention must be held. These will be conducted by a 'review officer', who must be an officer of at least the rank of inspector who is not directly involved with the investigation (s. 40(1), (2)). The first review will generally take place not later than six hours after detention was first *authorised* (s. 40(3)(a)). This means when the custody officer decided to detain under s. 37(3) (see 3.2.3), not 'the relevant time'. Subsequent reviews must take place at intervals of not more than nine hours (s. 40(3)(b), (c)). Generally, then, unless there is a significant gap (i.e. at least nine hours) between 'the relevant time' and the decision to detain, there will be at least two reviews during the standard 24 hour period of detention.

A review may be postponed if it is not practicable to carry it out at the required time (s. 40(4)). The Act does not limit the kinds of circumstances which may lead to impracticability, but does specify two particular situations where postponement will be justified. The first of these is where the detainee is being questioned by a police officer, and the review officer is satisfied that the interruption necessary for a review would prejudice the investigation. The investigating officer who is on the brink of obtaining a confession need not break off for the purposes of a review. The second situation is where there is no review officer readily available. Both these possibilities allow a fair scope for police discretion in carrying out reviews, though the reasons for any postponement must be recorded on the custody record (s. 40(7)), and the review must be carried out as soon as it becomes practicable to do so (s. 40(5)).

In carrying out the review, the review officer must consider the same issues, and follow the same procedures as the custody officer does in dealing with the initial decision to detain (see 3.2.3). Continued detention will only normally be justified therefore, where there are reasonable grounds for believing that it is necessary either to secure or preserve evidence relating to an offence for which the person is being detained, or to obtain such evidence by questioning

(s. 37(2)). Before reaching such a decision, however, the review officer must give the detainee (unless asleep), or the detainee's solicitor (if available), the opportunity to make representations about the detention (s. 40(12)). Such representations may be oral or in writing (s. 40(13)), although the review officer is not obliged to hear oral representations from the detainee, if the officer considers that the detainee is unfit to make such representations (s. 40(14)).

Code C recommends that where a detainee is likely to be asleep at the time when the next review is due, the review officer should bring it forward, so that the detainee will be able to make representations (Code C, Note 15A). It also recognises that in the last resort, it may be permissible to carry out a review over the telephone, provided that the other procedures required by the Act are followed (Code C, Note 15C).

There is, of course, likely to be tension in some cases between the requirements of the review officer, and those of the investigating officer, who may be of the same or higher rank than the review officer. If a conflict arises as to what is to be done in relation to a detainee, the review officer should immediately refer it to an officer of at least the rank of superintendent, who is responsible for the police station where the review is being carried out (s. 40(11)). This senior officer will presumably have the last word as to what is to happen in the case.

3.3.3   The extended period: serious arrestable offences

Detention without charge beyond the normal 24 hours is permissible in certain situations. One of these is where at least one of the offences for which the detainee has been arrested is a 'serious arrestable offence'.

3.3.3.1   Definition of serious arrestable offence   This is a sub-category of offences which are regarded as particularly serious, within the broader category of 'arrestable offences' (see 2.4.3.1). It is important to remember that no offence which is not 'arrestable' within s. 24 can ever be a serious arrestable offence, no matter what the consequences of it. The offence of dangerous driving, for example, under s. 2 of the Road Traffic Act 1988, may result in very serious injuries, or extensive damage to property. The maximum penalty for the offence, however, is two years' imprisonment. It is not, therefore, an arrestable offence, and so can never be a serious arrestable offence.

The definition of 'serious arrestable offence' is to be found in s. 116 of PACE and sch. 5. Certain offences are always serious arrestable offences. These include treason, murder, manslaughter, rape, and various other sexual offences (s. 116(2)(a); sch. 5, Part I). Various statutory offences, connected with drug trafficking, explosives, or firearms, for example, are in the same category (s. 116(2)(aa), (b); sch. 5, Part II). On the other hand, serious non-sexual assaults, such as causing grievous bodily harm with intent to do so under s. 18 of the Offences Against the Person Act 1861, are not automatically serious arrestable offences, nor are attempts or conspiracies to commit the offences listed in sch. 5.

Any arrestable offence has the potential to become a serious arrestable offence if its commission has led, or was intended to lead, to certain consequences specified in s. 116(3). It is not enough that those consequences were *likely* to occur. They must actually have occurred, or have been intended to occur.

The consequences are:

(a)   serious harm to the security of the State or to public order;
(b)   serious interference with the administration of justice or with the investigation of offences or a particular offence;
(c)   the death of any person;
(d)   serious injury to any person;
(e)   substantial financial gain to any person; and
(f)   serious financial loss to any person.

This list of consequences means that in practice offences such as conspiracy to murder, or the offence of causing grievous bodily harm under s. 18 of the Offences Against the Person Act 1861 mentioned above, will always be serious arrestable offences, despite the fact that they are not listed in sch. 5.

Two of the consequences are further defined. First, 'injury' in (d) is stated to include 'any disease and any impairment of a person's physical or mental condition' (s. 116(8)). This is very broad, but it must be remembered that the disease or impairment must be 'serious'.

Secondly, a financial loss under (f) will be serious if 'having regard to all the circumstances, it is serious for the person who suffers it'. The test is thus subjective, based on the effect on the victim. So in *R* v *McIvor* [1987] Crim LR 409, the trial judge ruled that the theft of dogs worth £880 which were owned collectively by a hunt could not be regarded as a serious financial loss to the hunt. If they had all been owned by one person, the result might presumably have been different (see also, *R* v *Eric Smith* [1987] Crim LR 579). As has often been pointed out, the subjective approach leads to the possibility that the theft of say, £20, from an impecunious old age pensioner, might be regarded as a serious arrestable offence. The test of substantial gain in (e), on the other hand, is apparently objective, so that the state of the thief's finances will be irrelevant. Since the test of whether the offence is 'serious' is there primarily to decide the issue of whether the police should have extended powers of investigation, rather than to do justice as between different victims, it is submitted that the objective approach makes more sense than the subjective. The use of specific financial limits, as is done in relation to deciding which offences under the Criminal Damage Act 1971 should be triable on indictment, would perhaps have been more sensible. This option was one which parliament was not, however, prepared to accept (see Birch, [1987] Crim LR 410).

3.3.3.2   Detention in relation to a serious arrestable offence   Where the detainee has been arrested for a serious arrestable offence, the maximum possible period of detention without charge is extended from 24 hours to 96 hours, that is up to four days. Such extensions are subject to special procedures, however, and detention beyond 36 hours will always require the approval of a magistrates' court.

The initial power to extend detention beyond 24 hours must be exercised by an officer of at least the rank of superintendent who is responsible for the police station at which the person is detained. As well as having reasonable grounds to believe that at least one of the offences for which the detainee is under arrest is a serious arrestable offence, the officer must also have reasonable grounds for believing that the continued detention is necessary to secure or preserve evidence relating to an offence (not necessarily the serious arrestable offence) for which the detainee is under arrest, or to obtain such evidence by questioning (s. 42(1)(a)). These, of course, are the same grounds which justify an initial decision by the custody officer to detain, and the decision by the review officer to continue detention up to 24 hours. The officer approving extended detention, however, must in addition have reasonable grounds for believing that the investigation is being conducted 'diligently and expeditiously' (s. 42(1)(c)). Before reaching a decision, the officer, as is also the case in relation to a review officer during the initial 24 hours, must allow the detainee or the detainee's solicitor to make representations orally or in writing about the detention (s. 42(6), (7), (8)). If after this the officer is satisfied on reasonable grounds of all the matters specified in s. 42(1), then the officer may authorise continued detention up to 36 hours from the 'relevant time' (see 3.3.1). The power cannot be exercised, however, before the second review of detention under s. 40 (see 3.3.2.1) has been carried out, or more than 24 hours after the relevant time (s. 42(4)). It cannot be used, therefore, pre-emptively at an early stage of detention, nor retrospectively, to legitimise unauthorised detention beyond 24 hours.

If a decision to continue detention is made, it is the duty of the officer authorising it to inform the detainee of the grounds, and to record them in the detainee's custody record (s. 42(5)).

At the expiry of 36 hours from the relevant time the detainee must either be charged, kept in detention in accordance with a magistrates' warrant under s. 43 (below), or released (s. 42(10)). If released, the detainee may not be re-arrested without warrant for the same offence, unless new evidence has become available justifying a further arrest (s. 42(11)).

After the initial 36 hours of detention, the control of continued detention changes significantly. Whereas up to this point it may be regarded as essentially an administrative procedure operated by the police, the introduction of supervision by the magistrates' courts at this stage indicates that it then becomes a judicial decision. This is important in the context of compliance with the requirements of the European Convention on Human Rights, Art. 5 (see 3.7).

The application for a warrant of further detention is governed by ss. 43–45. It must be made to a magistrates' court, which is defined as being 'a court consisting of two or more justices sitting otherwise than in open court' (s. 45(1)). The application may be made at any point before the expiry of 36 hours from the relevant time. If, however, it is not practicable for a magistrates' court to sit before the expiry of this time, but it will become so within the next six hours, the application may be made before the expiry of those six hours (s. 43(5)). In effect, therefore, a person can be detained, in certain circumstances, for up to 42 hours, before being brought before the magistrates. The court has a power to dismiss an application which it thinks it would have been reasonable to make before the expiry of the 36 hours (s. 43(7)).

The application must be supported by an information (a copy of which must be supplied to the detainee) outlining the reasons for arrest, the progress of the investigation, and the reasons for believing that continued detention is necessary (s. 43(14)). The detainee must be present at the hearing, and is entitled to be legally represented. The grounds for issuing a warrant of further detention are the same as those for authorising continued detention (s. 43(4); see 3.3.3.2). The warrant, if issued may extend the period of detention by up to 36 hours (s. 43(11)(12)). If it is refused, the detainee must be charged or released, unless there is still a period of previously authorised detention which has not expired (s. 43(15), (16)). No further application for an extension may be made after a refusal, however, unless new evidence has subsequently come to light (s. 43(17)). Similarly, a person who is released at the expiry of a warrant of further detention may not be re-arrested for the same offence unless new evidence has come to light since the release (s. 43(19)).

If the police wish to extend a warrant of further detention, this is possible, but a new application and information will need to be submitted, and there will have to be a further hearing before a magistrates' court, in relation to each extension (s. 44). The maximum period for any one extension is 36 hours, and no extension may extend the period beyond 96 hours from the relevant time. 96 hours is therefore the maximum period for which anyone can be detained without charge, other than those arrested under the Prevention of Terrorism (Temporary Provisions) Act 1989.

3.3.4 The extended period: the terrorism provisions

The detention of people arrested under s. 14 of the Prevention of Terrorism (Temporary Provisions) Act 1989 (see 2.4.4.1) is governed by the provisions of that section, and sch. 3 to the Act, rather than by PACE. Section 14(4) allows an initial period of detention of up to 48 hours on the authority of the police, and a further period of five days on the authority of the Home Secretary. The procedures governing the detention are to be found in sch. 3.

During the initial period of detention, regular reviews should be carried out by a review officer. This is an officer who is unconnected with the investigation, and who, for reviews carried out during the first 24 hours of detention, must be of at least the rank of inspector, and for later reviews, must be of at least the rank of superintendent (para.4).

The first review should take place as soon as practicable after the beginning of the detention (para.3(2)). This review is therefore comparable to the custody officer's initial decision in relation to ordinary criminal proceedings as to whether there are grounds to justify detention (see 3.2.3). Subsequent reviews must take place at intervals of not more that 12 hours (para. 3(2)), though there are powers of postponement equivalent to those applying under PACE (see 3.3.2)(para. 5). Once an application for extension of detention has been made to the Home Secretary, however, no further reviews need take place.

The grounds for authorising continued detention are that the review officer is satisfied (note that there is no requirement of 'reasonable grounds') that it is necessary in order to preserve or obtain evidence which relates to an offence under ss. 2, 8, 9, 10 or 11 of the Act, or which indicates that the detainee is or has been concerned in the commission, preparation or instigation of acts of terrorism (para. 3(3)(a)). The obtaining of evidence may be, though it does not have to be, by questioning. The review officer must also be satisfied that the investigation is being conducted diligently and expeditiously (para. 3(3)(b)).

Before reaching a decision the review officer must give the detainee (unless asleep), and the detainee's solicitor (if any), the opportunity to make representations (para. 6).

The review officer has a duty to record the outcome of each review, in the presence of the detainee (para. 8). If detention is being continued, the detainee should be told the grounds (which should also be recorded).

From the above it will be seen that within the first 48 hours the position of the detainee is very comparable to that of a person detained under the PACE provisions. The big change comes at the end of the 48 hour period. At that point the Home Secretary can immediately authorise a further five days' detention. No basis for such authorisation is given in the Act; it appears to be entirely at the discretion of the Home Secretary. Moreover, there are no further reviews of detention once the Home Secretary has authorised an extension. The lack of any judicial review of this extended period has brought the British government into conflict with the European Court of Human Rights, in the case of *Brogan* v *United Kingdom* (1989) 11 EHRR 117. This is discussed below at 3.7.

3.4 CONDITIONS DURING DETENTION

3.4.1 The right to have someone informed
One of the effects of police detention is isolation from friends and family. A person who has been arrested on the street, and taken to a police station, may well be concerned that no one will know what has happened. PACE deals with this by generally giving a detained person the right to let someone know of the arrest, and the place of detention (s. 56(1)). This right is one of those which the custody officer is obliged to draw to the attention of the detainee (Code C, para. 3.1; see 3.2.2). Only one communication is allowed. If the detainee is moved to another location, however, the s. 56 right may be exercised again (s. 56(8)). The communication may be to a friend, a relative, or any other person known to the detainee, or likely to take an interest in the welfare of the detainee. If the detainee's first choice cannot be contacted, two alternatives may be nominated: if neither of these can be contacted, it is at the custody officer's discretion whether further attempts are allowed (Code C, para. 5.1).

Delay in the exercise of this right is governed by s. 56(2)–(7). It will only be allowed where a person is detained under the 'terrorism provisions' (discussed at 3.4.3), or for a serious arrestable offence (see 3.3.3.1 for the definition of this). It can only be authorised by an officer of at least the rank of superintendent. The authorisation of delay may be given orally, but should be confirmed in writing as soon as possible (s. 56(4)). There are three sets of conditions which may justify delay in relation to a serious arrestable offence. The first is where the authorising officer has reasonable grounds for believing that telling the named person of the arrest would lead to one of four consequences which are:

(a) interference with, or harm to, evidence connected with a serious arrestable offence;
(b) interference with, or physical injury to, other persons;
(c) the alerting of other persons suspected of having committed a serious arrestable offence; or
(d) hindrance of the recovery of property obtained as a result of a serious arrestable offence.

All these consequences clearly have the potential for impeding the police investigations, but that does not have to be believed to be the case before delay is authorised.

The second set of conditions for delay relates specifically to drug trafficking. Where the serious arrestable offence for which the person is under arrest is a drug trafficking offence (for which see the Drug Trafficking Offences Act 1986), delay will be permissible if there are reasonable grounds to believe that the recovery of the proceeds of the trafficking will be hindered by telling the named person of the arrest (s. 56(5A)(a), PACE).

The third set of conditions for delay relates to confiscation orders under Part VI of the Criminal Justice Act 1988, which allows the courts to make such orders in relation to the proceeds of an indictable offence. Delay will be permissible where there are reasonable grounds for believing that the detainee has benefited from the offence (which must, of course, be a serious arrestable offence), and the recovery of that benefit will be hindered by telling the named person of the arrest.

The grounds for delay are also set out in Annex B to Code C, though it is not made clear there that the police objection to communication must relate to the person named. In other words the decision to delay should not be a general one that this detainee is not to be allowed to communicate with anyone. In each case the question should be asked: 'Would communication with this named person be likely to result in one of the consequences justifying delay?' It is not clear whether the detainee who, for example, initially names a suspected accomplice, should, if that is thought to be unacceptable, be allowed an alternative to whom the police would not object. The wording of the Act does not require the police to allow this, and the Code of Practice is silent on the issue

If delay is authorised, the detainee must be told the reason, which must also be noted on the custody record (s. 56(6), PACE). If the reason ceases to exist, the detainee should be told of this, and given the opportunity to exercise the right at this stage (Code C, Annex B, para. 4). In any case, delay in the exercise of this right where the detainee is under arrest for a serious arrestable offence must never extend beyond 36 hours from the 'relevant time' (see 3.3.1) (s. 56(3)).

The right in s. 56 will be satisfied by the passing of a message by the police, but Code C, para. 5.6 also provides that the detainee should normally be allowed to communicate with one person directly by telephone or letter. Before such communication takes place, however, the detainee should be told that, unless it is to a solicitor, it may be listened to or read, and used in evidence (Code C, para. 5.7). This privilege may be denied by an officer of at least the rank of inspector who considers that its exercise may result in one of the consequences listed above as justifying a delay under s. 56.

3.4.2   The right of access to legal advice

This right is contained in s. 58. It has proved to be one of the most significant provisions of PACE in terms of litigation relating to it. This is not surprising. The right of the detained citizen to legal advice and representation is fundamental to a fair system of criminal justice. The balance of power between a professional police force, highly trained in techniques of questioning, and operating on home ground (that is, the police station), and the private individual, in unfamiliar and threatening circumstances, can only be equalised by allowing the detainee professional legal advice.

The right arises where a person has been arrested and is being held in police custody in a police station or other premises (s. 58(1)). In *R v Kerawalla* [1991] Crim LR 252, in effect applying the definition of 'police detention' contained in s. 118(2), this was held to mean that the right only arises where a person has been taken to a police station and is under the supervision of a custody officer. Thus, in that case, where questioning had taken place in the hotel room where Kerawalla had been arrested, he had no right of access to legal advice. It is true that some other aspects of s. 58 would be difficult to comply with (for example, noting the request in the custody record), if it applied prior to arrival at a police station. Section 58(1) is, however, broad enough to allow for a different interpretation, and the result is unfortunate in that it may encourage the police to delay arrival at a police station (subject to the requirements of s. 30, see 2.4.5.2), simply with a view to being able to question before the detainee has had access to legal advice.

The detainee must be informed of the right of access to legal advice on arrival at the police station, and, as we have seen at 3.2.2, be given a written statement referring to it. A poster advertising the right is to be prominently displayed in the charging area of every police station (Code C, para. 6.3). The RCCJ has recommended that recording of a suspect's waiver of the right to consult a solicitor should be achieved by the ticking of boxes, in addition to the requirement of a signature (*Report*, chapter 3, para. 48). If the right is declined, the suspect should be given the opportunity of speaking to a duty solicitor on the telephone (*Report*, chapter 3, para. 49).

As with the right to have someone informed under s. 56, most of those who are in police custody will be entitled to exercise the right under s. 58 at any time. Where a person is under arrest for a serious arrestable offence, however, or under the terrorism provisions, delay is possible. The terrorism provisions are discussed below (3.4.3); what follows relates solely to those under arrest for serious arrestable offences.

The maximum period of delay is 36 hours from the 'relevant time'(see 3.3.1) (s. 58(5)). It may only be authorised by an officer of at least the rank of superintendent (s. 58(6)). The procedures to be followed, and the conditions justifying delay, are virtually the same as for the right to have someone informed under s. 56 (see 3.4.1). The fact that delay is justified in relation to one of the rights does not, however, automatically mean that it will be justified in relation to the other (*R v Parris* (1988) 89 Cr App R 68). In addition, the following differences in wording should be noted. First, whereas in s. 56 the conditions for delay refer to 'telling the named person', under s. 58 the more general formulation of 'the exercise of the right' is used. In other words, it would appear at first sight that the police objection should be a general one, and not related to the particular legal adviser the detainee wishes to consult. The Court of Appeal in *R v Samuel* [1988] QB 615, however, thought that the reasonable belief that, for example, the solicitor might transmit (albeit unwittingly) information useful to the detainee's accomplices, must be related to the particular adviser that the detainee wishes to consult. They thought that it would only be very rarely that the police officer could have such a reasonable belief in relation to a solicitor.

The second difference in wording arises where the police rely on the first set of conditions, dealing with the possible harmful consequences of exercising the right. Section 58(8) specifies that the reasonable grounds for belief that this will happen must relate to the exercise of the right 'at the time that the person detained desires to exercise it'. The police objection must therefore be more specific as to time in relation to this right, as opposed to the s. 56 right. The reason for this is that the right under s. 58 is a continuing one, which can be exercised at any time, whereas the right under s. 56 can only be exercised once (unless the detainee is moved to a different location).

Annex B to Code C specifies that access to a solicitor may not be denied on the grounds that the solicitor may advise the detainee not to answer any questions (para. 3). This is a most important provision, for this is one of the things which the police will be most concerned about if legal advice is allowed. Quite rightly, however, as long as the suspect's right of silence is regarded as an important right, the police should not be able to weaken it by preventing access to a lawyer who will make sure that the suspect knows exactly what the situation is, and will advise silence, if that appears to be the most appropriate course. As we shall see below (3.6.3.3), incriminating statements, made in the absence of a legal adviser, have frequently been excluded by the courts as 'unfair evidence' under s. 78 of PACE.

If delay of access to legal advice is authorised, then the detainee must be told the reason, and it must be recorded on the custody record (s. 58(9)). Once the reason for delay ceases to exist, then access to legal advice should be allowed immediately (s. 58(11)).

The detainee should be allowed to specify the solicitor who is to give advice (Code C, Note 6B). If the detainee does not have, or know of, a solicitor, the custody officer should draw attention to the duty solicitor scheme. If the duty solicitor is unavailable, or unacceptable to the detainee, a list of solicitors willing to give advice should be provided. Up to three selections may be made from this list. If attempts to secure advice in this way are unsuccessful, the custody officer has a discretion to allow further attempts, until a solicitor has been found who is willing to give advice (Code C, Note 6B).

When a solicitor arrives at the police station, there is currently no obligation on the police to provide any information. The RCCJ has recommended that solicitors should automatically see, and if possible be given a copy of the custody record on arrival, and on departure (*Report.* chapter 3, para. 51). They should also be able to hear the tapes of any interviews, and be informed of the general nature of the case, and the *prima facie* evidence against the suspect (*Report*, chapter 3, paras 52, 53).

3.4.3   The terrorism provisions

The powers of the police to delay exercise of the right to have someone informed, and the right to legal advice, are slightly different where the detainee is held under the terrorism provisions. Section 65 defines these to mean s. 14(1) of the Prevention of Terrorism (Temporary Provisions) Act 1989, and any provision of sch. 2 or 5 of that Act which confers a power of arrest or detention.

The differences in the way in which the two rights operate are set out in s. 56 (11) (right to have someone informed) and s. 58(13) (access to legal advice). In relation to the grounds of delay, two further consequences are added to the list contained in the first set of conditions for delay (see 3.4.1). These are that exercise of the right will:

(a)   lead to interference with the gathering of information about the commission, preparation or instigation of acts of terrorism; or

(b)   by alerting any person, make it more difficult

(i)   to prevent any act of terrorism; or

(ii)   to secure the apprehension, prosecution or conviction of any person in connection with the commission, preparation or instigation of an act of terrorism.

These are broader consequences than those relating to people held for ordinary criminal offences. The decision to delay must still be taken by an officer of at least the rank of superintendent, but it will be difficult to challenge an officer's stated belief that there were reasonable grounds to fear one of these consequences.

The prohibition on authorising delay on the basis that the legal advice will be to refuse to answer questions applies equally to those held under the terrorism provisions (Code C, Annex B, para. 10).

The maximum period for delay in relation to both rights is extended from 36 hours to 48 hours in relation to people held under the terrorism provisions (s. 56(11)(b); s. 58(13)(a)). This is also the maximum period for which a person may be held under these provisions on the authority of the police. As we have seen at 3.3.4, after 48 hours continued detention must be approved by the Home Secretary.

Finally, whilst the right to legal advice under s. 58(1) is specifically stated to be a right to consult 'privately', this is not necessarily the case with a person held under the terrorism provisions. An officer of at least the rank of commander or assistant chief constable may in certain circumstances give a direction that the detainee may only consult a solicitor in the sight and hearing of a uniformed officer of at least the rank of inspector. This officer should not, in the opinion of the authorising officer, have any connection with the case. The circumstances which will justify such a direction are that the authorising officer has reasonable grounds to believe that without this supervision one of the consequences justifying denial of access to legal advice for someone held under the terrorism provisions will follow (s. 58(14)). In other words, this allows for access to legal advice to be allowed under supervision, in circumstances which would otherwise justify refusal of access altogether.

3.4.4 Other conditions
Code of Practice C, paras 8 and 9, contain detailed provisions on the conditions of detention, and the treatment of detainees. Paragraph 8 covers such matters as the state of the cells, access to toilet and washing facilities, provision of meals, and exercise. It also states that detainees should be visited every hour, or, if drunk, every half hour (para. 8.10)

Paragraph 9 deals primarily with the provision of medical treatment, where a detainee appears to be ill, or otherwise in need of medical attention. It also contains a general provision (para. 9.1) relating to complaints by, or on behalf of, a detainee, of improper treatment. If such a complaint is made, or if an officer thinks that improper treatment may have occurred, a report must be made as soon as possible to an officer of at least the rank of inspector, who is not connected with the investigation. If the improper treatment concerns a possible assault, or unreasonable use of force, then the police surgeon should also be called.

The provisions in paras 8 and 9 are of great importance to the individual detainee, and promote a standard of civilised treatment which is clearly desirable. A person in detention for questioning is simply a suspect, and is entitled to be kept in conditions which are as comfortable as possible, and to be treated well. It must be noted, however, that there is very little in the way of sanctions in relation to breaches of these provisions. Failure to comply with them will not make the detention unlawful, nor will there be any remedy in damages against the police officers responsible. Even if it is argued that incriminating evidence was obtained while a person was detained in conditions which fall below those required, the evidence is unlikely to be excluded unless the breaches are serious, and it can plausibly be argued that the statements would not have been made had the breaches not occurred (see 3.6.3.2). A formal complaint under the police complaints procedure is probably the most that can be done to back up the rights given by paras 8 and 9 (see 3.6.2).

3.5 OBTAINING EVIDENCE DURING DETENTION

The purpose of detaining a suspect is almost always to obtain evidence. There are three principal ways in which this can be done: by questioning; by taking samples for analysis; and by identification procedures (identity parades, etc).

All three are governed by PACE and its Codes. Before looking at how they operate, and the extent to which the rights of the detainee are protected, however, the use of the 'caution' and the right to silence must be considered.

3.5.1   Cautions and the right to silence

3.5.1.1   Caution: content and procedures   At various stages in the investigation of a crime the police are obliged to issue a caution to a suspect, in effect reminding the suspect of the right to silence. The rules relating to cautioning are not contained in PACE itself, but in the Codes, particularly para. 10 of Code C.

A caution must be given whenever a suspect is to be questioned about an offence, for the purpose of obtaining evidence which may be used by the prosecution in any subsequent trial. Questioning for other purposes, such as to establish the suspect's identity or address, can take place without a caution as can an investigation which does not involve questioning, such as a search (Code C, para. 10.1). A caution will normally be required when a suspect is questioned prior to arrest; when a suspect is arrested; and where a suspect in police detention is to be questioned, or further questioned. It is the responsibility of the interviewing officer to make sure that when there is a resumption of questioning following a break, the detainee realises that the questioning is still taking place under caution. The safest procedure is probably for the caution to be repeated (para. 10.5).

The form of the caution is set out in Code C, para. 10.4. It is to be given in the following terms:

> You do not have to say anything unless you wish to do so, but what you say may be given in evidence.

The most important matter, however, is not the precise words used, but whether the suspect understands their significance. Minor deviations from the above formula will not matter, as long as the gist of the caution is communicated (para. 10.5). If it appears to the officer issuing the caution that the suspect does not understand what it means, then the officer should explain it (Code C, Note 10C), drawing attention to the general principle in English law against self-incrimination, and the fact that no adverse inference may be drawn at any trial from the fact that the defendant has exercised the right of silence (Code C, Note 10D).

A record of the caution should be made in the officer's pocket book, or in the interview record, as appropriate (Code C, para. 10.7). This is important, since evidence resulting from an interview not under caution may well be excluded (see 3.6.3.2).

Two recent cases have dealt with the need for the use of cautions in connection with police undercover operations. In *R v Christou* [1992] 3 WLR 228 the police had set up a shop which purported to be a genuine business dealing in jewellery. All transactions in the shop were video-recorded. The defendants were recorded dealing in stolen goods. It was argued that their conversations with the undercover officers managing the shop were in effect interviews, and that a caution should have been given (which would, of course, have destroyed the police officers' 'cover'). The Court of Appeal held that the conversations were outside the scope of the Codes, which were directed towards protecting the individual from abuse and pressure from police officers, who are perceived to be in a position of authority, leading to the possibility of the suspect being intimidated or undermined. The factual situation in this case meant that no such pressure or intimidation could possibly arise. In reaching this conclusion, however, the Court issued the following warning:

> It would be wrong for the police officers to adopt or use an undercover pose or disguise to enable themselves to ask questions about an offence uninhibited by the requirements of the Code and with the effect of circumventing it.

This warning was followed in *R* v *Bryce* (1992) 95 Cr App R 320. An undercover police officer visited the defendant who was selling a car. The officer asked a series of questions which were clearly directed towards establishing that the car was stolen. They culminated in the direct question: 'How long has it been nicked?', to which the defendant was reported to have answered 'Two to three days'. The defendant was then arrested. The Court of Appeal held that this series of questions ran the risk of offending against the caveat in *Christou*. Since the conversation was disputed, and, unlike the exchanges in *Christou* had not been recorded, it should not have been admitted.

The principles which lie behind the use of the caution derive from the idea of the 'right to silence'. That is, the right of any suspect not to answer questions, and not to give evidence at trial, and the fact that no adverse inferences may be drawn from this. What is the basis of the right to silence? It relates to two other principles which are regarded as being of fundamental importance in the English criminal justice system. The first is the presumption of innocence. No one is guilty, until *proved* to be so. Moreover, the burden of proof is always on the prosecution: *Woolmington* v *DPP* [1935] AC 462. Thus suspects or defendants are under no obligation to provide any explanation of their behaviour, or any other evidence: the prosecution must prove guilt beyond reasonable doubt.

The second, and related, principle is the one referred to above in Code C, Note 10D, that a person cannot be compelled to make a self-incriminating statement. It is thought wrong to put people into the position where they are forced to condemn themselves out of their own mouths.

The right to silence has been a controversial issue in recent years. A recent case which received much press publicity involved the death of a young child from injuries which were unlikely to have been caused accidentally. Both parents refused to make any statement, or to give any evidence. Although there was strong suspicion that one or other, or both, of them was responsible, there was no evidence on which either could be proved to be guilty beyond reasonable doubt. The problems arising from this type of case, and also of cases involving terrorist suspects who may be trained to withstand questioning, have given rise to calls for the right to be amended. This has been done to a limited extent in Northern Ireland (Criminal Evidence (Northern Ireland) Order 1988). Similar proposals for England and Wales put forward by a Home Office Working Party in 1989 have not, however, been acted upon. What is proposed is not, of course, that the suspect should be physically forced to speak. Rather, the suggestion is that a failure to answer questions, provide information, or give evidence, could be matters from which the court would be entitled to draw adverse inferences in appropriate cases. The knowledge that such inferences can be drawn might then be expected to lead to suspects, and their legal advisers, being less ready to rely on silence as a means of defence to police inquiries.

The majority of the members of the RCCJ recommended that the position as regards the right of silence, and the inferences to be drawn from silence, should remain unchanged (*Report*, chapter 4, para. 22). Nevertheless, on 6 October 1993, the Home Secretary, Michael Howard, announced at the Conservative Party Conference that he intended to remove the 'so-called right to silence'. It was not clear, however, exactly how this would be achieved.

As regards self-incrimination, an exception to this has been created by the Criminal Justice Act 1987, in relation to the investigation of serious frauds. The House of Lords in *Smith* v *Director of the Serious Fraud Office* [1992] 3 All ER 456 undertook a lengthy analysis of the right to silence, and the rule against self-incrimination. It concluded that the inquisitorial regime which parliament had approved in the Criminal Justice Act, allowed the Director of the Serious Fraud Office to obtain by compulsion (that is, it would be an offence to refuse to answer) responses to questions which might be self-incriminating (although the use to which such responses could be put is strictly limited: Criminal Justice Act 1987, s. 2(8)).

3.5.2 Interviews

The main method by which the police gain, or attempt to gain, evidence from a suspect is by means of interviews. Such questioning is controlled by various provisions in PACE and Code C. The protective provisions only apply, however, to something which is properly classified as an 'interview'. It is necessary, therefore, to start with the definition of this concept, before moving on to look at how it is regulated.

3.5.2.1 Meaning of an 'interview'

The concept of the interview was not defined in the original version of the PACE Codes. There was a certain amount of case law on the issue, some of which will still need to be considered, but the starting point is now Note 11A in Code C, which was added when the Codes were revised in 1991. It states that:

An interview is the questioning of a person regarding his involvement or suspected involvement in a criminal offence or offences. Questioning a person simply to obtain information or his explanation of the facts or in the ordinary course of the officer's duties, does not constitute an interview for the purpose of this Code. Neither does questioning which is strictly confined to the proper and effective conduct of a search.

The first sentence is clear enough and seems to envisage a very broad definition of an interview. It is, at any rate, established that an interview does not have to take place at a police station (*R* v *Maloney and Doherty* [1988] Crim LR 523; *R* v *Fogah* [1989] Crim LR 141); nor is it necessary for the officer concerned to be intending to conduct an interview. In *R* v *Sparks* [1991] Crim LR 128, what started out as an informal 'chat' between an officer not involved in the investigation and the suspect, was capable of being regarded as an interview when the conversation elicited damaging admissions from the suspect.

The difficulty lies in deciding how far this broad approach is cut down by the second and third sentences of the note. Questioning 'to obtain information' or the interviewee's 'explanation of the facts' is clearly capable of falling within the scope of the first sentence. What is excluded is presumably the situation where the questioning is directed to a person who is not *at that stage* a suspect, but who may become one, depending on the answer to the questions. This corresponds to the approach in *R* v *Absolam* (1989) 88 Cr App R 332 at p. 336, where Bingham LJ defined an interview as a 'series of questions directed by the police to a *suspect*' (emphasis added). On the other hand, in *R* v *Maguire* (1989) 90 Cr App R 115 the accused was arrested near the scene of a burglary, and was thus a suspect. In the police car, an officer said to him: 'Look, you've both been caught. Now tell us the truth'. This was held simply to be an invitation to the suspect to explain himself, and did not constitute an interview. This would presumably still be the case under Note 11A.

The meaning of Note 11A was considered by the Court of Appeal in *R* v *Cox, The Times*, 2 December 1992. After the suspect had been arrested, but before he was taken to the police station, an officer asked him whether he had been in a stolen lorry that had been observed on a previous evening. The suspect was said to have replied: 'If you saw me it's up to you to prove it, but I'll give you six to four I'll get off'. The evidence of this exchange was admitted at trial, and Cox was convicted. On appeal, it was argued that the evidence should not have been admitted. The Court of Appeal had great difficulty interpreting Note 11A. As McCullough J pointed out, the first sentence is clear enough, but the second is not. The phrase excepting questioning 'in the ordinary course of the officer's duties' from the definition of an interview, made no sense, since 'an officer conducting a formal interview with a view to obtaining evidence to be given at court in a prosecution was acting in the ordinary course of his duties'. Taken at face value the exception would mean that a formal interview was not an 'interview' for the purpose of para. 11, which cannot be what was intended. Furthermore, the exception for questioning only to obtain information or an explanation of the facts, was equally troublesome. Such questions were commonly part of a formal interview, and so:

It could not credibly be suggested that after a person suspected of murder by stabbing had been arrested and taken to a police station he could be interrogated without the protection of paragraph 11 so long as every question was directed to obtaining his explanation for the stabbing.

The Court recognised the possibility of drawing the distinction referred to above, between questions directed towards ascertaining whether a person ought to be arrested, and those asked with a view to the answers being used in evidence. If, however, that was the distinction which was intended, the Note did not make it clear. As a result, the Court found very little help in Note 11A. It turned instead to the general framework provided by PACE and Code C, which was based on the following sequence of events: decision to arrest; arrest; arrival at the police station; notification of the right to legal advice; legal advice; interview. It concluded that:

It is against this framework that one must ask, in any given set of circumstances, whether or not the questioning amounted to an interview.

Applying this approach to the facts of the case, the Court held that the exchange quoted above amounted to an interview for the purpose of paragraph 11. The only point of the question was to see if Cox would admit a vital part of the case against him. It should not have been asked until after he had arrived at the police station and had been informed of his right to legal advice. There had, therefore, been a breach of the provisions of paragraph 11. The evidence should have been excluded. The Court did not, however, think that exclusion would have affected the jury's verdict, and dismissed the appeal.

The decision in *Cox* has not helped the uncertainty over the meaning of an 'interview'. The approach, however, seems to be purposive. What was the point of a particular question? Was it a question which was appropriate to the stage of proceedings (as outlined above) that had been reached? In particular, was it the kind of question which should only be asked after the suspect has had the opportunity of receiving legal advice?

Finally, to conclude with one point of much greater certainty, Note 6C of Code C provides that procedures in relation to breath tests, etc, under s. 7 of the Road Traffic Act 1988, do not constitute interviewing for the purposes of the Code.

Not surprisingly, given the problems identified above, the RCCJ has recommended that the Note for Guidance 11A should be amended to clarify the confusion as to what constitutes an interview (*Report*, chapter 3, para. 10).

3.5.2.2 Conduct of an interview Code C para. 11.1 provides that once a decision to arrest has been taken, a suspect must not generally be interviewed about the offence other than at a police station. The only exceptions are where the delay involved in taking the suspect to a police station would be likely to lead to one of the consequences which justifies delaying exercise of the right to have someone informed under s. 56(5) (see 3.4.1).

The conduct of the interview, in terms of duration, breaks, provision of meals, etc is governed by Code C, para. 12. For example, in any 24 hour period the detainee should normally be allowed at least eight hours' rest (para. 12.2).

An important aspect of the interview procedure is the continuing right to private legal advice, and to have a legal adviser present during an interview (Code C, para. 6.1). Any request for legal advice, and the action taken on it, must be recorded (Code C, para. 6.16). The RCCJ has recommended that a suspect who declines advice should be asked to give the reasons for doing so (*Report*, chapter 3, para. 48).

The right to legal advice will apply unless a decision has been taken to delay access under s. 58(8) or (8A) (see 3.4.2). Otherwise, in relation to an interview with a detainee who wants legal advice, the interview should not start unless one of the conditions set out in Code C, para. 6.6 is satisfied. There are three of these. The first arises where an officer of at least the rank of superintendent has reasonable grounds for believing that delay will involve an immediate risk of harm to persons or serious loss of, or damage to, property (Code C, para. 6.6(b)(i)). A detainee suspected of having planted a bomb, for example, may need to be questioned about its location. Once sufficient information has been obtained to avert the risk, however, questioning should stop until the detainee has received legal advice (Code C, para. 6.7). The second condition is where an officer of at least the rank of superintendent has reasonable grounds to believe that to await the arrival of a solicitor who has been contacted and has agreed to attend would cause unreasonable delay to the progress of the investigation (Code C, para. 6.6(b)(ii)). Before reaching such a decision the officer should where practicable obtain an estimate of the likely delay from the solicitor. If the solicitor is on the way to the station, or about to set off, it will not normally be appropriate to begin the interview. If it appears that it will be necessary to start the interview before the solicitor's arrival, the solicitor should be told how long the police are prepared to wait, so that alternative arrangements for legal advice may be made by the solicitor (Code C, Note 6A).

The third condition justifying interviewing before legal advice has been given arises where the solicitor nominated by the detainee is unavailable. This may be because the solicitor cannot be contacted, or is unwilling to attend. The detainee must also have declined to see the duty solicitor, if one is available (Code C, para 6.6(c)). The interview may then start immediately, but the detainee's agreement to being interviewed without receiving legal advice must be recorded in writing or on tape, as must the fact that an officer of at least the rank of superintendent has given written agreement for the interview to proceed.

In all the above cases, where the detainee has asked for legal advice and the interview is begun in the absence of a legal adviser, this must be recorded on the interview record (Code C, para. 6.17).

If a solicitor arrives at a police station to see a particular detainee, there is an obligation on the police to inform the detainee of this, even if the detainee has previously declined legal advice (Code C, para. 6.15). It is not clear whether this will apply to a telephone inquiry by the solicitor. In *R* v *Chahal* [1992] Crim LR 124, the detainee, who had indicated that he did not want a solicitor, was not told of telephone calls from a solicitor who had been instructed by his family. It was held by the Court of Appeal that he had no right to be told of the calls. This decision was reached on the basis of the original Code, which did not have a provision equivalent to the current para. 6.15. The wording of para. 6.15 is in terms of the solicitor being physically present at the police station. This would suggest that the police have no obligation to inform the detainee of telephone calls. It is submitted, however, that the spirit of para. 6.15 suggests that as a matter of practice the police should do so.

It may often be the case that the legal adviser sent to provide advice is not a solicitor, but a clerk or legal executive. Code C, para. 6.12 makes it clear that the rights given by the Code strictly apply only to solicitors. A clerk or legal executive must, however, be allowed access to the suspect for the purpose of giving legal advice unless an officer of at least the rank of inspector directs otherwise on the basis that such a visit would hinder the investigation. Code C para. 6.13 suggests that grounds for reaching this decision may be that the officer is not satisfied as to the identity, status or character of the adviser. In particular, a person who has a criminal record is unlikely to be suitable. The officer should also take account of any matters contained in any written letter of authorisation provided by the solicitor for whom the adviser is acting. If a direction to refuse access is given, the solicitor on whose behalf the adviser attended must be notified, so that other arrangements may be made. The detainee should also be informed, and a note made on the custody record (Code C, para. 6.14). Once granted access in order to give advice a clerk or legal executive should be treated in the same way as a solicitor.

A solicitor who is present at an interview may only be required to leave if the conduct of the solicitor prevents the investigating officer properly questioning the detainee (Code C, para. 6.9). Challenging an improper question, or advising the detainee not to answer, or seeking to give the detainee further legal advice, are not grounds for requiring the solicitor to leave (Code C, Note 6D). On the other hand, answering questions on the detainee's behalf, or providing written replies for the detainee to quote, may well provide such justification. An investigating officer who thinks that a solicitor is behaving in a way which justifies exclusion, should stop the interview and consult either a superintendent, if available, or an officer of at least the rank of inspector who is not connected with the investigation. This senior officer should speak to the solicitor, and then decide whether to allow the solicitor to continue to be present at the interview. If the decision is taken to exclude the solicitor, the detainee must be given the chance to consult another solicitor, who will have the opportunity to be present when the interview continues (Code C, para. 6.10). These provisions indicate the seriousness with which the right to legal advice is treated within the Code. Only where there is clear misconduct is the solicitor of the detainee's choice to be excluded, and even then the detainee is not to be prejudiced more than necessary. The interview should not continue until a new solicitor is available to advise the detainee, and attend the interview.

3.5.2.3 Record of interview In most cases nowadays interviews are recorded on tape. Detailed procedures relating to this are contained in Code of Practice E. This is designed to encourage confidence in the procedure on the part of the detainee, and to ensure security. The system has advantages for both the detainee and the police, in that the police will not be able to put words into the detainee's mouth, but incriminating statements which appear on the tape will be difficult to deny.

Within police stations the use of tape recordings will satisfy the more general requirement under Code C, para. 11.5, of the contemporaneous recording of interviews. Where recording facilities are not available, however, a written record will need to be made. The details of the procedures to be followed are set out in Code C, paras 11.5–11.10. As is the case with a tape-recorded interview, a written record must give the details of the location of the interview, the time it starts and finishes (including any breaks), and the names of all those present. It may take the form of a precise record of the words used, or a summary. If it is not practicable to make the record during the interview itself, it must be made as soon as practicable thereafter. The person interviewed should be given the chance to read and sign the record. This allows the detainee to indicate any inaccuracies. The detainee's solicitor, if present, should also be given the opportunity to read and sign the record.

These procedures are regarded by the courts as very important. As will be seen, in discussing the exclusion of evidence under s. 78 (see 3.6.3.3) one of the most common grounds for excluding evidence of incriminating statements is that a proper contemporaneous record was not kept. Such a record is regarded as greatly increasing the reliability of the evidence. As a result, the revised version of Code C introduced a requirement of a written record even as regards statements made outside the context of an interview (Code C, para. 11.13). Any comments made by a suspect, even if unsolicited, should be recorded in writing. The record should be timed and signed by the officer making it. The suspect should also be given the opportunity to read and sign the record, in the same way as for an interview record. This extension of recording requirements to 'non-interview' statements reduces the possibility of the police relying on evidence of statements supposed to have been made at the time of arrest, or before arrival at the police station. The courts will not be prepared to accept the evidence of the police officer on its own; they will expect it to be backed up by a written contemporaneous record.

Further discussion of these requirements, and the effects of police failure to comply with them will be found at 3.6.3.3, in relation to exclusion of evidence under PACE, s. 78.

3.5.3 Fingerprints, searches, and samples

Fingerprinting has long been an important element in police detection, as a means of linking a specific individual to a crime. The development in recent years of so-called 'genetic fingerprinting', resulting from research carried out by Professor Alec Jefferys at Leicester University, has made blood samples of almost equal importance. The technique relies on matching DNA profiles, which are very unlikely to be the same for different people. It is not without its critics (see, for example, David Farrington, 'Unacceptable Evidence', (1993) 143 NLJ 806), but it has become an important part of prosecution procedures. Indeed, the RCCJ has recommended changes in powers and procedures to facilitate the acquisition and use of such evidence (*Report*, chapter 2, paras.

35–38). The issue looked at here is the extent to which the police have the power to take fingerprints, or samples, from a suspect to aid their inquiries. Extensive searching, including bodily orifices, may also be justified in looking for evidence of drug offences, for example. Such procedures of sampling and search obviously involve a major intrusion into the bodily integrity of the suspect. They would constitute serious assaults if carried out without consent, or specific lawful authority. The powers of the police in this area are covered by ss. 55 and 61–65 of PACE; para.4 and Annex A of Code of Practice C; and paras 3 and 5 of Code of Practice D. As will be seen, the way in which the appropriate balance between the rights of the citizen and the powers of the police is struck is by reference to recording and notification procedures, the level of seniority of the officer given the power of authorisation, and the seriousness of the offence. Thus the most intrusive procedures need the authorisation of an officer of at least the rank of superintendent, and are available only in relation to serious arrestable offences.

3.5.3.1 Fingerprinting The power to take fingerprints from a detainee is governed by s. 61. Normally this should only be done with the consent of the detainee, which must be given in writing (s. 61(2)). If consent is not given, then authorisation by an officer of at least the rank of superintendent is required. This officer must have reasonable grounds for suspecting that the detainee is involved in a criminal offence, and for believing that fingerprinting will tend to confirm or disprove this (s. 61(4)). Reasonable force may be used (s. 117). Any person who is fingerprinted should be told the reasons beforehand (Code D, para. 3.1), and these should be recorded on the custody record (s. 61(8)). They should also be told about the procedures for destruction, which are discussed at 3.5.3.5.

3.5.3.2 Strip searches and intimate searches The general power of search and seizure at the time when the initial decision to detain is made has been discussed at 3.2.4. A strip search, which means any search involving the removal of more than outer clothing, may be authorised by a custody officer who reasonably believes that it is necessary in order to remove an article which is subject to seizure (Code C, Annex A, para. 5). This includes articles of clothing or personal effects which the custody officer has reasonable grounds for believing may be evidence of an offence. Underwear stained with blood, or other substances requiring scientific analysis, might well fall into this category.

An intimate search, on the other hand, may only be authorised by an officer of at least the rank of superintendent. The definition of an intimate search is contained in s. 118, where it is defined as 'a search which consists of the physical examination of a person's body orifices'. This includes, therefore, searches of the ears, nose and mouth, as well as the vagina and rectum. The justifications for allowing an intimate search are two, namely to recover items which might be used to cause physical injury, or to recover a Class A drug (as defined in s. 2(1) of the Misuse of Drugs Act 1971) (s. 55(1)). The authorising officer must have reasonable grounds for believing that something falling into one of these categories will be found, and that it cannot be found without an intimate search (s. 55(2)). In relation to a search for drugs, the officer must also have reasonable grounds to believe that it was in the possession of the detainee with appropriate criminal intent prior to the arrest (s. 55(1)(b)(ii)). Only intention to supply, or to evade customs restrictions will be sufficient: mere possession is not enough (s. 55(17)). The authorisation must be given or confirmed in writing (s. 55(3)).

In general an intimate search may only be carried out by a doctor or nurse. If, however, in relation to a search which is not simply a search for drugs, the authorising officer thinks that it is impracticable (perhaps because of the urgency of the situation) to have the search carried out by a doctor or nurse, it may be made by a police officer of the same sex as the detainee. If the search is simply for drugs, it must not take place at a police station, but at a hospital, a doctor's surgery, or 'some other place used for medical purposes' (s. 55(8)).

Although the grounds justifying an intimate search are narrow, the range of items which may be seized as a result of such a search is rather wider. As regards evidence, the custody officer may seize anything found in the course of the search which the officer has reasonable grounds to believe may be evidence relating to *any* offence (s. 55(12)). In addition, items which the officer believes (reasonable belief is not necessary) may be used to cause injury, damage property, interfere with evidence, or assist escape, may be seized. The detainee must normally be told the reason for the seizure (s. 55(13)), but there does not appear to be any requirement to record this. On the other hand, the extent of any intimate search, and the justification for it, must be noted on the detainee's custody record.

The RCCJ has recommended that the power to remove substances (such as drugs) retained in the mouth of the suspect should be in effect treated as a 'non-intimate' search (*Report*, chapter 2, para. 30).

3.5.3.3 Intimate samples An intimate sample is defined in s. 65 as:

a sample of blood, semen or any other tissue fluid, urine, saliva or pubic hair, or a swab taken from a person's body orifices.

The RCCJ has recommended, responding to suggestions to this effect from the police, that saliva should be re-classified as a non-intimate sample, which can be taken without consent, primarily because of its usefulness in DNA profiling (*Report*, chapter 2, para. 29). It has also suggested that dental impressions, which at the moment are not dealt with anywhere, should be added to the list of intimate samples (*Report*, chapter 2, para. 31).

The taking of intimate samples, which is governed by s. 62, is such an intrusion into a person's bodily integrity, that they may only be taken with consent, which must be given in writing. Even then it will only be lawful if authorised by an officer of at least the rank of superintendent, who has reasonable grounds for suspecting that the detainee is involved with a serious arrestable offence, and for believing that the sample will tend to confirm or disprove such involvement. The authorisation must be made or confirmed in writing, and the detainee must be informed of the authorisation and the grounds for it. If the detainee consents, the sample may then be taken, though if it is to be of anything other than urine, or saliva, it must be taken by a doctor (s. 62(9)). The authorisation, the grounds, and the consent, should be recorded in the detainee's custody record (s. 62(7), (8)).

The detainee, of course, may refuse to allow the sample to be taken. There is no power to override this consent and take a sample by force, nor does refusal in itself constitute an offence (unlike the position in relation to the drink/driving procedures under s. 7 of the Road Traffic Act 1988). The principles behind the right to silence, however, have not been extended to the refusal to give a sample. Whereas, as we have seen at 3.5.1, a detainee is perfectly entitled to refuse to answer questions, or to give any explanation of behaviour, in the knowledge that such refusal will not result in any adverse comments in later proceedings, the same is not true of a refusal to give a blood sample, which may turn out to be even more incriminating than a statement. If there is such a refusal to give an intimate sample, then in any subsequent criminal proceedings the court is specifically empowered to draw 'such inferences from the refusal as may appear proper' (s. 62(10)). This may result in the refusal being treated as corroboration of any evidence against the detainee in respect of which the refusal is material. Because of this, Code of Practice D, para. 5, requires the detainee to be warned of the effects of a refusal, and sets out an appropriate form of words (Code D, Note 5A):

You do not have to [provide this sample] [allow this swab to be taken], but I must warn you that if you do not do so, a court may treat such refusal as supporting any relevant evidence against you.

The provisions relating to intimate samples as they stand do not allow such samples to be taken, even with consent, where the offence is not a serious arrestable one. The RCCJ has recommended that it should be possible for the police to have such a sample taken with consent (*Report*, chapter 2, para. 32). Moreover, it is recommended that if the suspect declines to consent in such circumstances, the courts should be able to draw inferences from the refusal, and, if appropriate, treat the refusal as corroboration of any other evidence (*Report*, chapter 2, para. 32). These recommendations, if enacted, would almost totally undermine the special status given to the taking of intimate samples, and would give insufficient weight to the intrusive nature of such procedures.

3.5.3.4 Non-intimate samples   These are defined in s. 65 as:

(a) a sample of hair other than pubic hair;
(b) a sample taken from a nail or from under a nail;
(c) a swab taken from any part of a person's body other than a body orifice;
(d) a footprint or a similar impression of any part of a person's body other than a part of his hand.

The taking of a non-intimate sample is less intrusive than an intimate sample, but may still involve unpleasant, painful, or degrading procedures. As a result, the normal procedure will be to seek consent, which must be given in writing (s. 63(2)). If such consent is not forthcoming, then an officer of at least the rank of superintendent may authorise the taking of the sample, and reasonable force may be used. The RCCJ has recommended that this should include the power to take a sample of non-pubic hair by plucking, as opposed to cutting (*Report*, chapter 2, para. 28).

The grounds for authorising the taking of a non-intimate sample without consent are the same as those in relation to taking an intimate sample with consent (see 3.5.3.3). In other words, the power will not arise at all unless the detainee is suspected of involvement in a serious arrestable offence. The RCCJ, however, has recommended that, for this purpose only, assault and burglary should be reclassified as serious arrestable offences (*Report*, chapter 2, para. 33). The notification and recording procedures under s. 63 are the same as for the taking of intimate samples under s. 62.

There is no sanction for refusal to provide a non-intimate sample by a detainee who is being held in relation to an offence which is not a serious arrestable offence. Suppose, for example, that X is being held for a relatively minor theft, and the police wish to take a swab from X's hands to show contact with some item of stolen goods which would have left traces. If X refuses to allow the swab to be taken, there is nothing that the police can do; and since there is no specific provision in s. 63 comparable to that in s. 62 allowing adverse inferences to be drawn from a refusal, it must be assumed that the court would have no power to draw such inferences. The RCCJ has recommended that there should be power to draw adverse inferences following a refusal to supply a non-intimate sample (*Report*, chapter 2, para. 32).

A more controversial proposal is that the police should have the power to take, without consent, non-intimate samples from all those arrested for 'serious criminal offences' (undefined), for the purpose of DNA analysis, whether or not DNA evidence is relevant to the offence. If the person is convicted, the records would be kept, and could be used in future investigations, in the same way that fingerprints are now. If the person is acquitted, the record should only be kept for statistical purposes (for example, maintaining a 'frequency data base' to provide estimates of the likelihood of a DNA sample matching a sample in the data base) (*Report*, chapter 2, paras 34–36).

3.5.3.5 Destruction of fingerprints and samples Where a person is cleared of an offence, or if it is decided not to prosecute, or to discontinue a prosecution, any fingerprints or samples which have been taken must be destroyed. The detailed procedures in relation to this, and the circumstances in which a person can witness the destruction of the fingerprints, are set out in s. 64. (Note the recommendations of the RCCJ, noted in the previous paragraph, concerning the retention of samples for the purpose of DNA statistics.)

3.5.4 Identification by witnesses

In some situations the police will want to confirm their suspicions by asking for identification of a suspect by a witness or victim. There are four ways in which this can be done. The relevant procedures are set out in Code of Practice C, para. 2, and Annexes A-C. The four methods are:

  (a) an identification parade;
  (b) a group identification;
  (c) a video film; or
  (d) a confrontation.

It is clear from the Code of Practice that these are presented in order of desirability. In other words, the methods lower down the list should only be used if none of the methods higher up are practicable. The order of the list also relates to the level of consent required from the suspect.

The procedures will be under the control of a uniformed office of at least the rank of inspector, who is not involved in the investigation, and who is referred to as 'the identification officer' (Code D, para. 2.2).

Identification by means of photographs may not be used where a suspect is in police custody. This procedure, which is governed by Annex D, may only be used where the identity of the suspect is not known. It is not discussed further here, since it is unlikely to involve any infringement of civil liberties. A person who is arrested and taken to a police station may generally only be photographed after giving written consent (Code D, para. 4).

3.5.4.1 Identification parades

An identification parade must if practicable be held, if it is requested by the suspect in a case where identification is in issue (Code D, para. 2.3). This will be the case whenever there is a dispute as to whether the suspect was present at the scene of the crime at the relevant time. An identification parade can also be held if the investigating officer considers that it would be useful, provided that the suspect consents. Thus, the suspect who is unwilling to participate in an identification parade cannot be forced to do so. If a parade is held the identification officer must, before it takes place, tell the suspect both orally, and by means of a written notice, about the purposes and procedures of the parade, the suspect's right to legal advice, and the right to have a solicitor or friend present during the parade. The suspect must also be told that refusal to participate may be given in evidence in any subsequent trial (Code D, paras 2.15, 2.16). A suspect who is willing to proceed must sign a copy of the written notice. Detailed rules as to the conduct of the parade are set out in Annex A, and deal with matters such as the minimum numbers (eight), and the fact that the suspect may choose where to stand in the line. Immediately before the parade, a caution in the terms of para. 10.4 of Code C (see 3.5.1.1) must be given.

The RCCJ has recommended that before a parade is held, the police should provide the suspect's solicitor with details of the description given of the offender by the witness or witnesses who are due to attend the parade (*Report*, chapter 2, para. 10).

3.5.4.2 Group identification

If a parade is impracticable, or the suspect refuses to participate, a group identification may be used. The suspect's consent should be sought, and notice given under paras 2.15 and 2.16, in the same way as for identification parades (see 3.5.4.1). If consent is refused, the identification officer has a discretion to proceed without it. The identification should normally take place away from a police station, in a place where there will be likely to be numbers of other people, such as a shopping centre or underground station (Code D, para. 2.9). In other respects, the procedures should, as far as possible, follow those for an identification parade.

3.5.4.3 Video film identification Where neither a parade nor a group identification is practicable, the witness may be shown a video film of the suspect. The suspect must be asked for consent, and given the para. 2.15 and 2.16 notifications and warnings, but the identification officer may proceed without the suspect's consent if it is practicable to do so. The procedures are governed by Annex B. At least eight people must appear in the video, as well as the suspect, and as well as being of similar appearance, they must be filmed, as far as possible in the same way and under identical conditions. What is clearly envisaged is a series of sequences of each person in turn, including the suspect, rather than a shot of the group as a whole. The suspect and the suspect's solicitor should have a chance to see the video before it is shown to the witness, and to raise any objections, which should either be met, or recorded together with the reason why they cannot be met. The suspect's solicitor should be present when the video is shown to the witness.

3.5.4.4 Confrontation This may take place without the suspect's consent, if none of the other three procedures is practicable. The procedure is governed by Annex C. It should normally take place in the police station, and in the presence of the suspect's solicitor (unless this would cause unreasonable delay).

3.6 CHALLENGING THE POLICE

The recognition of rights is of little value to the citizen unless the infringement of such rights is backed up with effective sanctions. In English law the remedies for police misbehaviour are threefold, namely, civil action, official complaint, or exclusion of evidence.

3.6.1 Civil action
The traditional remedy of the citizen unlawfully detained by State authorities is the writ of *habeas corpus*. It is, however, of little practical use in relation to police powers of stop and search, arrest, or detention, however, for two reasons. First, the writ is mainly concerned with whether the correct procedure has been followed. As will have been noted, many decisions in this area are based on reasonable suspicion or belief, and this is notoriously difficult to challenge. Secondly, the periods of detention without charge are in most cases relatively short, a matter of a day or two at most. An application for the writ will normally be adjourned for 24 hours. Once a person has been released or charged, then the writ of *habeas corpus* becomes irrelevant. It has, however,

been much more frequently used in relation to detention prior to deportation and extradition proceedings, and so a more detailed consideration of the writ is left to chapter 9 which is concerned with these issues.

Civil actions in tort for trespass to the person, in the form of an assault, or false imprisonment may also be possible. These may be taken after the event, and may provide damages for the plaintiff. Their success will depend on showing that the police have acted beyond the scope of any statutory or common law power. A failure to comply with the provisions of one of the PACE Codes of Practice will not be sufficient. The most likely bases for the claim will be either that there was no justification for an arrest, search, or detention, or that excessive force was used. If the tort is proved, however, exemplary damages may be available. The rules relating to the award of exemplary damages are set out in the two House of Lords decisions of *Rookes v Barnard* [1964] AC 1129, and *Cassell & Co. v Broome* [1972] AC 1027. These cases limited the availability of such an award to two situations. The one that is relevant here is where there has been oppressive, arbitrary or unconstitutional action by servants of the government. 'Servants of the government' will include police officers. The most recent reported consideration of this issue is the decision of the Court of Appeal in *Holden v Chief Constable of Lancashire* [1986] 3 All ER 836. The plaintiff had been unlawfully arrested, and held in a police cell for 20 minutes. There was no use of excessive force, or other improper conduct, other than the fact that the arrest had no lawful justification. The judge withdrew the issue of exemplary damages from the jury (this is one area where it is common for a civil action to be heard before a jury), on the basis that there was no 'oppressive' or 'arbitrary' conduct by the police. The Court of Appeal ruled that this was wrong. The categories set out by the House of Lords were disjunctive. In other words, there could be an award of exemplary damages where there was unconstitutional conduct, even though this was not accompanied by any oppression or arbitrariness. In coming to this conclusion, the Court of Appeal was also reluctant to hold that every unlawful action by the police, no matter how well-intentioned, justifies exemplary damages. If the conduct was unconstitutional, then exemplary damages could be considered, but there should probably be some other impropriety on the part of the police before such an award would be appropriate. If exemplary damages are not awarded, then, as is shown from the cases listed in the leading work on this topic (R. Clayton and H. Tomlinson, *Civil Actions Against the Police*, 2nd edn, Sweet & Maxwell, 1992, pp. 411–431), the amount awarded in terms of compensation is likely to be relatively small. Generally speaking the awards have been in terms of hundreds, rather than thousands, of pounds.

3.6.2 Official complaints

PACE provides the framework for a system of complaints against police misconduct. Insofar as the individual complainant is concerned it is of limited use, in that it does not provide compensation, or any other redress, for those who are the victims of such misconduct. Victims may, of course, as with those who have suffered from the criminal activities of others, gain some satisfaction simply from seeing the malefactor brought to book. The existence of an effective complaints procedure can, however, in a more general way be an instrument for the promotion of civil liberties, in that it may act as a deterrent to the police from stepping outside their legitimate powers. Its most significant role may therefore be in controlling temptation, rather than punishing offenders.

As has been noted above, breach of the provisions of one of the PACE Codes of Practice does not in itself provide the basis for a legal action against the officer concerned. It is, however, automatically a disciplinary offence, and therefore a proper ground for complaint on the part of someone who has suffered from it. The procedures for dealing with complaints are contained in Part IX of PACE, ss. 83–105.

3.6.2.1 Police Complaints Authority Section 83, and sch. 4 to the Act, provide for the establishment of a Police Complaints Authority ('PCA'). The PCA has a general role in overseeing the operation of the complaints system. It is an independent body, consisting of a chair person and at least eight other members. It does not have the staff to carry out its own investigations, but will supervise police investigations into complaints. The first level at which a complaint will be dealt with is, however, that of the chief constable (or in London the Commissioner) of the police force of which the officer against whom the complaint is made is a member. (In the following paragraphs, references to the 'chief constable' should be taken to include the Metropolitan Police Commissioner, and the Commisioner of Police for the City of London.)

3.6.2.2 Procedures for complaints The chief constable who receives a complaint must take steps to obtain or preserve relevant evidence, and must then decide who is the 'appropriate authority' to deal with it (s. 84(1) and (2)). In general this will be the chief constable. The only exception is where the complaint is against an officer above the rank of chief superintendent. In this case the appropriate authority, other than within the Metropolitan Police area, is the local police authority for the chief constable's area. The Act makes provision for informal resolution of complaints in certain circumstances. This is not available, however, unless the complainant consents, and the appropriate authority is satisfied that even if the complaint was proved no criminal or disciplinary charge against the officer would be appropriate (s. 85(10)). Since, as we have seen, any breach of a provision of a Code of Practice, and *a fortiori*, any breach of the Act itself, will constitute a disciplinary offence, it seems that complaints in the context of significant breaches of the procedures discussed in this chapter, and chapters 2 and 4, will be unlikely to be appropriate for informal resolution. In that case, the appropriate authority must appoint an officer to carry out a formal investigation. This officer, who can be from the same or another force, must be of at least the rank of chief inspector, and at least of equal rank to the officer being investigated.

Certain investigations must be supervised by the PCA. This is where the misconduct alleged resulted in death or serious injury (ss. 87(1), 89(1)), or where the Home Secretary has by regulation provided that the investigation of the complaint should be so supervised. Currently this applies to complaints of misconduct which constitutes an assault occasioning actual bodily harm; constitutes an offence under s. 1 of the Prevention of Corruption Act 1916; or constitutes a serious arrestable offence (Police (Complaints) (Mandatory Referrals, etc.) Regulations, SI 1985 No 673). Other complaints may be referred to the PCA, and it may decide to supervise the investigation of those, or indeed any other complaints, if it considers that it is desirable in the public interest to do so (ss. 87(1), 89(2)).

Where the PCA is supervising, it has the power of approval and veto over the investigating officer appointed by the appropriate authority (s. 89(4)). Its powers are otherwise more indirect than direct. It cannot carry out its own investigations, though it may issue directions as to the conduct of an investigation, and a member of the PCA may attend when witnesses, complainants, or officers under investigation are being interviewed or asked to give statements (*R v Police Complaints Authority, ex parte Thompson, The Times*, 24 October 1989).

Once the investigation is complete, a decision will be taken as to whether disciplinary, or criminal proceedings should be taken. The PCA has a role in supervising whether the right decision is taken in this respect, though the decision as to whether to charge an officer with a criminal offence must be referred to the Director of Public Prosecutions (ss. 90–92).

The PCA also has certain supervisory powers in relation to whether disciplinary proceedings are held (s. 93). In some cases, members of the PCA may serve on a disciplinary tribunal.

3.6.2.3 Position of the complainant A complaint is unlikely to lead to either disciplinary or criminal proceedings. In 1990 there were 16,712 complaints which resulted in only 305 cases of criminal or disciplinary charges (Annual Report of the Police Complaints Authority for 1990). Even if it does, then it provides nothing in the way of direct compensation for the officer's wrongdoing. Moreover, statements made during the formal investigation will not be available in any subsequent civil action, since they have been held to be protected by public interest immunity: *Nelson v Laugharne* [1981] 1 QB 736; *Conerney v Jacklin* [1985] Crim LR 234; *Peach v Metropolitan Police Commissioner* [1986] QB 1064.

A further hazard for the complainant is that the complaint may be regarded as defamatory, and action taken for libel by the police officer concerned: *Conerney v Jacklin* [1985] Crim LR 234. This, and certain other difficulties noted by Clayton & Tomlinson (*Civil Actions against the Police*, Sweet & Maxwell, 2nd edn, 1992, pp. 56–63) lead to the conclusion that there is very little advantage in making a formal complaint against the police. Moreover, the low level of success of such complaints can only mean that the threat of one being brought is unlikely to be a deterrent for a police officer considering bending or breaking the rules set out in PACE and its Codes.

3.6.3 Exclusion of evidence
The fact that in certain circumstances a court may be prepared to exclude evidence produced by the prosecution is important for the citizen. Of course,

a court should primarily be concerned with issues of relevance and reliability; but even where evidence is relevant and reliable, there may be circumstances where the defendant can justifiably claim that it should not be used, because of the manner or the circumstances in which it has been obtained. A power to exclude in these circumstances may go some way to ensuring that the rights of the citizen to be treated properly by the police are upheld. There are two sections under PACE which give the courts the power to exclude evidence. Section 76 is concerned solely with confessions, broadly defined in s. 82(1) as including:

> any statement wholly or partly adverse to the person who made it, whether made to a person in authority or not and whether made in words or otherwise.

Section 78, on the other hand, is concerned with all types of evidence, including confessions.

3.6.3.1 Section 76(2)(a): oppression If a confession appears to have been obtained as a result of oppression, then, whether or not it is thought to be reliable, it should be excluded, unless the prosecution can prove beyond reasonable doubt that it was not so obtained. The matter may be raised either by the defence, or by the court itself (s. 76(3)). 'Oppression' is defined as including 'torture, inhuman or degrading treatment, and the use or threat of violence (whether or not amounting to torture)'. Fortunately, the thumbscrew and the rack are not commonly found in British police stations. Interrogation procedures involving prolonged physical discomfort, or sensory deprivation, would almost certainly be regarded, however, as constituting 'inhuman or degrading treatment'. This was the view of the European Court of Human Rights in relation to procedures of this kind used in Northern Ireland (see, *Ireland* v *UK* (1978) Eur Court of HR, Series A, Vol 25). In *R* v *Fulling* (1987) 85 Cr App R 136 the Court of Appeal expressed the view that it was unlikely that oppression could occur without some impropriety on the part of the police. The Court referred to the Oxford English Dictionary definition of it as involving:

> exercise of authority or power in a burdensome, harsh, or wrongful manner; unjust or cruel treatment of subjects, inferiors, etc, or the imposition of unreasonable or unjust burdens.

In this case the alleged oppression was that a police officer had told the defendant, who had been held in police custody for two days, that her lover had been having an affair with another woman, who happened to be in the next cell. The defendant then confessed, on the basis that this was the only way in which she would be released from custody. The Court of Appeal held that the trial judge had been right to rule that this was not a case of oppression.

There are, in fact, very few examples of the courts finding the existence of oppression. One is *R* v *Beales* [1991] Crim LR 118, where the confession was obtained as a result of an interview in which the defendant had been 'hectored and bullied from first to last', and which had included deliberate misstatements of the evidence by the interviewing officer in order to put pressure on the defendant. The trial judge ruled that this constituted oppression, though the confession might also have been excluded on grounds of unreliability.

3.6.3.2 Section 76(2)(b): unreliability As with oppression the issue of unreliability may be raised by either the defence or the court. It arises where a confession was or may have been obtained from a person:

in consequence of anything said or done which was likely, in the circumstances existing at the time, to render unreliable any confession which might be made by him in consequence thereof.

Once the issue is raised, the burden is on the prosecution to prove beyond reasonable doubt that the confession was not obtained in this way. It is not enough to show that the confession is reliable. The test is whether what happened to produce the confession was *likely* to render it unreliable. Thus in *R v Cox* [1991] Crim LR 276, the Court of Appeal quashed a conviction because the judge had allowed evidence of a confession which he considered reliable, whereas he should have considered the question of whether the failure to follow the correct procedures (in this case interviewing a juvenile in the absence of an appropriate adult) made it likely that a confession made in those circumstances would be unreliable.

It is clear that one situation to which s. 76(2)(b) will apply is where there has been conduct by the police, in the form of threats or inducements, which puts pressure on a defendant, but which falls short of oppression. It need not necessarily involve any impropriety: *R v Fulling* (1987) 85 Cr App R. 136. An indication that the offence would be treated as one 'more for the attention of doctors than judges' might well have been regarded as an inducement to admit guilt: *R v Delaney* (1988) Cr App R 338 (indecent assault).

The statement or behaviour which leads to the confession need not come from the police. It will be most likely to lead to unreliability if it emanates from a person in authority, such as a parent, or a teacher, but it does not have to do so. In *R v Harvey* [1988] Crim LR 241 it came from the co-defendant. The defendant's own conduct, however, cannot trigger the operation of the section: *R v Goldenberg* (1988) 88 Cr App R 285 (defendant was a drug addict).

Other conduct which has led to exclusion under s. 76(2)(b) includes a failure to comply with the requirements of Code of Practice C. In *R v Doolan* [1988] Crim LR 747, for example, there was a failure to caution before interview. Failure to allow access to a solicitor may also render a confession unreliable: *R v Chung* (1991) 92 Cr App R 314.

3.6.3.3 Section 78: unfairness Section 78 was included in PACE at a relatively late stage in its parliamentary proceedings, as a government response to an attempt by Lord Scarman to get an even broader exclusionary power included. Its effect is to give to any court a discretion to exclude evidence if:

it appears to the court that, having regard to all the circumstances, including the circumstances in which the evidence was obtained, the admission of the evidence would have such an adverse effect on the fairness of the proceedings that the court ought not to admit it.

There was some scepticism at the time as to the extent to which the courts would be prepared to use this discretion, particularly in the light of the very limited exclusionary rule which existed under the common law on the basis of the House of Lords decision in *R* v *Sang* [1980] AC 402. All the members of the Lords in this case were prepared to recognise that there should be the possibility of excluding evidence on the basis of unfairness, but did not present any uniform view as to what circumstances might justify this. Oppression was probably enough, but the fact that the evidence was obtained as a result of the activities of an *agent provocateur* would not in itself merit exclusion.

In fact, contrary to expectations, s. 78 has been used in many cases. Part of the reason for this is that it quickly became established that the section could be used to exclude *any* evidence, including confessions and other incriminating statements, which might at first sight have seemed to be the exclusive preserve of s. 76. It also became established fairly early on, in *R* v *Samuel* [1988] QB 615, that the section was a self-contained provision which should be interpreted within its own terms, rather than being regarded as simply re-stating the common law (as had been suggested by Watkins LJ in *R* v *Mason* [1987] 3 All ER 481).

R v *Samuel* was also important in establishing one of the main grounds on which exclusion has subsequently been justified: that is, on the basis that there have been 'significant and substantial' breaches of the Act, or a Code of Practice, or both. The case was in fact concerned with breach of a statutory provision (that is, the right of access to legal advice), but it was subsequently confirmed by the Court of Appeal in *R* v *Keenan* [1989] 3 All ER 599, that a breach of the Code could in itself justify exclusion (in this case, failure to keep proper records of interviews, under paras 11 and 12 of Code C).

The fact that the breach must be 'significant and substantial' means that it is unlikely that breaches of the detailed provisions of the Codes concerning such things as the provision of meals will be sufficient (see, for example, *R* v *Brine* [1992] Crim LR 122). In fact, the vast majority of cases under s. 78 have been concerned with just two types of breach, namely, breach of the provisions concerning access to legal advice under s. 58, and breach of the provisions of Code C concerning the requirements to make contemporaneous records of interviews, and to show these to the suspect (for example, *R* v *Canale* [1990] Crim LR 329, *R* v *Walsh* (1990) Cr App R 161, *R* v *Scott* [1991] Crim LR 56, *R* v *Sparks* [1991] Crim LR 128). Other breaches as regards, for example, breath tests (*Hudson* v *DPP, The Times*, 28 May 1991; *DPP* v *Godwin* [1991] RTR 303), or identification procedures (*R* v *Nagah* [1991] Crim LR 55) can, however, lead to exclusion.

Even if there has been a significant and substantial breach this does not, however, lead to automatic exclusion. In a number of cases the courts have refused to exercise the power to exclude evidence the breach did not 'make any difference' to what had happened, and the evidence was not therefore unfair. In reaching this decision the courts are not saying that the evidence is *reliable* despite the breach: reliability or not is generally irrelevant to s. 78. What they are saying is, for example, that the confession would have occurred even if the correct procedures had been followed. In *R* v *Alladice* [1988] Crim LR 608, for example, the defendant had wrongfully been refused access to a solicitor. His own evidence at the trial, however, made it clear that he was well aware of the right to remain silent, and that a solicitor might well have advised him to say nothing. There was no reason to suppose that he would not have confessed if he had had access to a solicitor. The same view was taken in *R* v *Dunford* (1990) 140 *NLJ* 517, and in *R* v *Dunn* (1990) 91 Cr App R 237, where the presence of a solicitor's clerk during an interview which was not recorded justified admitting the evidence of the interview.

Finally, the courts will be considerably influenced by the presence or absence of 'bad faith'. Trickery by the police will in some cases lead to exclusion under s. 78 even if there has been no breach of the Act or Codes. In *R* v *Mason* [1987] 3 All ER 481, the police had told the defendant and his solicitor that the defendant's fingerprints had been found near to the scene of the crime. This was quite untrue, and the defendant's subsequent confession was ruled inadmissible. 'Bad faith' does not necessarily consist of a deliberate trick, however. Awareness on the part of the police that they are acting outside their lawful powers may well be enough: *Matto* v *DPP* [1987] Crim LR 641. Conversely, in some cases, the courts have been prepared to condone deceit by the police. In *R* v *Bailey* [1993] 3 All ER 513, a blatant piece of play acting was approved by the Court of Appeal. The investigating officers and the custody officer played out a conversation in front of the defendants, in which the custody officer, appearing to act against the wishes of the investigating officers, insisted in placing the two defendants in the same cell. In fact, the investigating officers wanted the defendants together, as the cell was bugged. The defendants, lulled into a false sense of security, engaged in a conversation which contained a number of damaging admissions, and was recorded. The Court of Appeal found nothing wrong in what the police had done, even though it was clearly a means of circumventing the fact that they could not question the defendants further (because they had both already been charged).

If bad faith is shown, however, this will often override the fact that a breach might not otherwise be regarded as substantial, or that it made no difference. In *R* v *Alladice* (1988), for example, where, as we have seen, the confession was held admissible because the breach was thought to have made no difference to the defendant, Lord Lane commented that 'if the police had acted in bad faith, the Court would have had little difficulty in ruling any confession inadmissible under s. 78'. This approach shows that, despite protestations to the contrary, the power to exclude evidence is at times used to discipline the police. The knowledge that a deliberate failure to follow the correct procedures may well lead to evidence being excluded under s. 78 must have some effect in encouraging adherence to them, and the influence of the section must be regarded as having been a very beneficial one in respect of the protection of the rights of the suspect while in police custody.

3.7 THE EUROPEAN POSITION

The provisions of Art. 5 of the European Convention on Human Rights have been discussed in the previous chapter (see 2.6), insofar as they may be applicable to powers of stop and search and arrest. Here we need to consider whether the procedures for detention prior to trial meet the requirements of Art. 5. As with the powers considered in chapter 2, the provision which may justify the undoubted deprivation of liberty involved in these procedures is Art. 5(1)(c).This permits:

the lawful arrest or detention of a person effected for the purpose of bringing him before the competent legal authority on reasonable suspicion of having committed an offence or when it is reasonably considered necessary to prevent his committing an offence or fleeing after having done so.

Alongside this, reference must also be made to Art. 5(3), which deals with the need for judicial supervision of detention authorised by Art. 5(1)(c). This states:

Everyone arrested or detained in accordance with the provisions of paragraph 1(c) of this Article shall be brought promptly before a judge or other officer authorised by law to exercise judicial power . . .

The requirements of this paragraph were recently given detailed consideration in a British context in *Brogan* v *United Kingdom* (1989) 11 EHRR 117.

The case arose out of the use of the extended power of detention available in respect of those detained under s. 12 of the Prevention of Terrorism (Temporary Provisions) Act 1984. Virtually identical powers now exist under the Prevention of Terrorism (Temporary Provisions) Act 1989 (see 3.3.4). There were four applicants who had been detained, on the authorisation of the Home Secretary, for periods of between four days and six hours, to six days and sixteen and a half hours. As we have seen, the maximum period of detention without charge under these powers is seven days. Unlike the ordinary powers under PACE, where magistrates must approve detention beyond 36 hours (see 3.3.3.2), the detention under the terrorism legislation is in the hands of the police for the first 48 hours, and thereafter at the discretion of the Home Secretary. No judicial authorisation is required at any stage.

The Court recognised the particular problems presented by terrorist offences. It also acknowledged that these difficulties might have the effect of prolonging the period during which a person suspected of serious terrorist offences may, without violating Art. 5(3), be kept in custody before being brought before a judge. They might also result in special procedural precautions in relation to the judicial control (para. 61). Presumably the Court was referring here to possibilities such as the court sitting *in camera*, or dealing with the matter *ex parte* (that is, hearing the police case for detention, but not giving the detainee an opportunity to rebut it at that stage).

In the end, however, it had to be recognised that Art. 5(3) called for 'promptness' in bringing the detainee before a judge. In the French text of Art.

5(3) the word used was 'aussitôt', which confirmed the connotation of immediacy. This meant that the scope for flexibility was very limited. It was the view of the Court, by a vote of 12 to 7, that even the shortest period of detention under consideration, that is four days and six hours, was too long to fit with the notion of promptness. All four applicants had therefore been unlawfully detained, in breach of Art. 5(3), and should have had an enforceable right to compensation under Art. 5(5).

The British government's response to this was to use its power under Art. 15 to derogate from the provisions of Art. 5(3) on the grounds of the public emergency in relation to Northern Ireland. This was a disappointing response. The concerns of the Court could surely have been met by allowing a review of detention beyond 48 hours in such cases (of which there are never going to be a large number) to be in the hands of an appropriate senior judge. This would be unlikely to lead to a flood of terrorists on to the streets, or in any serious way to hinder legitimate police investigations. What it would do would be to make clear that the procedure was properly part of a criminal process undertaken with a view to prosecution, rather than a form of short-term executive detention having the primary aim of gathering intelligence by interrogation. The derogation has, however, subsequently been approved by the European Court of Human Rights in *Brannigan and McBride* v *United Kingdom, The Times*, 28 May 1993, so that it cannot be expected that there will be any move to amend the procedures under the Prevention of Terrorism Act 1989.

The broader implication of the *Brogan* case is that the ordinary criminal procedures under PACE are probably in accordance with Art. 5(3). The Court did not attempt to set out time limits which should apply, but the standard period of 24 hours before release or charge would surely be acceptable, given that a person charged and kept in custody is to be brought before the next sitting of the magistrates (PACE, s. 46). The additional twelve hours for which a person can be held in relation to a serious arrestable offence is likely to be regarded as being justified by the seriousness of the offence. Beyond that, the detainee is held on the authority of a magistrates' court, and is thus under the supervision of a judicial authority, which clearly meets the requirements of Art. 5(3).

It seems then, that in this area the Convention is unlikely to be of help to the detainee, provided that the provisions of PACE have been followed correctly.

FOUR

Property Rights: Entry, Search and Seizure

4.1 INTRODUCTION

In this chapter the focus is on rights of ownership of property. In general, the owner of property is entitled to defend it against interference by others. Such interference will normally amount to a criminal offence (for example, if property is stolen or damaged), or a tort (for example trespass, or conversion). In this way the law recognises the existence of an individual's rights over property. In some circumstances, however, such rights can be overridden. This chapter is concerned with the situations where the law allows the police, or other officials of the State, to enter a person's land, or to seize a person's property, without permission, and the justifications for such infringements of the individual's rights.

4.1.1 Property rights: reasons for protection

'An Englishman's home is his castle' is a powerful rhetorical assertion of the individual's right of property. What are the justifications for such an assertion? There are two principal ones. First, there is the recognition of the rights of private ownership of property. This is, of course, a politically charged right, which has by no means received universal or comprehensive acceptance. Modern Western democracies, however, including the United Kingdom, take it as given that the private ownership of land, as well as personal possessions, is desirable, and something which the law should protect. There is not space here to go into the political and philosophical debate on the validity of this position, and it will simply be accepted as one of the principles which underpins the rights discussed in this chapter. There may also, of course, be legal rights of exclusive possession which fall short of ownership. The tenant, in relation to land, and the hirer under a hire purchase agreement, for example, will be able to take legal action against those who infringe their possessory rights. Such rights will generally be based on contract.

The second argument does not depend on legal rights of ownership and possession. This is based on the idea that individuals have rights of privacy, that there is, in other words, a right of private space, infringement of which by others may justifiably lead to complaint. Such a right is recognised, for example, by Art. 8 of the European Convention on Human Rights (see 4.7). The privacy right has a considerable, though perhaps not comprehensive, overlap with rights to possession based on ownership or contract. The private householder who is the subject of an unlawful entry may complain both about the infringement of property rights, and the invasion of privacy which is involved. The privacy argument, however, applies more easily to domestic, as opposed to commercial premises. As regards the latter, an individual's personal office, for example, may have some of the characteristics of a private residence, but it is hard to see this extending to, say, a warehouse full of pornographic magazines. In this situation, the property rights will predominate over those based on privacy. There are also some situations, on the other hand, where privacy may predominate. The lodger in a private house, for example, may have no legal right to exclude the owner, but may justifiably claim an invasion of privacy if the owner starts rummaging through the lodger's belongings.

Both these bases for complaint about interference with property need to be borne in mind in looking at the position under English law. It will be found, however, that the rights based on ownership and contract have traditionally been given far greater recognition than those based on privacy. For the purposes of this chapter the phrase 'property rights' is used to encompass all three.

4.1.2   Property rights: justifications for infringement

The justifications for infringement of property rights are several. First, it may be regarded as necessary in the detection of crime. If it is believed that evidence of a criminal offence is to be found on certain premises, it may well be justifiable to allow the police to enter against the wishes of the occupier to search for it. A balance may need to be drawn, however, between the likely value of the evidence, the seriousness of the offence, and the degree of infringement involved. It may also be relevant whether the evidence is in the possession of a suspect or an innocent third party. In some situations it may be preferable to obtain the evidence by means of a court order, rather than by forcible search (see 4.4).

Another justification for entry to premises is the need to arrest or re-capture a person thought to be on those premises, or to intervene to stop an offence being committed by one person against another. In other words, there are some situations which justify entry to deal with *people* rather than *things*.

As far as goods are concerned, they may not only be required as evidence. It may be that they are seized with a view to their forfeiture or destruction. This will be the case where the items themselves are illicit, for example, obscene publications, or controlled drugs, and so should be removed from circulation, or where they constitute the proceeds of crime, and should be forfeited as part of the punishment of the person convicted of the offence.

Finally, it may be justifiable to allow forcible entry to premises for the purposes of inspection. Officials concerned with enforcing standards in relation to environmental health, or trading standards, for example, may need to have the power to enter premises without permission, in order to do their jobs properly.

This justification highlights the fact that many other officials apart from the police can obtain warrants authorising entry, or may in some cases be able to enter without warrant. One of the leading cases on search warrants prior to PACE involved an investigation by the Inland Revenue (that is, *R v IRC, ex parte Rossminster* [1980] 1 All ER 80). As well as those who are, like the police, involved in investigating crime, such as the Inland Revenue, and Customs and Excise, there are many central and local government departments with powers of entry, in particular in relation to business premises (see R. Stone, *Entry, Search and Seizure*, 2nd ed (London: Sweet & Maxwell, 1989), chapters 6 to 9). The protective provisions of PACE and its Codes apply to some of these powers (for example, those used by the Customs and Excise), but in many cases the powers are expressed widely, and allow considerable opportunity for oppressive use. That this does not by and large happen is a tribute to the integrity of those officials entrusted with these powers. The scope of the powers which exist, however, indicates a fairly low status being given to the rights of property and privacy referred to above. This is particularly true of business premises, as opposed to private dwellings. This might in turn suggest that privacy is rated more highly than property rights, if it is accepted that privacy applies more strongly to domestic, as opposed to business, premises.

There is not scope within this book to deal with any of these powers in detail. The concentration in this chapter is solely on the police. It is important to remember, however, that police powers, although in many cases the most intrusive, are only a small part of the full range of powers which exist authorising entry on to premises against the wishes of the occupier.

In looking at the variety of powers which are discussed in the rest of this chapter, the justifications noted above which might be said to apply in each case should be kept in mind, in order to answer the questions: 'Is this power necessary?', or 'Are the infringements of rights which it involves justifiable?'. It may be thought that an unacceptable approach to the use of forcible search powers appears in a recently reported quote from the Metropolitan Police Commissioner. Asked to comment on an operation against burglaries which had involved simultaneous raids on 617 addresses, and in relation to which some of the intelligence was criticised as being inadequate, he was reported as saying (*The Times*, 4 June 1993):

> Whenever you carry out a series of raids for anything, there will be a hit and miss element to it. It is a fact of life. It is not particularly disappointing. The aim of this operation is for burglars to feel some of the fear they have generated with law-abiding members of the public in the past.

This may be criticised on a number of grounds, such as its acceptance of a blunderbuss 'hit and miss' approach, or its presumption of guilt in relation to those whose premises were being searched. In particular, it cannot be acceptable that search warrant powers should be used as a means of intimidation of those subject to them, rather than as a process for obtaining evidence. It is disappointing, to say the least, to find the country's most senior police officer apparently taking a different view.

4.2 LAND AND PREMISES: RIGHTS OF ENTRY

The first group of powers to be considered relate to land and premises. We are looking here at powers which allow the police or others to enter premises against the wishes of the owner, or other person having exclusive possession, and, in some cases, to search those premises. The powers to seize things which are found on the premises are considered at 4.3.

4.2.1 Trespass and licence

We are concerned in this chapter with entries without permission, which will, if they take place without lawful authority, amount to the tort of trespass. The tort will not be committed, however, if there is an express or implied licence to enter. Express licences do not create too many problems. A police officer may be invited in, for example, to discuss a possible criminal offence. It should be noted, however, that an express licence can be created by conduct. In *Faulkner* v *Willetts* [1982] Crim LR 453, the invitation to a police officer was deemed to have been made when the appellant's wife, having opened the door, and been told the reason for the officer's visit, left the door open and walked back into the house. No words of invitation to enter were uttered, but there was held to be an express licence to enter, created by conduct. PACE Code of Practice B, para. 4.1, however, requires that where a police officer wishes to carry out a *search* with consent, such consent should be given in writing on a special Notice of Powers and Rights. This notice is to be used, if practicable, wherever premises are to be searched by the police (Code B, 5.7; see 4.2.3.2).

A licence to enter may also be implied in some situations. The scope of such an implied licence is limited, however. In *Robson* v *Hallett* [1967] 2 QB 939 it was held that there is an implied licence to go to the front door of a house where the entrant has legitimate business with the occupier. Entry to a front garden for this purpose will not therefore be a trespass. The purpose of the licence is to enable the entrant to deliver things to the premises, or to attract the attention of the occupier, and will presumably, therefore, also apply to the common parts of blocks of flats, insofar as these are not already 'public places' (see, for example, *Knox* v *Anderton* (1983) 76 Cr App R 156).

Code of Practice B, para. 4.4 appears to assume that there would be an implied licence where seeking consent would cause disproportionate inconvenience to the person concerned. The example given in the Code (Note 4C), is where an arrest took place at night, after a pursuit, and the police wished to check gardens along the route of the pursuit, to see if stolen or incriminating articles had been discarded. As will be seen below, there is no statutory power of search following an arrest, other than in respect of premises on which the arrest took place; or which the suspect left immediately prior to the arrest; or which are under the occupation or control of the suspect. The search of premises in the situation suggested would not fit into any of these categories, and so could only be carried out on the basis of a warrant, or consent. Where the search follows immediately on the arrest, it can only be on the basis of an implied consent, that is, that the occupier, knowing of the circumstances, would be likely to have consented. This must therefore be regarded as a form of implied licence.

An implied licence will not arise if the occupier makes it clear that particular visitors are not welcome. A notice stating 'Police Keep Out' would seem to be likely to be effective for this purpose. Both an express or implied licence can be terminated by clear words indicating that it has been withdrawn. In *Lambert v Roberts* [1981] 2 All ER 15, for example, the words 'This is private property: you are trespassing' were held sufficient to terminate a licence. Mere verbal abuse of the visitor, however, may not be enough: *Snook v Mannion* [1982] Crim LR 601.

Once a licence has been withdrawn, the visitor who is already on the premises must be given a chance to leave. Reasonable force may then be used to expel the trespasser: *Davis v Lisle* [1936] 2 KB 434. If the trespasser is a police officer, forcible ejection will not amount to the offence of assault on a police constable in the execution of his duty, because the failure to comply with the termination of the licence will take the officer outside the scope of any lawful duty (*Davis v Lisle*, above).

(The whole issue of licences in this context is discussed more fully in R. Stone, *Entry, Search and Seizure*, 2nd edn, Sweet & Maxwell, 1989, pp. 1–6.)

4.2.2 Entry without warrant: common law

As far as the police are concerned, the position as to entry to premises under the common law, against the wishes of the occupier, is governed by s. 17(5) and (6) of PACE. Section 17(5) states that, subject to subsection (6), 'all the rules of common law under which a constable has power to enter premises without a warrant are hereby abolished'. Subsection (6) then preserves 'any power of entry to deal with or prevent a breach of the peace'. The only power under the common law which is available to the police is therefore the power in relation to breaches of the peace. The meaning of 'breach of the peace' has been discussed in chapter 2 (see 2.4.1). The same definition will apply here. How exactly does the power operate?

The power was considered in some detail in *Thomas v Sawkins* [1935] 2 KB 249. A public meeting was being held on private premises. It had previously been made clear to the police that their presence was not welcome. Nevertheless, two officers attended, and entered the premises where the meeting was held. It was clear that they did not have the permission of the organisers to be there, and so were not present on the basis of any licence. Indeed, one of the stewards of the meeting attempted to eject one of the officers, who resisted, with the assistance of his fellow officer. This led to a private prosecution for assault being brought against one of the officers. The Divisional Court was called on to decide whether the police officers' presence was lawful. It was held that it was. The case established that the police have the power to enter premises to deal with actual, or *reasonably anticipated*, breaches of the peace.

The officers had such a reasonable apprehension in this case, so their presence was lawful, and their resistance to being expelled could not constitute an assault on the steward.

It seems that this power applies not only to premises to which the public has been invited, but also to purely domestic situations. In *Lamb* v *DPP* [1990] Crim LR 58, a constable had been invited on to premises by a woman who wished to remove some of her property, but feared attack by the occupier with whom she had been living. The occupier told the police officer to leave. This clearly terminated any right to remain on the basis of licence (see 4.2.1). Before the officer left, however, the occupier started to attack the woman, and the police officer intervened. It was held that he was acting in the execution of his duty in so doing. Although his licence to remain had been terminated, he was entitled to stay to deal with the breach of the peace. He had no obligation to withdraw and then re-enter the premises.

As a result the position is that a police officer can enter, and remain on, any premises, for the purpose of dealing with a breach of the peace which is taking place, or which is reasonably apprehended.

The common law also recognised a general power of entry available to any citizen where a person called out for assistance against an attacker: *Handcock* v *Baker* (1800) 2 Bos & P 260. The powers of the police in this context, to the extent that they go beyond the power to deal with a breach of the peace, are now governed by PACE, s. 17(1)(e) (see 4.2.3.1). People other than police officers, however, presumably still have a power of entry on this basis under the common law.

4.2.3   Entry and search without warrant: PACE
PACE gives powers of entry and search without warrant to the police under three sections, namely, ss. 17, 18 and 32. The first of these is concerned primarily with powers of arrest, the latter two deal with powers to enter and search premises in order to obtain or secure evidence.

4.2.3.1   Entry for the purpose of arrest, etc   Section 17 gives a number of powers of entry and search, mainly in connection with the exercise of powers of arrest. In each case the constable entering the premises must have reasonable grounds for believing that the person sought is on the premises (s. 17(2)(a)). First, the power is given to effect an arrest under warrant, or to execute a warrant of commitment under s. 76 of the Magistrates' Courts Act 1980 (this concerns those in default to the court, for example, for not paying a fine). Secondly the power may be used to arrest for any arrestable offence (s. 17(1)(b)); see 2.4.3.1. Thirdly, there are two named, non-arrestable, public order offences in relation to which premises may be entered to effect an arrest, (s. 17(1)(c)). These are offences under s. 1 of the Public Order Act 1936 (prohibition on wearing political uniforms, see 8.4.8.1), and s. 4 of the Public Order Act 1986 (fear or provocation of violence, see 8.4.5). It is not clear why these particular offences justify this special power of entry, particularly given the powers in relation to a breach of the peace noted at 4.2.2. Fourthly, various 'squatting' offences under ss. 6, 7, 8, and 10 of the Criminal Law Act 1977,

although non-arrestable, carry a power of arrest. Section 17(1)(c) of PACE gives a power of entry to carry out the arrest to an officer in uniform. It is easier to see the justification for this than the power relating to the public order offences, since 'squatters' are almost inevitably going to be on private premises. Finally, a power of entry is given to recapture a person who is 'unlawfully at large' and whom the police officer is pursuing. This will apply to those who have escaped from arrest, imprisonment, or other lawful custody. The application of the provision to persons detained under the Mental Health Act 1983, and the meaning of 'pursuit' were considered by the House of Lords in *D'Souza* v *DPP* [1992] 1 WLR 1073. A woman, who had a history of mental illness, had discharged herself from hospital after being detained under s. 6(2) of the Mental Health Act 1983. She went home. The police decided that she was 'unlawfully at large' and went to her home to 'recapture' her. The woman's husband and daughter forcibly resisted the police's entry, and were charged with assaulting a police officer in the execution of his duty. They were convicted, and the daughter appealed. The House of Lords held that the mother was within the scope of s. 17(1)(d), but the power under that section had to be exercised while 'in pursuit'. There was no evidence of a pursuit in this case. The police had simply formed an opinion as to where the woman was, and had gone to those premises to apprehend her. They were not in the execution of their duty when forcing entry, and the case was remitted to the Crown Court with a direction to dismiss the charge against the daughter. This case confirms that the provision applies to mental patients. It also limits the scope of the power, however. It cannot be used unless there is some pursuit of the fugitive. The result seems to be that the position under PACE is much the same as under the common law concept of entry in 'hot pursuit': *McClorie* v *Oxford* [1982] QB 1290.

In relation to all the above powers, if they are exercised in relation to premises consisting of two or more separate dwellings (for example, a block of flats), the power is limited to the common parts, and any specific dwelling in which the constable has reasonable grounds for believing that the person sought may be.

As has been noted above, in relation to all these powers, there must be reasonable grounds for believing that the person is on the premises. The cases are in conflict as to whether in relation to the power under s. 17(1)(b) (arrest for an arrestable offence), a court considering the valid exercise of that power must have proved to it that there existed valid grounds justifying the *arrest* of the suspect (for example, under PACE, s. 24). In *Kynaston* v *DPP* (1987) 87 Cr App R 200 one Divisional Court said that this was not necessary. The officers on arriving at the premises had indicated that they intended to arrest the suspect for robbery. This was held to raise an inference of reasonable grounds justifying the arrest. Since the officer concerned had not been cross-examined on this point, the inference had not been rebutted, and the justices were right to conclude that no positive evidence of the grounds justifying arrest was necessary. In *Riley* v *DPP* (1991) Cr App R 14, however, another Divisional Court held that because the justices had not been told the basis of the arrest, they could not judge whether it was lawful, and this in turn meant that they could not tell whether the entry under s. 17 was lawful either. This decision was taken without reference to *Kynaston*. The only way of reconciling them appears to be on the basis that in *Kynaston* the offence for which arrest was sought was known to the justices, and it was an arrestable offence, whereas in *Riley*, not even this information was available. It makes for a very fine distinction, however, and it is to be hoped that an opportunity will arise at some stage for the matter to be clarified by the Court of Appeal or House of Lords.

There is a final power of entry and search under s. 17(1)(e) which is not related to arrest. This is for the purpose of saving life or limb, or preventing serious damage to property and obviously covers the area which fell under the common law power recognised in *Handcock* v *Baker* (1800) 2 Bos & P 260 (see 4.2.2). It is unusual in that its exercise is not dependent on any reasonable belief or suspicion on the part of the police officer. Presumably, then, a genuine belief that entry without consent is necessary for one of the specified purposes is sufficient. There is no reason why the power should be this broad. It would have been perfectly satisfactory to make the power available here, as with the other powers in s. 17(1), only where the constable had reasonable grounds for believing it was necessary. There is, however, no evidence that this is a power which is in any way abused by the police.

All the powers to search under s. 17 are limited to what is reasonable for the purpose for which the power of entry is exercised. Once the person sought, for example, has been discovered and apprehended, no further search will be justified under s. 17. If the police wish to search further in order to find evidence, or a weapon used by the person arrested, for example, they will have to rely on one of the other powers justifying search without warrant, under s. 18 or s. 32 (see 4.2.3.2, 4.2.3.3).

4.2.3.2 Entry and search after arrest for an arrestable offence
Where a person has been arrested for an arrestable offence, s. 18 gives a power of entry and search. It seems that about half of all searches of premises take place under this power (V. Bevan and K. Lidstone, *The Investigation of Crime*, Butterworths, 1992, p. 112). The premises to which it relates are those which are occupied or controlled by the person who has been arrested. The word 'controlled' is not defined. It may well cover a person's place of work, for example, thus permitting the search of an office, or locker. Does a landlord, however, 'control' premises which are let out to tenants? The word is not clear, and is potentially wide in scope. The vagueness that it entails is unfortunate. The power is to be supervised by an officer of the rank of inspector or above (s. 18(4)). Unless the power is exercised immediately following an arrest away from a police station, the inspector should give the officer who is to carry out the search a written authorisation which can be taken and shown to anyone on the premises to be searched (s. 18(4); *R* v *Badham* [1987] Crim LR 202). Code of Practice B, para. 5.7 provides for a standard form of Notice of Powers and Rights which should, if practicable, be used for this purpose. This is discussed further below. It is not sufficient for the authorisation simply to be recorded in the inspector's notebook. Section 18(7) also requires the inspector to record

the grounds for the search and the evidence sought. Where the person in occupation or control of the premises is in police custody at the time of the search, a record of the authorisation, the grounds for the search, and the evidence sought, should be included in the custody record (s. 18(8)).

It will often be the case that the police officer arresting a suspect away from a police station will want to search premises under the s. 18 power immediately, and before taking the suspect to the police station. This is permitted by s. 18(5), where it is necessary for the effective investigation of the offence. In this case the officer conducting the search must, as soon as practicable, inform an officer of the rank of inspector or above that the search has taken place. That officer will then make the records relating to the search referred to above.

The power under s. 18 is to search premises on which there are reasonable grounds to believe there is evidence of the offence for which the suspect has been arrested, or of an arrestable offence connected with or similar to that offence. 'Connected with' would include, for example, searching for evidence of the theft of a gun which had been used in a robbery for which the suspect was arrested. 'Similar to' would cover the situation, for example, where a person arrested for using a stolen credit card was suspected of having other stolen cards at home. It will not apply if, after arrest, the police, perhaps as a result of questioning the suspect, have reasonable grounds to believe that evidence of some totally unconnected offence will be found on premises. If the police wish to search under the s. 18 power in that situation they will have to arrest for the second offence.

The power may not be used to search for evidence which is subject to legal privilege (see 4.4.1.1). It can, however, be used to search for evidence for which it will not normally be possible to obtain a search warrant, that is, 'excluded' material (see 4.4.1.2) or 'special procedure' material (see 4.4.1.3).

The search must not extend beyond what is reasonably required for the purpose of discovering the evidence sought (s. 18(3)). If it is stolen computers, it will not be legitimate, therefore, to search desk drawers. If the items sought are small and easily hidden, however, for example, documents or drugs, there will be virtually no limit to the search. Once the items sought have been found the search should cease (Code of Practice B, para. 5.9).

In addition to the requirements of s. 18, Code of Practice B, para. 5, sets out various provisions which apply to all searches. Searches should take place 'at a reasonable hour', unless this would be likely to frustrate the purpose of the search (para. 5.2). No definition is given of what is 'a reasonable hour'. Note 5A, however, says that in deciding this, regard should be had as to when there is likely to be anybody on the premises. Times when people are likely to be asleep should be avoided, unless this would be likely to frustrate the purpose of the search. In other words, unless there is good reason to act otherwise, searches should take place during the day time, at a time when the premises are likely to be occupied by someone with power to grant entry.

On arrival at the premises the officer in charge should normally attempt to communicate with someone who is entitled to grant access, and explain the authority under which entry is sought (Code B, para. 5.4). The officer's identity should be given, and, if the officer is not in uniform, the officer's warrant card shown. The purpose of the search, and the grounds for undertaking it should also be stated (Code B, para. 5.4). None of the above need be done, however, where the premises are known to be empty, or there are reasonable grounds for believing that to alert the occupants would frustrate the object of the search, or endanger the police officers or others (Code B, para. 5.4 (i) to (iii)). Reasonable force may be used to gain entry in such cases, or where the occupier has refused to allow entry, or cannot be communicated with (Code C, para. 5.6).

Once entry has been gained, the officer in charge should, if practicable, give the occupier a Notice of Powers and Rights, in the standard form set out in Code B, para. 5.7. This should be done before any search begins, unless there are reasonable grounds for believing that to do so would frustrate the object of the search, or endanger the police officers or others (Code B, para. 5.8). If the premises are unoccupied a copy of the Notice should be left in a prominent position.

The Notice should set out the power under which the search is taking place, and the extent of the powers of search and seizure being relied on. The rights of the occupier, and of the owner of any property seized, should be explained, as well as the possibility of compensation for damage, and where applications for this should be directed. Finally the Notice should state that a copy of the Code is available for inspection at any police station (Code B, para. 5.7).

Paragraph 5.10 of Code B emphasises that searches should be conducted 'with due consideration for the property and privacy of the occupier', and with 'no more disturbance than necessary'. If the occupier wants a friend, neighbour or other person to witness the search this should generally be allowed (Code B, para. 5.11). There is no need to delay a search for this purpose, however, and the officer in charge may refuse the request if there are reasonable grounds for believing that to comply would seriously hinder the investigation.

Finally, premises which have been entered by force, should be left secure (Code B, para. 5.12).

We see here the general pattern of protection under PACE and its Codes repeated. The citizen is protected against the police by the requirements that the exercise of the powers is supervised by an officer of a particular rank (in the case of s. 18, an inspector); that the police follow certain procedures; and that the citizen is given the fullest possible information. All of the protective provisions are subject to exceptions, however, and it must be debatable how effective they are likely to be in deterring abuse by police officers.

4.2.3.3 Entry and search after arrest for any offence

Where a person has been arrested for *any* offence, arrestable or non-arrestable, other than at a police station, s. 32 of PACE confers a power to enter and search certain premises. The premises in this case are those on which the arrest took place, or which the arrested person left immediately prior to the arrest. The power is broader than that under s. 18 in this respect, in that the premises do not have to be under the occupation or control of the arrested person. They may belong to an innocent third party who is not in any way subject to suspicion on the part of the police.

The power is to enter and search for evidence of the offence for which the person was arrested, and the officer concerned must have reasonable grounds for believing that such evidence will be found on the premises. This is narrower than s. 18, which, as we have seen, allows searches for evidence of 'connected' or 'similar' arrestable offences.

The wording of s. 32 does not indicate when the power may be used. In particular, it is not stated whether it must be used immediately following the arrest. In *R v Badham* [1987] Crim LR 202 the police tried to rely on the power as justifying an entry and search some four hours after the arrest. The Crown Court judge refused to accept this as a legitimate use of the power. Although it will be difficult to tell exactly where the line is to be drawn, the section does not confer an open-ended power to return to search premises where an arrest took place. It is intended to be an 'immediate' power. Any delay on the part of the police will therefore need very clear justification. It is submitted that once the arrested person has been taken to a police station the power under s. 32 should be regarded as expired. If the police subsequently wish to carry out a search, they will have to rely on s. 18 (if available), or seek a warrant.

The provisions of para. 5 of Code of Practice B (see 4.2.3.2) will apply to searches under s. 32 in the same way as to searches under s. 18.

4.2.4   Entry and search under warrant: general provisions

In this section we are considering further the situations where the wishes of the occupier of premises may be overridden by the need for the police to obtain evidence in relation to an investigation. Whereas the powers under s. 18 and s. 32 are dependent on there having been an arrest, in some cases the police may wish to search for evidence which is likely to form the basis of an arrest. Alternatively, other restrictions on the availability of the powers to search without warrant may apply, even though the police have a suspect in custody. The premises in question may not be those on which the arrest took place, and may also not be under the occupation or control of the person arrested. In these situations, in order to gain access to the premises other than by consent, the police will have to seek some sort of judicial authority, generally from a magistrate, for entry and search, in the form of a 'warrant'.

Sections 15 and 16 of PACE set out procedures which should be followed in relation to all applications for, and exercise of, powers of entry and search under warrant. Section 15(1), which is headed 'Search warrants – safeguards', states that 'an entry on or search of premises under a warrant is unlawful unless it complies with this section and section 16 below'. The Court of Appeal in *R v Longman* [1988] 1 WLR 619 had some difficulty in deciding to what 'it' referred. Was it the warrant, or the entry, or the search? It was, however, accepted in *R v Chief Constable for Lancashire, ex parte Parker and McGrath* [1993] Crim LR 204 that a breach of the provisions in s. 16 as to the information to be provided to the occupier at the time of the search, could render the whole search unlawful. The implication is that 'it' in s. 15 refers to all three elements, that is the warrant, the entry, and the search. All must comply with the various requirements of ss. 15 and 16 for the entry and search to be lawful.

4.2.4.1 Procedures for application for a warrant   Section 15 is primarily concerned with the procedures to be followed in applying for a warrant. These are supplemented by the provisions of para. 2 of Code of Practice B. No application should generally be made without the authority of an officer of at least the rank of inspector (Code B, para. 2.4). In a case of urgency, however, the senior officer on duty may give the authorisation. An application should not be made on the basis of anonymous information for which corroboration has not been sought (Code B, para. 2.1). In any case, the officer concerned should take reasonable steps to check the accuracy of the information. Reasonable inquiries should be made to establish the nature of the premises, whether anything is known about the occupier, and whether the premises have been previously searched, and if so how recently (Code B, para. 2.3). The nature and location of the articles sought should be ascertained as specifically as possible (Code B, para. 2.2). All this should be done before the application is made. The application will be made *ex parte*, so the person whose premises are to be searched will have no opportunity to challenge the application at this stage. It must be supported by an information in writing (s. 15(3)). The constable applying must make clear the power under which the warrant is sought, the grounds for the application, the premises to be entered and searched, and, so far as is possible, the articles or persons being sought (s. 15(2)). The judge or magistrate receiving the application may ask questions which the officer should answer on oath (s. 15(4)), though there is no provision for recording such exchanges. Questions may be asked about the reliability of the police sources, but there is no need to disclose the identity of an informant (Code B, Note 2A).

No particular form is required for a warrant (*R v IRC, ex parte Rossminster Ltd* [1980] AC 952). It must state, however, the name of the applicant; the date of issue; the enactment under which it is issued; the premises to be searched; and, as far as practicable, what is being sought (s. 15(6)). Two copies must be made, and certified as such (s. 15(7) and (8)).

4.2.4.2 Execution of warrant   The provisions of para. 5 of Code of Practice B, discussed at 4.2.3.2, apply to an entry and search under warrant. In addition, the following particular provisions apply to the execution of a warrant. A warrant will authorise entry on one occasion only (s. 15(5)), which must take place not more than one month after the issue of the warrant (s. 16(3)). Unless it is a case of urgency, if the search might have an adverse effect on relations with the local community, then the local police/community liaison officer must be consulted before the search takes place.

A warrant may be executed by any constable (that is, not necessarily by the officer who obtained it) (s. 16(1)). It may authorise others to accompany the constable (s. 16(2)). This allows for experts to go on to the premises with the police in appropriate cases. They should be there to assist, however, rather than to direct the search. The control of the search, and decisions as to what is to be seized, must remain that of the police: *R v Reading Justices, ex parte South West Meat Ltd* [1992] Crim LR 672.

The occupier, if present at the time, must be given a chance to inspect the warrant (*R v Longman* (1988) 88 Cr App R 148), and be given a copy of it (s. 16(5)). If the original warrant had schedules attached to it, specifying the items sought, a failure to supply these with the copy of the warrant given to the occupier renders the search unlawful: *R v Chief Constable of Lancashire, ex parte Parker and McGrath* [1993] Crim LR 204. If the occupier is not present, but some other person appears to be in charge of the premises, the obligation in s. 16(5) applies to that person (s. 16(6)). If the premises are unoccupied, a copy of the warrant must be left in a prominent place (s. 16(7)).

A warrant which has been executed should be endorsed with the results of the search, indicating whether what was sought was found, and whether anything else was seized (s. 16(9)). An endorsed warrant, or one which has expired before being executed, must be returned to the court which issued it, and kept for 12 months (s. 16(11), (12)). During that period it must be made available for inspection on request by the occupier of the premises to which it relates (s. 16(12)).

4.2.5 Entry under warrant: the powers
In *Entick* v *Carrington* (1765) 19 State Tr 1029; 95 ER 807, Lord Camden CJ emphasised that if a power of entry is alleged, then the judges must decide by looking 'into the books' to see 'if such a justification can be maintained by the text of the statute law, or by the principles of common law'. The case was one of a number (see also *Wilkes v Wood* (1763) 19 State Tr 1153; *Leach v Money* (1765) State Tr 1002; *Wilkes v Lord Halifax* (1769) 19 State Tr 1406) in which the government had tried to use general search warrants to enter and search the premises of publishers of anti-government newspapers. The courts had no doubt that such general warrants had no legal validity, and that the entries therefore constituted trespasses. These cases were one of the highlights of the courts' upholding of individual rights against the power of the State. They led to a situation in English law whereby the power to obtain search warrants was strictly limited, and arose only where specifically granted by statute for a particular purpose.

This situation was obviously advantageous as far as civil liberties were concerned, but gave rise to certain anomalies. In particular, where an offence existed at common law, rather than under statute, there would not generally be any power for the police to obtain a warrant to search for evidence. In *McLorie v Oxford* [1982] QB 1290, for example, it was held that the police had no power to enter private premises to seek evidence relevant to an offence of attempted murder. The Royal Commission on Criminal Procedure which was the precursor to PACE recommended that in relation to serious offences this gap should be filled (*Report*, Cmnd 8092, 1981, para. 3.42). This was done, though not in precisely the way in which the Royal Commission recommended, by PACE, s. 8.

4.2.5.1 PACE, s. 8
The section allows the police to obtain a search warrant from a justice of the peace. The procedures in ss. 15 and 16, and Code of

Practice B, outlined above, will apply. It only applies where there are reasonable grounds for believing that a serious arrestable offence (see 3.3.3.1) has been committed. The power is to enable a search to be made for material which is likely to be of substantial value to the investigation of the serious arrestable offence, and which will be admissible evidence at trial (s. 8(1)). The material must not fall into one of the protected categories, that is legally privileged, excluded, or special procedure (see 4.4.1).

In addition to being satisfied that there are reasonable grounds for believing that material satisfying the above conditions is to be found on premises specified in the application, the magistrate must also be satisfied, on reasonable grounds, that one of a number of further conditions is met. These conditions relate to the necessity of using a warrant to gain access to the material, and are set out in s. 8(3). They are:

(a)   that it is not practicable to communicate with one or other of the persons entitled to grant entry to the premises, or access to the material;

(b)   that entry to the premises will not be granted without a warrant being produced;

(c)   that unless the police can gain immediate entry on arrival at the premises, the purpose of the search may be frustrated, or seriously prejudiced.

In *R* v *Guildhall Magistrates' Court, ex parte Primlaks Holdings Co.* (1988) 89 Cr App R 215, the Divisional Court emphasised the 'draconian' nature of the power under s. 8. As a result it is imperative that the magistrate to whom the application for a warrant is made does not simply accept assertions by the police that there are reasonable grounds for belief in relation to the various matters set out above. The magistrate must be satisfied independently of such assertions, on the basis of the information presented. In the instant case, where the premises in relation to which the warrant was sought were the offices of a firm of solicitors, the material was almost certain to be legally privileged, or special procedure material. Moreover, it was very difficult to accept that it was impossible to communicate with the solicitors in order to gain access, or that the solicitors would have been likely to dispose of the material on being given notice of the police's interest. The correct procedure on the part of the police would have been to seek a production order under s. 9 (see 4.4). A different approach may be justified where it is the firm of solicitors itself which is under investigation: *R* v *Crown Court at Leeds, ex parte Switalski* [1991] Crim LR 559 (discussed further at 4.4.2.1).

4.2.5.2 Other statutory powers

Many statutes give the police powers to obtain warrants to enter and search premises (see, for example, R. Stone, *Entry, Search and Seizure*, 2nd edn, 1989, chapter 4). The most frequently used are those relating to stolen goods (Theft Act 1968, s. 26), drugs (Misuse of Drugs Act 1971, s. 23), and pornography (Obscene Publications Act 1959, s. 3, see, 7.4.1.2). The procedures set out in PACE, ss. 15 and 16 must be followed. All the provisions are in a fairly standard form, requiring the police to convince a justice of the peace that there are reasonable grounds for believing that the items sought are on the premises specified. In relation to these powers, the use of a search warrant is not so much a 'last resort' as it is under s. 8 of PACE. In other words, there is no need for the justice to be convinced that the use of a search warrant is the only way in which access to the items will be obtained; it is enough that they are believed, on reasonable grounds, to be on the premises.

There are also various powers which allow the police to obtain a warrant to enter in order to inspect premises. Examples include the Local Government (Miscellaneous Provisions) Act 1982, sch. 3, para. 25 (in relation to sex shops), and the Theatres Act 1968, s. 15 (where a performance of a play is suspected of involving the commission of an offence under the Act). Since these powers do not involve any *search* of the premises, they are not covered by ss. 15 and 16 of PACE. There is no reason, however, why the relevant provisions of Code B should not be followed as indications of 'best practice', even though there is no statutory obligation to do so.

4.2.6 Entry and search of vehicles
There are three ways in which the police may have a power of search in relation to vehicles.

4.2.6.1 Search for stolen and prohibited articles The power under s. 1 of PACE to search people for stolen or prohibited articles (see 2.3.3), and to detain them while doing so, is also available in relation to vehicles and their contents (s. 1(2)). A constable in uniform will be entitled to stop a vehicle for this purpose (s. 2(9)). The procedures are virtually identical to those which apply in relation to the stop and search of persons, but the following points should be noted.

First, where the vehicle is in a garden, yard, or other land 'occupied with and used for the purposes of a dwelling', a search may only take place where the constable has reasonable grounds for believing that the person in charge of the vehicle does not reside in the dwelling, and that the vehicle is not where it is with the permission of a person who resides in the dwelling. A car that is parked in the owner's driveway, or that of a friend or relative, is thus immune from search under this power.

Secondly, reasonable force will be available to search an unattended vehicle (s. 117). If such a vehicle has been searched, however, a notice must be left, preferably inside the vehicle (s. 2(7)), stating:

(a)   that it has been searched,
(b)   the name of the police station of the searching officer,
(c)   that any application for compensation for damage should be made to that police station, and
(d)   the right (under s. 3(8)) of the owner to obtain a copy of the search record (s. 2(6)).

(The power to stop and search for drugs under s. 23(2) of the Misuse of Drugs Act 1971 (see 2.4.3.1), similarly extends to vehicles.)

4.2.6.2 Search following arrest 'Premises' are defined in s. 23 of PACE as including 'vehicles'. The powers of search following an arrest under ss. 18 and 32, which have been described at 4.2.3, will therefore also be available in relation to vehicles.

4.2.6.3 Search under warrant Whether a search under warrant covers search of a vehicle will depend on the particular statute giving the power. As we have seen, PACE defines premises as including vehicles, so the power under s. 8 (see 4.2.5.1), and the procedures for access to excluded or special procedure material (see 4.4.1.2 and 4.4.1.3) will all, at least in theory, be available in relation to vehicles. The power under s. 23(3) of the Misuse of Drugs Act 1971, however, contains no definition of 'premises' so that it will not extend to vehicles. The position would appear to be the same in relation to the power under s. 26 of the Theft Act 1968. This section refers, however, to the issue of a warrant where a person is reasonably believed to have stolen goods 'in his custody or possession *or* on his premises' (*emphasis added*). It may be that the reference to 'custody or possession' would allow the issue of a warrant in relation to a vehicle. By contrast, the power to search under s. 3 of the Obscene Publications Act 1959 specifically extends to vehicles.

4.3 PERSONAL PROPERTY: SEIZURE POWERS

In this section the focus is on the powers of the police to seize personal property. Whereas an entry and search of premises involves an intrusion into the individual's physical space, a seizure power has the effect of removing property from the possessor's control at least temporarily. In some cases the seizure, if it is of illicit goods rather than simply evidence, may be a precursor to forfeiture or destruction.

4.3.1 Seizure following personal search
The powers of the police in relation to seizing items found in the exercise of stop and search powers, or following arrest, have been noted in chapter 2 (2.3). Seizure of items found on persons in police detention has been covered in chapter 3 (3.2.4).

All items seized under any of the above powers are subject to the general provisions in PACE concerned with the retention of seized property, which are discussed at 4.3.3.

4.3.2 Seizure following lawful entry
To some extent the power of police to seize property after lawful entry will depend on the power which is being relied on. Most statutory powers will indicate what items the police may search for and seize. In the case of the Theft Act 1968, s. 26 for example, the power is to seize any items which the constable believes (the belief does not have to be reasonable) to be stolen goods. Under the Obscene Publications Act 1959, s. 3, it is to seize any articles which the constable has reason to believe to be obscene, and kept for publication for gain, and any documents relating to a trade or business carried on at the premises.

Under s. 23 of the Misuse of Drugs Act 1971, controlled drugs may be seized if the constable has reasonable grounds to believe an offence *has been* committed in relation to them. Documents relating to a transaction which was or would be an offence under the Act may also be seized. Finally, under s. 8 of PACE the power is simply to seize anything for which a search has been authorised, that is 'relevant evidence', likely to be of substantial value to the investigation, and not consisting of protected material (see 4.4.1). As will be seen there are subtle variations between all these powers. It is necessary in every case to check the detail of the particular statutory provision giving the seizure power.

In addition to the powers attached to each provision, however, a general seizure power is given in s. 19 of PACE. This arises whenever a constable is lawfully on premises. This may be on the basis of consent, entry without warrant (see 4.2.2 and 4.2.3), or entry under a warrant. The constable does not need to be aware of the lawful basis for being on the premises: *Foster* v *Attard* (1985) 83 Cr App R 214. Two categories of items may be seized. The first is items which the constable has reasonable grounds for believing have been obtained in consequence of the commission of an offence (for example, stolen goods) (s. 19(2)). The second category is items which the constable has reasonable grounds for believing is evidence in relation to any offence (not necessarily one which the constable is investigating) (s. 19(3)). Thus, the constable executing a warrant to search for stolen goods who comes across a gun, or controlled drugs, will almost certainly be entitled to seize them. The only other requirement, which applies to both categories, is that the constable must have reasonable grounds for believing that seizure of the items is necessary in order to prevent them being concealed, lost, altered or destroyed, or in the case of items in the first category, damaged.

There is a general limitation in s. 19(6) applying to all powers of seizure under any enactment. This is that the power may not be used to seize items which a constable has reasonable grounds for believing to be subject to legal privilege (see 4.4.1.1). There is no mention of the other categories of protected material, that is excluded, or special procedure material. Items coming within these categories may be seized under the s. 19 power, even though it is generally impossible to obtain a search warrant in relation to them (s. 9; see 4.4.1). There seems no good reason why the s. 19 power should extend to such items. The fact that it does gives a clear encouragement to the police to gain entry to premises where they feel that excluded or special procedure material may be found, on the basis of some other lawful pretext, and then hope to 'come across' the material in the course of their searches.

Code of Practice B adds little to the Act's provisions in relation to seizure. The one addition is in para. 6.3. This deals with where an officer decides not to seize an item because of an explanation given by the person in possession of it. If the constable nevertheless has reasonable grounds for believing that the item has been obtained in consequence of the commission of an offence, the person must be told of this, and that if the property is disposed of, this may give rise to civil or criminal proceedings. The most likely situation for this to occur is where goods which are believed to be stolen are in the hands of an innocent purchaser. Whether the purchaser has acquired rights of ownership over the goods will depend on the civil law; if they are still stolen, any dealing with them may amount to the tort of conversion, or the criminal offence of handling.

Somewhat surprisingly, and contrary to the recommendations of the Royal Commission on Criminal Procedure (*Report*, Cmnd 8092, para. 3.47), there is no obligation on the police to provide a receipt for seized items as a matter of course. Under s. 21(1), however, a person who was the occupier of the premises at the time of seizure, or who had custody and control of any item immediately prior to seizure, is entitled to demand a record of what was seized. There is no time limit on this demand; it may be made at the time of the search or at any time thereafter. The police must provide the information within a reasonable time of the demand (s. 21(2)). The information may enable the individual concerned to enforce rights of access to the material under s. 21 (see 4.3.3), or to make a claim for recovery of it, for example under the Police (Property) Act 1897.

Code of Practice B requires a detailed record of every search to be kept at the relevant sub-divisional police station (para. 7.1, 7.3). The record should include details of the place, time, and authority for the search, and the names of the officers who conducted it. The names of any persons on the premises at the time should be noted, and a list made of all articles which were seized, and why. Finally, if force was used, the reason for this should be given, and details provided of any damage caused, and the circumstances in which it occurred. This record would clearly be very useful to any person who subsequently wishes to make a claim or complaint against the police. There is, however, no statutory right of access to it, so it must be regarded as being primarily intended for use by the police. Of course, once a legal action has been started, access to the record could no doubt be obtained through the normal procedures of discovery.

4.3.3 Retention of, and access to, seized property

In relation to property seized by the police under any statutory power, the right of the police to retain the property, and the right of the individual to have access to it, are governed by s. 22 and s. 21 respectively. This covers seizures as a result of a personal search, as well as in the course of a search of premises. The initial seizure must have been lawful for the powers of retention under s. 22 to arise: *R v Chief Constable of Lancashire, ex parte Parker and McGrath* [1993] Crim LR 204. The basic principle set out in s. 22(1) is that the police may retain seized property for as long as is necessary in all the circumstances. This vague formulation gives the police a fair degree of room to exercise discretion. Section 22(2) gives some examples of situations where retention will be justified. These are where the property is required as evidence, or for forensic examination or other investigation in connection with an offence. If this is the reason for retention, then the original property may not be kept if a copy or photograph would be sufficient (s. 22(4)). Property may also be retained in order to establish its lawful owner, where there are reasonable grounds for believing that it has been obtained in consequence of the commission of an offence.

Where the justification for the original seizure was that the property might be used to cause physical injury, to damage property, to interfere with evidence, or to assist in escape from police detention, it may only be retained while the person from whom it was seized is in police custody, or the custody of a court, and has not been released on bail (s. 22(3)).

If property is retained for the purpose of investigating an offence then s. 21 provides for rights of access to it. If it is retained for other purposes, for example because it is thought to constitute an obscene article and therefore to be liable to forfeiture, the statute gives no right of access, though the wording of para. 6.9 of Code B is wide enough to cover all situations in which property is retained. The rights in s. 21 are given to the person who had custody or control of the property before it was seized. Such a person, or someone acting on their behalf, has two rights. First, there is a right, on request, to have access to the seized property under the supervision of a constable. Secondly, there is a right, on request, to a photograph or copy of the property. This may be done by allowing the person making the request access to the property for this purpose, again under the supervision of a constable, or by providing a photograph or copy within a reasonable time (s. 21(4), (7)).

Challenge to the police's retention of property, or a refusal to allow access to it, should be made by application for judicial review (*Roandale* v *Metropolitan Police Commissioner* [1979] Crim LR 254; *Allen* v *Chief Constable of Cheshire, The Times*, 16 July 1988), or by recourse to the Police (Property) Act 1897. These remedies are discussed further at 4.6.

4.4 PERSONAL PROPERTY: PRODUCTION ORDERS

In certain situations an individual can be compelled to produce material for inspection by, or surrender to, the police. This may arise under general police powers, for example in relation to obtaining evidence from computers (PACE, s. 20; see 4.4.2.1), or from an order issued by a court as a result of an application by the police. PACE significantly extended the police's powers to obtain evidence by means of a search warrant (that is, under s. 8; see 4.2.5.1). This raised concern in certain quarters that the power might be used to search for confidential material in the offices of solicitors, social workers, doctors or voluntary agencies. This concern was met by creating three statutorily defined categories of protected material. In relation to this material, the police would not be able to obtain an ordinary warrant, under PACE, or any other statute, but would have to go through a special procedure laid down in PACE, which, if successful, would result in a court order for production of the material to the police. The rest of this section looks at the categories of protected material, and the orders which can be made.

This type of procedure is, of course, less intrusive than the search warrant. It still involves infringements of both property and privacy rights. The property is not seized, but has to be handed over under compulsion, with refusal generally constituting contempt. It will in most cases contain confidential information, disclosure of which may infringe the privacy of the person producing the material, and anyone mentioned in it. It is important, therefore, to look carefully at the protected categories, and the procedures for disclosure, to make sure that they go no further than is necessary in meeting the legitimate aims of police investigations.

4.4.1 Protected material

The three categories of protected material recognised in PACE are legally privileged material, excluded material, and special procedure material. Access to items which are subject to legal privilege cannot be obtained at all. Excluded and special procedure material cannot be obtained by means of an ordinary search warrant, though, as we have seen, it may be seized if discovered in the course of a lawful search (PACE, s. 19; see 4.3.2).

4.4.1.1 Legal privilege   The definition of 'items subject to legal privilege' is contained in s. 10. The category is intended to protect the confidentiality of communications between client and legal adviser. In relation to such communications the view is taken that the public interest in allowing advice to be given as freely as possible, outweighs the advantages which might accrue to police investigations if access to such communications were allowed. The policy may be seen as being linked to the right to silence, and the privilege against self-incrimination. A person must be free to communicate with a solicitor or barrister without restraint, including the admissions of facts which might appear incriminating. The same policy underlies the right of access to legal advice in PACE, s. 58 (see 3.4.2).

The definition in s. 10 is primarily concerned with 'communications'. This word is undefined, but presumably covers letters, recorded telephone calls or conversations, and electronic messages. Two categories of communication are covered. First, there are those which are made between a professional legal adviser and the client, or any person representing the client, in connection with the giving of legal advice. The advice does not have to relate to any proposed legal proceedings. Secondly, there are communications made for the purposes of actual or contemplated legal proceedings. In relation to this category, the range of people who may be involved is wider. As well as communications between the client, or the client's representative and the legal adviser, those between the client, representative, or adviser and *any other person* are covered. Communication between the legal adviser and a prospective witness would, for example, come within this definition.

A third category covers items which are not in themselves communications, but are enclosed with or referred to in such communications. The items must have been made in connection with the giving of legal advice, or for the purposes of actual or contemplated legal proceedings.

In relation to all three categories the privilege only arises where the items concerned are in the possession of a person who is entitled to possession of them; but it extends to any such person, not just the legal adviser and client. Suppose that a solicitor who is acting for a client charged with causing death by dangerous driving, sends a letter, together with a specially prepared plan of the scene of the accident, to prospective witnesses, asking the witnesses to mark where they were standing at the time of the accident. The solicitor then sends copies of the replies to the client. The letters and the maps would be legally privileged in the hands of the solicitor, the witnesses, and the client.

The case law on s. 10 has generally been restrictive of its scope. In *R* v *Crown Court at Inner London Sessions, ex parte Baines and Baines* [1987] 3 All ER 1025, it was made clear that not every document on a client's file will be subject to legal privilege. Straightforward records of transactions, such as conveyancing documents, do not fall within s. 10. The communications or items must relate to the giving of advice, or to legal proceedings. This is in line with the policy reasons for the privilege outlined above. A person cannot therefore keep material out of the hands of the police by the simple expedient of giving it to a solicitor for safe-keeping. The material may attract some protection as being within the 'excluded' or 'special procedure' categories discussed below, but it will not receive the much stronger protection of legal privilege.

A broader restriction of the scope of the privilege derives from the decision of the House of Lords in *Francis and Francis* v *Central Criminal Court* [1988] 3 All ER 775. This case arose under the provisions of the Drug Trafficking Offences Act 1986, which uses the definition of legal privilege from s. 10 of PACE. The focus here was on s. 10(2) which removes the privilege from items 'held with the intention of furthering a criminal purpose'. The police were seeking correspondence and attendance notes held by a firm of solicitors relating to property transactions undertaken by one of their clients. The suspicion was that, although the client was probably innocent of any impropriety, the money for these transactions derived from drug-trafficking activities on the part of one of the client's relatives. The question was whether the relative's criminal purpose could remove the privilege from the documents, which were in the possession of the solicitors. The majority in the House of Lords followed the common law decision in *R* v *Cox and Railton* (1884) 14 QBD 153 which denied the protection of legal privilege where communications were intended to further the client's criminal purpose, even where the communications were in the possession of the innocent solicitor. The House felt that the 'holding' and the 'intention' in s. 10(2) should similarly be considered disjunctively. On this basis, the fact that a third party had an intention to further a criminal purpose was sufficient to remove the privilege. This has a potentially very restrictive effect on the scope of s. 10. Where police are searching for evidence of a criminal offence it is likely that *someone* will have a criminal purpose in relation to it. Lord Goff, however, thought that the privilege would still apply to communications by a client to a solicitor which, unknown to the solicitor, contained false statements, which might lead to the offence of perjury being committed in legal proceedings. On this basis he was able to uphold the decision, though not the reasoning, in the Divisional Court's decision in the earlier case of *R* v *Crown Court at Snaresbrook, ex parte DPP* [1988] 1 All ER 315. Here the police had argued that a legal aid application which was in the hands of the local Law Society was not privileged, because it was thought to contain untrue statements. The Divisional Court had held that the criminal intention under s. 10(2) must be that of the 'holder'. Following *Francis and Francis* this is clearly wrong, but the decision would still stand on the basis of the approach by Lord Goff, noted above.

4.4.1.2   Excluded material   This is the second most highly protected type of material. As will be seen, in general, excluded material can only be obtained by the police where there was a search warrant power prior to PACE which would have allowed access to it. The fact that it constitutes evidence of a serious arrestable offence will not in itself be enough to allow access. Its protected status arises from the fact that it is held in confidence, and that it consists either of personal records, human tissue or tissue fluid, or journalistic material. It is defined in s. 11.

The first type of excluded material consists of personal records. They must have been acquired or created in the course of a person's work, or for the purposes of a paid or unpaid office, and they must be held in confidence. 'In confidence' means held subject to an express or implied undertaking as to secrecy, or to a statutory restriction on disclosure (for example, under the Official Secrets Acts, or the Data Protection Act 1974). Personal records for this purpose are records of any kind concerning an identifiable person (living or dead), which relate to the person's physical or mental health; spiritual counselling or assistance given or to be given to the person; or other counselling or assistance given or to be given to the person for the purposes of personal welfare, by a voluntary organisation, or by someone who from their work has responsibilities for the person's welfare, or is responsible for supervising the person under a court order. All medical records, and those held by clergymen, probation officers, social workers, or voluntary organisations such as the NSPCC or the Samaritans, are likely to be covered. Educational records, and personnel files will only be covered if their contents fall within the above categories, which will by no means always be the case. The details of a person's salary, or bank account would not be excluded material.

The second category of excluded material is human tissue or tissue fluid (this includes blood, semen, saliva, etc). It must have been taken for the purposes of diagnosis or medical treatment, and be held in confidence. If a sample has been taken for the purposes of a criminal investigation, rather than for treatment or diagnosis, it will not be excluded material.

The third category of excluded material is journalistic material, consisting of documents or records, which is held in confidence. 'Journalistic material' is, rather unhelpfully, defined in s. 13 as material acquired or created for the purposes of journalism. This obviously covers the work of reporters working for newspapers, radio or television, but does it cover the freelance writer collecting material for a book, or the person producing a newsletter for a club or a small group of enthusiasts? The Act provides no help in answering these questions. It does make it clear, however, in s. 13(3) that it includes unsolicited material sent to a journalist by someone who intends that it should be used for the purposes of journalism. For journalistic material to be excluded material, as well as being held in confidence when access is sought, it must have been held in confidence continuously since it was first acquired or created for the purposes of journalism. It has to be in the possession of someone who acquired or created it for the purposes of journalism (s. 13(2)). It does not, however, have to be held continuously by a journalist. A document received by a journalist in confidence for the purposes of journalism, and then passed in confidence to an expert for an opinion, and then returned to the journalist, will be excluded material while it is in the hands of the journalist. It will lose this status while with the expert, but will during that time almost certainly be special procedure material.

4.4.1.3 Special procedure material This is the material with the lowest level of protection. It is defined in s. 14. Any journalistic material which is not excluded material is special procedure material. It does not have to be held in confidence. Photographs of people engaged in a riot have, for example, been held to fall into this category: *R* v *Bristol Crown Court, ex parte Bristol Press and Picture Agency* (1986) 85 Cr App R 190. The other type of special procedure material consists of items which are not legally privileged or excluded material, but have been acquired or created in the course of a person's work, or for the purposes of a paid or unpaid office, and are held in confidence. There are special provisions relating to employees and associated companies in ss. 14(3)–(6), but these do not affect the basic scope of the protection. Examples of material which has been held to come into this category include the accounts of a Youth Association (*R* v *Central Criminal Court, ex parte Adegbesan* [1986] 3 All ER 113), conveyancing documents in the possession of a solicitor (*R* v *Crown Court at Inner London Sessions, ex parte Baines and Baines* [1987] 3 All ER 1025), and details of bank accounts (*R* v *Crown Court at Leicester, ex parte DPP* [1987] 3 All ER 654).

4.4.1.4 Reasons for protection The reasons for giving legally privileged material special protection have been considered at 4.4.1.1. As regards excluded and special procedure material the reasons are more complex. Leaving aside journalistic material for the moment, it might be thought that the central element is 'confidentiality', since both types of material require this. The special status given to this material is concerned with providing protection for the confidential relationship which exists, for example, between doctor and patient, probation officer and defendant, and, in some cases, employer and employee. This is not enough in itself, however, since it would not explain the difference between excluded and special procedure material. There cannot be degrees of confidentiality: either material is held in confidence or it is not. The additional factor is the privacy of the person who is the subject of the material. Here it does make sense to talk of degrees of privacy: the details of a person's sex life may well be regarded as deserving greater protection than the details of their bank account. The first will be likely to be excluded material; the second only special procedure material.

The justifications for protecting journalistic material are different. Privacy is not really an issue here. The protection is more based on the public interest in a free press. In this context, it is desirable that journalists should be able to gather sensitive information about possible criminal activities without needing to worry that the police will be able to search their premises. Furthermore, where information is given in confidence to a journalist, it is desirable that the source should be fully protected (compare s. 10 of the Contempt of Court Act

1981; see 6.2.7). If such protection were not available, the journalist would not get the information. The best way of giving the protection is by making the information 'excluded material', and thus making it very difficult for the police to gain access to it.

4.4.2 Orders for production

As has already been noted, material which is legally privileged is beyond the reach of the police. Excluded material or special procedure material consisting of documents or records cannot be obtained by means of an ordinary search warrant (s. 9(2)), but may be accessible by means of a production order, or in extreme cases a search warrant, issued by a circuit judge. This procedure for access was introduced by PACE, but has subsequently been applied in other contexts.

4.4.2.1 PACE The procedure for access to excluded or special procedure material under PACE is set out in sch. 1. The police must make an application to a circuit judge, rather than a magistrate. Notice of the application must be given to the person in possession of the material sought. It need not be given to anyone else, such as, for example, the person under investigation: *R v Crown Court at Leicester, ex parte DPP* [1987] 3 All ER 654; nor is a bank, for example, which receives notice of an application concerning a particular account obliged to notify its customer: *Barclays Bank v Taylor* [1989] 3 All ER 563. The notice should set out the general nature of the offences under investigation (for example, 'fraud', 'riot', 'wounding'), and the address of the premises where the material is alleged to be (*R v Central Criminal Court, ex parte Carr* (1987), unreported, *Butterworths Police and Criminal Evidence Act Cases*, II, 73). It should also give sufficient information identifying the material to enable the person on whom the notice is served not to 'conceal, destroy, alter or dispose' of it without the permission of either a judge or the police (sch. 1, para. 11; *R v Adegbesan* [1986] 3 All ER 113). There will then be an *inter partes* hearing, at which the police will try to convince the judge that one of two sets of 'access conditions' is met. It was stated in *R v Crown Court at Lewes, ex parte Hill* (1990) 93 Cr App R 60 that the judge has a discretion to allow the person under investigation to be heard, even if someone else is in possession of the material. Moreover, since where material is in the hands of a third party who is not under investigation, the respondent may well not have any interest in challenging the application at the *inter partes* hearing, there is a strong duty on the applicant to ensure that all relevant material, including material adverse to the applicant, is before the judge. The judge must have sufficient information on which to decide whether the access conditions have been met: it is not acceptable for the judge simply to accept police assertions to that effect.

The first set of access conditions (sch. 1, para. 2) applies only to special procedure material, and follows fairly closely the requirements of s. 8 of PACE (see 4.2.5.1). There must be reasonable grounds for believing that a serious arrestable offence has been committed, that special procedure material comprising relevant evidence is on the premises, and that it is likely to be of substantial value to the investigation. The judge must also be satisfied that other methods of obtaining the material, for example a straightforward request for access, have been tried without success, or have not been tried because it appeared that they were bound to fail. Finally, the judge must be satisfied that production of, or access to, the material would be in the public interest, having regard to the likely benefit to the police's investigation, and the circumstances under which the material is held.

The question of the public interest has been considered in two cases. In *R* v *Bristol Crown Court, ex parte Bristol Press and Picture Agency* (1986) 85 Cr App R 190, the police were seeking access to photographs of rioting taken by press photographers. It was argued that it was contrary to the public interest to allow access, because it would prejudice the impartiality of the press, and would increase the likelihood of attacks on journalists and photographers covering such events. It was held that the press's impartiality would not be compromised where the material was handed over under compulsion, and that since the photographs were presumably taken with a view to publication, people photographed engaging in criminal activity would be just as likely to attack the photographer on this basis, as on the basis that the photographs would end up in police hands. A similar line was taken in *Re an Application under s. 9 PACE, Independent,* 27 May 1988. These cases indicate a fairly restrictive role for the concept of public interest in these situations. That is confirmed on a more general basis by the comments of Glidewell LJ in *R* v *Central Criminal Court, ex parte Carr* (1987) (unreported, but see R. Stone, 'PACE: Special Procedures and Legal Privilege' [1988] Crim LR 498, at 502), where he said:

> If documents of the kinds referred to in the information are on any applicants' premises, it is *obvious* that they are likely to be of substantial value to the investigation, that some or all of them will be relevant evidence, and *therefore* that it is in the public interest that such documents should be produced. (*emphasis added*)

This suggests that the issue of 'public interest' may well be subsumed in the decision as to the usefulness and evidential relevance of the material sought. The suggestion was confirmed in *R* v *Crown Court at Northampton, ex parte DPP* (1991) 93 Cr App R 376. The judge to whom an application for a production order had been made had held that a receipt held by a firm of solicitors was special procedure material, which would be of substantial evidential value in relation to a serious arrestable offence. He refused to issue an order for production, however, on the basis that it would be contrary to the public interest in that it would be using a 'sledgehammer to crack a nut'. On the Director of Public Prosecutions's application for judicial review of this decision, it was held that once the judge had decided that a serious arrestable offence had been committed it was not consistent for him to reach the conclusion that it was contrary to the public interest to grant access. It seems, therefore, that although the wording of the schedule appears to be clearly worded so as to require the judge to consider whether, notwithstanding the fact that the material would be of substantial value to the investigation and relevant evidence, it might be contrary to the public interest to allow access to it, in practice the decisions reviewing the use of the power lead to the conclusion that the main issue with which the judge needs to be concerned is whether the material relates to a serious arrestable offence. Once this is answered in the affirmative, the other elements of the first set of access conditions, and in particular the finding that disclosure is in the public interest, will follow almost as a matter of course. This cannot be what parliament intended.

The second set of access conditions (sch. 1, para. 3) allows an order to be made in relation to either special procedure or excluded material. The conditions are satisfied if there are reasonable grounds to believe that the relevant material is on the premises specified, and that, but for s. 9(2) of PACE, it would have been possible and appropriate for a search warrant to have been issued. Section 9(2) makes ineffective any search warrant power in a statute passed before PACE, insofar as it would have enabled access to be gained to legally privileged, excluded, or special procedure material. So if, for example, a blood sample constituting excluded material has been stolen, then it would have been possible, but for s. 9(2), to have obtained a warrant under s. 26 of the Theft Act 1968 to search for it. An order may therefore be granted under the second set of access conditions. It is important to note that although the second set of access conditions is limited to situations where there was a pre-existing search warrant power, the offence being investigated does not have to be a serious arrestable one, the material sought does not need to be relevant evidence, and there is no question of the public interest to consider. It is also important to remember that where a search warrant power is contained in legislation passed after PACE, it will allow access to both excluded and special procedure material, unless the later Act itself states otherwise. The Public Order Act 1986, for example, makes no reference to excluded and special procedure material, so the search warrant power contained in s. 24 of that Act can be used to obtain access to such material, without needing to use PACE, sch. 1.

A circuit judge who is satisfied that one or other set of access conditions is fulfilled, may make an order directing the person who appears to be in possession of the material to produce it to a constable, or to give a constable access to it (sch. 1, para. 4). If the material is held on a computer, the order will be construed as directing the person to produce it in a visible and legible form in which it can be taken away (in other words, a print-out), or to give the constable access to the material in a form in which it is visible and legible (for example, as a display on a computer screen sch. 1, para. 5) The order must give at least seven days for compliance (sch. 1, para. 4). Failure to comply will be treated as a contempt of the Crown Court, thus enabling the person who refuses to be fined or imprisoned (para. 15).

Anything produced and taken away is to be treated as having been seized by a constable, so that the access and retention provisions under ss. 21 and 22 of PACE (see 4.3.3) will apply to it.

As a last resort, sch. 1 provides that in certain circumstances a search warrant may be issued in relation to excluded or special procedure material (para. 12). As Macpherson J commented in *R* v *Maidstone Crown Court, ex parte Waitt* [1988] Crim LR 384:

> The special procedure under s. 9 and sch. 1 is a serious inroad upon the liberty of the subject. The responsibility for ensuring that the procedure is not abused lies with circuit judges. It is of cardinal importance that circuit judges should be scrupulous in discharging that responsibility. The responsibility is greatest when the circuit judge is asked to issue a search warrant . . .

Before issuing a warrant the judge must first be satisfied that one of the sets of access conditions is met. In addition the judge must be satisfied that one of a number of further conditions set out in para. 14, and justifying the issue of a warrant has been met. The first two are similar to conditions which apply under s. 8, that is that it is impracticable to communicate with the person entitled to grant entry to the premises, or the person entitled to grant access to the material. It was held in *R* v *Crown Court at Leeds, ex parte Switalski* [1991] Crim LR 559 that 'practicable' does not mean simply feasible, or physically possible. The judge can consider not only the available means of communication but also all the circumstances, including the nature of the enquiries and the person against whom they are directed. In this case a warrant had been issued against a firm of solicitors which was itself under investigation, and this was upheld by the Queen's Bench division in an action for judicial review.

The third condition which may justify the issue of a warrant arises where the material sought is subject to a statutory restriction on disclosure, and is likely to be disclosed in breach of this if the warrant is not issued. This would apply, for example, to journalistic material which was covered by the Official Secrets Acts. The fourth condition is where service of notice of an application for an order might seriously prejudice the investigation. This would be the case where there was reason to believe that the person in possession of the material would destroy or dispose of it, notwithstanding the provisions of para. 11 or that the person would alert others involved in a criminal operation.

Finally, where the second set of access conditions is satisfied, and an order under para. 4 has not been complied with, a warrant may be issued (para. 12(1)(b)). This does not apply where the order was based on the first set of access conditions. In this case, as noted above, an action for contempt of court is the only sanction (para. 15).

If a warrant is issued it will be subject to the general provisions of PACE and Code of Practice B, in the same way as any other search warrant. In addition, however, Code of Practice B contains some special provisions which apply to searches under a warrant issued under sch. 1. First, no application for such a warrant should be made without the authority of an officer of at least the rank of superintendent (Code B, para. 2.4). Secondly, an officer of at least the rank of inspector should take charge of the search, which should be carried out 'with discretion and in such a manner as to cause the least possible disruption to any business or other activities carried out on the premises' (Code B, para. 5.14).

Once on the premises, the officer should make sure that material cannot be taken from the premises without the officer's knowledge, and then ask for the material to which the warrant applies to be produced. If there is an index to files on the premises, this may be consulted, and any files which from this appear to contain material sought may be inspected. A physical search should be a last resort, to be used only where there is a refusal:

> to produce the material sought, or to allow access to the index; or where the index appears to be inaccurate or incomplete; or if for any other reason the officer in charge has reasonable grounds for believing that a search is necessary to find the material sought. (Code B, para. 5.14.)

4.4.2.2 Prevention of Terrorism (Temporary Provisions) Act 1989 ('PTA')

The production order procedure first enacted in sch. 1 to PACE, has been adopted for other purposes in various other statutes. In sch. 7 of the PTA it is used in relation to excluded or special procedure material sought in the course of a 'terrorist investigation', as defined in s. 17(1) of the PTA. This basically means an investigation into terrorist activities, or the resources of a proscribed organisation. Paragraph 2 of sch. 7 gives a power to obtain a search warrant in relation to material, not being legally privileged, or excluded or special procedure material, which would be of substantial value to the investigation. It does not have to be relevant evidence. If the material is excluded or special procedure material, however, an order for production can be obtained from a circuit judge. The application will be *ex parte*, rather than the *inter partes* procedure under PACE, presumably because of the nature of the investigation, and the risk of material being destroyed. This was the view taken in *R* v *Crown Court at Middlesex Guild Hall, ex parte Salinger* [1993] 2 All ER 310, at 317, where Stuart-Smith LJ set out certain guidelines for such applications. The application should be accompanied by a written statement of the evidence which is relied on, but need not disclose the source of information, if this is sensitive. The *nature* of the information should be disclosed, unless 'there are grounds for thinking that it is too secret', and the constable making the application should be available to give oral evidence if necessary. If an order is made, the judge should decide what information is given to the person to whom it is directed as to the evidence on which the order has been granted: 'The information should be as full as possible without compromising security'. On an application for the variation or discharge of an order (which should preferably be before the judge who made the order), oral evidence from the police should be available to supplement the information already given to the applicant, if necessary, but the judge should not permit questions 'as to the nature or identity of the source of information'.

Before making an order, the judge must be satisfied that a terrorism investigation is being carried out, that there are reasonable grounds for believing that the material sought is likely to be of substantial value to the investigation, and that it is in the public interest (on the same basis as under the first set of access conditions under PACE; see 4.4.2.1) that access should be granted. There is no need for other means of obtaining access to the material to have been tried, or to be shown to be likely to fail. Otherwise the procedure is very similar to that under PACE, except that if the order relates to material which is not in the possession of the person to whom it is addressed, that person may be required to state where the material is believed to be (para. 3(2)). Moreover, if the material is expected to come into the person's possession within 28 days, the order can require that person to notify a constable as soon as it does so (para. 3(3)). As under PACE, a search warrant may be obtained where an order for production or access has not been complied with, or where communication with the relevant people is impracticable, or where the purposes of the investigation might be seriously prejudiced unless a constable is able to obtain immediate access (para. 5, PTA).

If material is produced in response to an order, or seized under a search warrant, a circuit judge may order a person to provide an explanation of it, unless this would involve disclosing information protected by legal professional privilege. This exception to the right of silence and the privilege against self-incrimination is limited by the fact that any statements made cannot be used in any criminal proceedings against the person, other than where the person, in a prosecution for some other offence, gives evidence inconsistent with the statement, or where the person is prosecuted for giving false information in the statement (under sch. 7, para. 6(4)).

A refusal to produce material in response to an order will amount to a contempt of court, to which it is no defence to plead that disclosure would prejudice confidential sources, even if there may be a grave risk of personal injury or death: *Director of Public Prosecutions* v *Channel Four Television* [1993] 2 All ER 517.

In a situation which a police officer of at least the rank of superintendent has reasonable grounds to believe is one of 'great emergency' and that immediate action is necessary 'in the interests of the State', the officer may authorise a search by a constable by means of a written order (para. 7). The Home Secretary must be notified 'as soon as may be' when this power has been used.

Although the provisions under sch. 7 are more intrusive than those under PACE, sch. 1, the search warrant powers are subject to the provisions in Code of Practice B, paras. 5.13–5.14 (noted in the previous section) as to the conduct of any search.

4.4.2.3 Drug Trafficking Offences Act 1986 ('DTOA')

Section 27 of this Act gives the police powers to obtain access orders in relation to material which is likely to be of substantial value to investigations into drug trafficking (as defined in DTOA, s. 38). The power to issue an order is again given to a circuit judge, on the basis of an *ex parte* application. The judge must be satisfied that there are reasonable grounds for suspecting that a specified person (not necessarily the person in possession of the material sought) has been involved in drug trafficking, and that the material is likely to be of substantial value to the police investigations. As with the PTA powers, it does not have to constitute evidence of an offence. Surprisingly, the provisions do not require the judge to be satisfied that there are reasonable grounds for believing that the material is on specified premises. Material which is subject to legal privilege, or which is excluded material cannot be obtained under this power, but special procedure material can be. The scope of legal privilege in relation to this power was discussed in *Francis and Francis* v *Central Criminal Court* [1988] 3 All ER 775 (see 4.4.1.1).

As with the other powers considered in this section, there is a search warrant power provided as a 'back-up' by s. 28. This power will be subject to the standard provisions of PACE and Code of Practice B, but, presumably because it does not cover excluded material, the special provisions in Code B, paras 5.13–5.14 do not apply.

4.5 FORFEITURE AND CONFISCATION POWERS

The powers of the police considered so far cover only the seizure and retention of property in connection with their investigations. In certain circumstances, however, such seizure may lead to permanent forfeiture. The decision to deal with the property in this way is almost always taken by a court. It is distinct from a sentencing power which entitles the court to punish by way of a fine. We are looking here at powers to forfeit a person's property because of its nature, or because of that particular property's relationship to some criminal activity. Obscene articles, for example, may be forfeited by a magistrates' court under the Obscene Publications Act 1959 simply because they are deemed to be obscene. This is not dependent on a conviction for publishing them (see further at 7.4.1.1). There is also, however, a general power under s. 43(1) of the Powers of Criminal Courts Act 1973 to forfeit property which has been used for the purpose of committing, or facilitating the commission of any offence. The power arises where a person convicted of an offence punishable on indictment with two years' imprisonment was in possession or control of the property at the time of arrest. In *R* v *Highbury Corner Magistrates' Court, ex parte Di Matteo* [1992] 1 All ER 102 it was held that the power could be used to forfeit a car which had been used for the offence of driving while disqualified. Moreover, the Road Traffic Act 1991, s. 36, specifically extends the power to various driving offences under the Road Traffic Act 1988. Finally, forfeiture may be used as a means of confiscating the proceeds of criminal activity, or property which may be used to support criminal activity. Three examples of this type of power are considered here.

4.5.1 Drug Trafficking Offences Act 1986

There is a power under s. 27 of the Misuse of Drugs Act 1971 under which, where a person has been convicted of an offence under the Act, a court may order the forfeiture of 'anything shown to the satisfaction of the court to relate to the offence'. In *R* v *Cuthbertson* [1980] 2 All ER 401 the trial judge had ordered the forfeiture of property identified as the profits of a conspiracy to deal in illicit drugs. The House of Lords overturned the judge's order, and confirmed two serious limitations on the s. 27 power. First, it was not available where a person was convicted of conspiracy, rather than an offence under the 1971 Act. Secondly, the power of forfeiture applied only to tangible items capable of being physically destroyed, and not to choses in action, or other intangible property. The legislative response, largely following the recommendations of a working party set up by the Howard League for Penal Reform under the chairmanship of Sir Derek Hodgson, (*The Profits of Crime and their Recovery*, Heinemann, 1984), was to include within the Drug Trafficking Offences Act 1986, a broad power to make confiscation orders. The power has now been amended by the Criminal Justice Act 1993, ss. 7–13. It arises where someone has been convicted of a 'drug trafficking offence' as defined in s. 38 of the 1986 Act. This covers various offences concerned with dealing with drugs under the Misuse of Drugs Act 1971, and the Customs and Excise Management Act 1979, as well as attempts and conspiracies to commit such offences. Where the person convicted is deemed to have 'benefited' from drug trafficking, s. 1 of the 1986 Act gives the Crown Court the power to confiscate an amount which the court 'assesses to be the value of the defendant's proceeds of drug trafficking' (s. 4(1)). It is up to the prosecution to prove this on the balance of probabilities (s. 1(7A)), but various presumptions as to the provenance of the defendant's property operate under s. 2, and this considerably reduces the prosecution's burden (see *R* v *Dickens* [1990] 2 All ER 626, which contains a very thorough survey of the operation of the Act). In order to prove, however, that a defendant who received property has 'benefited' from drug trafficking, it must be shown that the defendant knew the purpose for which the property was given: *R* v *Richards* [1992] 2 All ER 572. In this case a loan of £6,000 was made by the defendant's co-accused in connection with the purchase of a boat. The co-accused intended the boat to be used for smuggling drugs, but it was not proved that the defendant was aware of this at the time, and therefore it was wrong to regard him on this basis as someone who had benefited from drug trafficking.

The confiscation power applies not only to assets in the defendant's possession or control, but also to gifts made within the six years prior to the institution of the proceedings, or at any time if it was a gift of property (s. 5(9)):

(i)   received by the defendant in connection with drug trafficking carried on by him or another, or

(ii)   which in whole or in part directly or indirectly represented in the defendant's hands property received by him in that connection.

In *R* v *Dickens* [1990] 2 All ER 626, the defendant had bought a Range Rover, and this was, by virtue of s. 2, deemed to have been bought out of the proceeds of drug trafficking. It had been given by the defendant to his wife, but had subsequently been sold to an innocent third party in whose hands it remained at the time of the trial. The value of the car at the time of the confiscation order was £15,000, and this sum was held by the Court of Appeal to have been properly included within the order. Thus it is the *value* of gifts, rather than the property which is the subject matter of the gift, which is liable to confiscation.

The Act also contains a power under which the High Court can issue a 'restraint order', effectively preventing a person against whom proceedings for drug trafficking have been initiated from dealing with property, and thereby avoiding the confiscatory provisions (ss. 7 and 8). This may involve the appointment of a receiver to administer the defendant's realisable property (s. 8(6)).

The power of confiscation under the 1986 Act is a stringent one. The justification for it is the wish to avoid those who may have made a fortune out of dealing in drugs retaining the opportunity to benefit from their crime even after serving a lengthy prison sentence.

4.5.2   Criminal Justice Act 1988

Part VI of the Criminal Justice Act 1988 adapted the confiscatory powers introduced in the Drug Trafficking Offences Act 1986, and applied them more generally. The power can be used by the Crown Court in relation to a person convicted of any indictable offence. As far as the magistrates' courts are concerned they also have the power to make an order in respect of the offences listed in sch. 4. These are largely offences concerned with the commercial exploitation of sex: for example, concerning sex establishments under the Local Government (Miscellaneous Provisions) Act 1982 (see 7.8.1.2), unclassified video recordings under the Video Recordings Act 1984 (see 7.5.2), or unlicensed cinemas under the Cinemas Act 1985. In all cases, the power will only arise where the defendant has benefited to a mininum amount, currently set at £10,000 (s. 71(7)).

The 1988 Act also contains provision for restraint orders of the same type as under the 1986 Act (s. 77).

The extension of the confiscatory powers to all types of criminal offence runs counter to the recommendations of Sir Derek Hodgson's Working Party (see 4.5.1) which saw the role of confiscation as lying primarily in the area of 'non-victim' crimes, and 'regulatory' offences, though it found it difficult to define the appropriate categories. The powers in the 1988 Act are all-encompassing at the indictable level, and include crimes of violence.

4.5.3   Prevention of Terrorism (Temporary Provisions) Act 1989

A power which has some similarities to the confiscation powers under the Drug Trafficking Offences Act 1986, and the Criminal Justice Act 1988, but which operates for a rather different purpose is contained in the Prevention of Terrorism (Temporary Provisions) Act 1989. Where a person has been convicted of certain offences under ss. 9, 10 or 11 of the Act which concern receiving or organising support for terrorism in the form of money or other property, a power to order forfeiture is given by s. 13. The power applies to money or other property which the person intends, or has reasonable cause to suspect, will be applied 'for the commission of, or in furtherance of, or in connection with, acts of terrorism' related to Northern Ireland, or to other terrorism not solely connected with the affairs of the United Kingdom (excluding Northern Ireland). A similar power is given where a person has been convicted of an offence under s. 10(1)(a) or (b) in relation to support for a proscribed organisation, and it is thought that the money or other property may be used to fund terrorism (defined as above) (s. 13(4)). Where someone other than the person convicted claims an interest in property which may be subject to forfeiture, it may still be forfeited, but that person must be given an opportunity to be heard before it is (s. 13(6)).

The detailed procedures in relation to forfeiture orders are set out in sch. 4 to the Act, and are very similar to those applying to confiscation orders. As with such orders there is a power to apply to the High Court to obtain a 'restraint order' preventing property from being dealt with pending consideration of the making of a forfeiture order.

The purpose of these provisions is not to prevent people from benefiting from crime, but to make the operation of terrorist groups and organisations more difficult, by forfeiting assets which might be used to support their activities. The fact that they are concerned with terrorism will no doubt be regarded as justification for the wide powers which they give to the courts.

4.6 REMEDIES

If there have been breaches of proper procedures by the police in relation to any of the powers discussed in this chapter a formal complaint is, of course, possible, as described in chapter 3 (3.6.2). It is also possible, however, to use civil remedies. In particular, it is necessary to consider actions in tort, judicial review, and the Police (Property) Act 1897.

4.6.1 Tortious actions
Where there has been an unlawful entry on to property there will clearly be the possibility of an action for trespass. A police search under such circumstances, however, may well also involve the unlawful use of force against occupants, and so lead to actions for assault, or false imprisonment. This was the basis of the action in *White* v *Metropolitan Police Commissioner, The Times*, 24 April 1982, where £20,000 exemplary damages was awarded to both the plaintiffs as a result of the use of 'excessive, unreasonable and unnecessary force' by the police in the course of a search. Where trespass is relied on, it is not necessarily the case that the entry needs to be unlawful from the beginning. If the police act in excess of their powers following a lawful entry, this may well have the effect of turning them into trespassers: *Six Carpenters' Case* (1610) 8 Co. Rep 146a. Despite some comments of Lord Denning to the contrary in *Chic Fashions* v *Jones* [1968] 2 QB 299, there seems no doubt that as far as the retrospective effect of unlawful actions after entry is concerned, as Clayton and Tomlinson conclude (*Civil Actions Against the Police*, Sweet & Maxwell, (1992), p. 222), 'the doctrine remains good law'. Once the police are regarded as trespassers, this may well have the effect of rendering any further action taken by them unlawful. As indicated in the *White* case noted above, exemplary damages will be available if the police were aware of the fact that they were exceeding their powers, or use excessive force (see also 3.6.1).

Tortious actions may also be brought in relation to seizure of, or damage to, property which has occurred in the course of an unlawful search and seizure. The torts of trespass to goods, conversion, and negligence, may all be relevant here. Whatever the basis of the action, the remedies are governed by the Torts (Interference with Goods) Act 1977, which provides for three categories of remedy (s. 3(2)):

(a)   an order for the delivery of the goods, and payment for any consequential damage; or

(b)   an order for the delivery of the goods, but giving the defendant the alternative of paying damages by reference to the value of the goods together in either case with payment for any consequential damage; or

(c)   damage.

The first of these is available only at the court's discretion, but the plaintiff may choose between the other two (s. 3(3)(b)).

4.6.2   Judicial review

The case of *O'Reilly* v *Mackman* [1983] AC 237, has caused problems in relation to the selection of remedies where the actions of public officials are involved. The case indicated that where the improper use of discretion by a public official is the basis of a legal claim, then the plaintiff should always proceed by seeking judicial review, rather than by issue of a writ. This is a distinction which is easier to state than to apply. If, for example, the police enter premises on the basis of a warrant which has been improperly issued by a magistrate, should the action be for trespass, against the police, or judicial review, in relation to the magistrate's decision? The precise scope of *O'Reilly* v *Mackman* has been discussed in a number of cases, culminating in *Roy* v *Kensington and Chelsea FPC* [1992] 1 All ER 705. The House of Lords ruled that where a claim in relation to a private law right incidentally involves the consideration of a public law issue, it is nevertheless quite acceptable for a litigant to proceed by means of the issue of a writ. It is only where an issue 'depends exclusively on the existence of a purely public law right' (Lord Bridge, at pp. 707–708) that it has to be determined by judicial review proceedings.

As a result, it would seem that wherever there is unlawful entry to premises, involving trespass, or other torts, then it is appropriate to use the ordinary civil action. Where, however, following a seizure, property is being retained by the police in a way which is alleged to be unlawful, then judicial review would be the appropriate remedy. This was the view taken by the Court of Appeal in *Allen* v *Chief Constable of Cheshire Constabulary, The Times,* 16 July 1988, where the issue was refusal of access to seized documents (see 4.3.3). A similar approach was taken in the pre-*O'Reilly* v *Mackman* cases of *R* v *IRC, ex parte Rossminster* [1980] AC 952, and *Roandale* v *Metropolitan Police Commissioner* [1979] Crim LR 954 (see 7.4.1.2).

4.6.3   Police (Property) Act 1897

Where goods are in the possession of the police as a result of investigations into a suspected offence, this Act provides a summary procedure whereby the owner can reclaim them. This will be most relevant where property which has been lawfully seized is retained after the conclusion of legal proceedings, without being made subject to any order for confiscation or forfeiture. The owner can apply to the magistrates' court for an order for the delivery of the property (s. 1(1)). If ownership is in doubt the court must order delivery to the person appearing to it to be the owner. The existence of the Act does not, however, preclude the use of ordinary civil proceedings to determine ownership, and these are to be preferred if there is a real legal dispute as to who is the owner: *Lyons* v *Metropolitan Police Commissioner* [1975] QB 321. Equally, if an order under s. 1(1) of the Act has been made, any person claiming to be the true owner can challenge this by initiating civil proceedings. There is, however, a time limit of six months from the making of the order for such proceedings to be taken (s. 1(2)).

3.7   EUROPEAN CONVENTION AND PROPERTY RIGHTS

The relevant provision of the ECHR in relation to entry, search and seizure, is Art. 8, which provides for a right to respect for a person's 'family life, his home and his correspondence'. As long ago as 1959, however, the Commission, in rejecting a claim as inadmissible, recognised that lawfully authorised searches and seizures would generally fall within Art. 8(2), which permits invasions of such rights where 'necessary in a democratic society . . . for the prevention of disorder or crime' (*Application 530/59, Yearbook*, Vol 3, p. 190). More recently in the *Chappell* case (30 March 1989 (Series A, No. 152)) the Court held that the exercise of an Anton Piller order (which is a kind of 'civil search warrant' commonly used in connection with intellectual property actions: see, for example, R. Stone, *Entry, Search & Seizure*, 2nd ed. (London: Sweet & Maxwell, 1989), chapter 5) did not involve any infringement of Art. 8, despite the fact that there were some breaches in procedure. It seems unlikely, therefore, that the lawful exercise of any of the powers discussed in this chapter would be held to involve a breach of the ECHR. If the power is exercised unlawfully, there is, as we have seen, a range of possible remedies under English law, and so action on the basis of the ECHR would be unnecessary.

FIVE

Freedom of Expression I: Official Secrets and Freedom of Information

5.1 THE MEANING OF 'FREEDOM OF EXPRESSION'

This is the first of several chapters in which issues relating to the control of freedom of expression are discussed. It is appropriate at this point to indicate what is meant here by 'expression', and why that word has been chosen in preference to 'speech'.

'Speech' may be taken to refer to the most obvious forms of expression, such as writing books, or articles, making speeches, or broadcasting. It is clear, however, that in most modern democracies, access to forms of expression for the most effective promotion of ideas, or points of view, is limited. In particular, the control of content in relation to newspapers, and broadcasting, is in the hands of a very small group of people, even at the editorial level. At the level of ownership, the range is reduced even further, with a small number of individuals and organisations owning the major newspapers, and controlling significant areas of broadcasting. In this situation, the possibility of an individual, or group of individuals, being able to promote a particular idea, or point of view, becomes very limited. In order to do so, the attention of the mass media has to be attracted, so that they are prepared to give time or space to the reporting of the arguments being put forward. One important way in which this may be done, is by organising a 'demonstration'. Events in Eastern Europe over the past few years have clearly indicated the power of the street demonstration as a force for democracy. Even in the UK, the strength of feeling shown against the 'poll tax' or 'community charge' in the form of marches and processions, was probably a contributing factor to the government's decision to change its policy. It seems right to include these forms of putting forward views alongside 'speech' in the strict sense, and to use the wider term 'expression' (see further 8.1).

The use of this word also makes it clear that 'artistic' expression, such as painting, photography, sculpture, and music, is included. Such work may at times carry an overt or explicit political message, but even if it does not do so, arguments for its restriction should be clearly justified.

In this book, therefore, the term 'expression' is used to include virtually all ways in which a person may put forward a point of view, an argument, or an artistic idea, or show support for a cause. Two types of action which might come within this definition are, however, specifically excluded. First, the donation of money to support a political cause is not treated here as expression. This is in contrast to the position taken by the Supreme Court in the United States, where in *Buckley* v *Valeo* (1976) 424 US 1, limits on expenditure on political campaigns were held to restrict freedom of speech. The position is taken here that the connection with speech or expression is in this case too indirect to justify its inclusion. Secondly, any action where a primary aim is to cause harm or damage to other people or property, for example, by planting a bomb, is excluded from 'expression', even though the objective of such an action may be to attract attention to a cause, and show support for it. Although it would be possible to treat such actions as 'expression' but to use their consequences, or intended consequences, as a justification for restriction, the view is taken here that they should not be regarded as having surmounted even the first hurdle towards achieving that special status that is generally given to speech, and expression.

5.2 ARGUMENTS FOR THE PROTECTION OF FREEDOM OF EXPRESSION

Many constitutions give protection of freedom of speech or expression a high status. In the United States Bill of Rights, for example, it appears in the First Amendment, and is included in the first substantive section of the Canadian Charter of Rights and Freedoms (that is, s. 2). This recognition early in these constitutional documents may well be taken to indicate that this freedom is regarded as having particular importance. Why should that be? What arguments can be put forward which suggest that the freedom of expression should have this degree of importance? A variety of such arguments may be proffered, but just three of the most commonly used are looked at here.

5.2.1 Argument from 'truth'
In his essay *On Liberty* John Stuart Mill devoted one chapter to 'the Liberty of Thought and Discussion' in which he discussed the freedom of the press, and freedom of speech in some detail. The argument which he developed at some length as to why this freedom should be protected has come to be known as the 'argument from truth'. The basis of the argument is that nobody has a monopoly on truth. In particular, he asserted that the majority in a society have no right to suppress the views of the minority, however much they dislike them. An example might be drawn from the area of science, where the prevailing orthodoxy on the nature of the Universe has changed over the centuries, and even now there are heated debates as to its origins between opponents and supporters of, for example, the 'big bang' theory. At no point would it have been right to say that just because a majority of people took the view that one particular theory was correct, all opposing theories were incorrect. Mill's argument is that this approach should apply to political,

moral, and philosophical views as well. Unorthodox and minority views must
be allowed to be expressed, because there is a chance that they may be 'the
truth' or may enable us to get nearer to it. If people disagree with them, they
should attack with counter arguments, not with suppression. Further, Mill
argues, even if it is the case that the orthodox view is correct, it is much better
that it should be tested against other possibilities than that it should be
accepted unquestioningly.

The one exception which Mill allows to this free expression of ideas and
opinions, is where it may lead to direct harm to others (*On Liberty*, chapter
III):

> An opinion that corn-dealers are starvers of the poor, or that private
> property is robbery, ought to be unmolested when simply circulated
> through the press, but may justly incur punishment when delivered orally
> to an excited mob assembled before the house of a corn-dealer, or when
> handed about among the same mob in the form of a placard.

Restriction of freedom of expression on these grounds is considered further in
chapter 8.

As will be seen, the argument from truth has most relevance to the
expression of ideas and opinions. It is more difficult to apply it to straightforward factual reporting, and very difficult in relation to artistic expression.
Nevertheless, within its limitations, the argument from truth is a powerful
one, and those who support the suppression of unpopular viewpoints need to
put forward convincing reasons (such as the likelihood of direct harm
resulting) why the argument should not apply to protect freedom of expression.

5.2.2   Argument from self-fulfilment

Another widely favoured argument in favour of freedom of expression is based
on the idea that such freedom is an important aspect of an individual's
self-fulfilment. This argument may be broader than the argument from truth,
in that it will clearly cover not only the expression of beliefs or opinions, but
also artistic expression. On the other hand, it will be more difficult to include
purely factual information within its scope. Does the freedom to publish the
details of government contracts for the purchase of office furniture really
contribute to anybody's self-fulfilment?

The argument is based on the assumption that individual self-fulfilment is a
desirable objective, and one that should take precedence over other considerations which might lead to restrictions on freedom of expression. It also has
connections with the idea that expression is intimately tied up with the nature
of humanity. We are distinguished from the animals because of our superior
abilities to communicate, and to express our feelings in a variety of ways. If we
restrict our ability to express ourselves in this way, we are to some extent
denying our humanity, and prejudicing our full development as individuals.

A limitation of this reason for justifying free expression is that it is difficult
to regard it as giving any special status to free speech, over and above other

activities which may contribute to self-fulfilment. The freedom to have children, or to learn a foreign language, may also contribute to this aim for particular individuals. Freedom of expression thus becomes just one amongst a number of civil libertarian objectives, and this does not seem to give it the status as a particularly significant freedom which many would argue that it should have.

5.2.3   Argument from democracy

The third argument looked at here is based on an assumption that there is an agreement in the value of democracy. Once that premise is accepted then certain consequences for freedom of expression will follow almost automatically. By democracy is meant a political system which in some way takes account of the wishes of the people in decisions about how they are to be governed and by whom. In the UK this is achieved by the right to vote in general elections to parliament, which must take place at least once in every five years.

If the participants in a democracy are to be able to exercise their rights as citizens effectively, there are two consequences for freedom of expression. First, there must be the widest possible scope for the exchange of opinion about the society in which the voters are living, the ways in which it operates, and changes which might be made. Only by having the opportunity to consider and debate alternatives to the *status quo* can the individual citizen be in a position to exercise the responsibilities attached to that membership of the sociey meaningfully and effectively. The repression of political and philosophical views (broadly defined) is the antithesis of democracy, and the two cannot properly co-exist. Secondly, the citizen in a democracy requires not only opinions and viewpoints, but also factual information. For example, the citizen cannot make an informed judgment about whether one system of health care is better than another, without the factual information which may make it possible to consider the costs and benefits of the two alternatives. This applies not only to information which may be produced or held by a government, but also to any information, whatever its source, which may have an input into the citizen's decisions about the manner and form of government which should operate, and who should be in charge of it. What is more difficult to include within this justification for freedom of expression is purely artistic work. Of course, many books, plays, films etc, may be said to have an influence on how the citizen views the world, and society; but it would be difficult to argue that this was the case in relation to every piece of sculpture, every painting, every magazine, every novel, every television show, which is available in a modern society. The argument from democracy is undoubtedly at its strongest in relation to material which has a clear political content, and becomes weaker the more divorced from relevance to the citizen's democratic responsibilities the expression becomes.

5.2.4   Conclusion

The arguments outlined above are not the only ones which can be put forward in favour of freedom of expression but they are some of the most commonly used. As will be seen, none of them supplies a complete case for allowing freedom to all categories of expression. Between them they cover most areas. At times, however, it has to be accepted that there is no special argument justifying freedom for a particular type of expression. At this stage, and the area of pornography may be one where this is the case, the supporter of freedom has to rely on more general civil libertarian arguments, such as that a State has no right to use force (for example, through the criminal law) to control behaviour, unless that behaviour causes harm to others. This line of argument can again be traced by to John Stuart Mill and *On Liberty* (see 1.1).

5.3   ARGUMENTS FOR AND AGAINST OFFICIAL SECRECY

The arguments in favour of a freedom to publish information about the workings of government are most obviously based on the argument from democracy. This justification for free speech clearly supports the making available of as much information as possible to enable citizens to exercise their democratic responsibilities. It also supports the acceptance of wide-ranging criticism of governments and government officials. This aspect of freedom of expression, will however be left to chapter 10, which deals with defamation and privacy.

The argument from truth may also be relevant to this area, in the sense that information gathered by the government may contribute towards the search for the truth on various matters. If, for example, a government department is conducting scientific research for military purposes, some of the results of that research may be of value to the wider scientific community. In this way it may contribute towards the avoidance of errors by others, and progress towards discovery of 'the truth' on a particular issue. It should therefore be possible to allow it to be published, unless there are clear reasons why this would, for example, be damaging to the national interest.

Those who argue for restrictions in this area (that is, most governments), generally do so on one of three grounds, or some combination of them.

First, it may be argued that certain types of government information need to be kept secret on grounds of 'national security'. This applies most obviously to matters of defence, where it can most convincingly be argued that disclosure of military secrets may put the whole country 'at risk'. The problem is, however, that the phrase 'national security' has no clear definition. Because the courts have for the most part been prepared to take the word of the government of the day that a particular matter involves issues of 'national security', without exploring that question for themselves, there is very little in the way of case law to provide any guidance. The only specific items which we can say that the concept covers are:

   (a)   the defence of the realm (*The Zamora* [1916] 2 AC 77);
   (b)   the prosecution of war (*The Zamora* [1916] 2 AC 77);
   (c)   the disposition of the armed forces (*Chandler* v *DPP* [1964] AC 763);
   (d)   nuclear weapons (*Secretary of State for Defence* v *Guardian Newspapers* [1984] 3 All ER 601);

(e)   the activities of the security and intelligence services (*Attorney-General v Guardian Newspapers Ltd (No. 2)* [1988] 3 All ER 852).

The first four of these are all related to 'defence'. The two main categories are thus defence, and security and intelligence. The courts are often prepared, however, to recognise that there may be a further category of 'other matters of national security'. It does not seem possible to define this category further, and so the limits of this argument for restriction of freedom of expression are destined to remain uncertain. (See further on this issue, R. Stone 'National Security versus Civil Liberty', in F. Patfield and R. White (eds), *The Changing Law*, Leicester University Press, 1990).

A second argument for control is that too free a flow of information may prejudice the government's dealings with other countries or international organisations. This would be to the detriment of the country as a whole. It may also give an unfair advantage to those who might seek to make a profit out of economically sensitive information (for example, the discussion with other countries about possible devaluation of the currency, or alteration of interest rates). This line of argument has some force, but it only relates to a fairly narrow area of government information.

The third, and more general, argument, is that for the process of government to be carried on too much in the open does not lead to good government. One aspect of this relates to the discussions and debates that may take place between civil servants, or between Ministers and civil servants, before a decision is taken on a particular policy, or course of action. It is argued that the participants in such discussions may be inhibited in what they will say, if they feel that this will be disclosed and open to scrutiny. Such inhibition will encourage cautious and self-conscious discussion which will not be in the interests of good government, and as a consequence, not in the interests of the country as a whole.

None of the arguments outlined above provides a convincing justification for wholesale restrictions on the freedom to publish information about government, though each of them has weight in relation to particular areas. They should, however, be kept in mind during the following discussion of the current restrictions which operate under English law, in order to consider the extent to which those restrictions may be able to be justified by one or other of them.

5.4   OFFICIAL SECRETS ACTS 1911–1920

The main controls over freedom of expression in relation to official secrecy are contained in various criminal offences contained in the Official Secrets Acts 1911–1989. The 1989 Act is the most recent response to pressure for reform, and establishes a system of controls which need to be looked at separately. It repealed parts of the earlier legislation. In this section, the focus will be on the surviving provisions of the 1911 and 1920 Acts.

5.4.1   Official Secrets Act 1911
The Official Secrets Act 1911 was a piece of legislation passed through parliament in a day, as a result of a panic about espionage, and the activities of

foreign, and specifically German, agents. It was, and to the extent that it is still in force, still is, a very widely drafted Act, creating a range of offences. The most important surviving provision in relation to freedom of expression is s. 1. This is labelled in the Act 'Penalties for spying', and it was towards espionage activities that it was clearly directed, providing, amongst other things, offences appropriate for those attempting to acquire sensitive information from military establishments, or communicating such information to agents of a foreign power. It was held in *Chandler* v *DPP* [1964] AC 763, however, that despite the heading, the scope of the section was wide enough to cover 'sabotage', certainly, and probably any activities that fell within its wording. It has, nevertheless, mainly been used in cases related to espionage. The communication offence is the one that is, of course, most relevant to freedom of expression. The offence is committed where:

> any person for any purpose prejudicial to the safety or interests of the State ... communicates to any other person any secret official code word, or pass word, or any sketch plan, model, article, note, or other document or information which is calculated to be or might be or is intended to be directly or indirectly useful to an enemy.

There are three main issues to consider in relation to this offence: first, what is meant by a purpose prejudicial to the safety or interests of the State; secondly, what is meant by 'communicates'; and thirdly, what type of information is covered.

In relation to the first issue, the Act itself provides some guidance as to how this may be established. Section 1 (2) makes it clear that no specific act showing such a purpose need be proved, and indeed that it may be inferred from 'the circumstances of the case', the defendant's conduct, or the defendant's 'known character'. Furthermore, where the communication offence is charged, and the information relates to a 'prohibited place' (as defined in s. 3), the burden of proof shifts, and a prejudicial purpose is assumed unless the defendant proves otherwise. A 'prohibited place' in effect means any premises used by the armed forces, or by the government for purposes connected with defence.

The meaning of the phrase was considered in *Chandler* v *DPP* [1964] AC 763. The defendants were members of the Campaign for Nuclear Disarmament ('CND'), who had been involved in the organisation of a demonstration at a military airfield occupied by the US air force. The plan was to enter the airfield and disrupt its operation by sitting on the runways, etc. The defendants were charged with conspiracy to commit an offence under s. 1(1)(a) of approaching, or entering, a prohibited place (which the airfield was) for a purpose prejudicial to the safety or interests of the State. One line of defence raised was that the activities of the defendants were not connected with 'spying', and were therefore outside the scope of s. 1. As we have seen, however, that point was rejected by the House of Lords. A second defence argument related to the fact that, from their own point of view, the defendants did not have a purpose which was prejudicial to the State's interests. On the contrary, their intention was to try to rid the country of nuclear weapons. They argued that this would make this country, and the world a safer place, and was therefore clearly 'in the interests of the State'. The reaction of the House of Lords to this argument was that, although it could not be said that in every case the courts should simply accept the word of the government as to what constitute the interests of the State, in this case they were concerned with the disposition of the armed forces. In this area, the courts had to accept that this was a matter which was within the exclusive discretion of the Crown. In other words it was not a justiciable issue suitable to be left to a jury. There was no scope, therefore, for consideration of the broader arguments of the defendants as to what were the interests of the State. The jury did have a role, the House felt, however, in that once the 'interests of the State' had been determined, the jury would have to decide whether or not the defendant's purpose was prejudicial to those interests. On the facts of the case this, in reality, left the jury with little to do. The government stated that it was in the interests of the state that the airfield should not be disrupted. The defendants' avowed intention was to disrupt the airfield. The way that the interests of the State were stated thus effectively pre-empted the only issue to be left to the jury, and made a verdict of guilty almost inevitable.

The second issue of interpretation in s. 1 is what is meant by 'communicates'? Again, the Act itself provides some indication. Section 12 states that communication includes 'transfer' or 'transmission'. It is not necessary, therefore, that the recipient of the communication should read it, or understand it. The physical handing over of a document from one person to another is enough to amount to 'communication' under this section. The reason for this interpretation is easy to see, since it would be clearly very difficult to prove that information given to an enemy agent, who might well simply be acting as a courier, was in all cases read and understood. Nevertheless, as with the interpretation of 'interests of the State' it allows a broader scope to the offence than might have been expected at first reading.

The third issue of interpretation relates to what information is covered. The basic requirement is simply that the information needs to be 'useful to an enemy'. In *R v Parrott* (1913) 8 Cr App R 186, the defendant was alleged to have communicated information to a person in Germany. He argued that since the UK was not at that time at war with Germany, and Germany was not therefore an 'enemy', he could not be said to have communicated information 'useful to an enemy'. This argument was rejected, Phillimore J ruling that:

> When the statute uses the word 'enemy' it does not mean necessarily someone with whom this country is at war, but a potential enemy with whom we might some day be at war.

This is again a wide interpretation. The real answer to Parrott's argument, however, is surely that the phrase 'useful to an enemy' refers to the nature of the information, not the person to whom it is communicated. Any information which, if it fell into the hands of an enemy would be useful, is within the scope of s. 1. The information does not, therefore, need to be 'official' information, or secret information. It can be of any kind, provided that an enemy might find it useful, and if it is communicated to *anyone* for a purpose prejudicial to the safety or interests of the State, then an offence will have been committed.

This means, for example, that if a civil servant goes home and tells her husband of some matter which she has come across at work, and this is something which an enemy would find it useful to know, then an offence under s. 1 may well have been committed. The only additional point that the prosecution has to establish is that the communication to the husband was for a 'purpose prejudicial'. This may be possible to prove, even if the husband is a perfectly loyal and discreet citizen, who would not think of passing on the information to anyone else. For all the government has to do is to certify that *any* disclosure of information of this kind is prejudicial, and on the basis of the approach in *Chandler*, a jury would be obliged to find the offence made out.

Given this wide scope, s. 1 of the 1911 Act is potentially a very restrictive provision, which could quite easily be used against a wide range of disclosures concerning the operations of government made by the press. It is arguable, for example, that *The Guardian*'s disclosures in the Tisdall case (see *Secretary of State for Defence* v *Guardian Newspapers* [1985] AC 339) about the arrangements for the announcement of the arrival of cruise missiles into this country could have come into this category. Control of prosecutions under the 1911 Act is, however, in the hands of the Attorney-General (by virtue of s. 8), and in general prosecutions have only been taken or approved in cases which would be agreed to concern espionage, or related activities. The two notable exceptions to this are firstly *Chandler*, and secondly the so-called 'ABC' trial in 1978 which arose out of an interview between a journalist (Campbell) and a former soldier (Berry), which had been arranged by another journalist (Aubrey). (This case is not reported, but see A. Nicol [1979] Crim LR 284.) At one stage Aubrey, Berry, and Campbell were all charged with s. 1 offences, despite the fact that there was no suggestion that any of the three intended to pass any information to an enemy. The judge at their initial, abortive, trial made it clear that he did not regard this as an appropriate use of s. 1, particularly as some of the information related to prohibited places, and the burden of proof thus shifted to the defendants. At the second trial the Attorney-General dropped the s. 1 charges, and proceeded only on the less serious offences contained in s. 2.

The existence of the offence under s. 1 of the 1911 Act is thus more of a potential threat to, than an actual restriction on, freedom of expression; but the fact that its use in a way that is not repressive is dependent on the discretion of the Attroney-General is unsatisfactory. There is no reason why the offence could not be reformulated in more specific language, so that it covered only those activities connected with espionage which were clearly its original and intended target.

5.4.2 Official Secrets Act 1920

Section 1 of the Official Secrets Act 1920 contains offences related to the unlawful retention of documents, and similar matters. These are of little practical importance, and in any case do not strike directly at freedom of expression. Section 7 of the Act is, however, a provision which should be noted, in that it has the potential of considerably widening the effect of s. 1 of the 1911 Act.

The section is headed 'Attempts, incitements, etc', and its concern is acts of preparation for, or assistance with, any of the offences under either the 1911 or 1920 Acts. It makes it an offence to attempt to commit any such offence, or to solicit, incite or endeavour to persuade another person to do so, or to aid or abet its commission. Thus far it adds little or nothing to the general criminal law provisions about participation in crime. In addition, however, it is an offence if a person 'does any act preparatory to the commission of an offence' under either of the Acts. It was confirmed in *R v Oakes* [1959] 2 QB 350 that this is a separate offence from the 'aiding and abetting' offence. An example of its use is to be found in *R v Bingham* [1973] QB 870. Mr Bingham was an RAF officer who had been convicted of various offences under the 1911 Act. His wife then published her story in various newspapers, revealing that it had been her idea that she and her husband should pass information to the Soviet Embassy, in order to try to resolve their financial problems. She had, in fact, made the first contact with the Embassy. She said that it had been their intention that only false information should be passed on. As a result of this disclosure, she was convicted of an offence under s. 7. The Court of Appeal upheld her conviction, ruling that provided that she realised the *possibility* that harmful information might pass, as they felt she must have done, she had sufficient *mens rea* for the offence. In the course of his judgment, Lord Widgery made clear the wide scope of the *actus reus* of this offence ([1977] QB 870, at 875):

> ... this is a very special kind of offence based on a section which was passed no doubt by parliament to fill what was otherwise a gap in the law. It contemplates something which is even more remote from the substantive offence than an attempt to commit it.

Under the general criminal law on attempts, now set out in the Criminal Attempts Act 1981, only actions which come very close to the commission of the full offence count as attempts. For example, if you leave home with a loaded gun in your pocket, intending to kill the prime minister, you will not at that stage be guilty of attempted murder. Nor will you be so, if having lain in wait for your victim, five minutes before he arrives you change your mind, and abandon your plan. The way that this is expressed in the Criminal Attempts Act, s. 1(1), is to say that the actions must be 'more than merely preparatory' to the commission of the offence. Under s. 7 of the Official Secrets Act 1920, however, merely preparatory acts *do* amount to an offence. The problem is to know exactly what this means. In Mrs Bingham's case, for example, when did she first commit an offence? When she tried to make contact with the Embassy? When she looked up the address of the Embassy? When she bought paper and ink in order to write to them? When she left the house in order to buy paper and ink for this purpose? It is submitted that all the above could be regarded as preparatory acts, and that provided that Mrs Bingham could be proved to have had the required intention at the relevant time, she could have been convicted.

This then, is another example of the way in which the criminal offences under the Official Secrets Acts are much wider in scope, and much easier for the prosecution to prove, than would normally be regarded as appropriate elsewhere in the criminal law. It has already been noted that this is the case in relation to the presumptions as to 'prejudicial purpose' in s. 1(2) of the 1911 Act. This difference in approach has been discussed fully by Professor D. G. T. Williams in 'Official Secrecy and the Courts' (in P. Glazebrook (ed) *Reshaping the Criminal Law* (1978)). It may be considered justifiable to the extent that the Official Secrets Acts are concerned with acts akin to treason, and which threaten the very security of the State. As we have seen, however, the offences are much broader in scope than that, and depend on prosecutorial discretion for their proper use. As a result, there is a strong argument that the normal standards of the criminal law should apply, or that the offences themselves should be much more narrowly defined.

5.5   OFFICIAL SECRETS ACT 1989

5.5.1   Background

The offences looked at in the previous section are, at least ostensibly, directed towards spying. There is, of course, concern, amongst governments in particular, that a wider category of official information than is encompassed by this should be subject to restrictions on disclosure. Under the 1911 Act this was achieved primarily through the provisions of s. 2. This was a very widely drafted section which in effect made it an offence to disclose *any* official information without authority. 'Official information' covered any information to which 'Crown servants' (for example, a civil servant, army officer, or police officer) obtained access in the course of their work. The information did not need to have anything about it which would render its disclosure harmful to the nation. In *R* v *Crisp and Homewood* (1919) 82 JP 121 it was held that details of army clothing contracts could not be revealed without authorisation, even though this information had no military significance. As long ago as 1972, after a thorough review of the section, the Franks Committee (*Report*, Cmnd 5104) recommended its repeal because of its 'catch-all' nature, and its unacceptably wide drafting. The Committee recommended its replacement with a new statute containing much more closely defined offences, which would not depend on prosecutorial discretion for its proper operation. Several attempts were made during the 1970s and 1980s to achieve this, both by government and by private members, but all failed, for a variety of reasons. Increasing pressure from the press for reform was fuelled by three cases. The first of these was the 'ABC' trial, referred to in the previous section. The outcome of this trial was that after six weeks all three defendants were found guilty, but the two journalists were given a conditional discharge, and the former soldier a suspended six month prison sentence. Since the costs of the trial were estimated at something in the region of £150,000, many felt that the case represented a considerable overreaction by the authorities, and emphasised the problems with s. 2 of the 1911 Act.

The other two cases both concerned civil servants in the Ministry of Defence. Sarah Tisdall was a relatively low-ranking official who was unhappy about the way in which information about the arrival of US cruise missiles into this country was being presented to parliament. She leaked certain documents to *The Guardian*, which published one of them. Ms Tisdall was traced as the source of the leak and was charged under s. 2. She pleaded guilty, and was sentenced to six months' imprisonment. Many felt that even if it was right that she should be convicted, the sentence was disproportionate to the offence.

The third case, which arose shortly afterwards, concerned a high-ranking civil servant, Clive Ponting, who was an Assistant Secretary. He was again concerned about the way information was being given to parliament, in this case concerning the sinking of the Argentine ship, the *General Belgrano*, by a British submarine during the Falklands war. Ponting passed information, not to the press, but to a sympathetic member of parliament. Once again, the ministry managed to identify Ponting as the source, and he was charged with the unauthorised disclosure of official information under s. 2. He attempted to run a defence that it was his public duty to disclose the information. The trial judge, however, ruled that his official duty overrode any such duty, and that the 'interests of the State' under s. 2 could be equated with the interests of the government of the day. It appeared that a conviction was inevitable, but the jury acquitted. This was taken as indicating that the jury felt that it was inappropriate for Ponting to have been charged with a criminal offence for acting as he did.

The cases of Tisdall and Ponting indicated the severe difficulties that lay in the way of a civil servant 'whistleblower' who wanted to draw attention to wrongdoing, or malpractice, within a government department. The criticisms which the cases aroused also made it very difficult for the Attorney-General to continue to use s. 2. It had been almost totally discredited. The government once again tried to grasp the nettle of reform. A White Paper was published on *Reform of Section 2 of the Official Secrets Act 1911* (Cm 408, 1988), and an Official Secrets Bill based on it was introduced into parliament. This became the Official Secrets Act 1989 ('the 1989 Act').

5.5.2 Categories of information

The 1989 Act, and the White Paper on which it was based, take the same basic approach to reform as was suggested by the Franks' Committee. Instead of trying to provide a single comprehensive definition of 'official information', the Act sets out a number of specific categories of information, the disclosure of which may need to be controlled. If a certain piece of information falls within a category it may also need to be considered whether its disclosure would be 'damaging'. Finally there may be a defence available in some circumstances.

There are four main categories of information dealt with under the Act, namely:

    (a)   security and intelligence (s. 1);
    (b)   defence (s. 2);
    (c)   international relations (s. 3);
    (d)   criminal investigations (s. 4).

5.5.2.1 Security and intelligence This covers any 'information, document or other article' which relates to 'security or intelligence'. 'Security or intelligence' means 'the work of, or in support of the security and intelligence services or any part of them': s. 1(9). Any information held or transmitted by those services is covered. The Act does not, however, make it clear which services are meant. The Security Service Act 1989 relates to MI5, which is concerned mainly with counter-espionage, and this would certainly be covered. It is reasonable to suppose that 'intelligence' includes the work of the so far non-statutory MI6, or Secret Intelligence Service, which is mainly concerned with operations abroad. Whether the activities of the police Special Branch, or its anti-terrorist squad, or the intelligence divisions of the armed forces, are also covered, is uncertain. It is submitted, however, that the wording of the Act is wide enough to cover the work of any State service which is concerned with matters similar or related to the work of MI5 or MI6.

5.5.2.2 Defence This is defined in s. 2(4). It covers virtually all matters relating to the armed forces, their weapons and equipment. It also covers the more general matters of 'defence policy and strategy and military planning and intelligence'. This obviously includes all the work of the Ministry of Defence. A final category brings in all arrangements for the maintenance of essential supplies and services that would be needed in time of war. Arrangements of this kind are to some extent dealt with by local authorities. As we shall see, however, local government employees are not generally within the scope of the Act's provisions.

5.5.2.3 International relations This category is defined in s. 3(5). It means relations between States and international organisations, or between either or both. It includes matters which are internal to another State or organisation, but which are capable of affecting the UK's relations with another (not necessarily the same) State or organisation. Two types of international organisations which would clearly be covered would be any of the organs of the United Nations, or any of the institutions of the European Community. It is assumed, though the opposite interpretation is at least possible, that international organisations does not include multi-national companies.

5.5.2.4 Crime and special investigations There are three categories of information here, though they are to some extent related. The first category is unlike any of the other categories is ss. 1–4, in that it is defined in terms of the effects of disclosure. It covers any information, document or article the disclosure of which has, or if unauthorised would be likely to have, one of three results, namely:

(a) the commission of an offence; or
(b) the facilitation of an escape from legal custody, or prejudice to the safekeeping of persons in custody; or
(c) impeding the prevention or detection of offences, or the apprehension or prosecution of offenders.

The second main category within s. 4 relates to information obtained as a result of the interception of communications under a warrant issued under s. 2 of the Interception of Communications Act 1985. This Act gives the Home Secretary the power to authorise phone 'taps', in fairly closely defined circumstances. It is discussed further in 10.3.3. This category within s. 4 also covers any information relating to an authorised interception, or any document or article held or used in connection with such an interception.

The third category within s. 4 covers any information obtained through the exercise of a warrant issued under s. 3 of the Security Service Act 1989, any information relating to the obtaining of information under such a warrant, and any document or other article held or used in connection with the exercise of such a warrant. Section 3 of the Security Service Act 1989 allows the Home Secretary to issue warrants authorising members of MI5 to enter on, or otherwise 'interfere with', other people's property. This power might be used, for example, to inspect or photograph documents, or to plant a bugging device. Any information thus acquired would fall within the scope of s. 4 of the Official Secrets Act 1989.

5.5.2.5 Information not covered It is important to note that certain categories of information which might have been expected to appear are omitted from this list. The Franks Committee, for example, recommended that Cabinet documents should be subject to restriction. The government, however, took the view that to include them as a category in their own right would suggest that the criminal law was being used to protect against political embarrassment (White Paper, Cm 408, para. 32). Similarly economic information, and information provided to the government in confidence (for example, tax returns), is not covered unless it falls within one of the specific categories listed above (White Paper, paras 33–35).

5.5.3 Concept of 'damaging' disclosure

It was an important plank in the government's reform of s. 2 of the 1911 Act, that under the new legislation, only disclosures which were 'damaging' would be caught by the criminal law. The existence of this limitation on the scope of the Act was used as a justification for saying that there was therefore no need for defences of 'public interest', or 'prior disclosure'. It could not be in the public interest to disclose damaging information. It must be noted, however, that the converse is not true. Just because a disclosure is in the public interest does not mean that it will not be 'damaging' within the meaning of the Act. As regards prior publication, the government suggested that this would be a factor, though not a conclusive one, in deciding whether a further disclosure could be regarded as damaging (White Paper, paras 62–64).

The concept of the damaging disclosure operates differently in relation to the four categories of information in ss. 1–4 of the Act, so each of them must now be looked at again in turn to see exactly what publications are prohibited. As will be seen the emphasis here is not primarily on the nature of what is disclosed, but the effects of disclosure. It may, therefore, be relevant to look at the questions of to whom the disclosure is made, and where it takes place.

It should also be noted that 'disclosure' of a document or article is defined in s. 12 so as to include 'parting with possession' of it. There is a similarity here with the defintion of 'communication' under the 1911 Act (see 5.4.1).

In this section the phrases 'Crown servant' and 'government contractor' are frequently used. These are defined in s. 12 of the Act, and discussed further at 5.5.4.

5.5.3.1 Security and intelligence   There are two situations to consider here, depending on who is doing the disclosing. Where the discloser is a member of the security services, or a person who has been notified as being subject to the provisions of s. 1(1), then there is no need for the prosecution to prove actual or potential damage. Disclosure by such a person of any information falling within the category of 'security and intelligence', and acquired in the course of the person's work, is automatically an offence. It would be an offence under this section, therefore for James Bond to tell Pussy Galore the colour of the tie that 'M' had been wearing that morning (see Ian Fleming, *Goldfinger*). Such a result comes close to retaining the catch-all nature of the old s. 2 of the 1911 Act, and does little to support the government's commitment only to criminalise 'damaging' disclosures. The justification is that the work of a member of the security or intelligence services is so confidential that any breach of that confidentiality must be regarded as damaging, no matter what is disclosed. This assertion remains as unconvincing in relation to s. 1 of the 1989 Act as it did in relation to s. 2 of the 1911 Act.

The second situation is where the disclosure is by a person who is, or has been, a Crown servant or government contractor, but is not a member of the security or intelligence services. This would cover civil servants working in the Home Office or the Foreign and Commonwealth Office, for example, who might be engaged on matters related to security or the gathering of intelligence. A disclosure by such a person will be damaging if it causes damage to the work of the security and intelligence services (s. 1(4)), or if it is of information, or a document or article, the unauthorised disclosure of which would be likely to cause such harm. It will also be damaging if, although the disclosure of the particular information, document or article would not in itself cause harm, it falls within a class or description of information, documents or articles the unauthorised disclosure of which would be likely to have such an effect. This final category has the potential of greatly widening the scope of the Act, and considerably reducing its liberalising effect. Its inclusion is presumably based on a similar line of argument to that used in *Secretary of State for Defence* v *Guardian Newspapers* [1985] AC 339. Here the view was taken that although disclosure of the document leaked by Sarah Tisdall and published by *The Guardian* was not in itself prejudicial to national security, *any* unauthorised disclosure of documents by civil servants working in the Ministry of Defence would potentially have this effect. It was in the interest of national security, therefore, that no such disclosures should occur, no matter what the content of the particular document disclosed. The adoption of this line of reasoning in s. 1(4) of the 1989 Act, in defining the damaging nature of a disclosure by reference to the 'class' to which the information, document or article, belongs, rather than by its content, is unfortunate, in that it considerably weakens the government's argument that disclosures in the public interest need no special protection, because only disclosures which are clearly damaging will be caught by the Act.

5.5.3.2 Defence The offence under s. 2, concerning information relating to defence, is committed where there is a damaging disclosure of any information, document or article falling within this category, to which the discloser has or had access by virtue of being, or having been, a Crown servant or government contractor. A disclosure of information in this category is damaging if it has, or is likely to have, any of the following effects:

    (a) damage to the capability of any part of the armed forces to carry out their tasks;
    (b) loss of life, or injury to members of the armed forces;
    (c) serious damage to the equipment or installations of those forces;
    (d) danger to the interests of the United Kingdom abroad;
    (e) serious obstruction to the promotion or protection by the United Kingdom of those interests; or
    (f) danger to the safety of British citizens abroad.

It is not clear whether the 'loss of life' in (b) relates only to members of the armed forces. The strict grammatical reading would lead to its covering *any* loss of life, but the rest of the sub-section is entirely concerned with the armed forces.

5.5.3.3 International relations Once again, it is current or former Crown servants, or government contractors, who may commit the offence of making a damaging disclosure of information falling within the category of 'international relations'. The discloser must have or have had access to the information, document or article, as a result of holding such a position. The damaging effects here are those listed under (d), (e) or (f) in 5.5.3.2, in relation to defence.

    Where the offence is based on the fact that the material is likely to have one of these effects if disclosed (rather than having had such an effect), the fact that it was received in confidence from another State, or an international organisation, may be sufficient in itself to establish this likelihood (s. 3(3)(a)). It is also possible, of course, to establish the likely damaging effect from the 'nature or contents' of such material (s. 3(3)(b)).

5.5.3.4 Crime and special investigation powers Reference to the definition of material within the category of 'crime' (see 5.5.2.4), will show that it is based on the effects of disclosure. As a result, there is no further definition of 'damaging' disclosure in relation to this class of material. In a formal sense this is untidy, in that it is out of line with the general approach of defining a broad category of material, and then identifying damaging disclosures within that category, which is used in ss. 1–3. It has little significance of substance, however, and this part of s. 4 fits in with the general policy of the White Paper and the Act, that disclosures should be judged by their effects, or potential effects, as much as by the type or origin of the material which is disclosed.

In relation to special investigation powers, however, the position is different. As regards information relating to interception of communications, or warrants under the Security Service Act 1989, the definition in s. 4(3) of the material covered is purely in terms of the type of material or its content. There is no reference here to the effects of disclosing the material. It is surprising, therefore, to find that there is no definition of damaging disclosure as regards material within s. 4(3). The justification for this approach as regards interceptions appears in paras 30 and 53 of the White Paper. Paragraph 30 gives two reasons why disclosure might be harmful. The first is that: 'The effectiveness of interception would be much reduced if details of the practice were readily available'. The second is that interception involves interference with the privacy of those whose communications are subject to it: 'Such interference is acceptable in the public interest only if those responsible for interception maintain the privacy of the information obtained'. Paragraph 53 refers to the reasons set out in para. 30, and then asserts that 'no information obtained by means of interception can be disclosed without assisting terrorism or crime, damaging national security or seriously breaching the privacy of private citizens'. Therefore, it is concluded, no specific test of harm is needed in relation to the disclosure of this category of material. This argument would have more force if s. 4(3) was concerned solely with the content of any interception. As we have seen, however, the section also covers 'any information relating to the obtaining of information by reason of any such interception'. The government cannot seriously argue that all disclosures of information falling within this definition are damaging, since the Commissioner appointed under the Interception of Communication Act 1985 to monitor its operation annually issues reports indicating, for example, the number of warrants issued under the Act, the general areas to which they related (drugs, serious crime, etc), and their effectiveness (that is, the number of arrests which resulted). In the light of this it is hard to accept that a definition of damaging disclosure in respect of this category could not have been devised.

Much the same arguments apply to information relating to warrants issued under the Security Service Act 1989. The government would presumably argue that, as with information emanating from members of the security and intelligence services, under s. 1, any disclosure is harmful. Here again, however, the Security Service Act 1989 itself provides for a Commissioner who is to supervise, amongst other things, the operation of the warrant system, and make annual reports to the Prime Minister which are laid before parliament. Disclosure of the information contained in these reports is, presumably, not harmful. There seems no reason, then, why there should not be in this section a definition of 'damaging disclosure' as well.

5.5.4 Crown servants and government contractors
The principal obligations under ss. 1–4 of the Official Secrets Act ('OSA') 1989 are placed on Crown servants and government contractors. These are defined in s. 12 of the Act.

Crown servants include all government Ministers, but not all members of parliament. MPs who act as part of a Ministerial private office will not therefore fall in this category. Anyone employed in the civil service in whatever capacity, from a permanent secretary in the Foreign and Commonwealth Office, to a counter-clerk in a local office of the Department for Social Security, is a Crown servant. Less obvious groups who come within the s. 12 definition, are all members of the armed forces, and all police officers. Civilians employed by the police are also specifically included (s. 12(1)(e)), thus giving statutory recognition to the view taken in *Loat* v *Andrews* [1986] ICR 679 in relation to s. 2 of the 1911 Act. Section 12(1)(f) and (g) give a power to 'prescribe' that other people, or groups of people, are to be regarded as Crown servants for the purposes of the Act. This has been used, for example, to bring within its scope people concerned with nuclear energy, such as employees of British Nuclear Fuels plc, and the Atomic Energy Authority. It has also been used in respect of non-governmental organisations or bodies, such as the staff of the National Audit Office, and the Parliamentary Commissioner for Administration (Official Secrets Act 1989 (Prescription) Order 1990 (SI 1990 No 200)).

A 'government contractor' is defined as any person (not being a Crown servant) who 'provides, or is employed in the provision of, goods and services' to the people or organisations specified in s. 12(2)(a). This includes all government departments, and the armed forces. Under s. 12(2)(b) the Secretary of State may certify that suppliers under certain international agreements or arrangements should also be regarded as government contractors.

5.5.5   The private citizen and the Press

As we have seen, the offences under ss. 1–4 of the OSA 1989 are all directed against members of the security service, Crown servants, and government contractors. While stopping such people from disclosing information is a restriction on freedom of expression, these provisions do not operate as a direct attack on the Press. The fact that civil servants and others are reluctant to leak information may, of course, mean that the Press cannot get access to, and publish, some stories that it would like to. More direct controls are, however, contained in ss. 5 and 6 of the OSA 1989. These apply to disclosures by people other than Crown servants and government contractors.

5.5.5.1   Information resulting from unauthorised disclosures or entrusted in confidence   The test of whether a private individual of any sort, including a journalist or editor, commits an offence by disclosing material, depends primarily on how the material was acquired. There are four ways in which information, or a document or article is acquired which may mean that a further disclosure will amount to an offence:

(a)   where the material was acquired as a result of a disclosure in contravention of s. 1 of the Official Secrets Act 1911 (see 5.4.1) (s. 5(6));

(b)   where the material was acquired as a result of an unauthorised disclosure at some stage by a Crown servant or government contractor (s. 5(1)(a)(i));

(c)   where the material was entrusted to the recipient in confidence, or with a reasonable expectation of confidence, by a Crown servant or government contractor (s. 5(1)(a)(ii));

(d)   where the material was acquired as a result of an unauthorised disclosure at some stage by a person to whom it had been entrusted as in (c) above (s. 5(1)(a)(iii)).

The disclosure of material falling within (a) is an offence if it is made without lawful authority, and the discloser knows, or has reasonable cause to believe, that it has been communicated in breach of s. 1 of the 1911 Act. As will be recalled, this means it must be material which is communicated for a purpose prejudicial to the safety or interests of the State, and which is, or is intended to be, useful to an enemy (see 5.4.1).

In relation to material falling within categories (b), (c) or (d), above, the offence will depend to some extent on the content of the material. If it comes within ss. 1, 2 or 3 of the Act, that is security and intelligence, defence, or international relations, it will be an offence to disclose it without lawful authority, if the disclosure is 'damaging' as defined in ss. 1, 2 or 3, and the discloser has the required mental element. This is that the discloser knows, or has reasonable cause to believe, that the material is protected against disclosure under the 1989 Act, and that the disclosure would be damaging.

If the material falls within s. 4 of the Act, that is, crime and special investigation powers, then the offence is the same as outlined in the previous paragraph, except that the prosecution has no need to prove that the disclosure was damaging, or that the discloser knew or had reasonable cause to believe that it would be damaging. The discloser must still be shown to have been aware, or to have had reasonable cause to believe that the material was protected against disclosure under the 1989 Act.

How might these offences work in practice? Suppose a Minister gives an MP information relating to defence, in confidence. This might well be authorised, since Ministers will be taken to have wide powers of self-authorisation. What would be the position if the MP then leaks the information to a journalist, and it is published in a newspaper? If the disclosure of the information is damaging, then the MP will commit an offence because of the breach of confidence (category (c), above), and the journalist and newspaper will commit an offence, because of the earlier breach of confidence (category (d), above), provided that in each case the prosecution can prove the relevant mental element.

To take another example, *The Guardian*, in publishing the document sent to it anonymously by Sarah Tisdall (see 5.5.1), might well commit an offence under the new Act. The document was disclosed without authority by a Crown servant, and so fell within category (b) above. It clearly related to defence. The editor of *The Guardian* would only escape liability if its publication of the document was found not to be damaging, or the editor was found not to have had reasonable grounds to believe that it had been sent to him without lawful authority (which is unlikely), or not to have known, or had any reasonable grounds to believe, that the disclosure would be damaging (which is more possible). It was clear from *Secretary of State for Defence* v *Guardian*

Newspapers [1985] AC 339, that there was general agreement that the disclosure of the document which *The Guardian* published was not harmful to the national interest, and it would be difficult to see it as being 'damaging' within s. 2(2) of the OSA 1989. On the other hand, there is the risk that a court might interpret s. 2(2)(c) as covering such a situation. This makes damaging the disclosure of any material the unauthorised disclosure of which would be *likely* to be damaging under s. 2(2)(a) or (b). That is, it might be argued that although this particular disclosure of this particular document was not damaging, the disclosure of documents of this kind was always potentially damaging. This was the kind of argument which found favour with the House of Lords in *Secretary of State for Defence* v *Guardian Newspapers* (1985). It is not so obviously applicable to s. 2 of the 1989 Act as it is to s. 1, where there is specific reference to the likely effects of disclosing material of the same 'class' as that actually disclosed (s. 1(4)(b)), but the general history of statutory interpretation in relation to Official Secrets Act provisions does not lend encouragement to an expectation that a narrow interpretation would be adopted (see, for example, D. G. T. Williams, 'Official Secrecy and the Courts', in P. Glazebrook (ed), *Reshaping the Criminal Law*, Stevens, 1978).

As will be seen, then, the question of whether the Press is significantly less subject to restraint under s. 5 of the OSA 1989 than it was under s. 2 of the 1911 Act, will depend to a large extent on the concept of the 'damaging' disclosure, and in particular how this is interpreted by the courts.

5.5.5.2 Information entrusted in confidence to other States or international organisations

The government was concerned about the possible risks of disclosure where information was given to other States or international organisations, and then found its way back into the British Press. This was not dealt with in the White Paper, but is addressed in s. 6 of the OSA 1989. The section applies to material relating to security or intelligence, defence, or international relations. Material falling within s. 4 of the OSA 1989 (crime and special investigations) is not therefore covered. The material must have been communicated in confidence by or on behalf of the United Kingdom to another State or international organisation. If it comes into a person's possession as a result of having been disclosed without the authority of that State or organisation (or a member of it), then a disclosure by that person may constitute an offence, if it is a damaging disclosure. The discloser must know, or have reasonable cause to believe, that it is material to which the section applies, and that its disclosure would be damaging.

Unusually for the OSA 1989, there is here a defence of prior disclosure. Under s. 6(3) if the material has previously been made available to the public (and presumably this does not simply mean the public within the United Kingdom) with the authority of the relevant State or organisation, then no offence will be committed.

5.5.6 Defences
The Act is fairly limited in the defences which it allows, and for most offences there is only one that is available.

5.5.6.1   Awareness of nature of material or likelihood of damage   For Crown servants, and government contractors it is generally a defence for the discloser to prove lack of knowledge, or reasonable cause to believe, that the material disclosed was in one of the restricted categories of restricted within ss. 1–4, or that, where relevant, the disclosure would be damaging (see ss. 1(5), 2(3), 3(4), 4(4) and (5)). Note that this is a true defence, in that the burden of proof of this state of mind lies (on the balance of probabilities) on the person charged. In relation to disclosures by the public or the Press under ss. 5 or 6, the proof of the relevant state of mind remains with the prosecution (to be proved beyond reasonable doubt).

5.5.6.2   Lawful authority   All the offences under the Act so far considered require the prosecution to prove that the disclosure was made, as a matter of fact, 'without lawful authority'. In addition, s. 7(4) provides that there is a defence if the discloser proves:

> that at the time of the alleged offence he believed that he had lawful authority to make the disclosure in question and had no resonable cause to believe otherwise.

The concept of 'lawful authority' is dealt with in s. 7 (1), (2) and (3). The definition differs according to who is the discloser. Where the disclosure is by a Crown servant, or a person subject to a notification under s. 1(1) (see 5.5.3.1), it is only made 'with lawful authority' if it is made in accordance with the discloser's 'official duty'. This carries echoes of the Ponting case, where Clive Ponting tried to argue in relation to his disclosure, that it was his 'moral duty' in the public interest, to reveal what was going on in his department. The trial judge, however, ruled that the word 'duty' in s. 2 of the 1911 Act had to be interpreted as meaning a civil servant's official duty. The same approach is perpetuated by the definition in s. 7(1).

Where the disclosure is by government contractor, lawful authority means 'in accordance with an official authorisation', or:

> for the purposes of the function by virtue of which he is a government contractor and without contravening an official restriction.

'Official authorisation' and 'official restriction' are further defined in s. 7(5), as essentially meaning an authorisation or restriction duly given or imposed by a Crown servant or government contractor.

Finally, where the dislosure is made by any person who is not a Crown servant or government contractor, a disclosure will only be made with lawful authority if it is made to a Crown servant, or in accordance with an official authorisation (s. 7(3)).

5.5.6.3   Public interest   The Act makes no provision for a defence of public interest in relation to any type of disclosure. The White Paper considered the possibility but rejected it for two main reasons. First, to introduce such a defence would inevitably reduce the clarity of the law, because its availability would be likely to lead to a broad range of arguments as to when it should be available. Secondly, the reforms were intended to limit the scope of the criminal law to disclosures which are damaging, and therefore contrary to the public interest. The White Paper continues (para. 60):

> It cannot be acceptable that a person can lawfully disclose information which he knows may, for example, lead to loss of life simply because he conceives that he has a general reason of a public character for doing so.

This is no doubt true, but it goes too far. Those who support a public interest defence do not argue that it should override the danger of loss of life; but as we have seen, 'damaging' disclosures can involve conseqences considerably less serious than this, such as 'endangering the interests of the United Kingdom abroad' (s. 2(2)). In relation to consequences such as this it is hard to accept that there could be no circumstances in which a public interest in disclosure would outweigh the possible damage that might be caused.

5.5.6.4 Defence of prior publication This too was considered in the White Paper, but again rejected. It was pointed out that in some cases repetition of a story may in fact be more harmful, if for example it involved a senior official in a government department confirming what had previously been a rumour based on little evidence. Moreover, in certain circumstances the gathering together of information previously published in different places may create a much more damaging disclosure. The example used in the White Paper is of a list of addresses of persons in public life, which in its compiled form might be of considerable use to terrorist groups (para. 62).

The White Paper also claims that where it is necessary for a disclosure to be proved to be damaging, the fact of earlier disclosure of the same information will be a relevant factor. If no further harm is done by the second publication, it will not be damaging. This argument would be more convincing if it were not for the fact that it is difficult to see that the relevant provisions of the OSA 1989 will be interpreted in this way. Many of them refer to a damaging disclosure as covering the situation where the unauthorised disclosure would be 'likely' to have damaging consequences. This seems to leave it open to the courts to ignore any earlier publication, and the actual effects of publication, and simply to consider the hypothetical possibility of disclosure.

Finally, the Act itself does not follow the White Paper's line consistently. As we have seen in 5.5.5.2 in s. 6 it is recognised that in certain circumstances prior disclosure of material should prevent a subsequent disclosure from constituting an offence, even if that subsequent disclosure is itself damaging (s. 6(1)). It is difficult to see why this exception to the general approach should have been allowed here, and not in relation to any other similar circumstances.

5.5.7 Miscellaneous

5.5.7.1 Other offences Section 8 of the OSA 1989 creates various offences relating to the unauthorised retention or failure to take care of documents.

These are not really of much relevance to freedom of expression. Section 8(4) and (5), however, are more directly applicable to Press freedom. They apply where a person has under their possession or control a document or article which it would be an offence to disclose under s. 5 or s. 6, respectively. It is an offence to fail to return such a document or article, where there has been an official direction to do so. An official direction is one that has been issued by a Crown servant or government contractor (s. 8(9)). This means, presumably, that in a situation such as that which occurred in *Secretary of State for Defence* v *Guardian Newspapers* (1985), there would no longer be any need to rely on tortious remedies to recover the document. A direction for return could be issued to the newspaper, and if it failed to comply, an offence would be committed. It is to be hoped that the courts would, however, be prepared in appropriate circumstances to allow the defence under s. 10 of the Contempt of Court Act 1981, which was recognised, though not applied, in the *Guardian* case (for further discussion of this, see 6.2.7).

5.5.7.2 Arrest and search powers Section 11(1) makes all offences under the Act, except for those under s. 8(1), (4) and (5), 'arrestable' under s. 24 of the Police and Criminal Evidence Act 1984 (see 2.4.3.1). Section 11(2) extends the search warrant powers under s. 9 of the Official Secrets Act 1911, to offences (other than those under s. 8) under the OSA 1989.

5.5.7.3 Prosecution For all prosecutions, the consent of the Attorney-General or, in the case of s. 4(2), the Director of Public Prosecutions, is required.

5.5.7.4 Penalties All offences, other than those under s. 8 (1), (4) and (5), are triable either way. On indictment the maximum penalty is a fine, plus imprisonment for up to two years. On summary conviction the maximum is six months' imprisonment, or a fine not exceeding the statutory maximum, or both. This is the same level of penalties as applied to offences under s. 2 of the Official Secrets Act 1911.

Section 8 offences (other than s. 8(6)) are summary only, punishable by three months' imprisonment, or a fine not exceeding level 5 on the standard scale.

5.6 BREACH OF CONFIDENCE

So far in this chapter we have been primarily concerned with the criminal law, that is, restrictions on freedom of expression which operate by punishing those who publish. In recent years, however, the government has also attempted to exercise controls in this area by means of the civil law, and the use of injunctions. This type of restriction on prior disclosure is not generally available under the criminal law. The courts take the view that if a publisher is not deterred by the threat of penalties imposed under the criminal law, the threat of imposing similar penalties for contempt of court as a result of non-compliance with an injunction is likely to be similarly ineffective. The injunction is, however, often used as part of the range of remedies under the civil law. The area of civil law which is of particular relevance to the issues discussed in this chapter is 'breach of confidence'.

5.6.1   The background

The action for breach of confidence has its origins mainly in the law relating to trade secrets, for example, *Morison* v *Moat* (1851) 9 Hare 241, though the case of *Prince Albert* v *Strange* (1848) 2 De G & Sm 652 shows it also being used in a quasi-copyright situation raising privacy issues. As Lord Keith pointed out in *Attorney-General* v *Guardian Newspapers Ltd (No 2)* [1990] 1 AC 109, however, most of the cases on confidentiality have been concerned either with actual or threatened disclosures by 'an employee or ex-employee of the plaintiff, or where the information about the plaintiff's business affairs has been given in confidence to someone who has proceeded to exploit it for his own benefit'. The extension of the action into the more general 'privacy' area is discussed further in chapter 10. Here the focus is on the use of the action to protect politically sensitive information.

The starting point for discussion is the case of *Attorney-General* v *Jonathan Cape* [1976] QB 752. Richard Crossman was a Cabinet minister in the Labour governments under Harold Wilson in the 1960s and 1970s. He had a keen interest in the processes of government, and made no secret of the fact that he was keeping detailed diaries, with a view to eventual publication. After his death, his literary executors proposed to publish an edited version of these diaries, covering the period 1964–1966. They were to contain details of discussions with fellow Ministers, both inside and outside Cabinet, and also of dealings with civil servants in Crossman's department. Crossman's own frank opinions of his colleagues, and his subordinates, were also included. The Attorney-General sought an injunction to restrain breach of confidence. He claimed *locus standi* as guardian of the public interest, in the same way as it is well-established that the Attorney-General can intervene to prevent the disclosure of evidence in a trial if such disclosure would be contrary to the public interest (*Conway* v *Rimmer* [1968] AC 910). He also argued that the disclosures would constitute a 'breach of confidence', by analogy with *Argyll* v *Argyll* [1967] Ch 302 where it was established that disclosure of secrets arising from a marriage could be restrained on this basis. This principle could be extended to government information on the basis of conventions, such as the doctrine of the collective responsibility of the Cabinet, and the more general argument, that 'confidentiality is an inherent and essential part of the administrative machinery of government'. The defence rejected this extension of the breach of confidence action, and argued that even if information was given to Crossman in confidence, it was up to the person aggrieved (that is, other Ministers, or civil servants) to bring an action.

Lord Widgery accepted that the Attorney-General had a role in protecting the public interest in this area. This was not enough in itself, however. To obtain an injunction the Attorney-General needed to show a breach of confidence. In relation to Cabinet discussions, Lord Widgery said these were clearly confidential; but the confidence was not owed to other members of the

Cabinet, but to the Sovereign, as head of the Privy Council. There was no question, therefore, of other members of the Cabinet releasing Crossman from his obligation of confidence. In sum, what the Attorney-General had to show in order to obtain an injunction to stop a publication was:

(a) that such publication would be a breach of confidence; (b) that the public interest requires that the publication be restrained, and (c) that there are no other facets of the public interest contradictory and more compelling than that relied upon.

Even where restraint was justified on this basis, the court must be careful not to impose a restriction which goes beyond 'the strict requirement of public need'.

Applying this approach, Lord Widgery found that the delay of ten years between the events described in the diaries, and their publication, meant that there was no risk to the doctrine of collective responsibility, or of inhibition of discussion at the present time. Nor was there any need to restrict disclosure of Crossman's discussions with, or comments on, his civil servants. This was a matter of taste only, and did not affect the public interest. No injunction should be granted.

The Crossman case thus resulted in a victory for the publishers, but at the same time established the possibility of the Attorney-General using breach of confidence to restrain the publication of government secrets in an appropriate case. The later Austalian case of *Commonwealth of Australia v John Fairfax & Sons Ltd* (1980) 147 CLR 39, which was concerned with the publication of information about the Australian government's dealing with other countries, confirmed that it was a question of balancing two public interests: the interest in 'keeping the community informed and in promoting discussion of public affairs', and the interest in secrecy where otherwise 'national security, relations with foreign countries or the ordinary business of government will be prejudiced'. As Mason J concluded, this will not always be an easy process:

There will be cases in which conflicting considerations will be finely balanced, where it is difficult to decide whether the public's interest in knowing and in expressing its opinion, outweighs the need to protect confidentiality.

This, then, was the background to the most important case on the question of the use of breach of confidence by the government, which arose out of the attempt by Peter Wright to publish his book *Spycatcher*.

5.6.2 The *Spycatcher* saga

Peter Wright was a member of MI5 from 1955–1976. He then retired to Australia. He there wrote a book about his experience within MI5, entitled *Spycatcher*, which he proposed to publish in Australia. The book contained allegations, among other things, of a plot to assassinate President Nasser of Egypt at the time of the Suez crisis in the 1950s; various illegal burglaries and related activities carried out as part of surveillance operations; and a conspiracy within MI5 to 'destabilise' the Labour government of Harold Wilson in the 1970s. Publication of the book in the United Kingdom would undoubtedly have been an offence under the Official Secrets Act 1911. Since the initial publication was proposed for Australia, however, the Attorney-General started an action in the Australian courts, in New South Wales, seeking an injunction to restrain publication on the basis of breach of confidence. This action was started in 1985, though the trial did not begin until November 1986. In the meantime, undertakings were given by all concerned not to publish any relevant information from the book pending the trial.

In June 1986 *The Observer* and *The Guardian* published articles reporting on the forthcoming proceedings, and outlining some of Wright's allegations. The Attorney-General at once obtained interlocutory injunctions restraining the newspapers from disclosing any information obtained by Wright as an MI5 officer: see *Attorney-General* v *The Observer* (1986) 136 NLJ 799.

In March 1987 the New South Wales court dismissed the Attorney-General's action, but the undertakings not to publish or disclose were continued, pending an appeal.

In April 1987 *The Independent*, the *Evening Standard* and the *London Daily News* published articles based on the book. These publications led to lengthy contempt proceedings, which are not discussed further here (see 6.2.2.3).

In July 1987, *The Sunday Times* obtained a copy of *Spycatcher* which was about to be published in the United States. On 12 July *The Sunday Times* publised in its *second* edition, an extract from the book, as the first instalment of a serialisation. The extract was not put into the *first* edition, because it was thought that this might have prompted legal proceedings to stop distribution of the paper. By leaving it to the second edition, the newspaper ensured that the paper was on sale on Sunday morning. The Attorney-General at once sought and obtained an interlocutory injunction preventing publication of any further extracts. By this stage *Spycatcher* was freely on sale in the United States, and the government made no serious attempt to prevent copies being imported into this country. Nevertheless, on 30 July 1987, the House of Lords confirmed all the interlocutory injunctions: *Attorney-General* v *Guardian Newspapers Ltd* [1987] 3 All ER 316.

In September 1987 the New South Wales Court of Appeal dismissed the Attorney-General's appeal, and refused to restrain publication pending a further appeal to the High Court of Australia. As a result *Spycatcher* was published in Australia in October 1987. At the same time, it was also published in Ireland. In June 1988, the High Court of Australia dismissed the Attorney-General's appeal, thus concluding the Australian proceedings.

Against this background the House of Lords came to consider, in October 1988, the appeals in relation to the breach of confidence actions against *The Observer*, *The Guardian*, and *The Sunday Times*. Their decision, which was concerned with whether the interlocutory injunctions should be made permanent, is reported as *Attorney-General* v *Guardian Newspapers Ltd (No 2)* [1990] 1 AC 109.

A first issue which needed to be clarified in this case was the obligations, if any, of those who receive confidential material in a situation where they themselves have given no undertaking of confidence. Peter Wright may well have owed a duty of confidence to his former employers, the British government, but he had disclosed the information without any requirement that those to whom he disclosed it should keep it secret. On the contrary, his whole point in disclosing was that they should publish it. As far as *The Observer*, and *The Guardian* were concerned, their information came primarily from the legal proceedings in Australia. The House of Lords were clear that the recipient of information in this situation may well be subject to an obligation of confidence. As Lord Goff put it, as a broad general principle:

> a duty of confidence arises when confidential information comes to the knowledge of a person (the confidant) in circumstances where he has notice . . . that the information is confidential . . .

Since the newspapers were quite aware of the background to the *Spycatcher* material they must be taken to have had notice its confidentiality, and thus were themselves under an obligation of confidence. That did not determine, however, whether they could be restrained from disclosure. As Lord Keith pointed out, in relation to private confidences it may well be possible to take action without proof of damage, but as far as the government is concerned, some harm to the interests of the nation must be shown to follow, or to be likely to follow, from disclosure. Where the discloser was a Crown servant, such as Wright, then it would probably be relatively easy to show that it was contrary to the public interest that disclosure should occur. Lord Goff, with some support from Lord Brightman, however, thought that even Wright would lose his obligation of confidence in relation to information which was in the public domain. They were in a minority on this view, however, the majority assuming that Wright would be subject to a lifelong duty not to disclose anything about his work, even if others had done so. This is on the basis that it is always contrary to the public interest for members of the security services to make such disclosures. This has clear parallels with the approach taken in the Official Secrets Act 1989, s. 1 (see 5.5.3.1). As regards the newspapers, however, there was a need to show that their disclosures were specifically damaging to the public interest.

The articles in *The Observer* and *The Guardian* in 1986 simply gave some account of the proceedings in Australia, and repeated some of the allegations contained in the book. The majority of the House of Lords, with Lord Griffiths dissenting, did not feel that this could be said to be contrary to the public interest. The allegations referred to were not new, and the attribution of them to Peter Wright did not make them any more likely to be damaging; nor was there any need to try to stop similar reporting in the future.

In relation to *The Sunday Times* serialisation, however, the House was unanimous that this was a breach of confidence which was actionable. The newspaper had been deliberately trying to 'steal a march' on the imminent American publication of the book, but the fact that that publication was about to take place provided no excuse. *The Sunday Times* had published detailed material which they knew had been communicated in breach of confidence.

The fact that someone else was also about to breach the confidence did not give them any defence. The House viewed the likelihood of damage to the public interest differently here from *The Observer* and *The Guardian* publications, because of the information concerning the detailed working of the security service which was revealed, and because the newspaper went beyond simply reporting allegations, to publish substantial parts of the text of the book.

Was there any countervailing public interest which might justify publication? All the members of the House recognised that 'disclosure of iniquity' may be a valid defence to an action for breach of confidence. In other words, if the confidential information is revealed in order to expose the wrongdoing of others, this may outweigh any public interest in keeping it secret. This did not help *The Sunday Times*, however. To establish the defence, as Lord Keith pointed out, it was not enough simply to report that allegations of wrongdoing had been made: 'There must at least be a *prima facie* case that the allegations have substance'. The mere fact that the allegations emanated from a former member of MI5 was not enough to do this. Moreover, as Lord Goff and Lord Griffiths made clear, the disclosure of iniquity defence does not necessarily justify publication in the press. The first port of call for such disclosures should be those who may be in a position to investigate the alleged wrongdoing and, if necessary, take action against it. Only as a last resort, where no other avenue was likely to succeed, would publication in the national press be justified on this ground.

The unanimous conclusion, then, was that the 1987 *Sunday Times* article was a breach of confidence, in relation to which the paper should be liable to make an account of profits to the Crown. The majority, however, with Lord Griffiths again dissenting, thought that the fact that *Spycatcher* had by the time of the hearing been widely published, and that this was through no fault of *The Sunday Times*, meant that there was no longer any harm in publication. *The Sunday Times* should now be free to publish a serialisation of the book, if it so wished.

The effect of the *Spycatcher* litigation on the action for breach of confidence, and its relation to the freedom of the press, was thus as follows. The press may be restrained by an action for breach of confidence from disclosing government secrets, assuming that the newspapers concerned can be taken to know that the information was confidential. It must also be proved that some harm to the public interest will result from publication. This is unlikely to be the case where the information is already in the public domain, or is essentially useless or trivial. A defence of disclosure of iniquity is possible, but only where no other means of redress appears open.

The newspapers concerned in this case were unhappy with the House of Lords' decision, and took their complaint to the European Court of Human Rights. The European Court found against the government, in part, and awarded the newspapers substantial costs. These proceedings are discussed fully at 5.8.

5.6.3 After *Spycatcher*

The principles laid down by the House of Lords in *Attorney-General* v *Guardian Newspapers* (see 5.6.2) were applied when in 1987 a former member of MI6, Anthony Cavendish, proposed to publish a book of memoirs entitled *Inside Intelligence*, covering the years 1948–1953: *Lord Advocate* v *The Scotsman Publications Ltd* [1990] 1 AC 809. He initially sought permission for publication, but this was refused. He then arranged a private printing of 500 copies, some 279 of which he distributed to friends, etc, at Christmas 1987. A copy came into the hands of *The Sunday Times*, with the result that in January 1988 the Attorney-General obtained an injunction preventing further publication on the basis that this would amount to a breach of confidence. At about the same time, a leading Scottish newspaper, *The Scotsman* also obtained a copy, and proposed to publish extracts. The Lord Advocate sought an assurance that *The Scotsman* would abide by the terms of the injunction which had been obtained against *The Sunday Times*. When the paper refused, the Lord Advocate sought an interdict against *The Scotsman* itself. This was, however, refused by the Scottish courts, and by the House of Lords. The issue turned again on whether there was any risk of harm to the public interest from the publication. In this case the Lord Advocate had conceded that the publication of the contents of the book would in no way prejudice national security. His argument was the one that was apparently accepted by the House of Lords in *Spycatcher*, that to allow any publication by a former member of the security services would be contrary to the public interest. In this case, however, the House, with Lord Keith giving the main speech, felt that the Lord Advocate's concession, together with the fact that the circulation of the book meant that there had already been some disclosure, meant that in this case there was no reason to restrain publication by *The Scotsman*. Lords Templeman and Jauncey, in agreeing with this conclusion, referred to the Official Secrets Act 1989 (which was not at the time in force), and pointed out that under that Act, Cavendish would commit an offence by publishing the book, but that *The Scotsman* would only commit an offence if the disclosure was damaging. This reinforced their belief that it was right not to grant the interdict, since there was no clear harm that would result from this publication.

The courts have shown an encouraging willingness in this case and in *Spycatcher* to consider for themselves the issue of 'the public interest', and not to rely too heavily on the government's view of what this entails. This is in marked contrast to the approach under the Official Secrets Act 1911, where the 'interests of the State' were regarded as being resolved by Ministerial fiat. It is an approach which it is hoped will be applied in deciding the question of whether disclosures are 'damaging' under the OSA 1989. If it is, then this will lead to the possibility of freedom of expression interests carrying far more weight in this area than has previously been the case.

5.7 FREEDOM OF INFORMATION

Despite the reforms of the OSA 1989, the general attitude towards official information in the United Kingdom is still one of secrecy. Information is to be kept secret, unless there is a good reason for disclosing it. This attitude is reinforced by such extra-legal procedures as requiring civil servants to 'sign the Official Secrets Act'. This means signing a document containing provisions of the Act together with a declaration that the signor understands the effect of these provisions, and that it will be an offence to act contrary to them. This ritual has no legal significance whatsoever. A person cannot be more or less liable under the Official Secrets Acts according to whether they have, or have not, signed such a document. The procedure has the effect, however, of making people nervous of disclosure, and encouraging an attitude of 'if in doubt, keep quiet'.

The same type of criticism might be made of the 'D-Notice' system. Under this the Defence Press and Broadcasting Committee, which is composed jointly of officials from government departments concerned with national security, and representatives of the Press and broadcasting organisations, issues notices (there are currently eight in force), indicating that certain categories of sensitive information should not be published. The system is entirely separate from any legal procedures, and has no bearing on liability, or lack of liability, under the Official Secrets Acts. It smacks of collusion between the government and a compliant Press, and the need for its continued existence has been doubted by those working within and outside the media (see S. Bailey, D. Harris and B. Jones, *Civil Liberties Cases and Materials*, 3rd edn, London; Butterworths, 1991, pp. 430–435). It may be regarded as symptomatic of a system where there is a presumption of secrecy.

Many other countries across the world have adopted a different approach, operating an assumption that government information should be made available to the press and the public, unless there is a good reason for keeping it secret (see, for example, N. Marsh, *Public Access to Government-Held Information*, Stevens, 1987). A 'freedom of information' approach of this kind has been consistently rejected by successive British governments. Two arguments against are generally used. First, such a system is said to be very expensive to operate, and secondly, there is no need for it, since our particular brand of parliamentary democracy, which holds Ministers responsible for their departments, and directly accountable to parliament, provides adequate safeguards.

Neither of these arguments can be regarded as conclusive. Clearly there is an expense involved in operating a system of freedom of information. In other jurisdictions, however, it is common for at least part of such costs to be passed on to those who obtain information. In any case, advocates of this freedom would argue that it is a price worth paying for the more general benefits to the democratic process which would follow. As to the constitutional argument, in some cases this may have some weight. Sweden, for example, which has had constitutional recognition of the principle for over two hundred years, and the United States, which has had a Freedom of Information Act since 1966, are countries with very different traditions, and constitutions from that of the United Kingdom. During the 1980s, however, Australia, New Zealand, and Canada, all countries operating a parliamentary democracy based closely on that of the United Kingdom, introduced freedom of information legislation. Over the past ten years their experience has shown that such a system can work, and provide benefits, within such a constitutional framework. The argument that the United Kingdom can manage without it has started to wear very thin. The most recent response of the British government to the issue is contained in the White Paper *Open Government* (Cm 2290), published in 1993, which is considered below. Before looking at this, however, one of the freedom of information systems operating in another jurisdiction, that is Canada, will be looked at, as an example of how such a system can operate.

5.7.1   The Canadian Access to Information Act

Until 1982 Canada had an Official Secrets Act, passed in 1939, which was closely modelled on the British Official Secrets Act 1911. During the 1970s the Act came into disrepute as a result of a number of prosecutions culminating in one in 1979 against the *Toronto Sun* where the judge threw out the charges, and criticised the statute as 'vague, ambiguous and unwieldy'. He called for 'a complete redrafting'. The movement for reform was also supported by the Canadian Bar Association.

In 1980 the Liberal Party was returned to power, and committed itself to reforming the Official Secrets Act, and introducing access to information legislation. The result was the Access to Information Act of 1982, which came into force on 1 July 1983.

The Act applies to government information only, and this is fairly narrowly defined, so that, for example, the Canadian National Railways are not within its scope. It deals with *records* of information, rather than information itself, though records are defined sufficiently widely to cover those which are held in electronic form, as well as physical files. There is, however, no obligation to create a record simply because particular information has been requested. On the other hand the Act provides for the annual publication of an 'Access to Information Register', giving an indication of what information and records are held. This is obviously important. A right of access to information would be much weaker if the citizen simply had to guess at what kind of information might be available. The Register assists in the targeting of requests.

A request for access to a record must be made in writing to the government institution holding it, and be accompanied by a fee of $5. The institution has 30 days in which to respond (though this is extendable). Within this period the record must be supplied, or else the head of the institution must indicate why access had been refused.

Certain types of record are exempt from access. These categories are fairly predictable, covering areas such as defence, law enforcement, personal information, etc. One category which was included in the exemptions under the Act, but about which there has been some debate, is Cabinet documents. It is interesting that the Canadian government took a more restrictive line here than the British government under the Official Secrets Act 1989. In relation to most categories of exempt material, though again not in relation to Cabinet documents, there is a requirement of 'harm' in relation to disclosure of the content of the record before the exemption will apply. It is possible, also, for records to be severed, so that a potentially 'harmful' section may be excised from what is supplied.

The initial decision as to how to respond to the request for access is left to the government institution holding the record. The route of appeal against a decision to refuse access is thus very important. There are two aspects to this. First there is an independent Information Commissioner, who not only has the responsibility for the general supervision of the operation of the legislation, but also acts as the first port of call for an appeal against refusal of access. The Commissioner has wider powers of investigation, and can make recommendations. If a dispute is unresolved after the Commissioner's intervention, then there can be recourse to the Federal Court which will often be deciding whether or not a decision to refuse access was reasonable, rather than whether it was correct. Nevertheless, the courts have adopted a broad approach to interpreting the Act. Section 2(1) of the Act states that 'necessary exceptions to the right of access should be limited and specific'. This has led the courts to operate on the basis that there is a presumption of a right of public access, so that the burden of proof is on the party resisting access, and any doubts should be determined in favour of disclosure (*Re Maislin Industries Ltd and the Minister of Industry Trade and Commerce, Regional Economic Expansion* (1984) 1 DLR (4th) 411).

The Canadian Access to Information Act is not a perfect model. There have been criticisms of its expense. During the first eighteen months of its operation the Treasury Board Secratariat put the costs at over $5 million (see N. Marsh, *Public Access to Government Held Information*, Stevens, 1987, p. 169). The fees collected, however, amounted to only $35,855. On the other side, the blanket exclusion of Cabinet records from the scope of the Act has also been criticised, and the House of Commons Standing Committee on Justice has recommended that this should be amended (*Open and Shut: Enhancing the Right to Know and the Right to Privacy*, 1987).

We should not, therefore, simply take the Canadian Act as a basis for our own access to information legislation. What the Act shows, however, is that it is possible for a parliamentary democracy of our type to work satisfactorily with such legislation in place, and that it has the big advantage of making the presumption in relation to official information one of disclosure rather than secrecy. This presumption is one which, as we have seen, the courts have been prepared to enforce.

5.7.2 White Paper on *Open Government*

In July 1993 the Conservative government published a White Paper entitled *Open Government* (Cm 2290). It was the result of a review intended to 'identify areas of excessive secrecy in government and to propose ways of increasing openness' (para. 1.2). It is a relatively short document, dealing with a range of issues. The central question of a general right of access to government information is dealt with in chapter 4. What is proposed there (at para. 4.3) is that there should be a Code of Practice on government information, with a view to providing:

a clear statement of principle on what kinds of information will be available;
a clear statement of the circumstances in which information can justifiably be withheld;
detached, authoritative and independent supervision.

A draft Code of Practice is set out in Annex A to the White Paper. This would commit government departments to publishing (Code of Practice, para. 3):

> ... the facts and analysis of facts which the government considered relevant and important in framing major policy proposals and decisions; such information will normally be made available when policies and decisions are announced.

More importantly perhaps, there would be an obligation to respond to specific requests for factual information, including 'reasonable' requests for information relating to 'the policies, actions or decisions of departments and public authorities within the scope of the Code' (Code of Practice, paras 3 and 4). The obligation relates to the provision of information, rather than documents, and there is no obligation for a department to acquire information which it does not possess.

The obligations to disclose are contained in two paragraphs; the exemptions from those obligations run to over four pages. As well as the obvious areas of defence, law enforcement, privacy, and commercial or individual confidentiality, the following headings also appear (the list is not inclusive):

communications with the Royal Household;
immigration and nationality;
effective management of the economy and collection of tax;
effective management and operations of the public service.

Perhaps most generally there is a heading entitled 'Internal discussion and advice' which gives an exemption for all 'Information whose disclosure would harm the frankness and candour of internal discussion'.

These wide-ranging and broadly worded exemptions remove much of the positive aspects of the obligations of disclosure set out in the first part of the Code.

As for supervision of the operation of the Code, the suggestion is that it will be a matter of individual complaint, first to the department concerned, and then (via a constituency MP, in the normal way) to the parliamentary Commissioner for Administration (the Parliamentary Ombudsman). The Ombudsman would have no general supervisory function, but would simply respond to, and investigate individual complaints.

The verdict on this White Paper must be that while it is a step in the right direction, it is a very tiny step. In particular, the fact that there is no legally enforceable right to information covered by the Code means that it is likely to be very easy for government departments to hide behind the broad exemptions allowed. The possibility of investigation by the Ombudsman can be no substitute for the possibility of judicial review, and court orders to disclose. Moreover, there is no suggestion of any amendment of the Official Secrets Act 1989, or the law on confidentiality, so that all the legal controls operating against freedom of information described earlier in this chapter will remain in place. So far, the government's professed commitment to greater openness has not been matched with any very convincing progress in that direction.

5.8   EUROPEAN CONVENTION AND OFFICIAL SECRECY

The main consideration of the English law in this area by the European Court of Human Rights arose out of the *Spycatcher* litigation. The three newspapers primarily affected by the government's breach of confidence actions, that is *The Sunday Times, The Observer*, and *The Guardian*, all challenged the decisions to grant injunctions against them as a breach of Art. 10. The decision of the Court is reported as *The Observer and The Guardian v The United Kingdom* (1992) 14 EHRR 153, and *The Sunday Times v The United Kingdom* (1992) 14 EHRR 229. The court came to the same conclusions in both the actions (see (1992) 14 EHRR 153, paras 66–70, and (1992) 14 EHRR 229, paras 52–56).

The Court started from the basis that the injunctions amounted to a restriction of freedom of expression under Art. 10(1). The question was then whether this restriction was justified under Art. 10(2). In answering this, the Court adopted the approach which it had developed in earlier cases on Art. 10, such as *Handyside v United Kingdom* [1976] 1 EHRR 737 (see 7.9.2) and *Lingens v Austria* (1986) 8 EHRR 737. This involves considering as separate issues, first whether the interference was 'prescribed by law', then whether it has a legitimate aim under Art. 10(2), and finally whether it was 'necessary' in a democratic society.

5.8.1   'Prescribed by law'
The newspapers argued that although the injunctions were applied in accordance with English law, the principles upon which interlocutory injunctions were granted were unclear, and therefore neither adequately accessible, nor sufficiently foreseeable. The Court rejected this contention, considering that the guidelines laid down in *American Cyanamid v Ethicon* [1975] AC 396 as to the imposition of interlocutory injunctions were sufficiently settled that the newspapers must have been able reasonably to foresee a risk that such injunctions would be imposed.

5.8.2   'Legitimate aim'
This refers to the list of reasons contained in Art. 10(2) as possible justifications for interfering with freedom of expression. These are:

> national security, territorial integrity or public safety . . . the prevention of disorder or crime . . . the protection of health or morals . . . the protection of the reputation or rights of others . . . preventing the disclosure of information received in confidence . . . maintaining the authority and impartiality of the judiciary.

The first and last of these justifications were relevant in this case; that is, the Court had no doubt that one of the aims of the interlocutory injunctions was to preserve the Attorney-General's rights in relation to the alleged breach of confidence. If the confidential information were to be published pending trial of the full action, the whole point of the proceedings from the Attorney-

General's point of view would be lost. This came within the scope of 'maintaining the authority . . . of the judiciary', since the Court had previously interpreted 'the judiciary' as meaning in effect the whole judicial process (see further on this 6.4).

It was also accepted that one of the Attorney-General's aims was to protect national security interests. The Court commented, however, that 'the precise nature of the national security considerations involved varied over time' (para. 56).

On both these grounds, it was held that the restrictions were imposed in pursuit of legitimate aims within Art. 10(2).

5.8.3 'Necessary in a democratic society'

This is the most complex issue. The Court started by enunciating a number of general principles, drawing on its own previous decisions on Art. 10.

First it was noted that 'freedom of expression constitutes one of the essential foundations of a democratic society'. Because of this, the freedom must extend to information and ideas which may offend, shock or disgust. Exceptions to the freedom must be narrowly interpreted, and the necessity for restriction convincingly established.

Secondly, 'these principles are of particular importance as far as the press is concerned'. The press has a vital role as 'public watchdog'. It is incumbent on it to deal with ideas and information related to matters of public interest. Moreover the public has a right to receive them.

Thirdly, 'the adjective "necessary" . . . implies the existence of a "pressing social need"'. This was the test first stated in *Sunday Times* v *United Kingdom* (1979) 2 EHRR 245. Although the Contracting States have a certain discretion ('margin of appreciation') as to whether such a need exists, this is subject to an overall European supervision.

Finally, the Court's task is not to take the place of the national authorities, but to review their decisions. This does not mean simply asking whether the national authority exercised its discretion reasonably, carefully and in good faith. It must also be considered whether the interference was in all the circumstances 'proportionate to the legitimate aim pursued', and whether the reasons given to justify it were relevant and sufficient.

In addition to outlining the above principles, the Court pointed out that Art. 10 does not prohibit all forms of prior restraint on publication (such as the issue of an interlocutory injunction). Nevertheless, such restraints need to be carefully scrutinised, especially where the press is concerned. As the Court pointed out 'news is a perishable commodity, and to delay its publication, even for a short period, may well deprive it of all its value and interest' ((1991) 14 EHRR 153, para. 60).

Applying the above approach to the *Spycatcher* litigation, the Court divided the period of the operation of the injunctions into two. The first period was from the initial granting of the injunctions against *The Observer* and *The Guardian* on 11 July 1986, to the continuation of them by the House of Lords on 30 July 1987. The second period ran from 30 July 1987 to 13 October 1988, at which point the House of Lords discharged all the injunctions, including the one which had subsequently been obtained against *The Sunday Times*.

In relation to the first period the main question was whether the reasons for restraining publication noted above, that is protection of national security, and maintenance of the authority of the judiciary, were 'sufficient' to justify the restriction imposed. The Court considered that the national courts had not simply applied the *American Cyanamid* approach rigidly, but had recognised that there was a conflict between the public interests in preventing and allowing disclosure, and had weighed the relevant considerations carefully. In the light of this, and in particular the need to prevent potential prejudice to the Attorney-General's breach of confidence actions, the Court decided that the reasons for restriction were 'sufficient' ((1991) 14 EHRR 153, para. 63).

Were the actual restraints imposed 'proportionate' to the legitimate aims pursued? Again, the Court noted that the injunctions did not constitute a blanket prohibition. The newspapers were not restricted from pressing for reform of the security service, or from re-publishing information which had appeared elsewhere, relating to matters covered by *Spycatcher*, but emanating from other sources. The newspapers could, and did, seek variation or discharge of the injunctions. The Court concluded that, for this period, the restraint *was* proportionate.

Turning to the period from 30 July 1987 onwards, the Court took a different view. The significant change resulted from the publication of *Spycatcher* in the United States on 14 July 1987. This publication destroyed the confidential nature of the book's contents. Although the Attorney-General could argue that further publication in this country might still prejudice his actions against the newspapers, and this was a relevant reason for restraint, the Court did not think that in the circumstances it was 'sufficient'. As to the national security argument, the Court noted that this had shifted over time. At the outset, the argument was based on the secret character of the information contained in the book. Once the contents had been disclosed, however, the purpose of the injunctions had become confined to ((1991) 14 EHRR 153, para. 69):

promotion of the efficiency and reputation of the Security Service . . . by: preserving confidence in that Service on the part of third parties; making it clear that the unauthorised publication of memoirs by its former members would not be countenanced; and deterring others who might be tempted to follow in Mr Wright's footsteps.

The Court was not prepared to regard these objectives as sufficient to justify the continuing restrictions. There was some doubt as to whether attacking the newspapers, as opposed to Peter Wright himself, would further these aims. In any case, and most importantly, the restrictions prevented the newspapers from carrying out their right and duty to inform the public about matters, already available elsewhere, which were clearly of legitimate public concern.

For these reasons the Court found that there was a violation of Art. 10 in relation to the period 30 July 1987 to 13 October 1988. They ordered the United Kingdom government to make a substantial contribution to the newspapers' costs.

5.8.4 Conclusions
The decision of the European Court of Human Rights was hailed as a victory for the newspapers. It is important to note its limitations, however. The Court did not dispute that the government's original objective in preventing the publication of *Spycatcher* was legitimate, and that this could equally extend to stopping newspapers publishing information drawn from the book. It was only when the book itself was published elsewhere that the position changed, since that removed the confidential nature of the material. While the end result was in the newspapers' favour, the government can draw some comfort from the fact that the Court's decision in no way precludes the taking of similar injunctive action in the future to protect government secrets.

5.8.5 Wider implications
What does this decision tell us, if anything, about the likely reaction of the European Court of Human Rights to a challenge to the Official Secrets Acts, insofar as they restrict freedom of expression?

There seems no doubt that s. 1 of the 1911 Act would be regarded as an acceptable restriction to the extent that it is concerned with espionage, and therefore national security. If, however, the wider scope for this section opened up by *Chandler* v *DPP* [1964] AC 763 (see 5.4.1) were to be developed, then it might well be thought that the restrictions were going beyond what is necessary in a democratic society. As we have seen, however, there is at the moment fortunately little indication of the section being used in this way.

As far as the 1989 Act is concerned, the restrictions in ss. 1 and 2 would be likely to be regarded as dealing with the legitimate aim of protecting the interests of national security, and s. 4 would come within preventing disorder and crime. It is not clear, however, what justification, if any, can be argued for s. 3 (international relations). Some material within this category might fall into the category of 'national security', but not all of it would. To the extent that the disclosure of information might prejudice the safety of UK citizens abroad, it might be argued that 'public safety' is raised. Section 3 is, nevertheless, the hardest provision to fit within the legitimate reasons for restriction contained in Art. 10(2). The Act's general use of the concept of 'damaging' disclosure as a criterion for restriction would obviously increase its acceptability to the European Court. In three ways, however, it might well be found to be unacceptable.

First, to the extent that restrictions on freedom of expression are allowed without the need to prove any damage from the disclosure (that is, under ss. 1 and 4), it seems likely that the court might regard such restrictions as unnecessary. The Attorney-General's attempt to argue that the controls over the publication of material derived from *Spycatcher* were necessary in order to maintain confidence in, and the efficiency of, the security service, and to discourage others from following in Wright's footsteps, was received with little sympathy (see 5.8.3).

Secondly, the provisions of s. 5, which act as the control over the Press, take no account of the special position of the Press as guardian of the public interest, which was recognised as a basic principle by the Court ((1991) 1

EHRR 153, para. 59). The Press is treated under the Act in the same way as any other private individual in possession of government information.

Thirdly, and this relates to the second point, the lack of any general public interest in defence would surely be disapproved. The Court's approval of the action taken by the English courts between 11 July 1986 and 30 July 1987 against newspapers disclosing information from *Spycatcher* resulted in part from the fact that the Court recognised that the domestic courts had recognised the conflicting public interests involved, and had given them careful consideration ((1991) 1 EHRR 153, para. 63). No such process is possible under the OSA 1989.

It seems likely, then, that the Court would, in appropriate circumstances, regard the restraints on freedom of expression resulting from the OSA 1989 as going further than is necessary in a democratic society. If this prediction is accurate, then it would be as well for the government to act to amend the legislation, before such a formal challenge is made.

SIX

Freedom of Expression II:
Contempt of Court

Journalists and broadcasters frequently obtain copy from reporting or commenting on civil and criminal cases, or other matters involving legal issues. This might be, for example, a sensational murder trial, a defamation action involving a celebrity, or a challenge to the legality of actions taken by a government department. Local newspapers, too, regularly report even quite minor legal cases. Most of the time this causes no problems, but such reporting is not without its restrictions. In a number of situations there are specific statutory controls over the reporting of legal proceedings. More generally, such reports and discussions are subject to the law on contempt of court. Contempt operates more widely than simply as a restriction on freedom of expression, but it is on that aspect of the offence that this chapter will concentrate.

6.1 THE OFFENCE OF CONTEMPT

6.1.1 The nature of the offence
The offence of contempt of court is unusual. It can be both civil and criminal in character. In its civil form it is concerned with people who disobey court orders (e.g. injunctions). In looking at contempt as a restriction on freedom of expression, we are more concerned with it in its criminal form, which is concerned with protecting the proper administration of justice in court proceedings (both civil and criminal). Although contempt is a type of criminal offence, it is not dealt with by the normal criminal process. In some circumstances the court which has been affected by an alleged contempt will deal with the matter itself, even if it is not a court which normally has criminal jurisdiction. Often, however, the Attorney-General will initiate proceedings in the Queen's Bench Division. It is always dealt with summarily, rather than on indictment, and procedural matters are governed by Order 52 of the Rules of the Supreme Court. This strange character is perhaps a result of the rather obscure origins of the offence. It has been suggested that the power to deal

with contempts originated in the court of the Star Chamber, and was then appropriated by the ordinary courts (H. Street, *Freedom, the Individual and the Law*, 5th edn, Harmondsworth: Penguin, 1982, p. 147). Whatever the truth of this, it is clear that by the middle of the eighteenth century the offence was sufficiently well-established for the Lord Chancellor, Lord Hardwicke to identify three different ways of committing it. These were 'scandalizing the court itself', 'abusing parties who are concerned in causes', and 'prejudicing mankind against persons before the cause is heard' (*Roach* v *Garvan* (1742) 2 Atk 469). These categories can still be found to exist as types of contempt in the modern law. It is clear from them that 'contempt' is not being used here as a synonym for 'disrespect'. It is not the dignity of the judges which is being protected by contempt of court, but the authority and integrity of the judicial process.

6.1.2 Common law and statute
The origins of contempt lie in the common law. Onto this, however, a number of statutory provisions have been grafted, most notably the Contempt of Court Act 1981. Unfortunately, this piece of legislation, which was introduced as a liberalising measure following criticisms in the European Court of Human Rights (see 6.4), did not codify the law. Moreover, the courts have shown a willingness in recent years to breathe new life into the common law. As a result, the student of this area often has to grapple with a confusing mixture of statutory and common law rules. This is true, for example, of the next issue to be considered, i.e. what is a 'court'?

6.1.3 What is a 'court'?
For there to be contempt, there must be a court for the accused to be in contempt of. What is a 'court' for these purposes? Any of the standard courts of the civil or criminal justice systems will clearly be covered, from magistrates' courts, to the House of Lords. What of all the other bodies, however, which exist in the modern legal system to decide issues of fact and law? We have numerous specialist tribunals, e.g. industrial tribunals, social security appeal tribunals, mental health review tribunals, etc. They are part of our legal system, and may perform similar tasks to the general courts but they are not described as 'courts'. Does this remove them from the scope of contempt of court?

The answer to this is to be found in a mixture of case law and statute. The issue was first addressed in *Attorney-General* v *BBC* [1980] 3 All ER 161. The BBC were planning to show a film about a religious sect called the Plymouth Brethren. The Brethren alleged that this would prejudice a case which they had pending before a local valuation court. This was a body which decided issues relating to the rating of property ('rates' being a form of local taxation). The Attorney-General sought an injunction on behalf of the Brethren to restrain the alleged contempt. The main issue was whether the local valuation court could be regarded as a 'court' for contempt purposes. The Queen's Bench Division and the Court of Appeal both thought that it could. The House of Lords took a different view. They approached the issue on the basis that it was the *function* of the body which was important, rather than the *label* attached to it. The fact that this body was labelled as a 'court' could not be conclusive. In fact the House thought that it was exercising a purely *administrative* function within the rating system. To be a court, it would have had to be exercising a *judicial* role. On that basis, there could be no contempt of a local valuation court.

This approach was followed by parliament in the Contempt of Court Act ('CCA') 1981. Section 19 defines a court as 'any tribunal or body exercising the judicial power of the State'. This definition had to be applied in *Pickering* v *Liverpool Daily Post* [1991] 1 All ER 622. Pickering was trying to prevent publicity about a pending hearing by a mental health review tribunal, which was to decide on whether he could be released from a mental hospital. He argued that adverse publicity might influence the tribunal, prejudicing his chance of a fair hearing, and thus constituting contempt of court. The Court of Appeal overruled an earlier decision (*Attorney-General* v *Associated Newspapers Group plc* [1989] 1 All ER 604) of the Divisional Court that a mental health review tribunal was not a court within the definition of s. 19. The view of the Court of Appeal (with which the House of Lords agreed) was that since the tribunal was an independent body, which was required to act judicially on the basis of evidence, and had the power to decide matters affecting the liberty of individuals, it should be regarded as exercising the judicial power of the State. It was, therefore, a 'court' for the purposes of s. 19. Thus the proposed publications could potentially amount to contempt. On the facts, however, the House of Lords found that they would not, and refused the injunction.

The tests used in *Pickering* will be relevant in deciding whether other bodies are to be regarded as courts. On this basis it would seem that, for example, industrial tribunals, which decide issues on the basis of evidence from witnesses, and can impose penalties, would be courts, but that social security appeal tribunals, which are more concerned with the administration of a particular scheme of government support, would not.

6.1.4 Penalties and remedies for contempt
The traditional method of punishment for contempt was imprisonment. For civil contempts this could mean imprisonment until the contempt was 'purged', i.e. until the contemnor apologised and agreed to abide by the order of the court. A stubborn individual could languish in prison indefinitely. The position is now governed by s. 14 of the CCA 1981.

Section 14 provides that committal to prison for contempt shall always be for a fixed period. The indefinite aspect of purging contempt has thus disappeared, though a contemnor might still shorten the fixed term by apologising and agreeing to comply with the court's wishes. The maximum term for a committal by a superior court, which for these purposes includes a county court (s. 14(4A)), is two years. The limit for an inferior court is one month. There is also a power to fine for contempt, which is in practice the more commonly used penalty. Here the inferior court is limited to a fine of £1,000; there is no limit for superior courts.

It is also possible to seek an injunction to restrain a threatened criminal contempt. This is a further distinction between contempt and other criminal offences. In general the courts are reluctant to issue an injunction to restrain the commission of a criminal offence, on the basis that if the threat of the criminal penalties for committing the offence is not enough to deter the potential criminal, issuing an injunction is likely to be futile. In relation to contempt, the wish to ensure the due administration of justice apparently outweighs this argument, and both interim and permanent injunctions can issue. For interim injunctions, pending the full hearing of the case, the standard rules for balancing the interests of the parties derived from *American Cyanamid Co.* v *Ethicon* [1975] AC 396 apply. The plaintiff has to show an arguable case; once this is done the court must decide whether the 'balance of convenience' is for or against the issue of an injunction.

6.2 CONTEMPT AND THE PRESS

6.2.1 Arguments for and against restriction
The principal argument for freedom of expression in relation to reports and discussion of court proceedings is similar to that which is used for freedom of information about the activities of government (see 5.2.3). The courts, as we have seen, are said to be exercising the 'judicial power of the State'. In a democracy the citizens of the State are entitled to as much information as possible about how the organs of the State operate. This applies as much to the judicial branch of government as to the executive or the legislature. This goes beyond the simple requirements of 'open justice', and the idea that justice should not only be done, but seen to be done. It is, of course, generally in the interests of the parties to a legal action, and in particular the defendant in criminal proceedings, that trials should not, unless absolutely necessary, be held behind closed doors. Protecting this interest could, however, be satisfied by allowing the public access to the trial, without necessarily allowing the wider publication of what has been witnessed. Such publication is necessary to allow citizens to form judgments about the operation of the judicial process *in general*, rather than in relation to any particular case. As Lord Atkin put it: 'Justice is not a cloistered virtue: she must be allowed to suffer the scrutiny and the respectful and outspoken comments of ordinary men' (*Ambard* v *Attorney-General for Trinidad and Tobago* [1936] AC 322).

The arguments for restricting reports of and comments on actual or potential legal proceedings are of two main types. One type is based on arguments of privacy or confidentiality; the other on the requirements of the proper administration of justice.

The privacy and confidentiality arguments apply in those situations where it is necessary to keep all, or some aspect of proceedings, secret in order to protect personal rights of someone involved in them. Obvious examples here are cases involving sexual offences, or children, where it is thought appropriate to protect the privacy of some of those involved. Such cases are dealt with not by means of contempt, but by specific statutory restrictions, e.g. Sexual Offences (Amendment) Act 1976, s. 4(1)(a), which prohibits the identification of the complainant in a rape case.

Trade secrets, or government secrets, may similarly be protected by a decision to sit *in camera*. The rights being protected here are those of confidentiality rather than privacy.

The second type of argument for restriction is based on the public interest in the due administration of justice. This, of course, encompasses the individual's right to a fair trial. It is here that the law of contempt comes into play to restrict what can be published. The courts are looking at the effect of the publication not on the personal rights, such as privacy, which a person has independent of the legal proceedings, but on rights which derive from the proceedings themselves. The aim of the law should be to restrict publications which will adversely affect the way in which the legal process operates, or which will make the administration of justice in a general sense more difficult, or impossible. Of course, in practice, the law does not only attack those publications which can be proved to have had such an effect. The desire to protect the administration of justice means that publications which run the *risk* of causing such prejudice are also likely to be caught. Much of the debate about the scope of the law of contempt relates to this issue. To what extent should the law intervene to restrict freedom of expression on the basis of a risk, rather than an actuality, of prejudice to the legal process?

Finally, even where there is a risk of prejudice, it may be argued that there are countervailing arguments of public interest which mean that publication should nevertheless be allowed. As we shall see at 6.2.2.4, English law has only fairly recently recognised the validity of such an argument, and its precise scope is still uncertain.

6.2.2   Contempt of Court Act 1981 ('the CCA')

As has been noted above, this Act was introduced primarily as a liberalising measure following criticism of the English law of contempt in the European Court of Human Rights. It also took account of some of the recommendations of the Phillimore Committee on Contempt of Court (Cmnd 5794, London: HMSO, 1974). Its main liberalising provisions are the reduction in the scope of the *actus reus* of contempt (see 6.2.2.3), the shortening of the period of time when legal proceedings are deemed to be *sub judice* (see 6.2.2.2), and the introduction of a defence of public interest (see 6.2.2.4).

6.2.2.1   The strict liability rule   Contempt of court was always unusual in that it was one of the few common law offences of strict liability (i.e. there was no need to prove any intention or recklessness against the defendant in respect of the consequences of the actions alleged to amount to contempt). The 1981 Act retained this feature of the law, but limited its scope. The relevant provisions are ss. 1 and 2(1). Section 1 states that the 'strict liability rule' means:

the rule of law whereby conduct may be treated as a contempt of court as tending to interfere with the course of justice in particular legal proceedings regardless of intent to do so.

The phrase 'regardless of intent to do so' is slightly ambiguous. It could mean 'where there is no intent to do so', or 'whether or not there is intent to do so'. The second meaning is probably what was intended, so that the strict liability rule could be used in a situation where contempt *was* intended. Recently, however, the tendency has been to prosecute such cases as common law contempt by virtue of s. 6(c) of the Act (see 6.2.3). If this becomes general then the strict liability rule may end up only being used where the contempt is clearly unintentional.

Section 2(1) states that the strict liability rule applies 'only in relation to publications'. This means that in relation to other types of behaviour which might amount to criminal contempt, e.g. disrupting court proceedings, the prosecution will now have to prove intent. A 'publication' is defined in the section as including any:

> speech, writing, broadcast or other communication in whatever form, which is addressed to the public at large or any section of the public.

Private letters, conversations, telephone calls, etc, are not within the scope of the strict liability rule. Whether there is publication to a section of the public will be a question of fact in each case. Circularisation of a publication amongst a small group of people, e.g. the members of a club, might escape. On the other hand in *Re Lonhro plc* [1989] 2 All ER 1100 (see 6.2.2.3), a copy of a newspaper was circulated to between 2,000 and 3,000 people on a mailing list. There seems no doubt that this would have been regarded as a publication even if the newspaper had not also been put on general sale.

Most of the CCA is concerned with the strict liability rule. Accordingly, where the prosecution is prepared to prove intent, the Act will become largely irrelevant.

6.2.2.2 Active proceedings One of the main criticisms of the pre-Act law, particularly from the point of view of journalists, was its uncertainty as to when it started to operate. At what point did a case become *sub judice* so that any comment about it, or reporting of it, ran the risk of being in contempt? The most commonly used phrase to describe the position was that proceedings had to be 'pending or imminent'. This did not, however, require any formal steps towards the initiation of proceedings to have been taken. In *R* v *Savundranayagan and Walker* [1968] 1 WLR 1761 Salmon LJ thought that contempt could operate in a situation in which 'it must surely have been obvious to everyone' that a person was about to be arrested. The Press objected that this left it in an impossible situation as regards the investigation of suspected wrong-doing at a time when the authorities have not yet decided to act. The CCA, adapting a recommendation of the Phillimore Committee, attempts to avoid this uncertainty through the concept of 'active proceedings'.

Section 2(3) says that the strict liability rule applies only to 'active proceedings'. These are then defined in sch. 1 to the Act.

Criminal proceedings become active once any formal step has been taken. This can be an arrest, the issue of a warrant for arrest or a summons, the service of an indictment, or the charging of a suspect. They cease to be active after an acquittal, or conviction and sentence, or if the proceedings are discontinued in any other way, e.g. release without charge (otherwise than on bail).

Civil proceedings become active when arrangements are made for the hearing, or, if no prior arrangements are made, when the hearing begins. In relation to High Court actions, the effective date will generally be when the case is set down for trial. Note that this 'setting down' does not involve the fixing of a specific date for the hearing. Civil proceedings in other courts, e.g. the county courts, will become active when a date for the hearing is set. In either case, the proceedings will remain active until the action is concluded, or withdrawn.

Appellate proceedings, either criminal or civil, are treated as separate actions. They become active from the time at which an intention to appeal is formally indicated, i.e. by giving notice of appeal, or applying for leave to appeal. There may thus be a gap between the trial and the launch of an appeal when a case is for a time 'inactive'. Appeal proceedings cease to be active once concluded. If, however, the appeal court refers the case back to the lower court, proceedings in the lower court at once become active again.

Although the position under the CCA is a great improvement on the common law as far as certainty is concerned, journalists and editors may still need to take care, particularly in relation to criminal proceedings. The onus will be on them to make appropriate checks to make sure that no arrest warrant has been issued, and that no one has been charged in relation to a case. If, for example, a suspect is being questioned at a police station, but has not been arrested or charged, a newspaper may decide to publish a story about the case. If between the paper being printed, and its distribution around the country, a charge is made, the proceedings will become active, and the publication potentially liable for contempt. The newspaper may then only escape liability if it is possible to rely on the defence of innocent publication under s. 3, which is discussed at 6.2.2.5.

6.2.2.3 Actus reus of contempt A publication will not amount to contempt under the strict liability rule simply because it refers or relates to active proceedings. It must also run the risk of affecting those proceedings. The test is set out in s. 2(2) of the Act:

> The strict liability rule applies only to a publication which creates a substantial risk that the course of justice in the proceedings in question will be seriously impeded or prejudiced.

There are three elements of this definition which require discussion: the nature of a 'substantial risk'; the requirement that the risk relates to 'the proceedings in question'; and the type of publication which will give rise to a risk of serious impediment, or prejudice.

A 'substantial' risk does not mean a 'very big risk': *Attorney-General* v *English* [1983] 1 AC 116. It means a risk that is not remote. This was discussed in *Attorney-General* v *News Group Newspapers* [1986] 2 All ER 833. The England cricketer Ian Botham had brought an action for libel against a newspaper. At a time when this action was set down for trial, and thus 'active', he discovered that another newspaper was intending to publish similar defamatory statements. The Attorney-General sought an injunction to restrain this publication on the basis that it amounted to contempt, in that it would prejudice Botham's original libel action. The trial judge granted the injunction, but it was lifted by the Court of Appeal. The Court ruled that 'substantial' related to the proximity of the risk. A risk might be remote in place or time. For example an article published in a local newspaper in Devon would be unlikely to affect a trial taking place in Newcastle, many hundreds of miles away. In Botham's case the remoteness related to time. Although the case had been set down for trial, it was clear that it was not likely to take place for at least another ten months, by which time, as Sir John Donaldson MR commented 'many wickets will have fallen, not to mention much water having flowed under many bridges, all of which would blunt any impact of the publication'.

The risk must relate to the 'proceedings in question' (s. 2(2)). This refers back to the definition of the strict liability rule in s. 1, which says that it applies to interference with 'particular legal proceedings'. In other words, the strict liability rule, in contrast to the position under the common law (see 6.2.3), does not apply to publications which might have an adverse affect on the administration of justice in general, rather than in a particular case. For example, criticising judges for lack of impartiality could not be contempt under the strict liability rule, though it might on other grounds (see 6.2.5). The same would be true of a publication commenting on a completed case which might discourage potential witnesses from coming forward in future cases.

Thirdly, the risk must create a substantial risk of *serious impediment or prejudice*. The qualification 'serious', like the adjective 'substantial', was added to the common law test by the CCA. It indicates that the courts should not be concerned with trivial or technical contempts. Only when the outcome of a legal action is likely to be affected should contempt be found. What kind of publication is likely to have that effect? There are a number of categories:

  (a)   publications which prejudge the outcome of a case;
  (b)   publications which may prejudice a jury against a party;
  (c)   publications which criticise a party to a legal action;
  (d)   publications which pre-empt the legal rights of parties to an action.

In some situations a publication may have more than one of the above effects.

The risk from prejudgment will only arise where the case is to be heard by magistrates, or a jury. Judges are said to be able to ignore such publications, and are thus not likely to be prejudiced by them. Prejudging a civil action will therefore rarely amount to contempt under the strict liability rule. This is one of the changes introduced by the CCA. In *Attorney-General* v *Times Newspapers* [1974] AC 273 ('the thalidomide case') the House of Lords had held that prejudging a civil action could be contempt, since 'trial by newspaper' had an adverse effect on the administration of justice generally, irrespective of its effect on the particular case. Following criticism of this decision by the European Court of Human Rights (see 6.4), the CCA restricted strict liability contempt to the situation where particular proceedings are likely to be affected. In relation to criminal proceedings, any assumption of guilt on the part of the accused will almost certainly be regarded as contemptuous. In the pre-CCA case of *R v Bolam* (1949) 93 SJ 220, the *Daily Mirror* described the defendant in a murder trial as a 'vampire' and stated that he had committed other murders. This was regarded as a very serious contempt, warranting the committal of the editor to prison. There is no doubt that it would also be contempt under the strict liability rule. The Press needs to be particularly careful where there has been a well-publicised manhunt, culminating in an arrest. In 1980 the arrest of Peter Sutcliffe led to statements, encouraged by a police Press conference, that the so-called 'Yorkshire Ripper', who had murdered a number of women, had been caught. Sutcliffe subsequently confessed, so there was no actual prejudice to his trial, but the risk of prejudice was surely such that the Attorney-General could have obtained convictions if he had been prepared to act. (See G. Robertson, *Freedom, the Individual and the Law*, 6th edn, Harmondsworth: Penguin, 1989, p. 287.) More recently the Court of Appeal quashed the conviction of two sisters who had been convicted of murder, in part becuase of 'unremitting, extensive, sensational, inaccurate and misleading' press reporting at the time of the trial: *R v Taylor (Michelle), The Times*, 15 June 1993.

Prejudicing a jury against a defendant in criminal proceedings can occur without there necessarily being an implication of guilt. Revealing details of the defendant's past life may be enough. In the pre-CCA case of *R v Thompson Newspapers Ltd, ex parte Attorney-General* [1968] 1 All ER 268, it was held to be contempt to refer to the defendant in a trial for incitement to racial hatred, as a former 'brothel-keeper, procurer and property racketeer'. It may be, however, that the wording of s. 2(2) has relaxed the law in this area. In *Attorney-General v Times Newspapers Ltd, The Times*, 12 February 1983 ('the Fagan case'), actions for contempt were brought against a number of newspapers commenting on the prosecution of Michael Fagan who was accused of, among other things, burglary in Buckingham Palace. Descriptions of him as a drug addict, a glib liar, and a potential suicide, were held not to amount to contempt. Lord Lane commented that 'jurors were to be credited with more independence of mind than was sometimes suggested'. It may well be that the new qualifications of 'substantial' and 'serious' contributed to this decision. In *Attorney-General v Guardian Newspapers Ltd* [1992] 3 All ER 39, the Divisional Court held that a statement that a defendant in criminal proceedings was awaiting trial on other charges did not *necessarily* create a substantial risk of serious prejudice. The way in which the information had been presented in this case (the defendant was one of a group, and not named) meant that the risk of a juror being affected by it was insignificant.

Note that prejudice against a party can affect the prosecution as well as the defence. One of the newspapers involved in the Fagan case had stated that the prosecution had dropped a charge which was in fact being pursued. This could clearly have prejudiced the jury if the report had led them to think that the prosecution was so unsure of its case that it had at one point abandoned the charge all together.

The jury must also be protected against emotional reporting which might influence its attitude towards one of the parties. In 1981, soon after the CCA came into force, a trial took place in Leicester of Dr Leonard Arthur, who was accused of the attempted murder of a Down's syndrome baby (John Pearson) in his care. The prosecution alleged that the regime which the doctor had prescribed had hastened the baby's death. While the trial was in progress the *Sunday Express* published an article written by its editor, Sir John Junor. It read as follows (*The Times*, 17 November 1981):

> In the three grim days of his short, sad life, mongol baby John Pearson was given no nourishment. His parents had rejected him. So instead of being fed he was drugged. Even then, we know he fought tenaciously for life. Without a chance of success. And so he died. Unloved, unwanted. I blame no one. I condemn no one. And I make no comment on the case in Leicester Crown Court.

Although there was no direct suggestion of guilt, nor any comment on Dr Arthur himself, the Divisional Court had no doubt that this constituted contempt under the CCA. Watkins LJ thought that 'in this trial, more than most, it was essential that extraneous, irrelevant, and emotional influences should not reach the minds of jurors, lest they influenced the jury improperly, and denied Dr Arthur a fair trial'. Sir John Junor was fined £1,000, and Express Newspapers £10,000.

The third type of prejudice is where the publication criticises one of the parties to a legal action. This can operate in relation to either civil or criminal proceedings, and may be prejudicial in two ways. First it may deter potential witnesses from coming forward. For example, statements that a prosecution ought not to have been brought, or that a particular defence is morally unsupportable (though technically available), might have the effect of making potential witnesses for the prosecution or defence respectively reluctant to give evidence. Secondly, it may discourage the parties themselves from pursuing their legal rights. In this form it has been found more commonly in relation to civil proceedings. In *Vine Products* v *Green* [1966] Ch 484, Buckley J recognised that comment on a pending action could amount to contempt if it was:

> likely in some way or other to bring pressure to bear upon one or other of the parties to the action, so as to prevent that party from prosecuting or from defending the action, or encourage that party to submit to terms of compromise which he otherwise might not have been prepared to entertain, or influence him in some other way in his conduct in the action, which he ought to be free to prosecute or to defend, as he is advised, without being subject to such pressure.

This type of contempt was considered in detail in *Attorney-General* v *Times Newspapers Ltd* [1974] AC 273 (the 'thalidomide case'). The distributors of the drug thalidomide, which it was alleged caused the birth of malformed babies, were being sued for negligence by some of the parents of these babies. The pre-trial proceedings were very drawn out, and the *Sunday Times* decided to campaign on behalf of the plaintiffs. They published an article which was severely critical of the defendants, Distillers. It said that the thalidomide children shamed Distillers, and criticised them for relying on the strict letter of the law. Whatever the position as regards negligence, the *Sunday Times* asserted that the company could afford a much more generous offer of compensation than it had so far been prepared to make.

The House of Lords was unanimous that in some circumstances, criticism of parties could amount to contempt. Their Lordships were not in agreement, however, as to what type of criticism would have this effect, nor as to how the law should apply to the *Sunday Times* article. In relation to publications (as opposed to private pressure) the distinction was drawn between fair and temperate criticism, and holding a party up to public obloquy. The former was permissible, the latter contempt. To this extent the quotation from Buckley J given above was probably too widely stated. As Lord Reid pointed out, it would surely not be contemptuous to urge Shylock in Shakespeare's *Merchant of Venice* not to insist on his pound of flesh. The difficulty in drawing the line, however, is shown by the fact that three of their Lordships (Reid, Cross and Morris) felt that the *Sunday Times* was on the right side of it, whereas Lords Diplock and Simon felt that the article constituted contempt.

The final way in which the *actus reus* of contempt may be committed under the strict liability rule is if the publication pre-empts the rights of one of the parties to a legal action. This category of contempt arose out the litigation resulting from the British government's attempts to ban the publication of the book *Spycatcher* (see chapter 5, 5.6.2). It was first recognised by the Court of Appeal in *Attorney-General* v *Times Newspapers Ltd* [1987] 3 All ER 276 ('the *Independent* case'). The Attorney-General had obtained interlocutory injunctions against two newspapers, the *Observer* and the *Guardian*, restraining them from publishing information or extracts drawn from *Spycatcher*. While these injunctions were still in force, the *Independent*, and two other newspapers, published extracts and summaries from the book. The Attorney-General brought an action for contempt. In a preliminary action to determine whether contempt could occur in such a situation, the Court of Appeal held that it could, a view that was subsequently confirmed by the House of Lords (*Attorney-General* v *Times Newspapers Ltd* [1991] 2 All ER 398). This was not because the injunctions against the *Observer* and the *Guardian* had any direct effect on other newspapers: they did not. The potential liability of the *Independent* was based not on breach of an injunction, which would have been civil contempt, but on interference with legal proceedings, i.e. criminal contempt.

The reason for this was that the action against the *Observer* and the *Sunday Times* was for breach of confidence. The material contained in *Spycatcher* had been obtained in circumstances alleged to imply confidentiality, and the newspapers were breaking that confidence by their threatened publication. The *Independent*, by revealing the information which was said to be confidential, was prejudicing the Attorney-General's chance of success against the *Observer* and the *Sunday Times*. Once confidential material has been put into the public domain, even as a result of a wrongful action, its quality of confidence is lost, and the courts will not intervene to restrain further publication. The *Independent* had put some of the information into the public domain, and thus prejudiced the Attorney-General's action. The only remaining problem was that the proceedings against the *Observer* and the *Sunday Times* were not 'active' at the time when the *Independent*'s article was published. The Attorney-General had to argue therefore that the editor of the *Independent* had intentionally committed the contempt, and was liable at common law. This aspect of the case is discussed at 6.2.3.

The approach taken in the *Independent* case was followed in *Attorney-General v Observer Ltd* [1988] 1 All ER 385 (which concerned the question of whether a library could supply a copy of *Spycatcher* without being in contempt), and discussed further in *Re Lonrho plc* [1989] 2 All ER 1100. In this case the Secretary of State for Trade had decided not to publish a report by Department of Trade inspectors into a successful take-over bid for Harrods, the London department store, pending consideration of the case by the Director of Public Prosecutions and the Serious Fraud Office. He also decided not to refer the case to the Monopolies and Mergers Commission. Lonrho, who had been an unsuccessful bidder for Harrods, sought judicial review of these decisions. The application succeeded at first instance, but was overturned on appeal. While a further appeal to the House of Lords was pending, Lonrho received a copy of the inspectors' report, and arranged for its publication in a special edition of the *Observer* (which Lonrho owned). Some 200,000 copies were distributed, and some were sent to members of the House of Lords due to hear the appeal. The Attorney-General brought proceedings for contempt, which were heard by a special panel of the House of Lords, exercising original, rather than appellate jurisdiction.

The House held that the possible grounds for contempt were prejudgment and pre-emption. On prejudgment, the House took the view that in the light of the European Court of Human Rights decision in the *Sunday Times* thalidomide case (see 6.4), and the CCA, prejudgment on its own could not amount to contempt. It would only do so if it was likely to have an effect on the trial. Here there were no witnesses or jury to affect, and it was unlikely that the Secretary of State would be influenced in pursuing his appeal. That left pre-emption as the only possible type of contempt. Here the circumstances were superficially similar to the *Independent* case, in that information which the government wished to keep secret had been revealed. In this case, however, there was no injunction restraining publication, and the central issue was not 'confidentiality', but whether the Secretary of State had acted lawfully in deferring publication. There might be other remedies for what had been done, e.g. breach of copyright, but the publication did not constitute contempt.

The result of the House of Lords' decision in this case is that it seems likely that the pre-emption category of contempt will be limited to cases concerning confidentiality. In other cases, different remedies will probably be available. A useful comparison was drawn in the Court of Appeal in the *Independent* case ([1987] 3 All ER 277), with defamation. If an interim injunction is issued in a defamation action against one publisher, and a third party then publishes the same libel, there is no contempt. The plaintiff can sue the third party, and the action against the original defendant is in no way compromised. It is only where, as with breach of confidence, the action of the third party has the effect of destroying what is being protected by the injunction, and rendering the plaintiff's rights nugatory, that contempt has a role to play.

6.2.2.4 Defence of public interest One of the criticisms of the English law of contempt which was made by the European Court of Human Rights in the *Sunday Times* thalidomide case was that it paid too little attention to competing public interests, which might go in favour of publication. The government responded by including such a defence in s. 5 of the CCA. This is entitled 'Discussion of public affairs':

> A publication made as or as part of a discussion in good faith of public affairs or other matters of general public interest is not to be treated as a contempt of court under the strict liability rule if the risk of impediment or prejudice to particular legal proceedings is merely incidental to the discussion.

The section does not strictly speaking operate as a defence, in that the burden of proof is on the prosecution: *Attorney-General* v *English* [1983] 1 AC 116. In other words, once the defence has raised the issue of public interest it is up to the prosecution to try to prove that the publication was not in good faith, did not relate to public affairs or other matters of public interest, or that the risk of prejudice was not merely incidental to the discussion.

The operation of s. 5 has been discussed in several cases. The most important of these is the House of Lords decision in *Attorney-General* v *English*. This case, like the *Sunday Express* case discussed at 6.2.2.3, was concerned with the trial of Dr Leonard Arthur on a charge of attempted murder of a Down's syndrome baby. On the third day of the trial the *Daily Mail* published an article by Malcolm Muggeridge in support of Mrs Marilyn Carr, a 'pro-life' candidate in a parliamentary election. Mrs Carr had been born without arms, but had managed to lead a very normal life despite this handicap. The article asserted that if a baby like Mrs Carr was born today 'someone would surely recommend letting her die of starvation, or otherwise disposing of her'. Later in the article it was also suggested that 'mongoloid' (i.e. Down's syndrome) babies would be destroyed 'before or after birth'. The subject-matter of the article clearly related very closely to the allegations made against Dr Arthur. The House of Lords had no doubt that it created a substantial risk of serious prejudice under s. 2(2). Nevertheless, the House felt that it avoided being in contempt because it was protected by s. 5. To write an article supporting Mrs Carr without referring to the allegations about current medical practice would, as Lord Diplock put it, depict Mrs Carr as 'tilting at imaginary windmills'.

In the course of finding that the *Daily Mail* was not in contempt, the House made various other comments on s. 5. First, the requirement that the risk of prejudice is 'merely incidental' does not mean that the comments have to be necessary to the discussion. It does not matter that other words or phrases could have been used, as long as the risk is no more than an incidental consequence of expounding the main theme. Secondly, it was regarded as important that the article made no reference to the Arthur trial (indeed Malcolm Muggeridge claimed to be unaware that the trial was taking place). A contrast was drawn by Lord Diplock with the *Sunday Times* thalidomide case, where the whole point of the articles was to put pressure on Distillers. The suggestion seems to be that s. 5 would not have protected the *Sunday Times*. This is ironic in that one of the main reasons for including s. 5 was to meet the criticisms of the approach in the thalidomide case by the European Court of Human Rights.

In at least one later case, the courts have been prepared to allow s. 5 to be used even where a particular case is referred to. In *Attorney-General* v *Times Newspapers, The Times*, 12 February 1983 ('the Fagan case'), the *Mail on Sunday* had published an article suggesting that there had been a homosexual liaison between Fagan and the Queen's police bodyguard. The Divisional Court thought that could clearly create a risk of prejudice within s. 2(2). The issue of the safety and security of the Queen was, however, a matter of serious public concern, and the court was prepared to regard the risk of prejudice as merely incidental to the discussion of this matter.

In *Attorney-General* v *Guardian Newspapers* [1992] 3 All ER 38, the Divisional Court held, *obiter*, that in the context of a discussion about the propensity of judges to impose reporting restrictions in fraud trials (which was clearly a matter of public interest), a possibly prejudicial reference to a particular case where reporting had been restricted because the accused was awaiting trial on other charges, was merely incidental to the discussion.

The precise scope of s. 5 is still uncertain. The decision of the House of Lords in *Attorney-General* v *English* (1983) is the leading authority, but seems to envisage a fairly restricted role for the defence. The Divisional Court's approach in the Fagan case appears more liberal, but the extent to which other courts feel inhibited by the comments in the *English* case in using the section remains to be seen.

6.2.2.5 Other defences The CCA provides three other defences under the strict liability rule, in ss. 3 and 4. These are innocent publication (s. 3(1)), innocent distribution (s. 3(2)), and contemporary reports of proceedings (s. 4(1)).

The defences in s. 3 are substantial re-enactments of provisions previously contained in the Administration of Justice Act 1960, s. 11. They are true defences, in that the burden of proof is specifically stated to be on the defence (s. 3(3)).

Section 3(3) protects the innocent publisher of contemptuous material, who does not know, and has no reason to suspect, that proceedings are active at the time of the publication. This might protect the editor in the situation referred to in 6.2.2.2, where a charge takes place between the finalising of a story and its appearance on the streets. The editor will have to show, however, that all reasonable care has been taken. This might mean, for example, that the editor who knows that someone is helping the police with their inquiries, should check with the police as to the likelihood of a charge being made, before proceeding with a story on the case.

The defence of innocent distribution under s. 3(2) is aimed at protecting people like newsagents, who are 'publishers' of the newspapers, magazines, etc. which they sell, and so potentially liable under the strict liability rule if any of those publications contain prejudicial material. The section provides a defence if it can be proved that at the time of the distribution the distributor did not know, and had no reason to suspect, that the publication contained anything which would fall foul of the strict liability rule. As with s. 3(1), it must be shown that all reasonable care has been taken.

The third defence, in s. 4(1), is a new one. It removes from the scope of the strict liability rule fair and accurate reports of legal proceedings held in public, provided that they are published contemporaneously and in good faith. The requirement of contemporaneity means, for example, that a report of a case heard a year previously which is published at a time when someone involved in the case is again before the courts would not be protected by s. 4(1).

The section covers all proceedings held in public, so in theory this would allow the reporting of matters discussed in open court, but in the absence of the jury (such as an argument as to the admissibility of evidence). Such a publication would undoubtedly have been treated as contempt prior to the Act (cf *R* v *Evening Standard Co. Ltd* [1954] 1 All ER 1026). Now it will not be so, unless it can be said that the publication was not 'in good faith'. It seems likely that a court would expect an experienced reporter or editor to recognise the prejudicial nature of such a publication, and so regard such action as not in good faith. In addition, the court does have the power under s. 4(2) to issue a specific order postponing potentially prejudicial reports of proceedings. This is discussed further below at 6.2.4.

6.2.3 Common law contempt

The application of the common law of contempt to publications is preserved by s. 6(c). This states that nothing in ss. 1 to 5 of the CCA 'restricts liability for contempt of court in respect of conduct intended to impede or prejudice the administration of justice'. In other words, if the prosecution can prove intent then the question is whether the publication would have been contemptuous if it were not for the provisions of the CCA. If the answer is yes, then the provisions relating to the strict liability rule become irrelevant.

The significance of this was first recognised in *Attorney-General* v *Times Newspapers Ltd* [1991] 2 All ER 398 (the *Independent* case; see 6.2.2.3). The Court of Appeal was satisfied that the publication was prejudicial because it pre-empted the Attorney-General's action for breach of confidence against the *Observer* and *Guardian*; but there were no proceedings in that action which were 'active' within sch. 1. Nevertheless the Court of Appeal said that the *Independent* could still be liable if the editor could be said to have had an intention to prejudice. This meant a specific intention, not simply reckless-ness. On the other hand, the Court of Appeal said that intention must be approached here in the same way as in other areas of the criminal law. On the basis of the homicide cases of *R* v *Moloney* [1985] 1 All ER 1025, and *R* v *Nedrick* [1986] 3 All ER 1, intention could be (but did not have to be) inferred if the editor could be shown to have foreseen the prejudice as a virtual certainty as a result of the publication. On this basis the case was sent back to the trial judge, who found the editor of the *Independent* guilty of contempt (*In re Attorney-General* v *The Observer Ltd and Guardian Newspapers Ltd, The Times*, 9 May 1989). The editor's evidence had shown that although he did not desire to be in contempt, he was aware that the publication would do precisely what the court had said should not be done, and that a person should not knowingly frustrate the purpose of the court because this would interfere with the administration of justice.

Intention does not require that it should be the publisher's purpose or desire to cause prejudice. In *Attorney-General* v *Observer Ltd* [1988] 1 All ER 385, it was ruled, following the *Independent* case, that it would be contempt under the common law for a library to stock a copy of *Spycatcher*.

The common law has subsequently been relied on where there was a risk of prejudice to a criminal trial. In *Attorney-General* v *News Group Newspapers* [1988] 2 All ER 906, the *Sun* had taken up the case of an eight year old alleged to have been raped by a doctor, supporting both financially and through its columns a private prosecution (which in fact resulted in the doctor's acquittal). Before these proceedings became active the *Sun* published on successive days articles attacking the doctor in very emotive language. His photograph was printed on the front page. Watkins LJ could not accept that an experienced editor 'could have failed to have foreseen that the material which he published . . . would incur a real risk of prejudicing the fairness of a trial of Dr. B'. On this basis the editor of the *Sun* was guilty of contempt under the common law.

These cases dealt with the role of the common law when there are no active proceedings. It is unclear whether proceedings must nevertheless be 'pending or imminent' (the old common law test for strict liability contempts). Watkins LJ in the *Sun* case, doubted whether it was necessary, and a two-judge Divisional Court split on the issue in *Attorney-General* v *Sport Newspapers* [1992] 1 All ER 503.

Intentional contempt can operate alongside strict liability contempt. This possibility was recognised by the House of Lords in *Re Lonrho* [1990] 2 AC 154, though it was not applied as the House did not think there was any contempt at all. In *Attorney-General* v *Hislop* [1991] 1 QB 514, the Court of Appeal said that articles published by the magazine *Private Eye* were intended to put improper pressure on Mrs Sonia Sutcliffe (the wife of the 'Yorkshire Ripper') to discontinue a libel action against the magazine. The libel proceedings were active, and the articles therefore constituted contempt under both the common law, and the strict liability rule.

This increase in the use of common law contempt, particularly in situations where the strict liability rule can also apply, is worrying. One of the important reforms contained in the CCA was the introduction of the defences under ss. 4 and 5. Both of these only operate under the strict liability rule. If the Attorney-General chooses to use the common law instead, as in *Attorney-General v Hislop*, then these defences are unavailable. The danger of this happening is increased by the broad definition of 'intention', as capable of being inferred from 'foresight'. Although this definition is in line with that operating in other areas of criminal law, it is submitted that there is a case here (given that parliament has specifically provided for strict liability in certain circumstances) for limiting intention to 'purpose'. This would be in line with the restriction of the availability of the defences to the situation where the publisher acts in good faith. A deliberate attempt to affect the outcome of proceedings by improper means cannot be regarded as being published 'in good faith'. On the other hand, the fact that an editor has foreseen a possible risk of prejudice should not automatically preclude reliance on s. 5 if the matter is one of public concern.

The wide use of the common law also threatens another advantage of the CCA, i.e. the certainty introduced to the *sub judice* rule by the concept of 'active' proceedings. Indeed, if the *obiter* suggestions in *Attorney-General v News Group Newspapers* [1988] 2 All ER 906 (the *Sun* case), and *Attorney-General v Sport Newspapers* [1992] 1 All ER 503 that proceedings need not even be 'imminent' are taken up, the law will run the risk of being even more uncertain than prior to the CCA.

6.2.4   Disobeying court rulings

As noted at the start of this chapter, the main restrictions on publications arise out of criminal contempts, which are likely to have an effect on the outcome of proceedings. The CCA also recognises two situations where a publication may amount to civil contempt, in that it involves disobedience of a court order.

6.2.4.1   Section 4(2): Reports of proceedings   We have seen that under

s. 4(1) of the CCA, contemporaneous reports of legal proceedings may generally be published without fear of contempt. Under s. 4(2) the court has a power in certain circumstances to order the postponement of the publication of such reports. The grounds for postponement are that the report would create a substantial risk to the administration of justice in the proceedings which are the subject of the report, or to other proceedings pending or imminent. Note that the power is only to postpone, not to impose a permanent ban.

The circumstances in which it is envisaged that this power might need to be used is where, for example, evidence has been heard in the absence of the jury, in order to decide on its admissibility, or where there are other proceedings pending which involve one of the parties to the current proceedings, and which might be adversely affected by reports of them.

This new power was seized on with some avidity by courts at all levels, and in 1983 a Practice Note was issued to try to curb what was seen as an over-use of the section. The requirements laid down by the Lord Chief Justice were:

(a)   the order should be put into writing by the judge or the clerk of the court;

(b) it should be in precise terms, indicating its scope;

(c) it should state the time at which it will cease to have effect;

(d) it should state the specific purpose of making the order.

A 'blanket order' at the start of the trial postponing all reporting should not generally be made. The court should limit the scope of the order to what is necessary to prevent prejudice: *R v Horsham Justices, ex parte Farquharson* [1982] QB 762.

Where a valid order is made, any breach of it will amount to contempt. In the *Horsham Justices* case, Lord Denning argued that breach of a s. 4 order should only constitute contempt if it created a risk of prejudice. The majority of the Court of Appeal, however, ruled that the breach was in itself contempt, irrespective of any effects of the publication, and this must be regarded as representing the current position. It was accepted as being so by Brooke J in *Attorney-General v Guardian Newspapers* [1992] 3 All ER 38 (at p. 48), although this case also made it clear that criticising the making of a s. 4(2) order, rather than breaking its tems, cannot in itself be regarded as contempt.

Despite the attempts by the Attorney-General and the Lord Chief Justice to indicate that s. 4 orders should be made with caution, they continue to cause problems for the Press and broadcasters. In *Re Central Independent Television plc* [1991] 1 All ER 347, the judge made an order restricting reporting so that the jury who had to spend the night in a hotel considering their verdict, would be able to watch television and listen to the radio. The Court of Appeal ruled that this was not an appropriate use of the power. The objective of the order could have been achieved by restricting the jurors' access to the broadcasts, and it was not therefore necessary in the interests of the administration of justice. Similarly, in *Ex parte Telegraph plc* [1993] 2 All ER 971 Lord Taylor emphasised the careful nature of the balance to be made between the 'competing public considerations of ensuring a fair trial and of open justice' (at p. 976), and that restrictions should only be imposed where 'necessary'. This did not simply mean asking whether the imposition of restrictions was the only way to avoid the risk, but also whether the risk was one which was sufficiently serious for it to be necessary in the interests of justice to avoid it. Applying that approach, the Court of Appeal reduced the scope of the judge's order so that it applied simply to the identities of the accused, and not to any other material. The issue of postponing the reporting of any proceedings which took place in the absence of the jury should be considered if and when it arose.

6.2.4.2 Section 11: matters not disclosed in court

Section 4 deals with the restriction of the reporting of matters disclosed in court. Section 11 recognises a power in certain situations to forbid the publication of matters which were *not* disclosed in the course of a trial. The section says that where a court has the power to allow information to be withheld from the public during the course of proceedings, and exercises that power, then it may also give directions prohibiting the publication of that information outside the court. The section does not, however, give any guidance as to when the court has the power to keep things secret within the court. This falls to be determined by the common law. Such a power has been recognised in relation to blackmail trials (*R* v *Socialist Worker* [1975] QB 637), and trials involving national security issues (*Attorney-General* v *Leveller Magazine* [1979] 1 All ER 745), but the categories are presumably not closed.

In *R* v *Socialist Worker* witnesses in a blackmail trial were allowed to be identified as 'Mr X' and 'Mr Y'. The judge indicated that they were not to be identified in any publication outside the court. The *Socialist Worker* purported to identify the witnesses. This was held to amount to contempt under the common law in that it would deter potential blackmail victims from giving evidence in the future, and in any case flouted the authority of the court. It would now constitute contempt as a breach of a s. 11 direction. It is unclear whether it would *automatically* do so in the same way as a breach of s. 4. In *Attorney-General* v *Leveller* a failure to comply with a direction not to disclose the name of an army officer identified in court as simply 'Colonel B', was held by the House of Lords not to constitute contempt, since the direction was made before the colonel gave evidence, and that evidence had made his identity obvious. The court had not re-issued the direction after this evidence had been given, and there was therefore no contempt in publishing the colonel's real name. It is to be hoped that the courts would adopt the same approach to a breach of a s. 11 direction.

A direction under s. 11, if valid, may be permanent in its effect, and so there is no need to indicate how long it is to last. In all other respects, however, the issue of the direction should follow the requirements of the 1983 Practice Note, outlined at 6.2.4.1 in relation to s. 4.

6.2.4.3 Challenging orders under ss. 4(2) and 11   The method of challenging an order under either s. 4 or s. 11 will depend on the court issuing it. If it is made by magistrates, or some other inferior court which is subject to the jurisdiction of the High Court, the appropriate method of challenge is by judicial review. In *R* v *Arundel Justices, ex parte Westminster Press* [1985] 2 All ER 390, for example, a s. 11 direction issued by magistrates was held to be *ultra vires*, in that it related to information which had been disclosed in the proceedings. If, however, the order is issued during a trial on indictment, judicial review will not be available, because the High Court has no jurisdiction over the Crown Court: *R* v *Central Criminal Court, ex parte Crook, The Times*, 8 November 1984. There was for a time, therefore, no way of challenging an order issued by a Crown Court judge. Now, however, s. 159 of the Criminal Justice Act 1988, gives a right of appeal to the Court of Appeal in this situation.

6.2.5   Criticising the courts
In certain situations it may amount to contempt to criticise a court. This is sometimes referred to as 'scandalising the court'. The leading authority on it is the case of *R* v *Gray* [1900] 2 QB 36. At the conclusion of an obscenity trial, Gray published an article in which he referred to the judge, Darling J, as 'an impudent little man in horsehair, a microcosm of conceit and emptyheadedness'. He also commented that (following on from the judge's warnings to the

Press about its reporting of the trial) the judge 'would do well to master the duties of his own profession before undertaking the regulation of another'. The Divisional Court held that this amounted to contempt. Lord Russell made the distinction between 'reasonable argument and expostulation' criticising a judicial act as contrary to law or the public good, and 'scurrilous personal abuse of a judge as a judge'. The former was not contempt; the latter clearly was. Gray's article fell within this category.

Lord Russell's analysis has been consistently applied, generally in favour of the publisher: *Ambard* v *Attorney-General for Trinidad and Tobago* [1936] AC 322; *R* v *Metropolitan Police Commissioner, ex parte Blackburn (No 2)* [1968] 2 QB 150. Recently the Privy Council has confirmed that even 'scurrilous abuse' of a judge will not amount to contempt unless it relates to the judge's judicial role. A judge as chairman of a public inquiry, for example, is not protected in this way: *Badry* v *DPP of Mauritius* [1983] 2 AC 297.

The fairly relaxed approach of the courts to criticisms of them means that this head of contempt is of little practical importance nowadays (cf. C. Walker, 'Scandalising in the Eighties', (1985) 101 *LQR* 359).

6.2.6 Disclosing jury secrets

Section 8 of the CCA makes it a contempt to 'obtain, disclose or solicit' any information relating to what has happened during a jury's deliberations. It was confirmed by the Divisional Court in *Attorney-General* v *Associated Newspapers* [1993] 2 All ER 535, that 'disclose' should be interpreted as covering any type of publication, whether by a juror to his friend or neighbour, or to the world in a national newspaper. It was irrelevant whether the information was obtained direct from the jury member, or indirectly via a third party.

This provision was added at a late stage in the passage of the CCA through parliament, and is very draconian in its effect. The common law only made such disclosures an offence where they had an adverse effect on the administration of justice, either in the case in question, or generally: *Attorney-General* v *New Statesman* [1981] QB 1. Section 8 is absolute in its effect; there are no exceptions to it. Even information required for research into the ways in which juries operate cannot lawfully be obtained, even if it is to be used simply to compile statistical information.

There seems little or no justification for the breadth of this provision, and it has been the subject of much criticism. The Royal Commission on Criminal Justice has recommended that it should be amended to enable research to be conducted into juries' reasons for their verdicts (*Report*, Cm 2263, 1993, chapter 11, para. 8).

6.2.7 Protecting sources

Journalists will generally claim that it is necessary for the proper fulfilment of their role that they are allowed to keep their sources secret. The argument is that they will not get information, for example, about abuses of power within government, or dubious business practices, unless insiders feel able to reveal what is going on without the risk of their identity being disclosed. Journalists will, however, run the risk of being in contempt, if they refuse to reveal the

name of a source in legal proceedings. The need to provide journalists with
some protection has long been recognised, but this is now given statutory form
in s. 10 of the CCA.

The section allows a person to refuse to disclose 'the source of information
contained in a publication for which he is responsible', unless it is 'necessary
in the interests of justice or national security, or for the prevention of disorder
or crime'.

The precise scope of the section has been considered in a number of cases
since the Act. Some of the decisions have taken a broad view as to its
application. The overall effect, however, has been to narrow down the number
of situations in which the journalist or publisher will be protected.

Looking first at the positive side, it was held in *Secretary of State for Defence*
v *Guardian Newspapers* [1985] AC 339, that the section applied to an indirect
disclosure of a source. The Secretary of State had brought an action to recover
a document from the *Guardian*, which had been leaked from his department.
The *Guardian* resisted this action, although the document was clearly the
property of the Ministry of Defence, on the basis that markings on it would
probably enable the Ministry to identify the source of the leak. The House of
Lords agreed that, although in this case even the *Guardian* itself was unaware
of the identity of its informant, it was entitled to plead s. 10 to avoid indirectly
disclosing this information. As we will see, however, the House felt that on the
facts the Secretary of State was able to bring his claim within one of the
exceptions to the section.

The section requires the disclosure to be 'necessary' if one of the exceptions
is to apply. In *Maxwell* v *Pressdram* [1987] 1 All ER 656 the Court of Appeal
emphasised that this did not mean 'important' or 'relevant'. In this case the
information was sought in order to show that the defendants in a libel action
had made false statements either recklessly or knowingly, and had persisted in
a defence of 'justification' simply to avoid an interim injunction. The Court of
Appeal thought that these matters could adequately be dealt with by the trial
judge in his direction to the jury as to the availability of aggravated or
exemplary damages, and that disclosure was therefore not necessary.

The rest of the reported decisions on s. 10 go in favour of disclosure. First,
in *Secretary of State for Defence* v *Guardian Newspapers* (1985) the House of
Lords held that the interests of national security could prevail even if it was
agreed that the leaked document did not prejudice it. It was enough that a civil
servant in the Ministry of Defence might have leaked a document for the
national security issue to be raised.

Secondly, in *Re an Inquiry under the Company Securities (Insider Dealing)
Act 1985* [1988] AC 660, the House of Lords held that the interests of the
prevention of crime did not require the person seeking disclosure to identify
any particular crime or crimes that might be committed. It was enough if
disclosure might help generally in the prevention of future insider dealing, etc.

Finally, in *X Ltd* v *Morgan Grampian (Publishers) Ltd* [1991] 1 AC 1, the
House of Lords again held that the interests of justice were not limited to
interests arising in the course of legal proceedings. It covered also the ability
to exercise important legal rights. Lord Bridge gave the following example:

[I]f an employer of a large staff is suffering grave damage from the activities of an unidentified disloyal servant, it is undoubtedly in the interests of justice that he should be able to identify him in order to terminate his contract of employment, notwithstanding that no legal proceedings may be necessary to achieve that end.

With respect to Lord Bridge, this seems in itself to open a gaping hole in the protection afforded by s. 10. Taken together with the other two House of Lords decisions it means that the situations in which journalists will now be able to rely on the protection of the section are very small in number. (See also T.R.S. Allan, 'Disclosure of Journalists' Sources, Civil Disobedience and the Rule of Law' [1991] *CLJ* 131.)

6.3   CONTEMPT IN THE FACE OF THE COURT

The due administration of justice clearly requires that trials should be allowed to proceed without extraneous interruptions. Assaults on, or threats towards, those taking part in proceedings will amount to contempt, in addition to any other offence that may be involved. In relation to freedom of expression, however, the relevant type of behaviour is that which involves a general disturbance of court proceedings. There are three cases to consider in this context.

First, in *Balogh* v *St Albans Crown Court* [1975] QB 73, a solicitor's clerk decided to enliven some proceedings which he was attending by letting off a canister of 'laughing gas' through the ventilation system. He had the canister in his briefcase, but was apprehended before he could carry out his plan. The judge before whom he was brought sentenced him to six months' imprisonment for contempt. Balogh did nothing to help his case by replying to the judge: 'You are a humourless automaton. Why don't you self-destruct?'. Nevertheless the Court of Appeal allowed his appeal. Contempt could not be committed, the Court held, where there had been no actual disruption of the proceedings. The fact that Balogh had made a plan which would have disrupted the proceedings, and was intending to carry it out, was not enough.

The second case to consider relates more directly to freedom of expression issues. In *Morris* v *Crown Office* [1970] 2 QB 114, some twenty demonstrators supporting the use of the Welsh language disrupted the trial of a defamation action in the High Court in London. The case had nothing to do with their cause, but their actions were seen as a way of attracting publicity. The demonstrators scattered leaflets, chanted slogans, and sang songs. Lawton J, who was in charge of the case disrupted, fined those who apologised £50, and sent the rest to prison for three months. The Court of Appeal, while agreeing that the demonstration constituted contempt, reduced the sentences of imprisonment to binding over for twelve months. Two points emerge. First, that it is clear that arguments in favour of freedom of expression cannot prevail over the requirement of legal proceedings being allowed to carry on without interruption. Secondly, the case illustrates the danger of allowing the judge who has been the object of the contempt to impose the penalty. Here, as in

Balogh's case, the Court of Appeal had to intervene to protect the offender. *The Times* for 3 April 1992 reported a Crown Court judge sending to the cells 12 people who had, in his view, reacted too boisterously to the acquittal of their friend. A representative of Liberty categorised this as 'disgraceful example of a judge abusing his power'. It is perhaps rather just another example of the dangers of allowing a judge to sentence in case in a which he has too direct an interest. A similar view might be taken of *R* v *Powell, The Times*, 3 June 1993, where a man sitting in the public gallery 'wolf-whistled' at one of the jurors, who was 'an attractive, smartly dressed young lady'. The judge ordered the man to be arrested, and sentenced him to 14 days' imprisonment. This was reduced by the Court of Appeal to the one day of imprisonment that he had already served, the Court being of the view that a fine would probably have been a more appropriate punishment.

Finally, *Bodden* v *Metropolitan Police Commissioner* [1989] 3 All ER 833, confirms that the disruptive actions need not take place in the court, provided their effect is felt there. Mr Bodden was addressing a crowd outside Bow Street Magistrates' Court. He was protesting about a case taking place there, and was using a loudhailer. The result was that the magistrate in another case was unable to hear a witness. It was accepted by the Court of Appeal that this could amount to contempt under s. 12 of the CCA, which makes it an offence wilfully to interrupt the proceedings of a magistrates' court. The requirement of 'wilfulness' means that the offender must either intend, or at least be aware of the risk of, disruption to the proceedings. A noisy procession of people chanting slogans, which happened to pass a court, would not automatically lead to the participants being guilty of contempt if proceedings inside were disturbed. It would have to be shown that the demonstrators knew that their actions were likely to have that effect.

6.4   EUROPEAN CONVENTION AND CONTEMPT

Article 10(2) of the European Convention on Human Rights allows for restrictions on freedom of expression to the extent necessary in a democratic society to maintain 'the authority and impartiality of the judiciary'. The scope of this exception, and its application to English law was considered in detail in proceedings arising out of the House of Lords' decision in the *Sunday Times* 'thalidomide' case (*Attorney-General* v *Times Newspapers Ltd* [1974] AC 273, see 6.2.2.3). The publisher and editor of the *Sunday Times* took the case to the European Commission on Human Rights. The Commission found that there was a breach of Art. 10 and referred the case to the Court. The Court's decision ((1979) 2 EHRR 245) was, by 11 votes to 9, in agreement with that of the Commission.

The first issue which the Court addressed was whether the restriction in this case could be said to be 'prescribed by law'. The applicants argued that the idea that 'prejudgment' was in itself contempt, irrespective of the effect on any particular case, was a novel one. For a restriction on behaviour to be prescribed by law it must be possible for citizens to assess beforehand with a reasonable degree of certainty the consequences of their acting in a particular way. The

Court agreed with this approach (para. 49), but felt that in the circumstances there had been sufficient indication in previous cases (in particular *Hunt* v *Clarke* (1889) 58 LJQB 490) of the dangers of prejudgment, to alert the applicants to the risk of contempt on these grounds (para. 52).

Next the Court considered whether the restriction had an aim which was 'legitimate' under Art. 10(2). This involved a consideration of the meaning of the phrase 'maintaining the authority and impartiality of the judiciary'. The Court ruled that 'the judiciary' here does not simply mean 'judges'. It also encompasses 'the machinery of justice' and 'the judicial branch of government' (para. 55). This includes the rights of litigants (para. 56). On this basis the Court regarded the House of Lords' concern with protecting the parties from undue pressure, avoiding 'trial by newspaper', and avoiding disrespect for the processes of law, as all coming within the legitimate scope of the restrictions permitted by Art. 10(2) (para. 57).

The final issue was whether the interference was 'necessary in a democratic society'. The Court adopted the same approach as that which it had taken in the *Handyside* case (see 7.9.2) to this issue. Thus, while the Convention does not set out an absolute standard, and individual countries will be allowed a 'margin of appreciation', the restriction must respond to a 'pressing social need'; it must be 'proportionate to the legitimate aim pursued'; and the reasons given to justify it must be 'relevant and sufficient under Article 10(2)' (para. 62). To reach a conclusion on these matters the Court had to examine all the circumstances surrounding the issue of the injunction against the *Sunday Times*.

The Court noted that at the time of the injunction there had already been considerable pressure on Distillers from other quarters, including parliamentary debates, to settle the claim on more beneficial terms. The article itself was, the Court thought, couched in moderate terms, and was not completely one-sided. Moreover, at the time when the article was proposed to be published, negotiations had been proceeding for several years, and the case had not yet reached the stage of trial.

In this context, the Court's role was to balance the public interest in freedom of expression against the need to maintain the authority of the judiciary. This was in contrast to the view of at least some of the House of Lords that the prejudgment rule was absolute, and that the House could not get involved in trying to balance the competing interests. The Court was required to take a different approach, and consider the public interest in the debate on the thalidomide tragedy, which was a matter of undisputed public concern, raising 'fundamental issues concerning protection against and compensation for injuries resulting from scientific developments' (para. 66). The Court's conclusion was that taking into account all the matters noted above, there was in this case no pressing social need sufficient to outweigh the public interest in freedom of expression. The restraint was not proportionate to the legitimate aim pursued, and was not necessary in a democratic society for maintaining the authority of the judiciary.

As has been noted above, the response of the British government to this decision was, eventually, to pass the Contempt of Court Act 1981. To what extent has this Act met the criticisms of the European Court of Human Rights?

In some ways the Act went further than necessary. The European Court did not go so far as to say that prejudgment without prejudice to a particular case should not be contempt. On the contrary it specifically recognised the protection of the administration of justice in general as a legitimate aim of restriction. Nor was the introduction of the much clearer *sub judice* rule by means of the concept of 'active' proceedings a requirement of the Court, though the rule would have prevented action against the *Sunday Times* under the strict liability rule. The Court's main criticism, as we have seen, was the failure to balance the public interest issues. The response to this was the inclusion of s. 5 (see 6.2.2.4). This is certainly an improvement on the common law position, but it does not quite achieve what the Court was advocating. The defence, as we have seen, operates where the risk of prejudice is 'merely incidental', to the risk of prejudice. We have also seen that at least one member of the House of Lords (Lord Diplock in *Attorney-General* v *English*, see 6.2.2.4) has suggested that the *Sunday Times* thalidomide articles would not have been protected by this. The problem is that the section does not require the English courts to 'balance' one interest against another. In particular, it gives no special recognition to the interest in freedom of expression. The weight is still on the side of restricting publication. Only where the risks of prejudice are 'incidental' do other public interests prevail. There is a good chance that at some stage the operation of the Contempt of Court Act itself will be challenged under Art. 10, and there is no guarantee that the improvements in the law which it introduced will be enough to avoid further criticisms.

SEVEN

Freedom of Expression III: Obscenity and Indecency

The English law relating to the control of obscenity and indecency is a mess. As long ago as 1979 the *Report of the Committee on Obscenity and Film Censorship* (Cmnd 7772, London: HMSO) chaired by Bernard Williams ('the Williams Committee'), commented that (para. 2.29):

> The law is scattered among so many statutes, and these so often overlap with each other and with the various common law offences and powers which still exist in this field, that it is a complicated task even to piece together a statement of what the law is, let alone attempt to wrestle with or resolve the inconsistencies and anomalies to which it gives rise.

Over the past fourteen years further legislation and decisions of the courts have only added to the confusion. This is also an area in which arguments about policy have a tendency to become high on emotion and low on coherence. It is, however, with the policy issues which we shall start, looking at the arguments for and against restriction, before moving on to examine in detail the current state of the legal controls.

7.1 ARGUMENTS FOR AND AGAINST RESTRICTION

Explicit depictions of sex or violence, or both, in magazines or videos, which are the most common point of attack for the obscenity laws, are often difficult to justify in terms of arguments for freedom of expression *per se*. Of the arguments outlined in chapter 5, the argument from democracy has little relevance. Free access to sex magazines does not make one better able to exercise the responsibilities of a voting citizen. Similarly, the Millian argument for truth can provide little protection for material which carries no overt 'message', but is designed primarily for titillation, and entertainment. Self-expression and personal autonomy are perhaps more credible arguments for freedom in relation to sexual material, though they tend to concentrate on the author rather than the reader, whereas the debate about pornography tends to be concerned not so much with what people may write, but what others may read. It is for this reason that in recent years much of the debate in this area has centered on the question of the effects of sexual and violent material. Another, more general, civil libertarian principle derived from John Stuart Mill's *Essay on Liberty*, has often been brought into play in this context. This is the idea that, as summarised succinctly by the Williams Committee (para. 5.1), 'no conduct should be suppressed by law unless it can be shown to harm someone'. This approach rejects paternalism. As Mill himself put it (*On Liberty*, chapter 1), a person 'cannot rightfully be compelled to do or forbear because it will be better for him to do so, because it will make him happier, because in the opinion of others, to do so would be wise, or even right'.

The Williams Committee dubbed this concept 'the harm condition', and that convenient shorthand will be adopted in this chapter. The problem that it raises, of course, even if it is accepted as a guiding principle, is that its operation is dependent on the precise definition given to the word 'harm'. Does this mean simply physical harm, or are there other types of harm which should be included? It is clear that the supporters of the harm condition are in part drawing a distinction between law and morality, so that the fact that behaviour is immoral is not enough to justify restraint. It is not so clear that behaviour which might cause a general lowering of moral standards can equally be regarded as non-harmful. There is a range of possible harmful effects which might justify restrictions. For example, restrictions on pornography might be justified because its distribution caused:

    (a)   an increase in sexual assaults or rape; or

    (b)   an increase in non-violent criminal offences, such as indecent exposure; or

    (c)   an increase in non-criminal behaviour of which society disapproves, e.g. private homosexual conduct between consenting adults;

    (d)   a widespread acceptance of lower moral standards in sexual matters; or

    (e)   a reinforcement of undesirable attitudes towards one section of society, e.g. women.

This list is not exhaustive, but in each case a plausible argument can be made for saying that if pornography has this effect, then it is in some sense 'harmful'. The next problem is that it is notoriously difficult to obtain empirical evidence of the effects of pornography. Research has been done by both psychologists and sociologists, but is generally accepted as being inconclusive. The Williams Committee certainly found it so, and refused to accept that any harms had been shown as existing beyond reasonable doubt, other than harms involving the participants in the creation of pictorial pornography (see the *Report*, chapter 10, in particular para. 10.8). A more recent survey for the Home Office, by Howitt and Cumberbatch, concluded that: 'The research evidence is clearly inadequate, partial and incomplete', and thus provides no foundation for any firm conclusions (D. Howitt and G. Cumberbatch, *Pornography: impacts and influences*, London: Home Office, 1990, p. 93).

A rather different approach has been advocated in recent years by some feminist writers, in particular Andrea Dworkin (see, for example, *Pornography: Men Possessing Women*, Women's Press, 1981), and Catherine MacKinnon. They attack pornography (defined as 'the graphic sexually explicit subordination of women through pictures or words' (Mackinnon, *Feminism Unmodified*, Harvard University Press, 1987, p. 175)) not because it *causes* violence against women, but because it is *in itself* violence against women. It violates the rights of women as a group, and as individuals, and may be regarded as a form of discrimination on sexual grounds. A powerful collection of writing from this perspective is to be found in C. Itzin (ed), *Pornography: Women, Violence and Civil Liberties*, Oxford: Oxford University Press, 1992. Not all feminists subscribe to this analysis, however. See, for example, A. Assiter and A. Carol (eds), *Bad Girls and Dirty Pictures*, London: Pluto Press, 1993.

Dworkin and MacKinnon have advocated the availability of civil remedies rather than the use of the criminal law to control pornography, but the Canadian Supreme Court has recently adopted an approach closely related to that put forward by these writers as the basis for criminal liability. In *R v Butler* (1992) 89 DLR (4th) 449, the view was taken that pornography which portrays explicit sex with violence would usually fall within the definition of obscenity as the 'undue exploitation of sex'. Furthermore the portrayal of explicit sex without violence, but 'which subjects people to treatment that is degrading or dehumanizing', would also be obscene if it causes 'harm'. Harm is then taken to include offence to 'the fundamental values of our society' (at p. 479). The particular problem of the way in which women are portrayed in pornography is recognised in the following passage from Sopinka J's judgment (at p. 479):

> [I]f true equality between male and female persons is to be achieved, we cannot ignore the threat to equality resulting from the exposure of audiences to certain types of violent and degrading material. Materials portraying women as a class as objects for sexual exploitation and abuse have a negative impact on 'the individual's sense of self-worth and acceptance'.

'Harm' is thus being defined broadly. Catherine MacKinnon was reported as welcoming this decision as a recognition that 'what is obscene is what harms women, not what offends our values' (*New York Times*, 28 February 1992). It remains to be seen, however, how the Supreme Court's approach will operate in practice, and exactly what types of material will be regarded as 'dehumanising and degrading'.

Are there any positive arguments for allowing the production of pornography? The only one that has been put with any force in favour of work which has no pretensions to literary or artistic merit, is that it may have a 'psychotherapeutic' value. In other words, the availability of pornography may help people with sexual problems, and may, by providing an outlet for the release of sexual tension, actually decrease the likelihood of sexual violence. There is as little in the way of scientific evidence for this beneficial effect, as there is for pornography's harmful effects. The English courts have rejected any possibility of a defence for publication of obscene material on these grounds (see *DPP* v *Jordan* [1976] 3 All ER 775 at 7.4.1.3).

7.2 METHODS OF CONTROL

There are various ways in which the distribution and availability of obscene or indecent material can be controlled. Three main devices are used in English law, i.e. pre-censorship, criminalisation, and controlling outlets. The first two act as direct controls; the third is indirect.

7.2.1 Pre-censorship
By this is meant a system whereby any material which it is proposed should be published must be submitted to some person or organisation for approval before publication can take place. The censor may have strict guidelines laid down by law, or may operate with a broad degree of discretion. There may or may not be an appeal from the censor's decision.

This type of control is regarded by proponents of liberty as the most insidious, in that it refuses to allow material even to see the light of day, and generally puts the issue of what can and cannot be published into the hands of a small group of officials. It has produced some notable attacks, from Milton's *Areopagitica*, to Lord Chesterfield's speech in the debates on the Theatres Licensing Act 1737, to Blackstone's *Commentaries on the Laws of England*, Clarendon Press, 1769, Book IV, pp. 151–152. In current English law such a system operates in relation to films and videos (see 7.5).

7.2.2 Criminalisation
Control by means of criminal offences generally, but not always, operates after publication. This is regarded as more acceptable than pre-censorship, in that it allows a work to be put into circulation before it is controlled, and, perhaps more importantly, the decision as to control is in the hands of the courts. This means that controls must be imposed on the basis of legally defined categories or offences (rather than the often vague discretion of the censor), and that it is always possible to argue against restriction before a final decision is taken.

This is the most common form of control in English law. In particular, in relation to books and magazines, a range of offences exists to control different types of objectionable publication (see 7.4).

7.2.3 Controlling outlets
The third method of control does not try to restrict publications themselves, but operates against the ways in which they may be made available to the public. It may take the form of requiring shops or other premises dealing in certain types of material to display warning notices, or to restrict their clientele (see e.g. Indecent Displays (Control) Act 1981 at 7.8.1.1). It may go further and require establishments dealing in certain types of activity to be licensed (e.g. Local Government (Miscellaneous Provisions) Act 1982; see 7.8.1.2). It may appear to be in many ways a more liberal system than either pre-

censorship or criminalisation, but, as we shall see, in some circumstances it can be just as restrictive.

7.3 PROBLEMS OF DEFINITION

Any system of control needs to define to some extent the behaviour to be restricted. This is most necessary in relation to criminal offences, where it is not possible to rely on the discretion of a censor or a licensing authority to give content to a general set of guidelines. It is, however, very difficult to provide satisfactory, workable definitions in this area of the law. Indeed, one of the two main words used in English legislation, i.e. 'obscene', has two, mutually contradictory, legal definitions. The other, 'indecent' has no clear definition at all. The result is that there is a constant danger that controls will result from an approach based on the idea that 'I cannot define pornography, but I know it when I see it'. This is clearly unacceptable where people are being charged with criminal offences which may well carry sentences of imprisonment on conviction. What, then, are the current definitions?

7.3.1 Obscenity

7.3.1.1 The 'deprave and corrupt' test The definition of 'obscenity' used in the Obscene Publications Act 1959 and the Theatres Act 1968 derives from the case of *R* v *Hicklin* (1868) LR 3 QB 360, where Lord Cockburn defined it as a tendency 'to deprave and corrupt those whose minds are open to such immoral influences, and into whose hands a publication of this sort may fall'. In its modern form it has been recast to remove the emphasis, which Lord Cockburn felt was important, on the dangers to the young who might possibly see such material, even if this was unlikely. The wording in the Obscene Publications Act 1959, s. 1, states that an article is to be deemed obscene if:

> its effect or (where the article comprises two or more distinct items) the effect of any one of its items is, if taken as a whole, such as to tend to deprave and corrupt persons who are likely, having regard to all relevant circumstances, to read, see or hear the matter contained or embodied in it.

The re-wording means that only 'likely' readers, as opposed to all possible readers need to be considered. *All* likely readers must be taken into account, however, not simply the *most* likely readers: *DPP* v *Whyte* [1972] AC 649. In addition, the reference to taking the article 'as a whole' makes it impermissible to select a few pages out of a lengthy novel, and argue that they are obscene, without looking at their context. The central element of the definition is, however, still the tendency to deprave and corrupt. How have the courts interpreted this phrase?

First, it is well-established that the tendency is to be looked at objectively, i.e. without reference to the intention of the author or publisher. This had been the position under the common law. In *R* v *Hicklin* (1868) it was said that innocent motives or objects would not justify an otherwise obscene publication. This was followed in the first reported case on the 1959 Act, *R* v *Penguin Books* [1961] Crim LR 176, which concerned the publication of D. H. Lawrence's *Lady Chatterley's Lover*. Byrne J ruled that it was not open to the defence to establish that there was no intention to deprave and corrupt (though in the end the publishers were acquitted). The Court of Appeal took the same view in *Shaw* v *DPP* [1962] AC 220, commenting (at p. 227) that 'obscenity depends on the article and not upon the author'. This approach is clearly based on the concept that, as Blackburn J put it in *R* v *Hicklin* (at p. 375) that although the publisher may have had another object in view 'he must be taken to have intended that which is the natural consequence of [his] act'. Since the enactment of s. 8 of the Criminal Justice Act 1967, this method of establishing *mens rea* has been rejected generally within the criminal law, in preference for a requirement that it must be proved that the accused actually foresaw or intended the consequences of acting in a particular way. As far as obscene publications are concerned, however, there has been no serious challenge to the proposition that all that is needed is an intention to publish, and that awareness or intention as to the consequences of that publication is irrelevant.

The crucial question therefore remains that of what is meant by 'deprave and corrupt'. The decisions of the courts have provided a few guidelines, without coming up with a comprehensive definition. In *R* v *Calder and Boyars* [1969] 1 QB 151, for example, the Court of Appeal ruled that an article which shocked and horrified people, and thus turned them against the activities described or depicted, would not tend to deprave and corrupt them. In *Shaw* v *DPP* [1962] AC 220, it was held that it was wrong to have regard to what people might do after reading an article in deciding whether it was obscene. In other words, no particular acts were necessary in order to establish depravity and corruption. This point was especially relevant in *Shaw*, where the publication was a directory of prostitutes and their services, and the question was whether people were encouraged to visit the prostitutes as a result of reading the directory. The Court of Appeal held that this was irrelevant. The point was upheld in a more general way by the House of Lords in *DPP* v *Whyte* [1972] AC 849, where the view was taken that an effect on the mind was all that was required, and that there was no need for this to be established by any overt activity. The question of what precise effect on the mind is required is unfortunately not made clear in the cases, but will be discussed further below.

The issue of the number of people who must be likely to be affected by an article in order for it to be considered obscene was considered in *R* v *Calder and Boyars* (1969). The Court of Appeal stated that the question for the jury was 'whether the effect of the book was to tend to deprave and corrupt a *significant proportion* of those likely to read it' ([1969] 1 QB 151 at p. 168, *emphasis added*). What is a 'significant' proportion is a matter for the jury, or magistrates, to decide, but it is clear that it means more than a negligible number, but may be much less than half (Lord Cross, in *DPP* v *Whyte* [1972] AC 849 at p. 870).

It is apparently possible to be corrupted more than once. In *DPP* v *Whyte* (1972) the magistrates had accepted an argument put by the defendants, who owned a bookshop, that their customers were almost entirely middle-aged men who were already corrupt. The House of Lords ruled that this was wrong. They confirmed the view expressed by the Court of Appeal in *DPP* v *Shaw* [1962] AC 220 at p. 228, that such an argument is false in that 'it assumes that a man cannot be corrupted more than once and there is no warrant for this'. Moreover, the House of Lords in *Whyte* felt that the pornography 'addict' should be discouraged from feeding or increasing his addiction.

One other important point of interpretation is that the courts have made it clear that obscenity under the 'deprave and corrupt' definition is not limited to sexual material. In *John Calder Publications Ltd* v *Powell* [1965] 1 QB 509, it was held that a book dealing with drug-taking could be obscene in this sense. This has been confirmed more recently in *R* v *Skirving* [1985] QB 819. In *DPP* v *A & BC Chewing Gum Ltd* [1968] 1 QB 159 pictures, contained in packets of bubble-gum, depicting scenes of (non-sexual) violence, were also held to be covered. So far, however, there has been no extension of the scope of the definition beyond sex, drugs, and violence.

These rulings as to the scope of obscenity do not, however, get very far in helping to explain exactly what is meant by a tendency to deprave and corrupt. It must surely mean that the material has some sort of adverse effect on the reader, though not one which necessarily results in any undesirable conduct. It presumably also has something to do with moral perversion. Remembering that it must be assessed objectively, this suggests that the concept depends on there being some core of morality which is accepted by society as a whole. The existence of such a core is in itself an arguable proposition, but assuming it exists, 'deprave and corrupt' then comes to mean 'pervert from contemporary moral standards'. We now come to the question of what kind of article will have such an effect.

For an article to pervert someone from contemporary moral standards it must, either explicitly or implicitly, be persuasive in its effect. A book which expounded the theme that buggery is good for you would be explicitly persuasive (though it might also shock and disgust, and so not be obscene). Implicit persuasion might arise from a publication which depicted a homosexual as a happy, fulfilled human being, who was more successful in life than heterosexuals. This might have the effect of encouraging others to partake in what society as a whole deems to be an undesirable activity. Support for this approach to defining obscenity comes from the summing-up of Stable J in *R* v *Martin Secker and Warburg* [1954] 1 WLR 1138, where he said (at p. 1142):

> The theme of this book is the story of the rather attractive young man who is absolutely obsessed with his desire for women. It is not presented as an admirable thing, or a thing to be copied. It is not presented as a thing that brought him happiness or any sort of permanent satisfaction, and throughout the book you hear the note of impending disaster.

This analysis leads us to the conclusion, then, that an obscene article means one that presents deviation from contemporary moral standards in an attractive light. There are, however, three serious objections to such a conclusion.

First, there is the problem that in *Knuller (Publishing, Printing and Promotions) Ltd* v *DPP* [1973] AC 435 at p. 456, Lord Reid stated that one may 'lead persons morally astray without depraving and corrupting them'. On this basis, perversion from contemporary moral standards is not enough, and there must be some additional factor which renders an article obscene. This connects with the second objection to defining 'deprave and corrupt' as 'pervert from contemporary moral standards', which is that this does not explain why obscenity is limited to sex, drugs and violence. A book which explains how to pick pockets, or how to make bombs, or how to help people commit suicide, may be condemned as inciting to crime, but it is unlikely to be categorised as obscene. Yet such a book may well 'pervert from contemporary moral standards' as regards theft, for example, just as much as an explicit magazine perverts from such standards as regards sexual behaviour. Again, it seems that there must be some additional factor which explains the limitations of obscenity. The case law, however, provides no clue as to what it might be.

The third objection to the above analysis is that it does not match reality. The Obscene Publications Act 1959 is used in practice almost exclusively against explicit pictorial material dealing with what is generally regarded as deviant behaviour: in other words, sado-masochism, bestiality, paedophilia, bondage, etc. It is hard to believe that faced with such material a jury or magistrate spends much time in deliberation on nice points relating to the precise effect that it will have on the moral standards of those likely to read it. One suspects that the decision is much more likely to be based simply on a feeling as to whether the material is within the limits of acceptable adult reading, which will in turn be based on an assumption as to the general standards applying within society. This is a decision based on the nature of the material itself, rather than its effects.

If this is right, then the conclusion must be that the definition of obscenity in terms of a tendency to deprave and corrupt is both incoherent in theory, and of little help in practice. The words 'deprave and corrupt' serve to emphasise the seriousness of the issue, but do not actually function as a definition.

7.3.1.2 The 'shock and disgust' test   The test of obscenity described in the last section, based on the tendency to deprave and corrupt, is only used in two statutes: the Obscene Publications Act 1959 and the Theatres Act 1968. A number of other statutes use the word 'obscene', but without defining it, and usually in association with the word 'indecent'. Examples include the Post Office Act 1953, s. 11 (discussed at 7.4.2.1), and the Customs Consolidation Act 1876, s. 42 (discussed at 7.8.2). In *R* v *Anderson* [1972] 1 QB 304, in relation to a charge under the Post Office Act, it was argued that 'obscene' in s. 11 of that Act should be defined in the same way as in the Obscene Publications Act. The judge had directed the jury to consider whether the material under consideration was 'repulsive', 'filthy', 'loathsome' and 'lewd'. The Court of Appeal held that while this was a misdirection in relation to a charge under the Obscene Publications Act 1959, it was acceptable in relation to the Post Office Act offence. This was because here the word 'obscene' should be given its dictionary meaning, which includes things which are 'shocking, lewd, indecent and so on.' So, in direct contrast to the Obscene Publications Act test, material can be found to be obscene under these statutes if it shocks and disgusts the reader. As we have seen, if the 'deprave and corrupt' test applies, the fact that the likely effect of the material is to shock and disgust may well provide a defence. It is small wonder that juries can become confused, when the same word can have directly opposite meanings depending on which offence is being charged.

7.3.2 Indecency

The other word, apart from 'obscene', which is frequently used in this area is 'indecent'. In some statutes, as noted at 7.3.1.2, it is used in conjunction with 'obscene'. In *R* v *Stanley* [1965] 2 QB 327, Lord Parker tried to explain the difference (at p. 333):

> . . . The words 'indecent or obscene' convey one idea, namely, offending against the recognised standards of propriety, indecent being at the lower end of the scale and obscene at the upper end of the scale . . .

It would appear from this that 'indecent' means shocking and disgusting, but not as shocking and disgusting as 'obscene'. This is confirmed by the statement of Lord Reid in *Knuller* v *DPP* [1973] AC 435, at p. 458, that it includes 'anything which an ordinary decent man or woman would find to be shocking, disgusting or revolting'. There has been little else in the way of judicial definition of the word. Indeed, during debates on the Indecent Displays (Control) Act 1981, some MPs clearly thought it an advantage that the word was vague, in that this would allow magistrates to apply local standards in different districts (see, for example, *Hansard* H.C. Vol. 997 cols 1196 and 1207). Whether this is a proper basis for the formulation of a criminal offence is open to question.

Indecency is also used as the basis for some common law offences, such as presenting an indecent exhibition, keeping a disorderly house, or outraging public decency (see 7.4.3.2 and 7.6.2). In this context at least it is not limited to sexual indecency, as is shown by the recent case of *R* v *Gibson* [1991] 1 All ER 439. This concerned an item on display in an art gallery which consisted of a mannequin's head to which were attached earrings made out of freeze-dried human foetuses. The owner of the gallery and the artist were convicted of outraging public decency (see also 7.4.3.2).

This case, and the use of the word 'impropriety' by Lord Parker, point to the fact that essential elements of indecency seem to be offence, and inappropriateness. Pictures may be indecent if they depict behaviour which is quite acceptable in private (such as consensual heterosexual intercourse), but offensive and inappropriate if it takes place in public. A freeze-dried foetus is appropriate (though some might still feel offensive) in a medical laboratory, but clearly inappropriate in an art gallery. The problem with this, as with the word indecent itself, is that both offence and appropriateness are largely subjective concepts, which do not therefore provide a firm basis for legal definition. What is clear, however, is that, just as the innocent motives of the creator of an obscene article cannot prevent its obscenity (see 7.3.1.1), so an improper motive cannot render a decent article indecent. This was confirmed in *R v Graham-Kerr* [1988] 1 WLR 1098, a case on the Protection of Children Act 1978 (see 7.4.2.4). The judge had allowed at trial evidence as to the accused's purpose and motive in photographing a seven year old boy at a naturists-only session at a swimming pool. The Court of Appeal held that this was irrelevant to the issue of the indecency of the photographs. On what constitutes indecency, however, the Court only felt able to refer back to Lord Parker's 'recognised standards of propriety'.

All this suggests that, although the word 'indecent' has caused less controversy, it is just as vague a term as 'obscene', and therefore its scope depends heavily on the subjective reaction of the jury or magistrates to the material under consideration.

7.4 CONTROLS OVER BOOKS AND MAGAZINES

The main targets for the criminal law in England and Wales as far as allegedly obscene or indecent materials are concerned, are books and magazines containing photographs, and videocassettes. The specific controls over videos are considered further at 7.5. In this section the offences and other procedures which apply to printed material are considered.

The main statutes are the Obscene Publications Acts of 1959 and 1964, but various other more specific statutes, often enacted to deal with particular issues of concern at the time, are also relevant.

7.4.1 Obscene Publications Acts 1959 and 1964

The 1959 Act was enacted in response to concerns that the common law offence of obscene libel was inadequate to deal with modern literature. This issue had been considered by a committee set up by the Society of Authors, and by a parliamentary select committee. One point of criticism was that the law failed to take account of the literary or other merits of the work under consideration. Accordingly, the long title of the 1959 Act states its aim as being 'to provide for the protection of literature; and to strengthen the law concerning pornography'. Two means of attack are used, namely criminal offences, and a forfeiture procedure.

7.4.1.1 The offences
The main offence enacted in the 1959 Act is that of publishing an obscene article, under s. 2(1). The publication does not have to be for gain. All three elements of the offence are the subject of further definition within the Act. We have already considered the meaning of 'obscene' at 7.3.1.1, so here we need only look at 'publication' and 'article'.

The definition of publication is contained in s. 1(3) which states:

> For the purposes of this Act a person publishes an article who —
>   (a) distributes, circulates, sells, lets on hire, gives, or lends it, or who offers it for sale or for letting on hire; or
>   (b) in the case of an article containing or embodying matter to be looked at or a record, shows, plays or projects it.

This is a broad definition. An individual copy of a work which is simply handed by one person to another is 'published' for the purposes of the Act. On the other hand, 'offer for sale' has been interpreted as being limited by the contractual rules as to offer and acceptance. In *Mella* v *Monahan* [1961] Crim LR 175 there was a prosecution under s. 2 on the basis that a packet of photographs had been published by being offered for sale. The packet had been displayed in the window of a shop. The Divisional Court took the view that this was not an offer for sale, but an invitation to treat, and so the prosecution failed.

The only other ruling on the meaning of publication in this section relates to the showing of a video in a cinema. This is discussed in the section dealing with videos (see 7.5).

An 'article' is defined in s. 1(2) as:

any description of article containing or embodying matter to be read or looked at or both, any sound record, and any film or other record of a picture or pictures.

This is again a wide definition. Its limits were, however, indicated in *Conegate* v *Commissioners for Customs and Excise* [1987] QB 254, where the 'articles' in question were rubber sex dolls, inflatable to life-size. It was accepted that these were not within the s. 1(2) definition, presumably because they were intended to be used, rather than looked at. (This case is discussed further at 7.8.2.) In other cases, however, the courts have been prepared to interpret the phrase to cover new technology, in the form of videocassettes (as a 'record of pictures': *Attorney-Generals's Reference (No. 5 of 1980)* [1980] 3 All ER 816), and it would presumably also be interpreted to cover a computer disc containing obscene text or pictures.

What the prosecution has to prove for the publication offence under s. 2(1), then, is that an article was published to a person who was likely to be depraved or corrupted, or to a group of people, a significant proportion of whom were likely to be depraved and corrupted. In looking at the likely readers, the court need not only consider the initial publication. Section 2(6) makes it clear that any further publication that could be reasonably expected to follow can also be taken into account. So in the case of the distribution of a magazine by a publisher to a wholesaler, it might be difficult to establish that the wholesaler was someone who was likely to be depraved and corrupted. Section 2(6), however, allows the court to take account of the further likely publication to retailers, and thence to the general public.

In some situations, however, no further publication will be likely, and attention will then have to focus on the corruptibility of the initial recipient. This caused problems in *R* v *Clayton and Halsey* [1963] 1 QB 163. The publication took the form of the sale of a packet of photographs to two plain clothes police officers. These officers admitted in evidence that they had seen thousands of photographs of the type purchased, and were totally unaffected by them. No further publication by the police officers was likely. On that basis, the Divisional Court felt bound to quash the defendants' convictions under

s. 2 (though they were also convicted on a conspiracy charge). This decision
clearly raised considerable problems for the police, and the result was the
enactment in the Obscene Publications Act 1964 ('the 1964 Act') of an
amendment to s. 2 of the 1959 Act creating a further offence, that of 'having an
obscene article for publication for gain'.

The differences between this offence and the original publication offence are
two-fold. First, there is no need for any publication to be proved. Possession
with a view to publication is enough (see 1964 Act, s. 1(5)). Secondly, the
proposed publication must be 'for gain'. The gain does not have to be that of
the publisher, 'gain to another' is sufficient. 'Gain' is not defined. In practice
it will normally be financial gain, but there is no reason why other types of
benefit should not be considered. For example, a scheme for the exchange of
pornography amongst enthusiasts might well come within its scope.

This offence not only deals with the difficulty raised by *R* v *Clayton and
Halsey* (1963), it also avoids the problems of *Mella* v *Monahan* (1961) as
regards goods displayed in shop windows. As a result it is the offence most
commonly used against those involved in the commercial production and
distribution of pornography. As is the case with the original publication
offence, the court is not limited to considering the effects of the initial
publication which the possessor may reasonably be inferred to have had in
mind, but can also take account of any further publication which could
reasonably be expected to follow (1964 Act, s. 1(3)).

7.4.1.2 The forfeiture provisions Most of the legal actions taken against
pornographic books and magazines are not prosecutions under s. 2 but
forfeiture proceedings under s. 3 of the 1959 Act.

Section 3 gives the police the power to obtain a search warrant to look for
obscene articles. In order to be granted one, they will need to convince a
magistrate that there are reasonable grounds for suspecting that obscene
articles are being kept for gain on specified premises. Note that private
possession is not enough, the prospect of 'gain' must be present. The
procedures for obtaining and executing the warrant will of course be subject to
the relevant provisions of PACE (see chapter 4, 4.2.4). The warrant should
specifically refer to 'obscene' articles. In *Darbo* v *DPP* [1992] Crim LR 56, the
phrase used was 'material of a sexually explicit nature'. The Divisional Court
held that this rendered the warrant invalid, because the category of material
which was 'sexually explicit' was far wider than that which could be
considered 'obscene'.

Once on the premises, the officers may search them, and seize any articles
which they have reason to believe are obscene, and kept for publication for
gain. In addition, if any such articles are taken, the police may also seize any
documents relating to a trade or business carried on at the premises (s. 3(2)).
The reason for giving the police this additional power was presumably to
enable them to obtain evidence that the material was held for gain, though the
wording of the section does not limit the police to seizing documents relating
to the trade in obscene articles: the documents may concern any business
carried on on the premises. The power to seize them also gives the possibility

of providing information which might help to identify the chain of distribution of the articles seized.

Once items have been seized, the police will need to decide whether to bring a prosecution under s. 2, or go for forfeiture proceedings under s. 3. This may take some time. In *Roandale Ltd* v *Metropolitan Police Commissioner* [1979] Crim LR 254, the police had seized from a warehouse some 170,000 magazines, including 18,000 copies of one magazine which belonged to the plaintiff. The seizure took place on 22 November. On 11 December, the plaintiffs sought an injunction requiring the police to return their magazines. Their argument was that there was an obligation under s. 3(3) to bring the items before the magistrates, and that, although there was no specific requirement in the statute to this effect, this should be done within a reasonable time. The injunction was refused, and by the time the matter reached the Court of Appeal (on 26 January) the articles had been deposited with the magistrates. The Court of Appeal indicated, however, that the correct way to have challenged the police would have been by way of judicial review, rather than by seeking an injunction. They agreed that the police had to act within a reasonable time, but regard had to be had to the quantity of material seized, and they were not prepared to say that the delay in this case was unreasonable.

Assuming that the police decide to proceed with forfeiture proceedings, the magistrates will issue a summons to the occupier of the premises from which the articles were seized, to appear to show cause why all or any of the articles should not be forfeited. Those who are simply wholesalers, or retailers, of the material may well not bother to challenge the forfeiture order, and simply regard the disappearance of their stock as a business loss; but s. 3(4) allows, in addition, any person involved with the production or distribution of the articles to appear to show cause (s. 3(4)). This gives the possibility of enabling the author or publisher of a serious work which has fallen into the possession of someone trading in pornography to come forward to argue their case. Since they are not required to be given notice of the proceedings, however, they may well be ignorant of what is going on.

The arguments that may be raised against forfeiture are that:

(a) the articles are not obscene; or
(b) that the publication of them would be for the public good (s. 4, see 7.4.1.3); or
(c) that they were not kept for gain.

Section 3(3) requires the magistrates to decide in relation to each article whether or not it is obscene and kept for publication for gain. In practice, where large quantities of material are seized, short-cuts are taken. For example, in *R* v *Croydon Magistrates, ex parte Rickman, The Times*, 8 March 1985, a stipendiary magistrate, faced with the long and distasteful job of examining many thousands of books, photographs and films brought before him under s. 3, decided that he would reach a decision on the basis of a police officer's evidence, consisting of descriptions of the nature of the material. Both prosecution and defence objected. The Divisional Court agreed, considering this to amount to reliance on hearsay. They expressed approval, however, of a proposed sampling procedure, whereby the magistrate would take a decision on representative samples, agreed by prosecution and defence, of various categories of material. A similar scheme had been approved at the stage of appeal to the Crown Court in *R v Snaresbrook Crown Court, ex parte Commissioner of the Metropolis* (1984) 79 Cr App R 184. This method of dealing with large scale seizures is understandable, but it must be questionable whether it actually meets the letter of the requirements of s. 3. (See further on this, R. Stone 'Obscene Publications: the problems persist' [1986] *Crim LR* 139.)

If the magistrates decide that all or any of the articles are not obscene they must be returned to the person from whom they were seized. Any that are found to be obscene will be ordered to be forfeited. Any person who appeared, or who was entitled to appear, before the magistrates, may appeal against this order to the Crown Court, which will review the merits of the case. If the order for forfeiture stands, or is not appealed, then the articles will be destroyed. The same will be the fate of seized material which is found to be obscene in the course of proceedings for an offence under s. 2 of 'having for publication for gain' (1964 Act, s. 1(4)).

7.4.1.3 The defence of 'public good' As has been noted above, one of the objectives of the 1959 Act was to provide greater protection under the law for works of literature. One of the ways in which this was attempted was by the inclusion of a defence of public good, which is set out in s. 4. This states that there is to be no conviction under s. 2, or order for forfeiture under s. 3, if the defence proves:

> that publication of the article in question is justified as being for the public good on the ground that it is in the interests of science, literature, art or learning, or of other objects of general concern.

Note that as with the test of obscenity the emphasis here is not on the article itself, but on the publication of it. The court must look at the circumstances of publication and decide whether one of the interests mentioned outweighs any possible obscenity. It is also clear that the defence does not mean that the article is not obscene, but that it can be published despite the fact that it is obscene. The logic of this was accepted in *Olympia Press v Hollis* [1974] 1 All ER 108, where the magistrates refused to listen to arguments under s. 4 until they had decided whether or not the articles in question were obscene. The Divisional Court said that this approach, while unusual, was perfectly acceptable. This separation of the issues was approved by the majority of the House of Lords in *DPP v Jordan* [1976] 3 All ER 775.

The main arguments about this defence have centred on its scope. What interests are covered, in particular by the phrase 'other objects of general concern'? The matter came before the House of Lords in *DPP v Jordan* (1976). The background to this case was that during the 1970s a number of prosecutions under the 1959 Act took place in which the defence called doctors who were prepared to testify that the publications under consideration were 'for the public good' in that they helped people with sexual problems. More specifically it was argued that it was preferable that people should have access to sexual materials as aids to masturbation rather than that they should either act out their fantasies, or repress them, and therefore become neurotic or psychotic. This evidence was brought in as relating to 'other objects of general concern.' In *Jordan*, the trial judge had refused to allow evidence as to the 'psychotherapeutic' value of pornographic material. On appeal, the House of Lords agreed that it had rightly been excluded. There were two reasons for this. The first was that the evidence related to the effect that the material had on people. As such it was really more appropriate to the issue of 'obscenity' under s. 1 of the 1959 Act (in relation to which, as we shall see, expert evidence is not usually allowed), than to that of 'public good'. Secondly, the defence, if allowed, would apply to virtually all pornographic material. Since the long title of the Act made it clear that one of parliament's intentions in passing the Act was to control pornography, the s. 4 defence could not have been intended to operate in this way. For both these reasons, the evidence was rightly excluded. 'Other objects of general concern' does not therefore cover the alleged psychological benefits of the pornography, even if these could be established, nor is there any indication from the cases as to what else might be covered by this phrase. It is significant that when the equivalent public good defence was enacted in s. 3 of the Theatres Act 1968, 'other objects' were not included in the list of interests.

A further attempt to expand the scope of s. 4 was made in the *Attorney-General's Reference (No. 3 of 1977)* [1978] 3 All ER 1166. Here the argument was that 'learning' should be taken to encompass 'teaching' and that this should cover sex education. Expert witnesses were prepared to give evidence that the sex magazines which had been seized could be used in relation to sex education, or in teaching people about sexual matters. The Court of Appeal refused to endorse this, ruling that 'learning' in s. 4 was a noun meaning 'the product of scholarship', or 'something whose inherent excellence is gained by the work of a scholar'.

In practice, then, it seems that an argument for 'public good' is unlikely to succeed unless based on the scientific, literary, or artistic merits of the publication.

7.4.1.4 The use of expert evidence The main use of expert evidence under the Obscene Publications Acts is in relation to the public good defence. Section 4(2) specifically provides that 'the opinion of experts as to the literary, artistic, scientific or other merits of the article' may be admitted, for the defence, or the prosecution. In *R v Penguin Books* [1961] Crim LR 176, the Bishop of Woolwich was allowed to give evidence as to the 'ethical merits' of *Lady Chatterley's Lover*. The role of the expert is to speak to the qualities of the work, not directly to the issue of whether its publication is for the public good. This is a matter for the magistrates or jury, and they are perfectly entitled to ignore the expert evidence in reaching their decision: *Calder* v

Powell [1965] 1 QB 509. In practice, however, it may be difficult to prevent witnesses from expressing an opinion as to whether or not the article should be published.

In general, expert evidence is not allowed on the issue of 'obscenity'. This is what the jury or magistrates have to decide, and the view is that they should normally be able to do this on the basis of their own judgment of the material, and its tendency to deprave and corrupt, without any external assistance. This was the line taken in *R* v *Calder and Boyars* [1969] 1 QB 151, and *R* v *Anderson* [1972] 1 QB 304. It was confirmed by the House of Lords in *DPP* v *Jordan* [1977] AC 699 (see 7.4.1.3). In two reported cases, however, expert evidence on obscenity has been allowed, and there are *obiter dicta* which suggest other circumstances where this might be possible. The first case to allow this type of evidence was *DPP* v *A & BC Chewing Gum Ltd* [1968] 1 QB 159. The case concerned cards depicting acts of violence which were distributed in packets of bubble-gum and were thus likely to fall into the hands of young children. The Divisional Court approved the admission of expert evidence for the prosecution as to the likely effect of the cards on such children. The justification for this was that the likely effect was something outside the range of experience of the ordinary jury member. Lord Wilberforce has on two subsequent occasions suggested the extension of this principle to other areas. The first was in *DPP* v *Jordan*, where, having rejected the admissibility under s. 4 of evidence as to the 'psychotherapeutic' value of pornography, he suggested that if the material was published to a limited class of people, e.g. consisting entirely of sexual deviants, there might be room for expert evidence as to its effect on them: [1977] AC 699, at p. 718. The second, similar suggestion came in *Gold Star Publications* v *DPP* [1981] 2 All ER 257, where the court was concerned with material destined solely for export. Lord Wilberforce again suggested (at p. 259) that expert evidence might sometimes be admissible as to the effects of the material on its target audience. In both these cases the justification was that the ordinary jury member could not be expected to assess the effect of the material on a particular type of audience. The suggestions were both in the form of *obiter dicta*, however, and there are no reported examples of other judges adopting this approach. Indeed, until 1985, *DPP* v *A & B C Chewing Gum* remained the only case where expert evidence had been allowed on the s. 1 issue.

In *R* v *Skirving* [1985] 2 All ER 705 the Court of Appeal again approved the use of prosecution expert evidence in an obscenity trial. The publication in question was a pamphlet which apparently described various methods of ingesting cocaine, and compared the merits of one against another. We have already seen at 7.3.1.1 that the Obscene Publications Acts are not limited in their scope to sexual material, but may also be used against publications concerned with drug-taking. In *Skirving* the judge allowed expert evidence to be given as to the effects of taking cocaine. The justification, which was accepted by the Court of Appeal, was superficially the same as in the *Chewing Gum* case, and in Lord Wilberforce's *dicta*; that is, that the effects of taking cocaine were outside the experience of the ordinary jury members, and therefore something on which it was permissible for them to have expert guidance. This misses the point, however, that what the jury had to decide on was the effect of reading the pamphlet ('would it deprave and corrupt'), not the effect of engaging in the activities described in it. It is not at all clear that they would have been incapable of deciding this issue from their own experience, without needing expert guidance. The analogy in the sexual area would be if evidence were allowed to show that indulging in sado-masochistic practices causes lasting physical or psychological problems, or that being homosexual increases the risks of contracting AIDS. Whether or not such evidence is true, it is irrelevant to the issue of the obscenity of a publication, where, as we have seen in *DPP* v *Whyte* (see 7.3.1.1) the emphasis is not on what people do after reading the publication, but the effect on their minds. (This point is argued at greater length in R. Stone, 'Obscene Publications: the problems persist', [1986] *Crim LR* 139. For a contrary view, see D. Birch, [1985] Crim LR 318.)

7.4.1.5 Other defences Apart from the arguments that the article is not obscene, or that its publication is for the public good, the Obscene Publications Acts allow one other defence, which is most likely to be of use to distributors. This is that the person charged was ignorant of the nature of what was published. Section 2(5) of the 1959 Act makes it clear that the burden of proof is on the defendant. In relation to the publication offence, it must be proved that the defendant had not examined the article and 'had no reasonable cause to suspect that it was such that his publication of it would make him liable to be convicted of an offence' against s. 2. Section 1(3)(a) of the 1964 Act provides an equivalent defence to the charge of having for publication for gain. The requirement of non-examination means that the only defendants likely to be able to make use of it are wholesale distributors, or retailers who have not at the relevant time removed the article from its packaging. As a result, the defence is of little practical significance.

7.4.2 Other statutory offences
In addition to the Obscene Publications Acts there are a number of other statutes which create specific offences which can be used against books or magazines, generally on the basis that they are indecent. Several of these were passed to deal with particular types of publication which were thought to be a problem at the time. The most important are noted here, in chronological order.

7.4.2.1 Post Office Act 1953 Section 11 of this Act makes it an offence to send, attempt to send, or procure to be sent, a postal packet which encloses any indecent or obscene 'article'. The word 'obscene' here has its dictionary definition and does not mean having a tendency to deprave and corrupt' (see 7.3.1.2). The offence of 'procuring to be sent' means that the person who orders the book or magazine will be guilty of an offence, as well as the person who sends it.

There is an additional offence where the outside of a packet contains material which is grossly offensive, or indecent or obscene (s. 11(1)(c)).

7.4.2.2 Children and Young Persons (Harmful Publications) Act 1955 This Act was passed to deal with a perceived problem in relation to 'horror comics'. The full story of the events which led up to the legislation is told in Martin Barker's *A Haunt of Fears*, London: Pluto Press, 1984. The Act is directed against books and magazines which are likely to fall into the hands of children, and consist wholly or mainly of stories told in pictures, though there may be some written content as well. To be within the scope of the Act the stories must portray (a) the commission of crimes; or (b) acts of violence or cruelty; or (c) incidents of a repulsive or horrible nature. The effect of the publication must be to tend to corrupt a child or young person into whose hands it might fall (s. 1). The Act has in fact been little used. In many cases, the offences under the Obscene Publications Act 1959 could now be used in a situation where the 1955 Act might apply, particularly since the decision in the *A & BC Chewing Gum* (1968) case extended the 1959 Act to publications dealing with non-sexual violence (see 7.3.1.1).

7.4.2.3 Unsolicited Goods and Services Act 1971 The procedure known as 'inertia selling' was the main target of this Act. Unscrupulous publishers would send people books which they had not requested, and tell them that unless they returned them by a certain date they would have to pay for them. Although such an arrangement would not be enforceable in civil law (since silence cannot amount to acceptance of a contract: *Felthouse* v *Bindley* (1862) 11 CBNS 869), there was thought to be sufficient of a problem to require specific statutory intervention. At the same time, the opportunity was taken, in s. 4, to deal with a related issue, which is of more direct concern to the issues being looked at in this chapter. This was the sending of unsolicited explicit sexual material, or advertisements for such material. It is an offence under the Act to send or cause to be sent, an unsolicited book, magazine, or leaflet which describes or illustrates human sexual techniques. It is also an offence to send unsolicited advertising material for such a publication. It was confirmed in *DPP* v *Beate Uhse (UK) Ltd* [1974] 1 All ER 753, that the advertising material does not itself have to describe or illustrate human sexual techniques. It will be seen that the offence is very limited in the type of material it covers. The justification is presumably that other types of sexual material would often be covered by the Post Office Act offence (see 7.4.2.1), but that simply depicting consensual human sexual intercourse might well not be considered indecent, so that a special offence was needed.

7.4.2.4 Protection of Children Act 1978 This Act was passed in response to worries about a perceived growth in child pornography. Much of such material would, of course, fall foul of the Obscene Publications Act, but there was thought to be a need to create a separate offence with respect to photographs and films. The Act is concerned with photographs or films (it is assumed that this would also be taken to cover videocassettes) which show children (a 'child' being a person under the age of 16) and are indecent. The child does not necessarily have to be involved in any indecency, this element could be satisfied by something occurring elsewhere in the photograph or film.

This interpretation was approved in *Owen* [1988] 1 WLR 134. In practice, however, the Act is used in relation to pictures where the indecency involves the children. Section 1 of the Act made it an offence to take such indecent photographs, to distribute or show them, or to possess them with a view to distribution or showing. There is no need for there to be any actual or intended gain (financial or otherwise) from the distribution or showing.

The meaning of 'indecency' has already been discussed (see 7.3.2). There have been two cases on the Protection of Children Act which have dealt with the issue in this context. In *Owen* [1988] 1 WLR 134, it was held that the age of the child was a relevant fact which the jury could take account of when assessing the alleged indecency of a photograph. The subject of the photograph was a girl aged 14, who was scantily clad and displaying her bare breasts. She had wanted to become a professional model. The defence submitted that the jury should judge the photograph simply as it stood, disregarding the girl's age. Presumably, it was thought that the girl might well appear to be older than her actual age, and that the type of photograph, if it had been of a 17 or 18 year old, was not such that it would have been regarded as indecent. The judge ruled against the defence submission, and the Court of Appeal upheld this ruling. The jury could take into account the age of the girl as a relevant factor in deciding whether or not the photograph was indecent.

A slightly different approach was taken in *Graham-Kerr* [1988] 1 WLR 1098. Here the defendant had taken a photograph of a seven year old boy at a naturist swimming bath. The judge directed the jury that they could take into account the circumstances in which the photograph was taken, and the motivation of the defendant in taking it, when assessing the indecency issue. On this occasion the Court of Appeal ruled that evidence on these issues was not relevant to the question of whether or not the photograph was indecent, though it might have affected the issue of whether the photograph was taken intentionally or deliberately. Since the *mens rea* of the defendant was not disputed, the evidence was not relevant to any issue which was before the jury, and the judge should have directed them accordingly. To this extent the issue of indecency must be judged intrinsically on the basis of the photograph alone. The defendant's conviction was quashed.

Continued concern about the availability of child pornography led to the creation in 1988 of an additional summary offence of possession of an indecent photograph. This is contained in s. 160 of the Criminal Justice Act 1988. Unlike the possession offence in the 1978 Act, there is no need to show any intention to distribute or publish the photograph. Simple possession constitutes the offence. In all other respects, however, the new offence adopts the definitions and procedures of the 1978 Act.

7.4.3 The common law
Two common law offences need consideration, namely, conspiracy to corrupt public morals, and outraging public decency.

7.4.3.1 Conspiracy to corrupt public morals
It is generally agreed among academic commentators that in the case of *Shaw* v *DPP* [1967] AC 220,

the House of Lords created a new offence, i.e. conspiracy to corrupt public morals. This piece of judicial law-making was the subject of much criticism, but the existence of the offence was confirmed by the House in *Knuller* v *DPP* [1973] AC 435, and by parliament in the Criminal Law Act 1977, s. 5. The *mens rea* of the offence is an intention to corrupt (*Knuller* v *DPP*). The *actus reus*, as with all conspiracies, is the *agreement* to carry out a particular course of conduct. The offence can thus be used against the dissemination of articles which fall within the scope of the Obscene Publications Act 1959, since the prohibition of the use of common law offences contained in s. 2(4) of that Act was held in *Shaw* only to apply where the *actus reus* of the common law offence consisted in *publication* of the material. At one time it was in practice mainly used where the Obscene Publications Act was not available, for example in relation to private film clubs, before these were brought within the scope of the 1959 Act. More recently, it has been used against sex 'contact' magazines, particularly where these were concerned with paedophilia, or other deviant sexual activities. In this it is returning to its origins, since *Shaw* was concerned with a 'Ladies Directory' (i.e. a directory of prostitutes) and *Knuller* with the publication of homosexual contact advertisements in a newspaper.

Despite fears that the offence might be used to circumvent the public good defence in the 1959 Act (see 7.4.1.3), this has not proved to be the case. An assurance given by the Attorney-General in 1964 that the offence would not be used in this way has been honoured.

7.4.3.2 Outraging public decency

In *Knuller* the House of Lords recognised the existence of an offence of outraging public decency (and thus also an offence of conspiracy to outrage public decency). This has mainly been used, in its manifestations of 'presenting an indecent exhibition' or 'keeping a disorderly' house, against live performances of one kind or another (for which see 7.6.2). In *R* v *Gibson* [1991] 1 All ER 441, it was used against the display of an article falling within the scope of the 1959 Act. This was a model's head, to which were attached earrings made out of freeze-dried human foetuses of three or four months' gestation. It was displayed at a commercial art gallery. The Court of Appeal held that there was no need for the prosecution to prove an intention to outrage public decency; an intention to display the article was enough. Further, it was held that s. 2(4) of the Obscene Publications Act 1959 could not protect the defendant. This section states that:

> A person publishing an article shall not be proceeded against for an offence at common law consisting in the publication of any matter contained or embodied in the article where it is of the essence of the offence that the matter is obscene.

We have seen that in *Shaw* this section was regarded as inapplicable, because the *actus reus* of the conspiracy was the agreement, not the publication. In *Gibson* it was held that 'obscene' in s. 2(4) must be given the same meaning as elsewhere in the Act, i.e. having a tendency to deprave and corrupt. Since the essence of the common law offence charged here was not corruption, but shock or outrage, then s. 2(4) did not operate as a bar to the prosecution. The unfortunate result was that the defendant was unable to raise a defence of 'public good', which is not available to the common law charge, despite the fact that there were witnesses available who would have testified to the artistic merits of the display.

The decision clearly opens the door to the wider use of the common law offence against public displays, such as posters, book or magazine covers, compact disc covers, etc. In most such cases, however, the more appropriate charge would probably be under the Indecent Displays (Control) Act 1981 (see 7.8.1.1). This was not available in *Gibson* because the offence under the 1981 Act does not apply to displays within art galleries (s. 1(4)(b)).

7.5 CONTROLS OVER FILMS AND VIDEOCASSETTES

Both films and videocassettes are subject to many of the same controls as books and magazines. For example, the publisher of a film or videocassette may be liable for an offence under the Obscene Publications Acts, or for conspiracy to corrupt public morals. In addition, however, both are also subject to a system of censorship, in which the British Board of Film Classification ('the BBFC') plays a leading role. The system operates slightly differently as regards the two media, however, so they need to be considered separately.

7.5.1 Cinemas Act 1985
The control of the public showing of films is in the hands of local authorities. They have the responsibility under s. 1 of the Cinemas Act 1985 for licensing premises for the public showing of films. The original legislation (Cinematograph Act 1909) gave this power primarily in order to control safety, but it quickly became used as a means of imposing controls over the content of what was exhibited. The current Act recognises this explicitly by imposing a *duty* on the local authority issuing a licence to impose conditions prohibiting the admission of children to film exhibitions deemed unsuitable for children (s. 1(1)(3)). It also gives a *power* to impose similar conditions as regards adults. In practice local authorities generally rely on the classifications of films issued by the BBFC. This is an independent body, originally established by the film trade itself. It has no official status under the 1985 Act, but in practice exercises censorship control, specifying the minimum age of children who may view particular films, and in some cases refusing a certificate altogether. The Board may ask for cuts or other alterations to be made before it will grant a certificate for a particular age group, or at all. In *Mills* v *LCC* [1925] 1 KB 213 it was held that a local authority could in effect delegate its censorship powers to the BBFC, by requiring a licensee to follow the classifications of that body, provided that the authority retained the final say. At times a local authority will exert this power, usually to ban a film which has been passed by the BBFC. In 1988, for example, a number of local authorities banned the film *The Last Temptation of Christ* despite the fact that it had been granted a certificate by the BBFC.

The local authorities' censorship powers were fully considered by the Court of Appeal in *R* v *Greater London Council, ex parte Blackburn* [1976] 1 WLR

550. The Greater London Council had allowed the exhibition of a film which had been refused a certificate by the BBFC. The Court of Appeal re-affirmed the decision in *Mills* v *LCC* (1925) as to the relationship between the BBFC and the local authority, and that there is no compulsion to censor films for adults as opposed to children. If, however, the local authority does exercise censorship in relation to adults it must not do so in a way which might allow the exhibition of a film which would amount to an offence under the criminal law. At the time of the *Blackburn* case films were governed by the common law indecency offences rather than the Obscene Publications Acts, and so the GLC's use of a test based on the likelihood of a film 'depraving and corrupting' its audience was held to be *ultra vires*. By virtue of the Criminal Law Act 1977, films are now subject to the Obscene Publications Acts, so a test based on this wording would now be acceptable. In practice, however, as we have seen, local authorities are content to leave most decisions to the BBFC.

There are also special provisions covering 'sex cinemas' in the Local Government (Miscellaneous Provisions) Act 1982. These are dealt with at 7.8.1.2.

7.5.2 Video Recordings Act 1984

The boom in the sale and rental market for videocassettes during the 1980s brought with it concerns over the content of some videos. Up until 1984, videos sold or rented for use in the home were simply subject to the Obscene Publications Acts and the other relevant statutory and common law offences noted above at 7.4. All these offences still apply. In 1983, however, a campaign was started, led by various pressure groups and sections of the press, against so-called 'video-nasties'. These were videos of films such as *Driller Killer*, *I Spit on Your Grave* and *Death Trap*. They were all films which contained scenes of extreme violence, sometimes combined with sex. Some were the subject of prosecutions under the Obscene Publications Acts, but juries were inconsistent in their verdicts on them. Research findings (the methodology of which was later shown to be very suspect) were then produced purporting to show that as many as 37 per cent of children under seven had seen one of these videos. The issue was taken up by Graham Bright, MP, who introduced a private members Bill to deal with the problem. With government support, this eventually became the Video Recordings Act 1984. (For a full account of the events leading up to this see M. Barker (editor), *The Video Nasties*, London: Pluto Press, 1984.)

It is no doubt true that there were some very distasteful films circulating on video at the time, and that the Obscene Publications Act was not providing a consistent response to them. The Video Recordings Act, however, goes much further than the problem of video nasties. It in effect introduces a comprehensive censorship system for all videos supplied to the public, with only very narrow exceptions relating to education, sport, religion or music (s. 2(1)). Even these categories lose their exemption if the video depicts 'to any significant extent' human sexual activity (or acts of force or restraint associated with such activity), gross violence towards humans or animals, or human genital organs or urinary or excretory functions (s. 2(2)). All videos other than exempted videos must be submitted for approval to a body designated by the Home Secretary (currently the BBFC) prior to distribution. This body, in deciding whether to grant a certificate, and if so, what age restrictions to place on the video, is required to have 'special regard' to the likelihood of the video 'being viewed in the home' (s. 4). At first sight this focus on the home might seem to impose a general standard of what is suitable for 'family' viewing. In fact, as Robertson and Nicol have argued (*Media Law*, 3rd edn, London: Penguin, 1992, p. 578), the reason for including the phrase was because of the existence of the facility on video recorders to replay passages over and over again, and, on some machines, to slow them down or 'freeze' particular shots. A scene that is viewed once on the cinema screen may, it is argued, have a very different impact if treated in this fashion. For this reason, films which have been given a particular classification in the cinema may receive a more restrictive one, or only receive the same one after cutting, when released on video. This aspect of the Act, however, does seem to encourage the censor to take an unusual interest in what people do within their own homes. After all, passages in books can be re-read an infinite number of times, and photographs can be pored over at much greater length than is likely in relation to a video, yet no particular account has ever been taken of this factor. Indeed, when the removal of censorship on the theatre was being debated in parliament during the passage of the Theatres Act 1968 (see 7.6.1), those who wished to retain the existing system argued that the theatre needed greater control than books, because what was done in the theatre was done in public, whereas books were generally read in the privacy of one's own home. Yet the theatrical experience is if anything more transitory than the cinema.

The BBFC currently uses the following categories of classification for videos:

U   Universal: Suitable for all
Uc   Universal: Particularly suitable for children
PG   Parental guidance: Some scenes may be unsuitable for young children
15   Suitable only for persons of 15 years and over
18   Suitable only for persons of eighteen years and over
18R   Suitable only for restricted distribution through segregated premises to which no one under 18 is admitted.

In relation to films to be shown in the cinema, there is an additional category: '12: Suitable only for persons of 12 years and over'.

It is an offence under the 1984 Act to supply an unclassified videocassette, or to supply a classified cassette to a person under the age for whom it is deemed suitable. The penalties are purely financial, but nevertheless substantial: a maximum fine of £20,000. The supply does not have to be for gain: lending an unclassified video to a friend will constitute the offence. On the other hand, certain supplies are exempt, for example gifts, or supply for the purposes of broadcasting (s. 3).

There is a right of appeal against a decision of the BBFC, by the person who submitted the video (who will usually be the distributor), but not by any other interested party such as an author or director: s. 4. The appellate panel is independent in the sense that it is not comprised of members of the BBFC, but it is selected by the BBFC. It allows legal representation, may sit in public, and gives reasoned judgments.

The BBFC is in practice mainly concerned with sex and violence, or both. In some cases, however, it has strayed into other areas. In 1989, a video entitled *Visions of Ecstasy* concerning St Teresa was refused a certificate by the Board on the grounds that it was blasphemous, and this decision was upheld by a majority of the appeal committee. The committee felt that it could not allow a certificate to be granted to a film, the publication of which might constitute a criminal offence, but they were perhaps being rather cautious, given the infrequency with which the blasphemy laws have been used in recent times. The following year the Board's decision to refuse a certificate to *International Guerrillas*, which contained a clearly libellous portrayal of the author Salman Rushdie. The Appeal Committee on this occasion reversed the Board's decision, on the basis that it was unlikely that proceedings for criminal libel would be taken. Rushdie himself was in support of this decision.

The result of the 'video nasty' scare, and the consequent Video Recordings Act 1984, is an intrusive and fussy system of censorship, and it is doubtful whether it has any significant beneficial effect on the moral health of the nation. Those who seek hard-core porn can no doubt still find what they want on the black market in unclassified videos. Aficionados of the films of Alfred Hitchcock, however, can only be allowed a bowdlerised version of *Psycho* to view at home, because of the intervention of the BBFC (G. Robertson and A. Nicol, *Media Law*, 3rd edn, London: Penguin, 1992, p. 592).

7.6   CONTROLS OVER LIVE PERFORMANCES

There are two sets of controls which are relevant to the content of live performances. One set is to be found in the Theatres Act 1968, the other in the common law offences of presenting an indecent exhibition, or keeping a disorderly house. Which is applicable will depend on the type of performance. If it is a 'play' or a 'ballet' then the Theatres Act will apply. If it is not, then the common law offences will apply.

7.6.1   Theatres Act 1968
This piece of legislation was passed following the recommendations of a joint parliamentary committee that the previous system of theatre censorship operated by the Lord Chamberlain should be abolished (Joint Committee on Censorship of the Theatre, HMSO, 1967). At a time when the theatre was exploring its limits in the 1950s and 1960s through the work of playwrights such as John Osborne, Edward Bond, Joe Orton and Harold Pinter, the restrictive pre-censorship of the Lord Chamberlain was seen as old-fashioned and stifling. Apart from anything else, the Chamberlain's insistence (as required by the Theatres Act 1843) on a script to approve, prevented any improvised work from being lawfully presented. The Committee recommended that instead the theatre should become subject to the control of the criminal law, in the same way as books and magazines.

As has been noted above the Act applies to 'plays'. Section 18(1) defines a play as a dramatic piece where what is done by one or more persons actually present and performing 'involves the *playing of a role*' *(emphasis added)*. It also includes 'any ballet', whether or not the performance involves the 'playing of a role'. The effect of this definition is that live performances in the form of singing, dancing (other than ballet), strip-tease, or monologue (as by a 'stand-up comedian') are all unlikely to fall within the scope of the Act. Although the definition is not without ambiguity (would it include a puppet-show, for example?), and despite the fact that 'ballet' is not further defined, it does not seem to have caused problems in practice.

The main offence under the Act is to be found in s. 2, which prohibits the presentation of an obscene performance of a play. 'Obscenity' is defined in the same terms as under the Obscene Publications Act 1959, that is as a tendency to deprave and corrupt a likely audience. It is the *performance* rather than the *script* that must be considered. The offence is, however, committed by the presenter or director of the performance, rather than by the actors.

There is a defence of public good in s. 3, in similar terms to s. 4 of the Obscene Publications Act, though the list of 'interests' is appropriately amended, and excludes the troublesome phrase 'other objects of general concern' which led to difficulties under the 1959 Act (see 7.4.1.4).

Use of the common law, including indecency and conspiracy offences, against 'plays' is excluded by s. 2(4).

Prosecutions under the Act are subject to the approval of the Attorney-General (s. 8). He has shown great reluctance to initiate prosecutions, despite regularly having productions referred to him (for example *Oh! Calcutta!* (1971), *The Romans in Britain* (1981)). In fact, there has only ever been one prosecution under the Act, in relation to a revue by Sebastian Kane entitled *Dee Jay*, and presented in Manchester (see *R v Brownson* [1971] Crim LR 551). It is not entirely clear why this production was singled out for prosecution, though the account later given by one of the performers (V. Nicholson and S. Smith, *Spend, Spend, Spend!*, London: Jonathan Cape, 1977, pp. 163–166) suggests that some of the other performers taking part in simulated sex and rape scenes were very young (though over 16).

The fact that the Act has been so little used means that the theatre is in practice probably the least legally controlled of all the media. Extra-legal controls, however, such as the need not to alienate local audiences, and the need to retain the approval of funding bodies, probably operate as a curb on any tendency to excess amongst theatrical producers. It may also be significant that theatre-going is a relatively expensive, and predominantly middle-class activity.

7.6.2 Common law offences
The two common law offences which are relevant in this area are both closely related to the offence of outraging public decency, dealt with at 7.4.3.2. They both use the common law test of 'indecency' rather than the deprave and corrupt test.

7.6.2.1 Presenting an indecent exhibition
This derives from *R v Saunders* (1875) 1 QBD 15 in which two showmen were convicted of keeping

a booth on Epsom Downs for the purpose of presenting an indecent exhibition
to those who paid. It has also been used against non-sexual exhibitions, such
as the display of a photograph of a man suffering from eruptive sores in a
herbalist's window (*R* v *Grey* (1864) 4 F & F 72). An example of its more recent
use against a live sex show can be found in a case in 1975 which involved a
striptease and lesbian act by three women culminating in their having sexual
intercourse with three of the customers (*The Times*, 21 January 1975. See also
R. Stone, 'Indecent Performances: the Law Commission's Proposals', (1977)
127 NLJ 452).

7.6.2.2 Keeping a disorderly house   This has in recent years been the
more frequently used of the two common law offences. It has been directed
primarily at performances by strippers and 'exotic dancers', both male and
female (see, for example, *R* v *Farmer and Griffin* (1974) 58 Cr App R 229, and
Moores v *DPP* [1991] 4 All ER 521). The definition of the offence approved by
the Court of Appeal in *R* v *Quinn and Bloom* [1962] 2 QB 245, seems to have
achieved general acceptance. It was there defined as:

> a house conducted contrary to law and good order in that matters are
> performed or exhibited of such a character that their performance or
> exhibition in a place of common resort (a) amounts to an outrage of public
> decency or (b) tends to corrupt or deprave or (c) is otherwise calculated to
> injure the public interest so as to call for condemnation and punishment.

In practice the element of the offence most commonly relied on is (a). The
word 'keeping' implies some element of persistence. This was confirmed in
Moores v *DPP* [1991] 4 All ER 521, where evidence of a single indecent
performance was held to be insufficient to constitute the offence. As with the
Theatres Act, the offence is primarily directed against the presenter of the
performance, rather than the performers themselves.

Few would argue that the restriction of shows of the kind under consideration in *Moores* v *DPP* (1991), which involved a male 'exotic dancer' having
his penis rubbed with oil by a female member of the audience, would be a
significant blow to artistic freedom. To the extent, however, that these offences
are used against shows put on for a willing audience, and which are not thought
to be depraving and corrupting, there does not seem to be any clear public
benefit involved sufficient to outweigh the restriction of personal freedom.

7.7 CONTROLS OVER BROADCASTING

The Broadcasting Act 1990, s. 162, made television and radio subject, for the
first time, to the Obscene Publications Act 1959. This change, however, seems
unlikely to be of great practical significance. It is hard to believe that a jury
would convict any of the output of the BBC or independent television as
having a tendency to deprave and corrupt. Surveys of audience concern
regularly show that more offence is caused by bad language in television

programmes than by sex or violence. It is much more possible that the range of programmes which will become available as a result of the increase in satellite broadcasting will include obscene material. The problem here will be that the publisher of the material will almost certainly be based outside the jurisdiction, and if the origin of the broadcasts is from within Europe, the scope for action will be limited by the 1989 EC Directive on Broadcasting. The issue was raised in 1992 by the broadcast from Denmark of an 'adult' television channel under the name 'Red Hot Dutch' (see F. Coleman and S. McMurtrie, 'Too Hot to Handle', (1993) 143 NLJ 10). Rather than acting directly against the broadcasters, the government made it an offence to deal in the decoding equipment necessary to receive the transmissions. An initial challenge to the legality of this under European law failed in the English courts, and any further action was precluded by the subsequent insolvency of the broadcasting company. It may well be that international conventions and cooperation will turn out to be more effective controls in these circumstances, as opposed to the English criminal law offences relating to obscenity and indecency.

Of more practical significance to domestic broadcasting is the statutory recognition, in s. 151 of the Broadcasting Act 1990, of the Broadcasting Standards Council. This is an independent body, appointed by the Home Secretary. Its first chairman was Lord Rees-Mogg, a former editor of *The Times*; Lady Howe took over the chair from him in 1993. The duties of the Council under the Broadcasting Act are first, to draw up codes of guidance for domestic broadcasters relating to standards of taste and decency, and in particular the portrayal of violence and sex (s. 152). This has been done. Secondly, the Council has a duty to monitor programmes, including those transmitted from abroad, in relation to the above matters (s. 153). Thirdly, the Council has a duty to consider complaints (which it may itself initiate: s. 153(1)(b)) of alleged failure to attain standards of decency, or relating to the portrayal of violence or sex (s. 154). Any such complaint must be considered, with or without a hearing, but in either case, the body responsible for the broadcast (e.g. the BBC, or one of the independent television companies) must be sent a copy of the complaint, to which they are required to provide a written answer (s. 154). If a hearing is held, then in addition to the broadcaster and the complainant, any person who appears to the Council to have been responsible for the making or provision of the programme, or who the Council consider might be able to assist at the hearing, is to be given an opportunity to attend and be heard (s. 154(4)). The sanction, if a complaint is upheld, is simply that of publicity, including an obligation on the broadcaster to publish the complaint and the Council's findings, in a manner directed by the Council. The Council has already considered a fair number of complaints, and issues its adjudications in monthly bulletins. It has been criticised that in a number of cases it has 'displayed both an ignorance of the nature of television, and an intention to damage it as a medium for providing education, information and entertainment' (G. Robertson & A. Nicol, *Media Law*, 3rd edn, London: Penguin, 1992, p. 608. See pages 606–652 of *Media Law* for a full account of the operation of the Broadcasting Standards Council, and the enforcement of its Codes of Practice).

7.8   GENERAL CONTROLS

This section looks at two types of general controls which are not specifically linked to a particular type of publication or article. The first relates to the distribution of sexual material, and covers controls over premises. The second type of control considered here is that covering the import of materials, and exercised by H.M. Customs and Excise.

7.8.1   Control over premises

7.8.1.1   Indecent Displays (Control) Act 1981   This Act resulted from a private members bill, which received government support, and which picked up one of the concerns about pornography which was emphasised by the Report of the Williams Committee on Obscenity and Film Censorship (Cmnd 7772, 1979). The Committee had found that an issue which raised widespread objection was the display of pornographic magazines on the shelves of general newsagents, and in the windows of sex shops (Report, para. 9.1). In other words, what might be termed the 'public nuisance' aspect of pornography. Accordingly, the Act makes it an offence to display publicly 'any indecent matter'. The word indecent is not defined, and so the approach outlined at 7.3.2, based on the idea of what is found 'shocking', 'disgusting', or offensive, will be used. It was accepted in the debates on the Act that the vagueness of this approach might well result in magistrates in different parts of the country applying different standards. This was not thought to be a significant problem, either because it was right that local standards of decency should be applied, so that what was acceptable in London might be unacceptable in Manchester, or because the Act was only concerned with public displays, and would not restrict the *availability* of any material.

The Act covers the display of any matter, other than the 'actual human body' (s. 1(5)). By this is meant the human body itself, rather than a portrayal of it. This type of display was thought to be adequately covered by the offences noted in 7.6. On the other hand, pictures, book and magazine covers, drawings, photographs, sex-aids, and slogans, will all be within the scope of the Act.

The display must be 'public', which means that it must be visible from a place to which the public have, or are permitted to have, access (whether on payment or otherwise) (s. 1(3)). This will include the inside of shops. There is no public good defence, but there are specific exemptions for museums and art galleries, cinemas, and matter included within either a television broadcast, or the performance of a 'play' within the meaning of s. 18 of the Theatres Act 1968 (see 7.6.1). In addition, there is no offence if members of the public can only see the display by paying an entrance fee specifically to do so, or if it is in a shop, or part of a shop which cannot be entered without passing a warning notice (s. 1(3)). These latter two exceptions only apply if people under the age of 18 are excluded from entry. The text of the warning notice which must be displayed to give protection to a shop is set out in s. 1(6), together with a requirement that it must be 'easily legible'.

Although this Act was widely welcomed, it cannot be said that it has had any very significant practical effects. The range of sex magazines to be seen on the top shelf of most newsagents is just as wide, if not wider, that in 1981. It is true that sex shop window displays have ceased to be a problem, but this is more a consequence of the more general provisions controlling sex shops in the Local Government (Miscellaneous Provisions) Act 1982 (see 7.8.1.2), than of the 1981 Act. On the other hand, the Act has been used to prosecute, for example, the showing of a sex video on a coach travelling up a motorway, which was visible from other vehicles, and the wearers of T-shirts containing indecent words or pictures. It is unlikely that these are the kinds of behaviour which the sponsors of the Act had in mind as needing control.

7.8.1.2 Local Government (Miscellaneous Provisions) Act 1982 ('the 1982 Act')

At the start of the 1980s there were some 160 establishments in the Soho area of London which were engaged in one way or another in the commercial exploitation of sex. The Westminster City Council had shown that it was possible to use planning controls against some of these activities. Shops which had set up booths in which individuals could watch videos, for example, were found to have 'changed their use' under the planning laws from being a shop to being a 'cinema'. As a result, this type of activity was effectively outlawed. Sex shops, as such, however, were not in any separate planning category from other shops. A change from a clothing shop to a sex shop, therefore, was subject to no planning control. The proliferation of sex shops in the Soho area was thought to be threatening its whole character, as most other commercial enterprises were being driven out. Moreover, there was concern in other parts of the country that sex shops could be opened anywhere, even in close proximity to a school or a church, and there was nothing that could be done about it. The response of the government was not to amend the planning laws, but to legislate for a separate licensing scheme for 'sex establishments'.

Section 3 of the 1982 Act empowers a local authority (generally the district council) to set up a licensing scheme for sex establishments in its area. 'Sex establishment' means a sex cinema or sex shop. Cinemas have really ceased to be a problem since the enactment of the wider licensing provisions contained in the Cinemas Act 1985. The concentration will therefore here be on 'sex shops'. The detailed provisions of the licensing scheme are set out in sch. 3 to the 1982 Act. Under these, a sex shop is defined as premises used for a business which consists 'to a significant degree' in dealing in 'sex articles' or 'other things intended for use in connection with, or for the purpose of stimulating or encouraging (i) sexual activity; or (ii) acts of force or restraint which are associated with sexual activity' (para. 4 (1)). 'Sex article' is itself the subject of a rather complicated definition in para. 4(3) and 4(4). These state that a sex article means:

(a) anything made for use in connection with, or for the purpose of stimulating or encouraging (i) sexual activity or (ii) acts of force or restraint associated with sexual activity; or

(b) any article containing or embodying matter to be read or looked at, or any recording of sound or vision, which is concerned primarily with the portrayal of, or primarily deals with or relates to, or is intended to stimulate or encourage, sexual activity or acts of force or restraint associated with sexual activity, or is concerned primarily with the portrayal of, or primarily deals with or relates to, genital organs, or urinary or excretory functions.

As this definition shows, the approach in the 1982 Act, unlike that of most of the other legal rules which have been considered in this chapter, is not to attempt to define on the basis of the *effect* of the material. It is irrelevant whether it depraves and corrupts, or shocks and disgusts. The approach is instead to try to *describe* the material in terms of its content, or what it is used for. As will be noted, the definition of 'sex article' is wide enough to cover books, magazines, photographs, films, videos, audio tapes, records, compact discs, sex aids (vibrators, dildoes, etc), bondage equipment, and probably many other things, for those with vivid enough imaginations! It is certainly wide enough to cover condoms or other birth control equipment, and a special exemption has had to be included (in para. 6(2)) to exclude trade in such items from the scope of the licensing scheme.

The definition of 'sex shop' under the Schedule fell to be considered in *Lambeth London Borough Council* v *Grewal* (1985) 82 Cr App R 301. The Council had introduced a licensing scheme under the 1982 Act. The defendant owned a shop which sold 'newspapers, magazines, children's books and comics, greetings cards, toys, ice-creams, stationery, toiletries, tobacco, dairy produce and groceries'. Amongst the magazines were some which could clearly be regarded as 'sex articles'. The defendant was advised by council officials that if he intended to display more than five sex articles he should apply for a sex shop licence. He failed to do so, and on a number of occasions, 16–20 different sex magazines were found on display. He was charged with operating a sex shop without a licence. In the Divisional Court the argument turned on the phrase 'to a significant degree', in that the Schedule, as we have seen, defines a sex shop as one where the business consists 'to a significant degree' in dealing in sex articles. The Divisional Court rejected the prosecutor's argument that 'significant' here meant simply more than *de minimis*. The following approach was, rather diffidently, suggested by Mustill LJ (at p. 307):

The word 'significant' has more than one meaning. It is capable, in some contexts of meaning 'more than trifling'. It does not have this meaning in the present context. A higher standard is set: how much higher cannot be prescribed by any rule of thumb. The ratio between the sexual and other aspects of the business will always be material. So also will the absolute quantity of sales. Since the fundamental question is whether the establishment is a 'sex shop' . . ., the court will no doubt find it appropriate to consider the character of the remainder of the business. The nature of the display can be a relevant factor, and the nature of the articles themselves will also be material, since the definition . . . covers a wide spectrum of offensiveness. It would be wrong to say in law that any single factor is decisive.

Applying this approach to the facts, and bearing in mind that it was the proportion of the *business* that was devoted to sex articles that was important, the court found that since the weekly turnover of about £45 in relation to sex articles amounted to less than 1.5 per cent of the shop's business, it could not be said that the Crown Court's view that this was not a sex shop was wrong.

The result of this case is that local councils cannot operate a strict rule that a certain number of articles on display turns a shop into a sex shop. The test will have to relate to the proportion of the shop's business that is devoted to this type of item.

Once a shop is classified as a sex shop, then a licence will be required. The local authority is entitled to refuse a licence on a wide range of grounds, set out in para. 12 of the Schedule. Some of the grounds are mandatory, for example if the applicant is under 18, or not resident in the UK (para. 12(1)). Others are discretionary, and may relate to such matters as the suitability of the applicant, the character of the locality, or the number of sex shops in that locality (para. 12(3)). The authority is specifically given the possibility of deciding that the appropriate number of sex shops in a particular locality is 'nil' (para. 12(4)).

If a licence is granted it may, and almost certainly will, be subject to conditions relating to such matters as the hours of opening, window displays (or lack of them!), and visibility of the interior to passers-by. There is the possibility of some overlap with the Indecent Displays (Control) Act here, but compliance with the terms of a licence will not provide a defence to a charge under that Act, nor will the holding of a licence provide any immunity against the Obscene Publications Acts. Licensed sex shops can be, and not infrequently are, the subject of police searches under s. 3 of the 1959 Act (see 7.4.1.2).

There is no indication in the Act of the fee that may be charged for the issue of a licence. This has led some local authorities, including Westminster (in relation to Soho), to set fees of several thousand pounds a year. A licence may be withdrawn at any time on certain of the grounds which would have justified the refusal of a licence in the first place (though not those relating to the nature of the locality; para. 17). In any case, all licences must be renewed annually, allowing the local authority close control over sex shops.

This Act can be said to have been a considerable success in achieving its objectives. In Soho, for example, the number of sex establishments was reduced from 160 plus, to just six. In other parts of the country there has ceased to be concern at the proliferation, and location, of sex shops. Moreover, this form of control is less restrictive of freedom of expression than others considered in this chapter, in that it simply controls the outlets. People who wish to buy sex articles are still able to do so. They are simply put to the relatively minor inconvenience of perhaps having to travel a little further in order to find a licensed sex shop.

7.8.2 Import controls

One of the fears which recurs in public debates about pornography, particularly amongst politicians, is that of the influx of highly obscene material from overseas, originating in countries with less restrictive laws than ours.

The current controls are contained in the Customs Consolidation Act 1876 and the Customs and Excise Management Act 1979. Section 42 of the 1876 Act prohibits the import of:

Indecent or obscene prints, paintings, photographs, books, cards, lithographic or other engravings, or any other indecent or obscene articles.

In *Derrick* v *Commissioners of Customs and Excise* [1972] 1 All ER 993, this definition was held to be wide enough to cover cinematograph film (as being *eiusdem generis* with photographs) and no doubt it would also be interpreted as covering videocassettes. It has also been held to cover sex aids, such as inflatable sex dolls (*Conegate* v *Commissioners of Customs and Excise* [1987] QB 254, discussed at 7.9).

Powers of forfeiture, together with related offences, are contained in the Customs and Excise Management Act 1979, s. 49, and sch. 3.

It will be noted that the test in s. 42 of the 1876 Act is 'obscene or indecent'. 'Obscene' here has its dictionary meaning, rather than that of 'deprave and corrupt' (see 7.3.1). This means that a stricter control is available as regards the *importation* of 'articles' covered by the Obscene Publications Acts, than in relation to their publication. This has given rise to some potential conflict with the concept of free movement of goods under European Community law. This is considered further in the next section (7.9). Robertson and Nicol (*Media Law*, p. 154) state that as a result Customs and Excise officers do not now seize articles, whatever their country of origin, unless they would appear to fall within the 1959 Act 'deprave and corrupt' test. This is, however, a matter of practice rather than law, at least in relation to goods coming from outside the European Community.

7.9 EUROPEAN APPROACH TO OBSCENITY

There are two issues to look at here. First, the cases, referred to briefly above, which have concerned the application of the free movement of goods provisions of the Treaty of Rome to the importation of pornography into the UK. Secondly, the approach of the European Court of Human Rights towards the English obscenity laws.

7.9.1 European Community law

Article 30 of the Treaty of Rome states that 'Quantitative restrictions on imports and all measures having equivalent effect shall . . . be prohibited'. In *R* v *Henn* [1981] AC 850 it was argued that this meant that the rules restricting the importation of pornography into the UK were unlawful. The defendant had been convicted, in relation to the same material, under both the customs legislation, and the Obscene Publications Act 1959, and was appealing against those convictions. The House of Lords referred the issue to the European Court of Justice ('ECJ'). That court ruled that the import restrictions applying to pornography did constitute a quantitative restriction within Art. 30. However, Art. 36 of the Treaty provided that the provisions of Art. 30 'shall not preclude prohibitions or restrictions on imports . . . justified on grounds of public morality . . .'. The ECJ took the view that the UK's restrictions came within those permitted by Art. 36. The House of Lords therefore upheld Henn's conviction.

The subject matter of the prosecution in *Henn* was films and magazines, which are clearly articles falling within the scope of the Obscene Publications Act 1959. A slightly different issue arose in *Conegate v Commissioners of Customs and Excise* [1987] QB 254. The objects which were seized in this case were life-size inflatable rubber sex-dolls, complete with 'orifices, one with a vibrator . . . attached to the head . . .'. Some 'sexy vacuum flasks' were also seized. In this case, the ECJ, applying the same Articles as in *Henn* came to the conclusion that the seizure of these items was contrary to European law. This was because, while it could not be said in *Henn* that there was any lawful trade within the UK in the items seized because of the Obscene Publications Act, that Act did not apply to the type of articles under consideration in *Conegate*. There were thus no restrictions within in the UK on the manufacture or sale of such items. This prevented the British government in this case relying on Art. 36 to justify the seizure. As the ECJ put it (para. 20):

> a member State may not rely on grounds of public morality within the meaning of Art. 36 of the Treaty in order to prohibit the importation of certain goods on the grounds that they are indecent or obscene, where the same goods may be manufactured freely on its territory and marketed on its territory subject only to an absolute prohibition on their transmission by post, a restriction on their public display and, in certain regions, a system of licensing of premises for the sale of those goods to customers aged 18 or over.

It is for this reason that, as noted above, Customs and Excise officers now only seize goods which appear to be subject to the Obscene Publications Act 1959.

A further attempt to use European law in this area was made in *R v Bow St Magistrates, ex parte Noncyp* [1990] 1 QB 123. This concerned the seizure by Customs officers of books destined for a bookshop called *Gay's the Word* in London. They were of a homosexual nature, with titles such as *Men Loving Themselves*, and *Below the Belt*. The defence argument in this case was that the Customs officers should have taken into account the possibility of a defence based on the defence of public good under s. 4 of the Obscene Publications Act 1959. The Court of Appeal did not feel the need in this case to refer the issue to the ECJ. Applying the principles from *Henn* and *Conegate* it took the view that as long as there was a restriction on the trade in the UK as regards articles of the type seized (in this case books with a sexual content), then they could be forfeited provided that they were 'obscene' within the meaning of s. 42 of the Customs Consolidation Act 1876. There was no need, therefore, to consider the possible availability of a public good defence under s. 4 of the Obscene Publications Act 1959.

7.9.2 European Convention on Human Rights ('ECHR')

Article 10(2) of the ECHR allows for restrictions over freedom of expression for the protection of health or morals. The scope of this provision was tested in the case of *Handyside v United Kingdom* (1976) 1 EHRR 737. Handyside had published in England a book entitled *The Little Red Schoolbook*. This had

208 pages, and was aimed at schoolchildren aged 12 and upwards. Alongside sections on education, teachers, pupils and the system it had a 26 page section dealing with sexual matters. This included sections on such things as masturbation, orgasm, homosexuality, and methods of abortion. The book was seized under s. 3 of the Obscene Publications Act 1959, forfeited and destroyed. Handyside brought proceedings under the ECHR alleging, among other things, a breach of Art. 10. The government relied on the restriction on the basis of protecting morals. To fall within this allowable restriction the control would have to be found by the court to be 'prescribed by law', to promote a legitimate objective, and to be 'necessary in a democratic society' for the achievement of that objective. The court had no difficulty in finding that the procedures which had been taken under the 1959 Act were 'prescribed by law'. It was also of the view, despite Mr Handyside's claim that in reality the action against him was politically based, that the application of the restriction was carried out for the purpose of 'protecting morality' amongst the children towards whom the book was directed. As regards the 'necessity' of the action, Mr Handyside laid stress on the fact that the book had circulated freely (in translation) in many other States which were signatories to the European Convention. If these States had not thought it necessary to prevent the distribution of the book, how could the action taken in England be deemed to be 'necessary'? On this issue the Court relied on the 'margin of appreciation' or discretion which is allowed to member States (p. 759):

> The Contracting States have each fashioned their approach in the light of the situation obtaining in their respective territories; they have had regard, inter alia, to the different views prevailing there about the demands of the protection of morals in a democratic society. The fact that most of them decided to allow the work to be distributed does not mean that the contrary decision of the Inner London Quarter Sessions was a breach of Article 10.

The conclusion was, therefore, that there was no breach of Art. 10 by the action taken against *The Little Red Schoolbook*. The decision also has the effect that there would seem very little point in challenging any of the laws looked at in this chapter under the ECHR. Certainly in all of the situations where criminal offences are created it seems certain that the European Court of Human Rights would say that the restrictions fell within the allowable margin of appreciation. Whether the operation of the censorship systems for films and videos would receive similar approval may be more doubtful, but on balance, given the apparent unwillingness of the Court in *Handyside* to become involved in discussion of the merits of the issues in such cases, it is likely that they would be upheld.

7.10   PROPOSALS FOR REFORM

There have been many attempts over the years to suggest ways in which the laws in this area should be reformed. In practice, however, the changes in the law which have taken place have been reactions to particular perceived problems, and as a result piecemeal and lacking in coherence. It is disappointing that the most recent set of fully thought through proposals for comprehensive reform should date from as long ago as 1979. These are the proposals of the Williams Committee on Obscenity and Film Censorship. They are discussed here, not because there appears any great likelihood of those proposals being adopted, but as an example of one way in which the law could be re-designed, starting with a blank sheet, and arguing from basic principles.

The starting point for the Williams Committee was its acceptance of what it called 'the harm principle'. This is the idea, adapted from John Stuart Mill, that the law should only be used to prevent behaviour (in this case the publication of pornography) where it could be shown to cause harm to others. The Committee looked, therefore, at the available evidence of the harmful effects of pornography. It took, as another fundamental premise, that the presumption should be in favour of freedom, and the burden of proof in establishing harm should lie on those who wished to restrict expression. On this basis they concluded, as we have seen others have done (see 7.1), that the case was at best 'not proven'. The research evidence was equivocal, and it could not be said that any clear harm to individuals resulted from the reading of pornographic material, for example, encouraging criminal sexual activity. Nor was the Committee prepared to accept the alleged social or moral harms resulting from it, nor the idea of 'harm' caused to the consumer alone, as justifying prohibition. This meant that the only harm of which they were prepared to take account, was harm to the participants in the production of pornographic films or photographs. Two possible types of harm of this kind were identified, and were summarised in s. 19 of the Committee's summary of its proposals (*Report*, p. 161), which state that prohibited material should consist of photographs and films whose production appears:

> to have involved the exploitation for sexual purposes of any person where either
> (a) that person appears from the evidence as a whole to have been at the relevant time under the age of sixteen, or
> (b) the material gives reason to believe that actual physical harm was inflicted on that person.

There should be no restriction on the production or publication of any material falling outside these two categories. On the other hand, the Committee found a 'remarkable balance of opinion' in favour of controlling the availability and display of pornographic material. This led the Committee to accept that the availability of certain types of material should be 'restricted'. The test of restriction would be whether its *unrestricted availability* would offend a reasonable person. Three points must be noted about this test. First, the standard is that of the reasonable person at any particular time, and is thus, as the Committee recognised, liable to change with changing social mores. Secondly, it is the offensiveness resulting from the material's free availability, rather than its inherent character, that justifies restriction. Thirdly, the offensiveness refers not only to what is actually visible when, for example, a magazine is displayed on a shelf, but also to the content of the material. So the fact that the cover of a magazine is less explicit than the material inside, as is usually the case, would not protect it from restriction. As we have seen, the Indecent Displays (Control) Act 1982, which attempted to achieve some of the same objectives as the Williams Committee's restriction controls, does not operate in this way, but concentrates solely on what is visible to the public. Under the Committee's proposals, restricted material would only be available in specialist shops, from which persons under 18 would be excluded, and which would be required to display warning notices.

The third area considered by the Committee was film censorship. Here many commentators felt that the Committee lost its nerve. Rather than simply applying the principles outlined above to films, the Committee, concerned about the willingness of some film makers to 'exploit a taste for torture and violence', advocated the retention of censorship, with, however, specific statutory guidelines as to how the powers should operate (proposals 35–56, *Report*, pp. 163–166).

It should be noted that none of the Committee's proposals would apply to written as opposed to pictorial material. The printed word, since it cannot involve either of the harms recognised by the Committee, and was not felt to be capable of being 'offensive' within the Committee's definition, would not be subject to prohibition or restriction. For this reason, among others, the Committee rejected any idea of a 'public good' defence, since it was in relation to printed matter that such a defence was likely, in the Committee's view, to have most justification.

The reaction to the Committee's report was mixed. Conservatives saw it as too liberal, whereas liberals thought that it did not go far enough. There would also be considerable problems in the practical operation of the test of 'offensiveness' (see R. Stone, 'Obscenity Law Reform: Some Practical Problems' (1980) 130 NLJ 872). As a result, the report was shelved by the Conservative government, and there seems no prospect of its being revived.

EIGHT

Freedom of Assembly

8.1 INTRODUCTION

No one who has witnessed the events which have occurred in Eastern Europe over the past few years can have any doubts as to the power of the demonstration as a political weapon. With the *Solidarity* movement in Poland being the precursor of much that followed, in country after country people took to the streets to indicate that they had had enough of the existing political regime and that it was time for change. Two events in particular stick in the memory. First, President Ceaucescu of Romania standing on a balcony and being faced with the sudden realisation that the large and hostile crowd in front of him was no longer going to listen to what he had to say. The visible change from powerful dictator to frightened old man is even more chilling in hindsight, given the knowledge of the rather summary trial and execution which followed. The second event to linger in the memory is the reaction on the streets of Moscow to the attempted coup against President Gorbachev in 1991. Here the people took to the streets not to demand change but to defend freedoms which they felt that they had already gained, and were prepared to pitch their own physical safety against military force.

Even in England we have had a fairly recent example of mass demonstrations playing at least a part in forcing a government to change course. The reform of local taxation which introduced the Community Charge (more commonly known as the 'Poll Tax') led to meetings, processions, and other demonstrations around the country, and contributed to the opposition which forced the Conservative government to change what had been put forward as a central policy; a change which furthermore played some part in the enforced resignation of the Prime Minister at the time, Margaret Thatcher.

The Poll Tax demonstrations, however, also illustrated the dangers inherent in mass meetings. At times considerable disorder resulted from these events, including violence against people and property, and, in some cases, looting. As well as being counterproductive in terms of the demonstrators' political objectives, such behaviour also indicates the justification for the existence of legal controls designed to draw the line between legitimate mass action, and the breakdown of public order.

Two further related issues need consideration as preliminary matters. First, the demonstration has particular importance in a situation where the majority of the population has no access to the most effective means of communicating a political message, that is, through the mass media. The control of broadcasting and the Press is in the hands of a very small number of people. Moreover, national television, which is the most powerful of the mass media, is under a legal duty to provide 'balanced' programming. This tends to leave little scope for the presentation of viewpoints which fall outside those held by the main political parties. If, however, a demonstration is held, and sufficient numbers of people participate, then the BBC or ITN may feel obliged to cover the event, and therefore give publicity to the views of the demonstrators.

The second issue referred to above follows from this, and is that the freedom of assembly can in some senses be looked at as an aspect of freedom of expression. Many of the arguments which we have looked at in the chapters concerned with that topic will also be relevant here. This is particularly so where the demonstration is addressed by a speaker who may put forward views which only have minority support. To what extent should such a speaker be protected, on the basis of John Stuart Mill's argument from truth, or any of the other arguments for allowing freedom of expression (see 5.2.1)?

Finally, there are problems which arise in the industrial context, in trying to define the acceptable limits to 'picketing', that is the attendance in numbers at the gate of a place of work with a view to persuading people not to enter. These are noted at various points in the rest of the chapter.

With these considerations in mind we now turn to look at the traditional approach in English law to demonstrations and public order, and then at the background to the main piece of legislation which now governs this area: the Public Order Act 1986.

8.1.1 The courts' approach.
In *Hubbard* v *Pitt* [1976] QB 142 Lord Denning referred (at p. 176) to the comment of the Court of Common Council in 1819 recognising 'the undoubted right of Englishmen to assemble together for the purpose of deliberating upon public grievances', and continued:

> Such is the right of assembly. So also is the right to meet together, to go in procession, to demonstrate, and to protest on matters of public concern. As long as all is done peaceably and in good order, without threats or incitement to violence or obstruction to traffic it is not prohibited.

Although Lord Denning starts with a clear assertion of 'rights', it becomes clear in the later part of this quotation that he is not in fact talking about a very strong right. In Hohfeldian terms (see 1.3.1) it appears to be simply a 'privilege', that is a freedom to act in a particular way as long as no one else is affected by the behaviour. This approach has tended to be that generally adopted by the courts in relation to meetings and demonstrations. They are permissible, but if they constitute any type of interference with others' rights, even politically insignificant rights, such as the use of the highway, the courts will be quite prepared to intervene. A particular problem can arise where the cause of the problem is not the person who has organised the demonstration, but people who wish to oppose it. In *Beatty* v *Gilbanks* (1882) 15 Cox CC 138, a procession by the Salvation Army was being disrupted by an opposing group which styled itself the 'Skeleton Army'. Beatty, a Salvation Army captain leading the procession was arrested when he failed to obey a police instruction to stop, and that the procession should cease. The Divisional Court held that the Salvation Army procession could not be regarded as an 'unlawful assembly' simply because others were trying to disrupt it in a way which might well lead to a breach of the peace. This decision is, however, perhaps the high point in the recognition of rights of assembly. Later decisions, focusing more directly on the power of the police to deal with a breach of the peace, such as *Wise* v *Dunning* [1902] 1 KB 167, and *Duncan* v *Jones* [1936] 1 KB 218, have not accorded such rights any high status. Indeed in *Duncan* v *Jones* Lord Hewart CJ expressed the view that:

> English law does not recognize any special right of public meeting for political or other purposes. The right of assembly . . . is nothing more than a view taken by the Court of the individual liberty of the subject.

A slightly more robust approach to the right was taken in *Hirst* v *Chief Constable for West Yorkshire* (1986) 85 Cr App R 143. This concerned the offence of obstructing the highway contrary to the Highways Act 1980, s. 137. Some animal rights demonstrators were standing in a pedestrian precinct, outside a shop selling furs. The demonstrators were holding a banner, and distributing leaflets. They were convicted of obstruction, the magistrates taking the view that the only lawful use of the highway was to pass and repass about one's lawful business, and for any purposes incidental to that. This followed the views expressed in cases such as *Homer* v *Cadman* (1886) 16 Cox CC 51, and *Waite* v *Taylor* (1985) 149 JP 551. The Divisional Court in *Hirst* however, preferred the approach taken in *Nagy* v *Weston* [1965] 1 All ER 78 which simply stated that the use must be 'reasonable' to be lawful, which was a question of fact in each case. Applying this to the case, Otton J said that the magistrates had failed to consider this question. If they had done so the balance between the right to protest and demonstrate on the one hand, and the need for peace and good order on the other would have been properly struck, and 'the "freedom of protest on issues of public concern" would be given the recognition it deserves'. This recognises the right to demonstrate as a relevant factor to be considered in assessing the reasonableness of a person's use of the highway.

The traditional approach of the English courts can only be said to be ambivalent. On the one hand, the right to demonstrate and protest is recognised; on the other, obstruction to the traffic may well be enough to override it. It cannot be said that there is any strong support given to the right.

8.1.2   Background to the Public Order Act 1986

The sequence of events which led to the passing of the Public Order Act 1986 can probably be traced back at least to 1974 and the demonstration against the

National Front in Red Lion Square in London, which led to the death of one of the demonstrators. An inquiry was chaired by Lord Scarman, and its report (Cmnd 5919, 1975) made a number of recommendations for reform of the law, which were not, however, acted on at the time. In 1981 there was rioting in Brixton (and in other parts of the country), which again led to Lord Scarman being asked to report. Again his recommendations (Cmnd 8427, 1981) were not immediately acted on. Throughout the period there was also concern about football violence. In addition, a number of public order issues arose from industrial disputes, particularly the miners' strike of 1984–85. A feature of the Brixton disorders, and to some extent the miners' strike, was that, whereas in many situations of public disorder the conflict is between two groups of citizens (Salvation Army/Skeleton Army; fascists/communists (1930s); Mods/Rockers (1960s); National Front/anti-racists (1970s); football supporters/rival supporters (1980s)) with the police intervening as a third party, in these two cases the target for the demonstrations was largely the police itself. This was particularly the case in Brixton where the riots are thought to have been sparked off by a certain degree of insensitive and heavy-handed policing. This development in itself gave an additional impetus to the need for a fresh look at the public order laws. Moreover in 1983 the Law Commission had reviewed the existing public order offences, and proposed some significant amendments (*Criminal Law: Offences Relating to Public Order* (Law Com No. 123, 1983)). It was with this background that the government published in 1985 its White Paper, *Review of Public Order Law* (Cmnd 9510), which formed the basis of the Public Order Act 1986.

The Act was passed with very little controversy. Its effect was to put the law relating to public order almost entirely on a statutory basis, whereas before the relevant offences had been found in a mixture of common law and statute (principally the Public Order Act 1936). The one continuing exception is the group of powers which the police have available to deal with actual or apprehended breaches of the peace. These powers are still defined by case law rather than statute.

The Public Order Act 1986 ('POA') does two principal things. First it provides a framework of controls which apply to processions and demonstrations. These are aimed at the events themselves, and if, when, and how, they should take place. Secondly, it enacts a range of offences to deal with disorderly conduct of various degrees of seriousness, from riot, to behaviour causing alarm or distress. For our purposes we can look on these as controls over behaviour once an event is taking place. They relate to what people can say or do while participating in a procession or other form of demonstration.

The Act also contains some specific provisions aimed at football offenders (that is, 'exclusion orders'), which are not discussed further in this book, and at people unlawfully setting up camps on private land (the problem of the so-called 'hippie convoys'), which are looked at briefly at 8.4.8.2.

8.2 PROCESSIONS

The most dramatic form of demonstration is probably the procession. The sight of many thousands of people marching down a street, carrying banners, and chanting is a powerful image, whether viewed in person or on a television screen. It is also one of the most disruptive forms of demonstration. A large-scale march will prevent all other traffic from using that route, and may bring normal activities in a town centre to a standstill. For this reason the tightest controls in the POA relate to processions.

8.2.1 Definitions

Perhaps surprisingly there is no attempt to define a procession in the Act. In most cases this is unlikely to cause a problem. What, however, of the situation where processions have been banned for a period, because of, say, disturbances caused by anti-racist demonstrations against processions organised by a group opposed to immigration. If one member of the group marches through the town centre on a Saturday afternoon, is that a procession? If not, what if two or three members march together? The only case law on the issue is the statement by Lord Goddard in *Flockhart* v *Robinson* [1950] 2 KB 498 at p. 502 that:

> A procession is not a mere body of persons: it is a body of persons moving along a route.

The reference to a 'body' of persons rules out the 'one-person' procession, but does not conclusively require any minimum number beyond this.

The only processions covered by the provisions of Part II of the POA are public processions. These are defined in s. 16 as processions 'in a public place'. The section also defines 'public place' as:

(a)   any highway . . ., and
(b)   any place to which at the material time the public or any section of the public has access, on payment or otherwise, as of right or by virtue of express or implied permission.

The law is normally used in relation to processions taking place on highways. The definition of public place is wide enough, however, that it would cover a procession into a theatre or cinema, for example, to protest about the play or film being performed or shown. Nor is it necessarily limited to areas within such premises where the public have specific permission to be. In *Cawley* v *Frost* [1976] 3 All ER 743 an almost identical definition of 'public place' was held to be wide enough to cover the speedway track surrounding a football pitch. Spectators admitted to the stadium to watch a football match had no licence to be on the speedway track, but it was still regarded as a public place. If a group of fans decided to hold a procession around the track to protest about the manager's team selection, for example, this would therefore appear to be a public procession.

8.2.2 Notice requirements

A requirement to give the police notice of a public procession is imposed by s. 11 where the procession has one of three purposes. These are: to demonstrate support for or opposition to the views of any person or body of persons; to publicise a cause or campaign; or to mark or commemorate an event. A crocodile of schoolchildren being led from school to nearby playing fields is not therefore subject to the notice requirements. All processions which are in the nature of a 'demonstration' will, however, be covered. There are, however, also a number of exceptions even where the procession *prima facie* falls within one of the above purposes.

First, the notice requirement does not apply to a procession which is one that is commonly or customarily held in the police area (s. 11(2)). Two examples of processions of this type would be May Day processions, which are common in some parts of the country, and Good Friday processions which some churches hold in order to bear witness to Christ's crucifixion. The exception only applies to established processions, however. A person wishing to initiate a procession of this type within a police area would have to give notice. The exception is, therefore, not there to exclude certain types of event because of their purpose, but simply to indicate that where a procession has regularly occurred in the past the police will be presumed to have notice of it for the future. It will presumably simply be a question of fact as to how often a procession has had to be held to fall within the exception. Will it be five years or ten years or more? Organisers of events other than those of very long-standing will be well advised to give notice until such time as the police indicate that this is unnecessary.

Secondly, funeral processions organised by a funeral director in the normal course of business are also excluded from the notice requirements (s. 11(2)).

Finally, there is a more general exception to the notice requirement where it is not reasonably practicable to give any advance notice. This is intended to legitimise the instant reaction to a particular event. For example, people exiled from their home country might hear on the radio that the regime is now thought to be about to carry out summary executions of political prisoners. A procession organised for that evening to march to the country's embassy in London in protest would not be unlawful for failure to comply with the notice provisions.

The length of notice required is normally six clear days before the date on which the procession is to be held. The 'clear days' will exclude the day on which the notice is received, and the day of the proposed procession. Notice of a procession to be held on a Saturday must therefore be given by the previous Saturday. Section 11(6), however, recognises that in some situations it may not be practicable to give six days' notice. A procession may be organised on the Wednesday to take place on the following Friday. This might happen, for example, where a child is knocked down by a car outside a school on the Wednesday morning, and parents decide to hold a procession from the school to the council offices on the Friday, when a meeting of the council is to decide whether to install a pedestrian crossing outside the school.

The form of the notice is dealt with in ss. 11(3)-(6). It is not specifically stated that it must be in writing, but this is implied by the fact that it is to be given either by post or delivery by hand. It must specify the date of the procession, the intended starting time, the proposed route, and the name and address of at least one person responsible for organising it. There is no need to state the purpose of the procession. It is to be delivered, by hand or (if six clear days in advance) by post, to a police station in the police district in which it is proposed that the procession will start.

Failure to give the proper notice, or organising a procession which does not correspond to details given in the notice, is a summary offence, punishable with a fine not exceeding level 3 on the standard scale.

This requirement of notice may look as though the permission of the police is being required before someone can hold a procession. This is not strictly the case, however. As the exception for traditional processions shows, the requirement is primarily one of 'notice', so that the police can organise any necessary resources to cope with the proposed procession. Once the notice has been given the organiser does not need to wait for any 'go-ahead' from the police. As will be seen, however, the police may in some cases wish to impose conditions, and can also initiate procedures which may lead to a ban.

8.2.3   Conditions

The power to impose conditions applies to all public processions, not simply those organised for one of the purposes which gives rise to the requirement of notice. There must, however, presumably be at least some implied agreement between the people concerned for it to constitute a 'body of persons' and therefore a procession (see 8.2.1).

The power is given to the 'senior police officer' which means different things in different circumstances. Where conditions are being imposed before the event, the senior police officer means the chief officer of police (that is the chief constable, or the Commissioner; s. 12(2)(b)). In this case, the conditions should be given in writing (s. 12(3)), presumably to the organisers. If the procession is assembling, however, or is under way, the senior police officer simply means the most senior officer (in terms of rank) who is present (s. 12(2)(a)). If only a constable is present, then that constable is the senior police officer and has the power to impose conditions on the procession. The conditions do not have to be given in writing. They may be communicated verbally to those assembling, or taking part in the procession.

8.2.3.1   Grounds for imposing conditions   The power to impose conditions only arises where the senior police officer reasonably believes either that certain undesirable consequences may flow from the procession, or that the procession is being organised for an illegitimate purpose (s. 12(1)). The undesirable consequences and illegitimate purpose which will have this effect are set out in s. 12(1). The consequences are that the procession may result in:

(a)   serious public disorder; or
(b)   serious damage to property; or
(c)   serious disruption to the life of the community.

The only one of these which can be regarded in any way as controversial is the last. What exactly is meant by serious disruption? If the traffic in a town centre is brought to a standstill is this sufficient? If so, it runs the risk of failing to take account of the fact that the whole point of a demonstration may be lost if nobody is inconvenienced in any way. A certain amount of disruption is inevitable from any large-scale procession, and the power to impose conditions on this basis will need to be used sensitively if it is not to operate oppressively.

The illegitimate purpose which will justify the imposition of conditions is intimidation, with a view to compelling others either not to do an act which they have a right to do, or to do an act which they have a right not to do. The inclusion of this results directly from events which occurred during the miners' strike of 1984/85, where there were allegations that groups of striking miners processed outside the houses of those continuing to work, or accompanied them along the street on the way to work, with a view to intimidating them into joining the strike. It is difficult to see many situations where this ground for imposing conditions would apply outside the context of an industrial dispute (see also *Police* v *Reid* [1987] Crim LR 702 at 8.3.2).

8.2.3.2 Conditions which can be imposed A very broad discretion is given to the senior officer of police as to the type of conditions which can be imposed. Section 12(1) states that the officer may impose such conditions 'as appear to him necessary' to prevent the disorder, damage, disruption, or intimidation that is feared. This formulation does not require the officer's decision as to what is necessary to be based on reasonable grounds. There is no list of the types of conditions which may be imposed, but it is specifically mentioned that they may include conditions as to the route to be followed, and may specify that the procession is not to enter a particular public place. The power to alter the route is perhaps inevitable, but has the potential for significantly reducing the effectiveness of the procession. If the purpose of the procession is to draw attention to activities going on in a particular factory, or in a particular country, the diversion of the procession away from the factory, or the relevant embassy, may deprive it of virtually all purpose. Once again there is a heavy burden on the police to ensure that the aim of maintaining an orderly society does not entirely emasculate the opportunities for protest.

Offences are committed by those who organise, or take part in a procession, and knowingly fail to comply with a condition (s. 12(4) and (5)). Incitement of others to commit such an offence is in itself a specific offence under the POA (s. 12(6)). Moreover there is a power of arrest without warrant in relation to anyone whom a constable in uniform reasonably suspects of committing one of these offences. So, if a procession is under way, and the senior officer directs that it should change route, perhaps in order to avoid a confrontation with a rival demonstration, any person who does not follow the new route is liable to be arrested. It is not at all clear that this arrest power is necessary, given the existence of the power under s. 25 of PACE (see 2.4.3.2), and the common law power to arrest in relation to breaches of the peace (see 2.4.1).

8.2.4 The power to ban processions
The power to initiate the procedures leading to a ban is exclusively in the hands of the chief officer of police (s. 13(1),(4)). That officer must reasonably

believe that because of particular circumstances existing in the police area, or part of it, the powers to impose conditions under s. 12 will not be sufficient to prevent serious public disorder. Note that the risk of damage to property, disruption to the community, or intimidation, is not enough to justify a ban. The procedure that must then be followed is different for London as opposed to the rest of the country.

In London, the Commissioner for the City of London, or the Commissioner for the Metropolis, makes the banning order with the consent of the Home Secretary. Outside London, the chief constable must apply to the district council, which has the power to issue the ban, subject to the approval (which may be given with modifications) of the Home Secretary. There is, then, an element of political control over the issue of bans. In practice it is unlikely, however, that either a district council or the Home Secretary are going to risk 'second-guessing' a chief of police who says that unless a ban is imposed serious public disorder will ensue. The political consequences of a refusal to ban being followed by rioting in the streets suggests that most councils and Home Secretaries will be prepared to listen to the advice of the professional police officer in such matters.

The nature of the ban is that it may apply to the holding of all, or a particular class of, public processions. There is no power to ban a specific public procession, other than by defining the 'class' so narrowly that only one procession is covered. This was deliberate. Lord Scarman had in his Brixton report come out in favour of a power to ban a particular procession in certain circumstances (*Report*, Cmnd 8427, 1981, para. 7.41–7.49), having changed his mind since his earlier 'Red Lion Square' report. The government did not follow his recommendation because it was felt that the targeting of a specific procession might appear to be based too obviously on political considerations. There is also the problem of sufficiently identifying a particular procession. If it were named by the organisation under the auspices of which it is being held, it would be all too easy for virtually the same procession to take place ostensibly on behalf of a different, or even newly created, organisation.

The ban can cover all or part of a police area, and last for up to three months (s. 13(1)). The order containing the ban should be put into writing (s. 13(6)), but there are no other formal requirements. There is no obligation on the person issuing the ban to give it any particular form of publicity.

The issue of a ban is susceptible to judicial review, as shown by *Kent* v *Metropolitan Police Commissioner, The Times*, 15 May 1981, which arose under the very similar power to ban given by the Public Order Act 1936. The Commissioner had issued a ban on all processions for 28 days from 25 April, except those traditionally held on May Day, and those of a religious character customarily held. The applicant was a leading member of the Campaign for Nuclear Disarmament which had planned to hold public processions during this period. The Court of Appeal, while accepting the application as the proper way to challenge a ban, refused to interfere with the Commissioner's decision. The definition of a 'class' could be achieved by excluding certain types of procession, as had been done here. Moreover, although at least one member of the Court felt that the Commissioner's stated reasons for the ban were 'meagre', there was no evidence that the decision was capricious or unreasonable. It was taken in a context where there had been significant outbreaks of violence (that is, the 1981 Brixton disorders). The Court was reluctant to interfere with the Commissioner's exercise of discretion, particularly since his actions had been approved by the Home Secretary. We see here, perhaps, the same reluctance to 'second-guess' the police that we have already seen is likely to arise at other stages of the banning process. In truth, although there is in form the possibility of supervision of this power by the local authorities, the Home Secretary, and the courts, in practice the chief constables and Commissioners have a power which they are largely free to operate at their own discretion, and to which there is unlikely to be any serious challenge.

Organising, or participating in a banned procession are summary offences (s. 13(7), (8)), as is inciting such participation (s. 13(9)). There is a power of arrest on grounds of reasonable suspicion that a person is committing any of these offences (s. 13(10)). It is exercisable by a constable in uniform.

8.3 PUBLIC ASSEMBLIES

Prior to 1986 there was no statutory control over the holding of public meetings as opposed to processions. The addition of such a power in the POA was a recognition that the static demonstration may raise as many public order problems as the mobile procession. It can also be seen as a response to the particular problems caused by mass picketing during the printers' dispute at Warrington, and the miners' strike of 1984/85. The long-term 'peace camp' at Greenham Common was also mentioned in the White Paper (Cmnd 9510, para. 5.1) as an event which gave rise to serious public order concerns. The scope of the power is not, however, limited to such situations, as will be seen from the definitions. The power to control is limited to the imposition of conditions. There is no power to ban public meetings. The White Paper commented that (para. 5.3):

Meetings and assemblies are a more important means of exercising freedom of speech than are marches: a power to ban them, even as a last resort, would be potentially a major infringement of freedom of speech (especially at election time). It might also be difficult to enforce: and there was no strong request from the police for a power to ban.

For all these reasons, the power to impose conditions was thought to be sufficient.

8.3.1 Definitions

A 'public assembly' is defined in s. 16 of the POA as:

an assembly of 20 or more persons in a public place which is wholly or partly open to the air.

A public place is defined in the same way as for processions (see 8.2.1).

The definition is very wide. It would appear to cover, for example, a crowd gathered to listen to the patter of a street trader, or to the performance of a brass band, as much as people attending a political meeting. The purposes of the assembly are entirely irrelevant to the power to impose conditions which is given by s. 14.

Unlike the position as regards processions, a minimum number of participants is stated, that is, 20. This could lead to problems of evidence if there is a dispute as to the number present. In relation to someone prosecuted for breaking a condition (see 8.3.2), the burden would presumably be on the police to prove beyond reasonable doubt that 20 or more people were present. If the conditions are challenged by means of judicial review, again the burden would be on the police, but only on the balance of probabilities.

The assembly must be in the open air, at least in part. This seems to be a consequence of a view endorsed by the White Paper (para. 5.17), that it is in relation to open air assemblies that disorder is most likely to result. The extension to assemblies which are only partly in the open air removes potential difficulties as regards stadia which are partly covered. Problems of definition might arise, however, in relation to a meeting held within premises, with an 'overflow' (perhaps with closed circuit television coverage of the speeches) outside (see D. Bonner and R. Stone, 'The Public Order Act 1986: Steps in the Wrong Direction', [1987] *PL* 202, at 223).

8.3.2 Conditions

The procedures for imposing conditions on public assemblies (s. 14) are virtually the same as for public processions (see 8.2.3). Conditions may be imposed by chief officers of police before the event, or by the most senior officer present in relation to an assembly which is taking place (s. 14(2)). The grounds for imposing conditions are listed in s. 14(1) and are identical to those in s. 12(1) which apply to processions, that is a reasonable belief that the assembly will result in serious public disorder, serious damage to property, or serious disruption to the life of the community, or that its purpose is intimidation. It is possible, however, that there is more scope here for intimidation. Much industrial picketing takes the form of a static assembly rather than a procession. It might also apply, for example, in situations where crowds assemble outside the place where a meeting is being held, and try to stop people entering. There must be an intention to force people to act differently, however, not just to make it less pleasant to carry on as they originally intended. In *Police* v *Reid* [1987] Crim LR 702, there was an anti-apartheid demonstration outside South Africa House, where a reception was being held, with much shouting at guests as they arrived. The stipendiary magistrate ruled that the chief inspector who had tried to impose conditions had acted *ultra vires*, in that he had interpreted 'intimidation' as including 'causing discomfort'. There would have had to be an intention to compel the guests not to go into the reception for the activities of the demonstrators to amount to intimidation.

As with processions, it is a summary offence to organise or participate in an assembly and knowingly fail to comply with a condition (s. 14(4), (5)).

Incitement to such participation is also an offence (s. 14(6)). A power of arrest is given to a constable in uniform by virtue of s. 14(7).

8.4 PUBLIC ORDER OFFENCES

In this section we are looking at the controls over behaviour which is to a greater or lesser extent 'disorderly'. The offences are in many ways simply ordinary criminal offences, raising no special civil liberties issues. Three aspects, however, make them of particular significance in a book on civil liberties. First there is the possibility of the offences being used to restrict protest, rather than disorder itself. In other words, they are offences which may be particularly apposite for dealing with the consequences of demonstrations, or public meetings, where disputes have arisen between opposing groups, or between the demonstrators and the police. The dividing line between acceptable protest, and unacceptable disorder, is at times a fine one, and we need to consider whether the range of offences are, or have the potential to be, used in relation to behaviour which it might be argued falls on the acceptable side of the borderline.

Secondly, there is the problem of 'disorder' itself. To what extent is it acceptable for a society to insist on 'order', and to condemn 'disorderly' behaviour, unless that behaviour has resulted in some identifiable harm to others? As will be seen, a number of the offences are based on the potential of the behaviour for causing harm, rather than the fact that such harm has in fact resulted from it, and the range of harms recognised by the law are very broad.

Finally, the fact that the offences are sometimes directed at what people *say*, rather than what they *do*, clearly raises freedom of expression issues. These become particularly problematic in the context of 'incitement to racial hatred' (see 8.6), where it may be the offensiveness of what is said that forms the basis for condemnation. Parallels can be drawn between this area, and the area of obscene publications, where again the criterion of offensiveness rather than harm is sometimes put forward as the basis for legal controls (see 7.3.2).

The relevant offences are almost entirely contained in Part I of the POA, which was largely based on the recommendations of the Law Commission (*Criminal Law: Offences Relating to Public Order*, Law Com No. 123, 1983). These were in turn accepted in the White Paper (*Review of Public Order Law*, Cmnd 9510, 1985). The Law Commission's principal task was to produce a coherent set of offences appropriate for dealing with different levels of disorder, and in this it was largely successful. The offences contained in the POA range from riot (the most serious), to disorderly behaviour. Before considering them in detail, however, it will be convenient first to deal with one recurring concept, that is, 'unlawful violence'.

8.4.1 Unlawful violence
One of the central concepts in the common law in relation to public order offences was that of the 'breach of the peace.' (For a definition of this, see 2.4.1.) The Law Commission, however, regarded the concept as too vague and uncertain to continue to be used in the reformed law (*Report*, para. 5.14). In

its place is put the concept of 'unlawful violence'. 'Violence' is defined in s. 8 as meaning 'any violent conduct', whether or not intended to cause injury or damage. It specifically includes violence towards property, and throwing something capable of causing injury at another person (even if the missile does not hit its target).

8.4.2 Riot

The offence of riot is defined in s. 1 of the POA. It is the most serious offence, and is designed to deal with large groups acting together, in a way which causes, or could cause, violence. The way in which it achieves this is to define a setting or context in which riot may occur, and then to specify that certain behaviour taking place within that context will constitute an offence.

The required setting is that 12 or more people use or threaten 'unlawful violence'. They must be acting together for a common purpose. A fight involving six people on each side would presumably not meet the definition. On the other hand there seems to be no requirement that the purpose is itself unlawful. It could cover, therefore, a picket aimed to persuade people not to enter a place of work, established as part of a legitimate trade dispute. The behaviour can take place in public or in private. If 12 or more people at a private party on domestic premises decide, for example, to attack others at the party, this has the potential to constitute a 'riot'. The conduct of the 12 must be such as would cause a 'person of reasonable firmness present at the scene to fear for his personal safety'.

This test of the effect on a 'person of reasonable firmness' is the standard of 'disorderliness' that appears at a number of points in the POA as the test of criminality. It looks at the likely effect of the behaviour on the average adult who might be present. It excludes the particularly timid, or the especially bold. No such person has actually to be present, however, or be likely to be present (s. 1(4)). The test is purely hypothetical. If, however, people who could be categorised as 'persons of reasonable firmness' were actually present, no doubt their evidence as to the effect of the behaviour on them would be very relevant. On the other hand, the fact that an elderly person, or child, was in fact frightened by the behaviour does not turn it into a riot, if a person of reasonable firmness would not have been so affected. The fear has to be for the person of reasonable firmness's own safety; fear as to what might happen to the participants, their victim (if any), or other persons present is not relevant. In theory, this seems a reasonable standard to apply. People should not be put in terror by the violent activities of others. In practice, however, it may be difficult to assess exactly what level of behaviour has such an effect, particularly where there were no 'reasonably firm' people present at the time.

All the above only constitutes the setting in which the offence of riot can take place. The offence itself is only committed by those amongst the group of 12 or more who actually *use* unlawful violence; threatening such violence is not sufficient for criminal liability. There is also a mental element, set out in s. 6(1). This is that a person is guilty of riot 'only if he intends to use violence or is aware that his conduct may be violent'. While it is right that an offence of the seriousness of riot should have a clearly defined mental element, in practice it seems that this is unlikely to cause difficulty for the prosecution. The mental element relates not to the *consequences* of the behaviour, but to its *nature*. In other words, the prosecution does not have to prove that the rioter realised that the behaviour might have the effect of causing fear in a person of reasonable firmness, but simply an awareness that the behaviour was, or might be violent. There is a certain unreality in asking whether a person who is proved to have used violence was aware of the nature of this conduct, unless there is evidence of automatism. One situation in which such a defence might commonly be raised, that is, where the rioter was intoxicated, is ruled out by s. 6(5). This states that, unless the intoxication was not self-induced or was the result of taking medically subscribed substances, people's awareness is to be judged on the basis of what they would have been aware of when sober. Finally, the prosecution only needs to prove the mental element in relation to a person actually charged with riot. It is not necessary to show that there were at least 11 others who were similarly aware of the nature of their behaviour (s. 6(7)).

The consent of the Director of Public Prosecutions is required for a prosecution for riot. This indicates the seriousness of the offence, and the fact that there was some feeling that in relation to the 1984 miners' strike there was over-enthusiastic charging of the common law offence of riot, which resulted in a number of prosecutions being abandoned (see, for example, P. Scraton, (1985) 12 *Jo. of Law and Soc.* 385, at 390). The seriousness of the offence is also reflected in the mode of trial and penalty. It is an indictable offence, punishable with up to 10 years' imprisonment (s. 1(6)).

8.4.3 Violent disorder

This is a new offence, created by s. 2 of the POA, which is to some extent a replacement for the common law offence of 'unlawful assembly'. The White Paper anticipated that it would be used as the most usual charge in relation to 'serious outbreaks of public disorder' (para. 3.13).

The offence has some similarities with riot, but requires only a group of three people, rather than 12. Unlike the offence of riot, however, the three people do not have to be acting for any common purpose. The three must simply use or threaten unlawful violence, such that a person of reasonable firmness would 'fear for his personal safety'. Each of the people who uses or threatens unlawful violence will be guilty of the offence. The concept of the 'person of reasonable firmness' is exactly the same as in relation to riot (see 8.4.2), as are the following elements, which are not therefore discussed in detail again here. The offence may be committed in public or in private (s. 2(4)). The mental element is intention or awareness that the behaviour is or may be violent, or may threaten violence (s. 6(2)). Lack of awareness resulting from self-induced intoxication is no defence (s. 6(5)).

This offence does not require the Director of Public Prosecutions's consent. It is triable either way, with a maximum penalty on indictment of five years' imprisonment (s. 2(5)).

An early example of the use of this offence may be found in *R v Hebron* [1989] Crim LR 839. The accused was present during a fight in a city centre on New Year's Eve. Bottles and other missiles had been thrown at the police.

Hebron was simply proved to have shaken his fists and shouted 'Kill the Bill' (referring to the police). He was convicted of violent disorder. The conviction makes clear the fact that this offence can be committed by *threats*, as well as by the use of violence. Moreover, Hebron's participation was seen as sufficiently serious to justify a custodial sentence.

The other case law on violent disorder has mainly been concerned with the requirement that there should be three people involved. In *R* v *Abdul Mahroof* (1988) 88 Cr App R 317, three people were named in the indictment as committing violent disorder. Two were acquitted, but the third was convicted. The Court of Appeal held that since the jury had not been directed on the possibility that there were others involved not named on the indictment, and the issue had not been dealt with by the defence, the conviction must be quashed. This was followed in *R* v *Fleming* [1989] Crim LR 658, where of four people charged, one was acquitted, and on another the jury could not agree. The conviction of the remaining two for violent disorder was quashed, but the Court of Appeal noted, *obiter*, that in some circumstances a person may be convicted even though it is not possible to prove that two others were guilty, for example, where the others were in fact using threatening violence but lacked *mens rea* (see s. 6(7)), or have a defence of some kind. The same must be true where there is clear evidence that two or more others were using or threatening unlawful violence, but they are not before the court (perhaps because they evaded arrest). Problems may still arise, however, unless the judge puts the issue to the jury correctly. In *R* v *Worton* [1990] Crim LR 124, there was prosecution evidence of eight to ten people being involved in fighting. Only four were charged, however. Of these, one was acquitted, and in relation to another, the charge was simply left on the file. The two who were convicted appealed successfully because the judge had not specifically directed the jury that they could only convict if either they found three of the people before them guilty, or they were satisfied that others not charged had participated in the unlawful violence.

Great care needs to be taken, therefore, in directing on this offence. These technical problems aside, however, the main concern with the offence must be that it is possible for people who have had a very low level of involvement in any unlawful violence to be convicted of a serious offence. One threat will be enough, if at least two others have done the same. No one needs to have actually used any violence, and if others have used violence, the issue of threats alone may, as we have seen, lead to a custodial sentence (*R* v *Hebron* (1989)).

8.4.4 Affray

Affray existed at common law, and was regularly used to deal with any unlawful fighting. The Law Commission and the White Paper anticipated that this would continue to be the case (Law Commission Report, para. 3.5; White Paper, para. 3.15). As a result, the offence, although it follows in many ways the pattern established by the definitions of riot in s. 1, and violent disorder in s. 2, has certain limitations. Thus, as with violent disorder, a person commits affray by using or threatening unlawful violence so that a person of reasonable firmness would fear 'for his personal safety'. No minimum number of participants is required, but where two or more are involved, it is the effect of their joint behaviour which must be considered (s. 3(2)). Unlike riot, or violent disorder, however, the threats or violence must be directed towards another person. Violent conduct towards property is not sufficient for affray (s. 8). Moreover a verbal threat is insufficient: it must be accompanied by some threatening actions (s. 3(3)). A shaking of the fist would, however, presumably be enough.

One recently reported decision shows the offence being charged in a situation which was not really one of public disorder. In *R* v *Davison* [1992] Crim LR 31 the events took place in the accused's flat, highlighting the fact that affray, like the other offences so far considered, does not have to be committed in a public place. There had been a domestic incident, as a result of which the police had been called. One of the police officers was threatened by the accused, who was holding a kitchen knife. He waved the knife from side to side saying 'I'll have you'. He was arrested before any further assault took place. It was held that there was a case to answer on an affray charge, though it would have to be shown that the hypothetical person of reasonable firmness would have feared for their own safety, rather than that of the policeman. It might be thought, however, that a more appropriate charge would have been common assault.

Affray is a triable either way offence, with a maximum penalty of three years on conviction on indictment. Since this does not make affray an arrestable offence (above 2.4.3.1), unlike riot and violent disorder, a specific power of arrest is given in s. 3(6).

8.4.5 Fear or provocation of violence
Whereas affray does not seem particularly appropriate for dealing with problems arising out of assemblies and demonstrations, the offence under s. 4, headed 'Fear or provocation of violence', has considerable potential in relation to such events. Its predecessor, that is s. 5 of the Public Order Act 1936, was certainly used in this way (for example, *Jordan* v *Burgoyne* [1963] 2 All ER 225; *Brutus* v *Cozens* [1972] 2 All ER 1297), though, like s. 4 of the 1986 Act, it had a scope extending far beyond this.

The offence is committed by using threatening, abusive, or insulting words or behaviour, towards another person, or by distributing or displaying any 'writing, sign or other visible representation' which is threatening, abusive, or insulting. In what follows the phrase 'words or behaviour' is used to cover all the types of conduct which may give rise to the offence. Some of the language of the section is taken over from the 1936 Act and so we can safely assume that the case law on this will stand. The most important decision is that of the House of Lord in *Brutus* v *Cozens* (1972), which arose out of an anti-apartheid demonstration during the Wimbledon tennis championships. It was held that the word 'insulting', and therefore presumably the words 'threatening' and 'abusive' as well, must be given its natural meaning. Whether any particular words or behaviour are capable of being 'threatening, abusive or insulting' should be regarded as a matter of fact, not law.

The phrase 'towards another person' did not appear in the 1936 Act offence. In *Atkin* v *DPP* (1989) 153 JP 383 it was held that the 'other person' towards whom the words or behaviour are directed must be present when the threats, etc, are made. The fact that they were reported to him shortly afterwards, causing him to be frightened for his safety, was not sufficient.

The use of such words or behaviour towards another person does not in itself constitute an offence. They must be intended, or be likely, to provoke, or to cause fear of, immediate unlawful violence. The requirement of immediacy was emphasised in *R v Horseferry Road Justices, ex parte Siadatan* [1990] Crim LR 598, where there was an attempt to prosecute the publishers of a book which was alleged to constitute a blasphemy against the Islamic religion. Although the Divisional Court took the view that 'immediate' did not mean the same as 'instantaneous', there must be proximity in time and place. The approach seems similar to that taken in relation to imminent breaches of the peace (see *Moss v McLachlan* [1985] IRLR 77 at p. 251).

The precise intentions or likely consequences which will constitute the offence are as follows. First an intention (a) to cause the person towards whom the words or behaviour was directed 'to believe that immediate unlawful violence will be used against him or any other person'; or (b) to provoke that person or another to use such violence. Secondly, a likelihood (c) that that person will believe that such violence will be used; or (d) that such violence will be provoked.

As with the other offences under Part I of the POA there is a further mental element, over and above any intention to bring about either the consequences in (a) or (b), which is that the person using the words or behaviour must intend it to be threatening, abusive, or insulting, or be aware that it may be so (s. 6(3)). As will be seen below, this *mens rea* requirement may have more significance in relation to this offence than the equivalent requirement in relation to riot, violent disorder, or affray.

The easiest version of the offence for the prosecution to prove, and therefore perhaps the most likely to be used (it was the version attempted in *ex parte Siadatan*) is that based on consequence (d), that is, that it is likely that violence will be provoked. The question arises as to whether the likelihood has to be a reasonable one, or one that a reasonable person would foresee. There is no case law under the 1986 Act, but the decision in *Jordan v Burgoyne* [1963] 2 All ER 225 on a similar issue under s. 5 of the 1936 Act would suggest that the test is entirely a question of what was in fact likely to happen. In *Jordan v Burgoyne* the issue was the likely effect of a public speech which expressed support for Hitler, and condemned 'world Jewry', and in particular whether it would be likely to provoke a breach of the peace. The speaker knew that his audience contained representatives of Jewish organisations and left-wing groups who would be hostile to his view, but he argued that their violent reaction to his speech was unreasonable. It was held by the Divisional Court that once a speaker has used 'threatening, abusive or insulting' words or behaviour then, in Lord Parker's words:

> that person must take his audience as he finds them, and if those words to that audience are likely to provoke a breach of the peace, then the speaker is guilty of that offence.

There seems no reason why the word 'likely' as used in s. 4 of the 1986 Act should not be interpreted in the same way. It may be, however, that there would now be an escape route for a speaker like Jordan in that it might be possible to argue that there was no intention or awareness as regards the insulting nature of the words or behaviour. This would be particularly true where the speaker was not aware of the presence of the hostile group (though this was not the situation in *Jordan*).

The offence under s. 4 may be committed in a public or a private place, except that it does not apply where the conduct takes place inside a 'dwelling' (as defined in s. 8), and the person to whom the conduct is directed is also inside that or another dwelling. This means that it is of more limited scope than riot, violent disorder, or affray, but would still apply, for example, to threatening words or behaviour used at a private meeting being held on business premises, or in a hired room. It was held in *Rukira* v *DPP, The Times*, 29 June 1993, that communal landings in a block of flats do not come within the meaning of a 'dwelling' for the purposes of s. 4.

The s. 4 offence is summary only, punishable with up to six months' imprisonment (s. 4(4)). A power of arrest is given by s. 4(3).

8.4.6 Harassment, alarm or distress
There was considerable debate prior to the passing of the POA as to whether there was any need for a 'lower-level' offence than that under s. 4, to deal with 'disorderly behaviour' which may cause annoyance or disturbance, but is not likely to gives rise to fear or provocation of unlawful violence. In the end the government decided that there was, and the result is s. 5 of the POA, which is labelled 'Harassment, alarm or distress'. The kind of behaviour which it was intended to deal with was set out in the White Paper (Cmnd 9510) at para. 3.22:

> hooligans on housing estates causing disturbances in the common parts of blocks of flats, blockading entrances, throwing things down the stairs, banging on doors, peering in at windows, and knocking over dustbins;
>   groups of youths persistently shouting abuse and obscenities or pestering people waiting to catch public transport or to enter a hall or cinema;
>   someone turning out the lights in a crowded dance hall, in a way likely to cause panic;
>   rowdy behaviour in the streets late at night which alarms local residents.

The White Paper suggested that if the offence were introduced then it should only apply to behaviour that has actually caused *substantial* alarm, harassment, or distress, to someone, and not to behaviour that was simply likely to do so. As we shall see, the requirement of an actual victim has been weakened in s. 5, and the need for a *substantial* effect has been dropped.

There are two ways in which the offence under s. 5 can be committed. The first is by using 'threatening, abusive or insulting words or behaviour'. This phrase is, of course, exactly the same as that used in s. 4, and so must be interpreted in the same way (see 8.4.5). The second method of committing the offence is by engaging in 'disorderly behaviour'. This is undefined. Presumably the examples used in para. 3.22 of the White Paper, and set out above, may be used as guidance as to the kind of behaviour that is intended to be covered. In practice, however, the question will be treated as one of fact to be decided by the magistrates, who will therefore set the standard for 'orderliness'. It seems unlikely that simple participation in an organised demonstration (whether a procession or a meeting) could be regarded as disorderly. Much more likely is that individual participants who carry placards or shout things at passers by, or people opposed to the demonstration who try to disrupt it (but do so without using or threatening violence) will be found to be disorderly.

The behaviour, to constitute the offence, must have taken place 'within the hearing or sight of a person likely to be caused harassment, alarm or distress thereby' (s. 5(1)). The POA thus abandons here the 'person of reasonable firmness' used in ss. 1–3. The object of the offence is to protect the 'weak and vulnerable' (White Paper, Cmnd 9510, para. 3.26), and so the person who acts in a disorderly way must take the chance that there is an unusually sensitive victim in the vicinity. This assumes that 'likely' is interpreted in the same way as in *Jordan* v *Burgoyne* (1963) (see 8.4.5), so as to mean likely in fact, rather than reasonably likely. The person does not have to be proved to have been harassed, alarmed or distressed, as long as this consequence is likely. It was held to be sufficient in *Lodge* v *Andrews, The Times*, 26 October 1988, that the unidentified driver of a car might have been alarmed by the sight of the accused walking down the middle of the road late at night. There is unlikely to be a conviction, however, if the only potential victim admits to not having been affected by the behaviour. If the only witness to the accused's behaviour is a police officer, this does not preclude a charge. A police officer is capable of being harassed, alarmed or distressed for the purposes of the section. This was held to be the case by the Divisional Court in *DPP* v *Orum* [1988] 3 All ER 449, and was applied in *DPP* v *Clarke* [1992] Crim LR 60 (discussed further below).

The offence may be committed in public or private, but will not occur where the behaviour or display takes place inside a dwelling, and the person potentially harassed alarmed or distressed is also inside that or another dwelling (s. 5(2)). So, abusive language which is heard through the dividing wall of two houses cannot constitute this offence. If it is heard on the street outside, however, the offence may have been committed.

There are three specific defences set out in s. 5(3). The burden of proof is on the accused. The defences are (a) that the accused had no reason to believe that there was anyone able to see or hear the behaviour who might be harassed, alarmed or distressed; or (b) that the accused was inside a dwelling, and had no reason to believe that the behaviour would be seen or heard by someone outside a dwelling; or (c) that the conduct was reasonable. It is difficult to imagine, however, that courts are going to be very receptive to pleas that it was reasonable to cause people harassment, alarm, or distress.

A specific, but slightly unusual, power of arrest, is given by s. 5(4). The power arises where a constable (not necessarily in uniform) has warned a

person to stop engaging in 'offensive conduct', and the person immediately
engages in further such conduct (not necessarily of an identical kind).
Offensive conduct is conduct which the constable reasonably suspects constitutes an offence under s. 5. Thus, suppose the police receive complaints about
a noisy party which has spilled on to the street. The police arrive, and tell those
causing the disturbance to keep the noise down. One of the revellers, with
more alcohol than sense, swears loudly at the officers. This might well justify
an arrest under s. 5(4). (Situations of a similar kind were involved in both *DPP
v Orum* (1988), and *Lodge v Andrews* (1988).) The police can, of course, also
use the power of arrest under s. 25 of PACE (see 2.4.3.2) in relation to this
offence, provided one of the general arrest conditions is satisfied. In this case
there would be no need for an initial warning, and the arrest could occur after
the first occurrence of disorderly behaviour.

Section 5 was used in a situation involving a demonstration in *DPP v Clarke*
[1992] Crim LR 60. This case also illustrates the importance of the *mens rea*
requirement under s. 6(4) by virtue of which the prosecution must prove either
that the accused intended the conduct to be threatening, abusive or insulting,
or was aware that it might be; or that the accused intended the behaviour to be
disorderly, or was aware that it might be. The prosecution arose out of a
demonstration outside an abortion clinic. Anti-abortion demonstrators, including Clarke, were carrying pictures of an aborted foetus, which they
displayed to officers on patrol and passers-by. The demonstrators refused to
comply with police requests not to display the pictures. Clarke was charged
under s. 5. The magistrates found that the pictures were abusive and insulting,
and that their display caused alarm and distress to one of the police officers
present. They also found, however, that, applying the *mens rea* test in s. 6, the
demonstrators did not intend the pictures to be threatening, abusive, or
insulting, nor were they aware that they might be. They therefore acquitted.
The prosecutor appealed on the basis that the only reasonable conclusion open
to the magistrates was that the demonstrators were aware that the continued
display of the pictures might be abusive or insulting. The Divisional Court
held that the magistrates had approached all the issues correctly. Their finding
on the *mens rea* issue was simply an acceptance of the evidence put forward by
the defence. It could not be said to be unreasonable, and the acquittal should
stand. It was noted, however, that it would be difficult for the accused in this
case to argue in a subsequent case that they were unaware that the pictures
might be abusive or insulting.

In *DPP v Fidler* [1992] Crim LR 62, a case arising out of the same facts, the
same court ruled that a *prima facie* case under s. 5 could be made by evidence
that the accused was not only anti-abortion but a member of the group
organising the protest, without any need to prove any particular threatening,
abusive, or insulting act. There are considerable risks, therefore, for those who
wish to participate in demonstrations in favour of causes where an impact may
be sought by the display of striking and disturbing pictures, for example of
torture, or starvation, or cruelty to animals.

The penalty for the offence under s. 5, which is a summary offence, is a fine
not exceeding level 3 on the standard scale.

8.4.7   Conclusion on POA Part I offences

For the most part the offences under Part I of the POA seem to provide a reasonable set of controls at appropriate levels of disorder. Some doubts may be raised as to whether behaviour which occurs entirely on private property should be covered, as for example in *R* v *Davison* (1992) (see 8.4.4). Does such behaviour really affect *public* order? A distinction should probably be more clearly drawn between private property on to which the public, or a section of the public have been invited (which would be a 'public place' within the definition of the s. 16 of the POA), and purely private events. It is submitted that even the narrowing of scope in ss. 4 and 5 to exclude dwellings does not really go far enough. It is hard to see that the State has a legitimate interest in what happens between private individuals behind closed doors, unless it results in some injury to persons or damage to property which would in any case be covered by ordinary criminal law offences.

The other main point of criticism must be the inclusion of the s. 5 offence, and its associated power of arrest. Given the survival of the common law power to deal with breaches of the peace (see 8.5), and the existence of the general arrest power under PACE, s. 25 (see 2.4.3.2) it is hard to see the need for this section. Moreover it relies so heavily for its operation on the discretion and judgment of the police officer on the street that it opens up considerable opportunities for oppressive policing. This will do nothing to improve relations between the police and those sections of the community which are suspicious of, or hostile towards, them.

8.4.8   Other offences

8.4.8.1   Prohibition of uniforms: Public Order Act 1936, s. 1   This surviving section of the Public Order Act 1936 was originally enacted in response to the adoption of quasi-military uniforms by certain fascist organisations in the 1930s (such as Oswald Mosley's British Union of Fascists, who wore, and became known as, 'black shirts'). It makes it an offence to wear in any public place or at any public meeting a uniform signifying association with any political organisation or with the promotion of any political object. There is a proviso by which the chief officer of police may, with the consent of the Home Secretary, permit the wearing of such uniforms on occasions when there is not likely to be a risk of public disorder. Any prosecution must be brought with the consent of the Attorney-General.

What exactly constitutes a uniform for these purposes? The Act contains no definition or guidance, but the issue was considered in *O'Moran* v *DPP* [1975] QB 864, where the alleged uniform consisted of black berets, dark glasses and dark (though not identical) clothing. Lord Widgery thought that the 'wearing' of a uniform required some article of clothing, so that a lapel badge, for instance, could not on its own constitute a uniform. Thus the adoption by the Labour Party of the red rose would not fall foul of this section. Beyond this, however, it seems to be a question of looking at all the circumstances. Lord Widgery was of the view that the wearing of the beret could, in itself, constitute the wearing of a uniform. The link with a political group could be established either by evidence of previous association, or from the present circumstances.

The section could still be used against the adoption of uniforms by political factions. Its most likely target, however, would be members of quasi-military political organisations in Northern Ireland, which are proscribed in this country under the Prevention of Terrorism (Temporary Provisions) Act 1989. This Act contains its own broader provision making it an offence, in a public place to wear any item of dress, or wear, carry or display any article in such a way or in such circumstances as to arouse reasonable apprehension that the person is a member or supporter of a proscribed organisation (Prevention of Terrorism (Temporary Provisions) Act 1989, s. 3).

8.4.8.2 Assemblies of 'travellers' One type of assembly which has caused problems in recent years has arisen where groups of travelling people, living in caravans or other mobile homes, have camped out on private land, and there have been problems in moving them on. These are the so-called 'hippy convoys' or 'New Age travellers'. A particularly notorious case occurred at about the time the Public Order Act was under consideration in parliament, and as result a section (s. 39) was added to try to deal specifically with this problem. As is often the case with instant legislative reactions, there must be some doubt as to how successfully it achieves its objectives.

The section has the effect of making a certain type of trespass by a group (though it may be as few as two) into a criminal offence. It is subject to a number of limitations, however.

First, it does not apply to buildings, other than agricultural buildings or scheduled monuments. So the offence has no relevance to squatters in residential property, nor does it apply to land forming part of a highway.

Secondly, the section only applies where the initial entry was as a trespasser. If a farmer gives permission to a group to come on to the land for a limited period, and the group overstays its welcome, s. 39 cannot be used to get rid of it (s. 39(4)).

Even if these conditions are satisfied, no offence is committed until there has been a direction to leave, issued by a police officer. The power to issue a direction arises when the officer reasonably believes that certain other conditions are fulfilled. These are, first, that the officer reasonably believes that the occupier, or someone acting on behalf of the occupier, has taken reasonable steps to ask the trespassers to leave. Secondly, the officer must reasonably believe *either* that one or more trespassers has caused damage to property on the land, *or* has used threatening, abusive, or insulting words or behaviour towards the occupier, or the occupier's family, employee, or agent, *or* that the trespassers have brought 12 or more vehicles on to the land.

Once the direction has been given (there is no indication of the form it should take), anyone knowing of it who fails to comply as soon as reasonably practicable, or tries to re-enter the land within three months, will commit an offence. The offence is backed up by a power of arrest (s. 39(3)), by virtue of which a uniformed constable may arrest anyone reasonably suspected of committing an offence under the section. Thus if a direction is given, and there is no attempt to comply, *everyone* on the land can be arrested. The 'assembly' will be broken up, and the land cleared.

Given its rather limited scope, it is perhaps not surprising that s. 39 has not been greatly used in practice, landowners more often resorting to court orders to try to clear land of trespassing groups.

8.5   THE COMMON LAW: BREACH OF THE PEACE

The power that any constable has to take reasonable steps to stop an actual or imminent breach of the peace is clearly of considerable significance in relation to the policing of disorder. The definition of the concept and the power of arrest attaching to it have been discussed in chapter 2 (2.4.1). Here its specific use in the context of the freedom of assembly is considered.

The case of *Duncan* v *Jones* [1936] 1 KB 218 shows how the power might be used effectively to prevent a public meeting. The appellant had attempted to address a meeting of about 30 people protesting about the Incitement to Disaffection Bill. The meeting was taking place in the road, opposite the entrance to an unemployed training centre. There was some evidence that meetings previously held at the same location, and addressed by the appellant had led to breaches of the peace. A police officer (the chief constable, in fact), told the appellant that the meeting could not be held where she wanted it, but could be held some 175 yards away. When she refused to move, she was arrested, and was charged with obstructing a police officer in the execution of his duty. She was convicted, and appealed, by way of case stated to the Divisional Court. The Court refused to recognise that the case had anything to do with the rights to hold public meetings, or whether an assembly could become unlawful simply because a breach of the peace might be caused by people opposed to it. They had no doubt that the police officer was acting within his powers in trying to prevent an apprehended breach of the peace; indeed it was his duty to do so. The conviction was upheld.

A similar result occurred in *Piddington* v *Bates* [1961] 1 WLR 162, which was concerned with an industrial dispute. There was a picket of 18 outside a printers' works where eight men were working. A police officer tried to limit the pickets to two at each entrance. The appellant resisted this limitation, and gently pushed past the police officer. He was arrested, and charged with obstructing a police office in the execution of his duty. Once again, the Divisional Court upheld the conviction. Provided that there were *reasonable* grounds for anticipating that a breach of the peace was a *real* possibility, then the police officer had acted lawfully. While not being prepared to express an opinion on the appropriate number of pickets to allow in such a situation, the Court was also not prepared to interfere with the magistrate's decision of fact that the appropriate conditions for the exercise of the restriction existed.

The most significant recently reported use of this power in relation to a situation of disorder at a public assembly is also drawn from the context of industrial disputes, that is, the case of *Moss* v *McLachlan* [1985] IRLR 77. During the 1984 miners' strike the police regularly placed patrols near motorway exits on the M1, to try to prevent so-called 'flying pickets' from militant areas in Yorkshire, joining picket lines at more moderate pits in Nottinghamshire. On this occasion the police stopped a group of 25 cars containing 60 to 80 men. From badges and car stickers, the men were clearly identifiable as striking miners. Some of the men refused to obey an instruction from a police officer to turn back from the pits, and were arrested. They were convicted by the magistrates of obstructing a police officer in the execution of his duty. The Divisional Court held that the police had not simply a right, but a *duty* to prevent breaches of the peace occurring. In the words of Skinner J (at p. 78):

> Provided [the police officers] honestly and reasonably form the opinion that there is a real risk of a breach of the peace in the sense that it is in close proximity both in place and time, then the conditions exist for reasonable preventive acting [*sic*] including, if necessary, the measures taken in this case.

As to the proximity, the Court thought that the police, if satisfied that 'there was a real possibility of the occupants [of the cars] causing a breach of the peace one-and-a-half miles away, a journey of less than five minutes by car', would be under a duty to prevent the convoy proceeding further. It is clear, then, that the breach of the peace does not have to be likely to occur 'immediately' in the normal sense of that word. A delay of five minutes still justifies police action. Presumably the delay would in practice have been longer, unless it was thought that a breach of the peace would have occurred as soon as the miners arrived at the pits. It is more likely that such a breach would in fact only have occurred at a point where working miners were trying to get into or out of the pit, which might have been some time later.

The scope for the use of the powers relating to breach of the peace in relation to demonstrations and assemblies is shown by these cases. It enables the police to take whatever action appears reasonable to stop behaviour which might amount to a breach of the peace. Using these powers, the police could in many cases avoid the need to use the power under the Public Order Act (see 8.2.3) to control the route of a procession. If the reason for the need for such control is the fact that rival groups might otherwise come into conflict, then the breach of the peace power would certainly be an appropriate one to use. Similarly, when behaviour at a demonstration is becoming unruly, the breach of the peace power may allow those who are the cause of the disturbance to be arrested, even before they have reached the stage of committing any of the offences under Part I of the Act. This flexibility is a clear advantage for the police, but also raises concerns from the civil liberties point of view. To give the police so much discretion always raises the danger the powers will be misused, or overused. It is therefore unfortunate that the opportunity was not taken in the Public Order Act 1986 to put the powers relating to breach of the peace on a statutory footing. This would have enabled their scope to have been defined more precisely, and would have allowed the introduction of appropriate safeguards (perhaps along the lines of those which exist under PACE in relation to stop and search powers (see 2.3)) to guard against the problems of improper or over-enthusiastic use.

8.6   INCITEMENT TO RACIAL HATRED

This topic is difficult to place. It clearly has strong links with the issue of freedom from discrimination, and indeed, the offences in this area started life as part of the race relations legislation. There has always been the difficulty, however, with any suggestion that *all* racist statements should constitute a criminal offence. If, for example, a researcher purports to have found as a result of research, that a particular racial group is less intelligent than others, should it be an offence to publish it in an academic journal? To make it so would constitute a very serious encroachment on free speech. There has always been an understandable reluctance to restrict serious attempts to present asserted facts, or genuinely held opinions, however objectionable, provided they are put forward in a context which is not inflammatory. To impose controls on such speech would run counter to all the arguments against restriction outlined at the beginning of chapter 5. The compromise which the British government has made is to make it an offence to publish racist material only where it is presented in immoderate language, and in a context where it is intended or likely to stir up racial hatred. This has meant that the English law on this topic has more in common with the laws protecting public order, than with those aimed at preventing discrimination. This was formally recognised in 1986, when the 'racial hatred' offences were re-enacted, and expanded, within the framework of the Public Order Act. Part III of the Act contains the relevant provisions. That is the justification for dealing with the offences in this chapter, rather than chapter 11. As will be seen, the offences are apt to control racist speech at public assemblies, but in fact extend beyond that, and in particular cover written material, against which they have most commonly been used. This broader scope to the offences must be kept in mind in considering what follows.

8.6.1   Meaning of racial hatred
Racial hatred is defined in s. 17 of the POA. It means 'hatred against any group of persons in Great Britain defined by reference to colour, race, nationality (including citizenship) or ethnic or national origins'. This definition is similar to the definition of 'racial group' in the Race Relations Act 1976, which is discussed at 11.1.4.1.

8.6.2   The offences
The Act contains a number of offences, all of which have common elements. First, the words or behaviour used must be 'threatening, abusive or insulting' (compare ss. 4 and 5 of the POA at 8.4.5, 8.4.6). This is the way in which moderately phrased debate on issues of race is kept out of the scope of the offences. Secondly, the actions of the person charged must either have been *intended* to stir up racial hatred, or be *likely* to do so. The issue of 'intention' in this context has a strange history. In the original version of the offence, in the Race Relations Act 1965, intention was required. It was argued, however, that this placed too heavy a burden on the prosecution and made conviction difficult (see, for example, the comments of Lord Scarman in his *Report on the*

Red Lion Square Disorders, Cmnd 5919, 1975, para. 125). As a result, the offence was amended so that it was only necessary to prove that the consequence was likely. This was the form in which it appeared in the Race Relations Act 1976, s. 70. It was then argued, however, that this was also too restrictive, in that it meant that there could be no conviction if the only publication of the offending words which could be shown was to people who would not be incited to racial hatred (such as, perhaps, MPs or clergymen), or who were perhaps sympathisers who could not be incited further. So in the POA version of the offences, both the 'intention' and the 'likelihood' version of the offences appear.

In all offences, if the person is not shown to have intended to stir up racial hatred, it will be a defence if there was no intention or awareness that the words or behaviour would or might be threatening, abusive, or insulting (for example, s. 18(5)).

8.6.2.1 The publication offences These are contained in ss. 18–22. Section 18 is the one which deals with speeches at meetings, or demonstrations. It makes it an offence to use words or behaviour, or display written material, which fulfils the elements outlined above. The offence may be committed in private, but not within a dwelling (unless seen or heard outside; s. 18(2)). There is a power of arrest without warrant in relation to anyone a constable reasonably suspects is committing this offence (s. 18(3)).

The other offences all deal with different types of publication. Thus s. 19 covers publishing or distributing written material. It can be used against racist organisations which circulate pamphlets, newsletters, etc, intended or likely to stir up racial hatred. Section 20 deals with the performance of plays, s. 21 with the showing or playing of films, videos, or records, and s. 22 with broadcasting and cable services. It is unlikely that any of these will be used with any frequency. (For detailed discussion of these offences, see A. T. H. Smith, *Offences against Public Order*, London: Sweet & Maxwell, ch. 9.)

8.6.2.2 The possession offence The 1986 Act for the first time made it an offence simply to possess racist material (s. 23). The offence covers both written material, and films, videos, tapes, etc. The material must be held with a view to its being published in some way.

Section 24 provides a power of entry and search under warrant where it is suspected that a person is in possession of material contrary to s. 23. This power will be subject to most of the standard procedures under PACE (see 4.2.4), except that a warrant issued under s. 24 can be used to search for excluded or special procedure material, without the need to use sch. 1 to PACE (see 4.4.2.1).

8.6.3 Enforcement procedures
No proceedings for any of the offences outlined above may be brought without the consent of the Attorney-General. This indicates that this is an area where it is thought that prosecutions might be politically sensitive. It also means that a private individual who might take exception to, for example, a speech by an

MP advocating a policy of ending immigration because of the danger that traditional British culture is being 'swamped', will be unable to use the POA offences against the MP.

The offences are all triable either way, and punishable on indictment with up to two years' imprisonment, or a fine or both, or on summary conviction with six months or a fine not exceeding the statutory maximum, or both (s. 27).

Finally, there is a power of forfeiture of relevant material, where there has been a conviction under ss. 18, 19, 21 or 23 (s. 25).

8.7 EUROPEAN CONVENTION AND FREEDOM OF ASSEMBLY

There are two provisions of the ECHR which are relevant to the issues discussed in this chapter. Art. 11 recognises that 'Everyone has the right to peaceful assembly . . . ', which clearly covers the right to demonstrate and hold public meetings on controversial issues. As regards what happens at such events, Art. 10 is once again relevant, protecting the freedom of expression of the speaker at a meeting, or a person chanting slogans. Both the Articles have qualifying second paragraphs, however, in virtually identical terms. The provisions of Art. 10(2) have been noted elsewhere (see 5.8.2). The second paragraph of Art. 11 is slightly narrower in scope, and reads (in part; *emphasis added*):

No restrictions shall be placed on the exercise of these rights other than such as are prescribed by law and are necessary in a democratic society in the interests of national security or public safety, *for the prevention of disorder* or crime, for the protection of health or morals, or for the protection of the rights and freedoms of others.

Most of the restrictive provisions dealt with in this chapter would no doubt be held to be justified as being prescribed by law, and necessary for the prevention of disorder. Even those powers which may be argued to be at the limits of what may be necessary, such as s. 5 of the POA, or the common law powers relating to breaches of the peace, would probably be held to come within the margin of appreciation allowed to individual States. If it is felt, therefore, that civil liberties in the area of freedom of assembly are unduly restricted by the provisions of the POA, etc, there would seem to be little point in appealing to the provisions of the ECHR for help.

NINE

Freedom of Movement:
The Right of Residence

9.1 INTRODUCTION

The right that is under consideration in this chapter is the right of residence in the United Kingdom. It is concerned with rights that are often discussed under the more general heading of 'freedom of movement'. The primary focus here is not, however, the freedom to come and go, but rather the right to remain; in other words, the freedom from being forced, against one's will, to leave the country, or some part of the country. As a result the details of immigration procedures are not discussed, despite the fact that they may raise civil liberties issues. For reasons of space, the emphasis is on those who are lawfully here and wish to stay, rather than on those who are seeking entry. The law surrounding immigration control cannot be ignored entirely, however, because, at least in relation to deportation and exclusion, it helps to define who may be subject to these powers.

The order of treatment is to move from the most generally applicable of the powers (extradition), to the most limited (exclusion orders).

Note that throughout this chapter where powers are exercisable by 'the Secretary of State', this will in practice normally mean the Home Secretary.

9.2 EXTRADITION

The law of extradition is primarily concerned with the situation where a person is alleged to have committed a criminal offence in country A, but is currently residing in country B. It also applies where the person has been convicted of an offence in country A, but has escaped or evaded custody there, and is again to be found in country B. It seems reasonable at first sight that the suspect or convict should be returned to stand trial, or to serve the appropriate sentence. Complications arise, however, where there may be suspicions that the requesting State has improper motives. In particular, it may be alleged that the return is being requested in order to try the person for a 'political' offence, or for some offence other than that to which the request relates, or in order to persecute the person for religious or political beliefs. For that reason English law has always required a degree of formality before extradition will be allowed. The procedure is recognised to be entirely a creature of statute: extradition is not possible under common law powers.

It is a very significant power in that it is, as we shall see, the only way in which a British citizen can be forcibly removed from the United Kingdom. In relation to non-citizens executive deportation powers may be available, and in some cases it has been alleged that these have been used as a form of 'disguised extradition' (see 9.3.3.2).

The availability of extradition has always been, and still is, dependent on the idea of mutual arrangements between States, generally on the basis of a bilateral treaty, though the multi-lateral European Convention on Extradition now plays a significant role. In recent years, however, as a result of problems with the increase in international crime, particularly in the areas of fraud, drug-trafficking, and terrorism, significant changes have occurred in the English law. Suggestions in a Green Paper on extradition (Cmnd 9421, 1985) were taken up in a more general White Paper concerned with criminal justice (*Criminal Justice: Plans for Legislation* 1986 (Cmnd 9658)). Major reforms were first enacted in the Criminal Justice Act 1988, and then incorporated into a general consolidation in the Extradition Act 1989 ('the 1989 Act'). There are, in fact, currently three different procedures operating in relation to extradition. First there is the new procedure under the 1989 Act; secondly there are the previous procedures operating under the Extradition Acts 1870 to 1932 which will continue to apply to extradition to countries with whom the UK had arrangements in place prior to 1989, until such time as these are superseded by new agreements within the 1989 Act; thirdly, there are arrangements with the Republic of Ireland, which for the time being continue to be governed by the Backing of Warrants (Republic of Ireland) Act 1965. A further procedure operating under the Fugitive Offenders Act 1967 in relation to commonwealth countries has now been brought within the scope of the 1989 Act.

In this chapter, for reasons of space, and because it indicates the way in which extradition will operate in most cases in the future, only the new procedures under the 1989 Act are discussed in detail, though some reference to the previous law will be made by way of comparison. References to section numbers refer to the 1989 Act, unless otherwise stated.

9.2.1 Grounds for extradition
The question of whether extradition is available depends on the identity of the requesting State, and the offence for which extradition is sought.

9.2.1.1 The requesting State The State seeking extradition must either be one with which the UK has an extradition agreeement, or be a commonwealth State (s. 1(1),(2)). In either case there must be an Order in Council in place under either s. 4 (in relation to a non-commonwealth State, described in the Act as a 'foreign State'), giving effect to the arrangements, or s. 5 'designating' a commonwealth State. The distinction is not mutually exclusive, in that a commonwealth country which is a party to the European Convention on Extradition (such as Cyprus) may be treated as a 'foreign State' (s. 3(2)).

In addition to general arrangements of this kind, the Act also provides for 'special extradition arrangements' (s. 3(3)(b), s. 15). These may be agreed between the United Kingdom and any other country with which there are no general extradition arrangements, and allow for a kind of *ad hoc* extradition in relation to particular cases. This was not possible under the previous law.

Finally, under s. 22, countries which are parties to certain international conventions may be treated as having 'general extradition arrangements' with the United Kingdom, and Orders in Council may be made in relation to them, as if such arrangements had been agreed bilaterally, which will allow extradition for the offences under the Conventions specified in s. 22(3). The relevant conventions are:

The 1963 Tokyo Convention on Offences and other Acts committed on Board Aircraft

The 1970 Hague Convention for the Suppression of the Unlawful Seizure of Aircraft

The 1971 Montreal Convention for the Suppression of Unlawful Acts against the Safety of Civil Aviation

The 1973 UN Convention on the Prevention and Punishment of Crimes against Internationally Protected Persons

The 1979 International Convention against the Taking of Hostages

The 1980 Convention on the Physical Protection of Nuclear Material

The 1984 UN Convention Against Torture and other Cruel, Inhuman or Degrading Treatment or Punishment

9.2.1.2 The nature of the offence The offence for which extradition is sought must be an 'extradition crime'. This is defined in s. 2. It means 'conduct' in the requesting State which, if it occurred in the United Kingdom, would constitute an offence punishable with at least 12 months' imprisonment. The conduct must also be so punishable under the law of the requesting State (though the use of the word 'conduct' implies that it does not have to be categorised as 'criminal' under the foreign jurisdiction). The offence does not, therefore, have to be a particularly serious one. Any theft, for example, however minor, is capable of being an extradition offence. On the other hand if the only penalty available for an offence is a fine, no matter how large (as is the case, for example, in relation to certain offences concerning sex shops (see 7.8.1.2)), it will not be an extradition crime. In some circumstances conduct which has taken place outside the territory of the requesting State, but is regarded by that State as an offence under its law, can be an extradition crime (s. 2(1)(b), (2), (3)). The penalty must again be at least 12 months' imprisonment.

9.2.2 Restrictions on extradition
It has always been a part of UK extradition law that its target is genuine 'criminals'. It should not, therefore, apply to 'political offenders', or where the

object of the requesting State is to recover the person for some ulterior motive. The current law on this is set out in s. 6 of the 1989 Act.

9.2.2.1 The political offence exception Under s. 6(1), a person may not be extradited if the offence for which extradition is sought is 'an offence of a political character'. This phrase is not further defined in the Act, although s. 6(8) excludes from its scope offences directed against the Head of the Commonwealth, and s. 23 provides that genocide can never be an offence of a political character. In certain circumstances there are also limitations under the Suppression of Terrorism Act 1978 (1989 Act, s. 24; see 9.2.2.2). Otherwise the phrase is left to be defined by the common law. Pre-1989 case law will clearly be relevant. While this did not provide a comprehensive definition, it has given some guidelines as to what is, and more particularly is not, an offence of a political character.

In *Re Castioni* [1890] 1 QB 149, extradition to Switzerland was sought in relation to a person who had shot and killed a member of the government of one of the Swiss cantons, in the course of an uprising against that government. The court unanimously took the view that the definition put forward by Stephen J (who was a member of the Court) in his *History of the Criminal Law of England*, vol ii, pp. 70–71, should be accepted. This was that offences of a political character were those which 'were incidental to and formed part of a political disturbance'. Denman J (at p. 156) expanded on this a little in the following terms:

> to exclude extradition for such an act as murder . . . it must at least be shown that the act is done in furtherance of, done with the intention of assistance, as a sort of overt act in the course of acting in a political manner, a political rising, or a dispute between two parties in the State as to which is to have the government in its hands.

This requirement of a dispute between two sides over who is to govern was emphasised in *In re Meunier* [1894] 2 QB 415. The applicant was sought by France in respect of explosions at a café and a military barracks, which had resulted in two deaths. He was a self-confessed 'anarchist'. Cave J (with whom Collins J agreed) took the view that this prevented his offence being 'of a political character'. There was not a dispute as to who was to govern since the applicant's party 'the party of anarchy, is the enemy of all governments' (p. 419). Moreover anarchist offences are not directed against some particular government, but 'are mainly directed against private citizens'. Whether terrorist offences carried out as part of a political dispute over government, but directed at civilian targets, would be treated in the same way is unclear, but, as we shall see, of little practical importance under the modern law, because of the reduced availability of the political offence exception (see 9.2.2.2).

1954 saw what was perhaps the high-water mark of the political offence exception, when in *R v Governor of Brixton Prison, ex parte Kolczynski* [1955] 1 QB 540 Polish seamen who had mutinied against, and wounded, their captain were held to be able to take advantage of it. This was because their offences, while not overtly political, were carried out with a view to avoiding the tyranny of the communist government which was at that time in power in Poland. On the other hand, the House of Lords in *R* v *Governor of Brixton Prison, ex parte Schtraks* [1964] AC 556, while refusing to provide a precise definition, emphasised that non-political offences, such as perjury and child-stealing, did not become political offences simply because they subsequently became a 'political issue'.

Finally, in *Cheng* v *Governor of Pentonville Prison* [1973] AC 931, the House of Lords had to decide whether the attempted assassination of the vice-premier of Taiwan by a member of an organisation opposing his regime was a political offence. On the basis of the approach taken in *Castioni*, and *Meunier*, it would have seemed that it could be. However, the attempt had taken place, not in Taiwan, but in New York, and the State requesting extradition was the United States, with whom the applicant was not in political conflict. On this basis the House of Lords held, by a majority of three to two, that the offence was not an offence of a political character. In order to take advantage of the exception the offence had to be political in relation to the requesting State. Since the applicant's offence was political only as regards Taiwan, and not as regards the United States, his extradition could be ordered.

It will be seen from the above brief survey that the concept of the political offence is not susceptible to easy definition. This may be one reason why, although it still exists, it has been given considerably reduced significance in modern extradition law.

9.2.2.2 Suppression of Terrorism Act 1978 Concern about the increase in international terrorism, and that those involved in terrorist crimes might seek to escape extradition on the basis of their offences being 'political', led in 1977 to the European Convention on the Suppression of Terrorism ('ECST') (Cmnd 7390, 1978), to which the United Kingdom is a party. The obligations under the ECST were given effect by the Suppression of Terrorism Act 1978. The effect is that where this Act applies certain offences are automatically prevented from being regarded as offences of a political character. The provisions of the Suppression of Terrorism Act are applied to the 1989 Act by s. 24. The offences to which it applies are set out in sch. 1 to the 1978 Act. They include murder, manslaughter, rape, and virtually all other offences against the person, apart from assaults which do not cause actual bodily harm. Also included are abduction, hostage-taking, explosives and firearms offences, criminal damage with intent or recklessness as to endangering life, offences under the Aviation Security Act 1982 and the Aviation and Maritime Security Act 1990, and financing terrorism (Prevention of Terrorism (Temporary Provisions) Act 1989, Part III). Attempts and conspiracy to commit any of these offences are also included.

The effect is that where extradition is sought by a country which is a party to the ECST, or in relation to which an order has been made under s. 5 of the Suppression of Terrorism Act 1978 (for example, the United States), it cannot be refused on the basis that the offence was of a political character. The other restrictions contained in the 1989 Act and listed at 9.2.2.3 *will* apply. If, however, extradition is refused on one of these grounds, s. 4 of the Suppression of Terrorism Act 1978 gives the courts in this country the power to treat certain conduct in a convention country as if it had been committed in the United Kingdom, and thus to try the person for that offence here. This applies to the offences of murder, manslaughter, kidnapping, false imprisonment, abduction, hostage-taking, and the explosives and firearms offences listed in sch. 1. This might be the appropriate course of action where there is evidence that a person has committed an offence, but a fair trial in the requesting State may be in doubt because of, for example, racial, religious, or political prejudice.

9.2.2.3 Other restrictions on extradition A range of other restrictions on extradition are contained in s. 6(1)(b)-(d), and s. 6(2)-(4) of the 1989 Act. Thus, extradition is not allowed if it appears that the request is a pretext for punishing a person on grounds of race, religion, nationality or political opinions (s. 6(1)(c)), or that any trial might be unfair because of prejudice based on such grounds (s. 6(1)(d)). There is a restriction on returning people convicted *in absentia*, if 'it would not be in the interest of justice' to do so (s. 6(2)), which might be the case, for example, if the original trial had clearly been unfair (see also, European Convention on Extradition, Second Protocol, Art. 3). A person should not be returned to stand trial where, if similar circumstances occurred in the United Kingdom, a plea of *autrefois acquit* or *autrefois convict* would have been possible: in other words, a person should not be tried more than once for the same offence (s. 6(3)). Finally, s. 6(4) gives effect to the 'specialty' principle, whereby a person returned for one offence should not be tried for another alleged to have been committed before return without being given the opportunity to leave. The Secretary of State may, however, give consent to the person being dealt with in relation to another extradition crime for which return was not sought, provided that it appears that it was one for which extradition could in law, and would in fact, have been available (s. 6(4)(c), (5)). In considering an undertaking given by another State to comply with the specialty principle in a particular case, there is no need to consider future political or legal developments in that State. This was the view taken in *R v Governor of Brixton Prison, ex parte Osman (No 3)* [1992] 1 All ER 122, where the applicant's extradition had been requested by Hong Kong, and the applicant raised a concern as to how he might be treated if he was in prison in Hong Kong in 1997, when the People's Republic of China would resume sovereignty (see also *R v Metropolitan Stipendiary Magistrate, ex parte Lee, The Times*, 15 February 1993).

9.2.3 Procedure for extradition
The provisions outlined in the previous section indicate that there is a range of safeguards in place in relation to extradition, to try to ensure that people are dealt with fairly, though as we have seen these have recently been narrowed in some ways to reflect changes in the nature of offending, and in international relations between States. Almost as important as the rules themselves, however, are the procedures for extradition, and the way in which they

operate, and also the methods of challenging extradition (which are dealt with in 9.2.4).

The procedures for extradition were simplified for the requesting State by the Criminal Justice Act 1988. The relevant provisions are now contained in Part III of the 1989 Act.

The normal starting point is the making of an 'extradition request', by a representative of the requesting State, to the Secretary of State, though there is power to arrest on the basis of a 'provisional warrant' supported by information from a police officer, for example, in cases of urgency (s. 8(1)(b)). The request must specify the particulars of the person sought, and the offence for which return is requested (s. 7(2)). The Secretary of State will then issue an 'authority to proceed' unless it appears that an order for the return of the person could not in law, or would not in practice, be made (s. 7(4)). The authority to proceed will normally be directed to the chief metropolitan magistrate. It should (s. 7(5)):

> specify the offence or offences under the law of the United Kingdom which it appears to the Secretary of State would be constituted by equivalent conduct in the United Kingdom.

Care must be taken over its wording. In *Re Farinha* [1992] Crim LR 438 the authority stated simply that Farinha was:

> accused of the commission of the crimes of supplying a controlled drug within the jurisdiction of the government of Norway.

The Divisional Court held that this was inadequate, and the authority therefore defective, because it did not address the issue of the offence under the law of the United Kingdom which would be constituted by 'equivalent conduct'. This was a matter which it was important that the Court should be sure that the Secretary of State had properly considered. The Court recognised that, presumably because this was a matter having serious consequences for an individual's liberty, it was necessary to be 'vigilant to ensure that extradition procedures were strictly observed'. On the other hand, it was prepared to endorse a rather bland, and unrevealing form of words, such as:

> AB is accused of conduct in the territory of the government of CD which appears to the Secretary of State to be conduct which had it occurred in the UK would have constituted the offence of supplying a controlled drug to another.

This formulation will no doubt become the standard one to be used in relation to authorities to proceed.

On receipt of the authority to proceed the metropolitan magistrate may issue a warrant for the arrest of the person specified. The magistrate will need to be sure that the authority is in order, and that the conduct alleged against the person sought would constitute an 'extradition crime' (s. 8(3)). Sufficient evidence must also be provided to show that a warrant for arrest would be available in relation to a person accused or convicted within the magistrate's own jurisdiction. Once issued, the warrant may be executed in any part of the United Kingdom by any constable (s. 8(5)).

Following arrest, the person should be brought before the metropolitan magistrate for committal proceedings (s. 9(1)). The position used to be (prior to 1989) that the magistrate had to be satisfied that, where the person sought was a suspect rather than a convict, there was a *prima facie* case against the person, such as would have justified committal for trial in the United Kingdom. This is still stated as the general rule (s. 9(8)), and, where it applies, requires the magistrate to give full consideration to the evidence against the accused. It is now subject, however, to a massive exception which means that in the vast majority of cases no such inquiry will be necessary. The combined effect of s. 9(4) and s. 9(8) is that where there is an Order in Council giving effect to general extradition arrangements with the requesting State, which provides that evidence of a *prima facie* case is unnecessary, all that the magistrate has to be satisfied of is that the conduct alleged against the accused amounts to an extradition crime. This is the standard arrangement under the European Convention on Extradition, and so in the future it will rarely be the case that the magistrate will need to give full consideration to the evidence against the accused before committing. Such a procedure will still be necessary, however, where there are special extradition arrangements to deal with a particular case (s. 3(3); see 9.2.1.1), or where the extradition arrangements are derived from one of the Conventions covered by s. 22 of the 1989 Act (see 9.2.1.1, s. 22(5)).

Whichever procedure is followed, the magistrate is limited to considering the matters referred to in the relevant statutory provisions, and in particular has no jurisdiction to consider whether the proceedings amount to an abuse of process, or whether any extradition treaty relied on has been complied with: *Sinclair* v *DPP* [1991] 2 All ER 366 (this was a House of Lords decision on the Extradition Act 1870, but there seems no reason why it should not also apply to committal under the 1989 Act).

Committal may be in custody or on bail, to await the Secretary of State's final decision on removal (s. 9(8)). If committal is refused the requesting State can appeal on a point of law to the Divisional Court, and thence to the House of Lords, by way of case stated (s. (10)), and the accused may be detained pending the appeal (s. 10(2)).

Following a committal by the magistrate, the final decision to return is taken by the Secretary of State (s. 12(1)). Section 12 sets out various grounds on which the Secretary of State might exercise the discretion in favour of the accused, such as the trivial nature of the offence, lapse of time, or bad faith on the part of the requesting State, any of which might make it unjust or oppressive to order the return (s. 12(2)). It seems very unlikely that in practice any of these circumstances will arise with any frequency. The Secretary of State may also refuse to return a person to face the death penalty for an offence which is not so punishable in Great Britain (s. 12(2)(b)). In practice, the

Secretary of State may simply seek an assurance that the death penalty will not be imposed before agreeing to the return. This may well be included as part of the extradition treaty. In *Soering* v *United Kingdom* (1989) 11 EHRR 439 the European Court of Human Rights held that it would be an infringement of Art. 3 of the Convention, relating to inhuman and degrading treatment, to return the accused to the United States where following sentence of death there would be a:

> very long period of time spent on death row . . . in extreme conditions, with the ever present and mounting anguish of awaiting execution of the death penalty.

Soering was in the end returned on the basis of an assurance that he would not be tried for a capital offence. The comments of the European Court in this case will, however, no doubt continue to influence the Secretary of State in the exercise of the discretion under s. 12(2)(b).

9.2.4 Methods of challenging extradition

There are three procedures for challenging extradition that need to be considered: habeas corpus; representations to the Secretary of State; and judicial review. All three are recognised in the 1989 Act.

9.2.4.1 *Habeas corpus*

This is the ancient writ by which the legality of detention (on any ground) can be challenged. It is sought by means of an *ex parte* application to the High Court which takes precedence over all other business. If the court thinks that there is a case for the writ to issue, it will normally (unless there is a need to act with urgency) adjourn proceedings to enable an *inter partes* hearing to take place. The issue of the writ will have the effect of ordering the person to whom it is directed to release the applicant from detention immediately.

The possibility of applying for *habeas corpus* in relation to a person who has been committed in extradition proceedings is recognised in s. 11. Indeed, the section *requires* the person committed to be told by the court 'in ordinary language' of the right to make such an application. If an application is made, the person must not be returned until the proceedings are completed, and there is no further possiblity of an appeal (s. 11(5)).

The High Court does not act as a court of appeal when hearing an *habeas corpus* application. Its scope for review is quite limited. It will consider first of all procedural issues. Has the court committing the applicant acted within its powers, and followed the correct procedures? Secondly, it may consider whether the return of the applicant would be 'unjust or oppressive' because of the trivial nature of the offence, lapse of time, or the bad faith of the requesting State (s. 11(3)). These are factors which, it will be remembered, the Secretary of State may take into account in deciding whether or not to return the applicant. Fresh evidence, not before the court which committed, may be considered in relation to these issues. Thirdly, fresh evidence may be adduced to show that one of the general restrictions on extradition contained in s. 6 of the Act (political offence, etc), applies (s. 11(4)). Beyond this, however, the court will not review the facts which formed the basis of the decision to commit. In fact, as we have seen, in the majority of cases there would now be very little to review, since the principal issue is simply whether the conduct for which extradition is sought constitutes an extradition crime.

9.2.4.2 Representations to the Secretary of State

If the Secretary of State has it in mind to issue an order of return in relation to a person who has been committed in extradition proceedings, notice must be given to the person (s. 13(1), (2)), who will then have 15 days in which to make representations to the Secretary of State as to 'why he should not be returned to the foreign State' (s. 13(2)). No warrant for return may be issued before the expiry of those 15 days, unless the person waives the right to make representations. There is no limitation on the nature of the representations that can be made, and the Secretary of State is obliged to consider them (s. 13(4)). It seems unlikely, however, that the Secretary of State will be persuaded by the representations unless they raise issues or information which were relevant to the decision to commit, but were not before the court which committed, or which were not relevant to the court's decision, but might affect the Secretary of State's discretion (such as the trivial nature of the offence, the political situation in the requesting State, or, possibly, the effect on the applicant's dependants if the extradition takes place).

9.2.4.3 Judicial review

If the Secretary of State decides to issue a warrant for return, the person to whom it applies then has seven days in which to institute judicial review proceedings in relation to that decision. The warrant for return may not then be executed until the judicial review proceedings are concluded (s. 13(7)). Judicial review might, for example, raise the issues in s. 12(2) which the Secretary of State may take into account in exercising the discretion to make an order. The wording of the sections is subjective, however, in terms of how matters 'appear' to the Secretary of State. None of the provisions uses a 'reasonableness' qualification, and so only if the decision is *Wednesbury* unreasonable, will it generally be susceptible to challenge. It might be possible to argue, however, in relation to the provision in s. 12(2)(b) concerning the death penalty, that the Secretary of State should have regard to the provisions of the European Convention on Human Rights, as applied by the European Court of Human Rights in *Soering* v *United Kingdom* (1989) 11 EHRR 439 (see 9.2.3).

9.2.5 Conclusions on extradition

The procedures for extradition have become easier in recent years. The reasons for this are easy to see, in that improved communications make international crime, and movement between countries, much easier than in the nineteenth century when the rules relating to extradition developed. The scope for the political offence exception has been much reduced, and the requirement of proof of a *prima facie* case by the requesting State largely removed. It should not be forgotten, however, that extradition is a very powerful procedure, which applies to British citizens as well as foreign nationals. It can involve the forcible removal of people from the country in which they were born, and which has always been their home. It can result in the separation of families, and, where the person is convicted of an offence on return to the requesting State, the possible imposition of harsher penalties than would be imposed for an equivalent offence in this country. For all these reasons it is important that the power to extradite is used cautiously and carefully. With the reduction in the role of the court of committal in reviewing the substance of the case against the person sought, much depends on the discretion of the Secretary of State. It is unfortunate that the recent changes simplifying extradition have not been balanced by a more formal procedure for appeal or review which would allow some opportunity for consideration of the strength of the requesting State's case. At the moment, the only point at which any formal consideration is given to this is when the original request for surrender is made, and an authority to proceed is issued, at which point the evidence must be such as would justify the issue of a warrant for arrest in this country (see ss. 7(2), 8(3)). This means in effect 'reasonable suspicion' which, as has been noted in chapters 2 and 3, is a very vague concept which does not provide any very stringent control of powers to which it applies.

9.3 DEPORTATION

Deportation is very different from extradition. It has no necessary connection with the committing of criminal offences, and it involves no judicial process comparable with the committal proceedings in relation to extradition. The decision to deport is almost entirely a matter of executive discretion (though, of course, operating within a framework of legal rules, which may make the decision susceptible to judicial review). The other important distinction from extradition, is that deportation is not available in respect of British citizens. Those who have the right of residence in this country on that basis are excluded from deportation powers. It is therefore necessary to look at the rules relating to citizenship, before moving on to consider in detail the grounds for deportation.

9.3.1 The concept of citizenship
At one time everyone who held a British passport had a right to enter and settle in the United Kingdom, even if their only connection with this country was that they were a citizen of a commonwealth country, or colony. Immigration controls only applied to those who did not hold a British passport, and were categorised as 'aliens'. It was thought necessary, however, in the 1960s and 1970s, because of the numbers who wished to enter the United Kingdom, and the increasing racial tensions which were developing in this country, to impose restrictions on immigration to the United Kingdom even in relation to certain categories of people from commonwealth countries who held British passports. The Commonwealth Immigrants Act of 1962 for the first time imposed significant limitations on the rights of those from the commonwealth and colonies to enter and settle in the United Kingdom. The trend has over the last

20 years continued to be increasingly restrictive. The position is now largely governed by the Immigration Act 1971, as amended by the British Nationality Act 1981. The Immigration Act 1971 introduced the two concepts of the 'right of abode' and 'patriality'. The latter concept has now disappeared, but the 'right of abode' survives as the test of whether a person has a right to settle and work in the United Kingdom, without being subject to immigration controls (Immigration Act 1971, s. 1(1)). A person is defined by s. 2(1) of the Immigration Act 1971 as having a right of abode if:

(a) he is a British citizen; or
(b) he is a Commonwealth citizen who —

(i) immediately before the commencement of the British Nationality Act 1981 was a Commonwealth citizen having the right of abode in the United Kingdom by virtue of section 2(1)(d) or section 2(2) of this Act as then in force; and
(ii) has not ceased to be a Commonwealth citizen in the meanwhile.

It will be noted that the category in s. 2(1)(b) depends on rights existing under previous legislation. It is a complex business to work out exactly who is included in it, but since it is a limited category, in that no new members of it can now arise, it is not discussed further here. (For a full discussion see I. Macdonald and N. Blake, *Immigration Law and Practice in the United Kingdom*, 3rd edn, London: Butterworths, 1991, chapter 6.) The definition of who is a 'British citizen' is to be found in Part I of the British Nationality Act 1981. All those citizens of the United Kingdom and Colonies who had a 'right of abode' prior the 1981 Act are included. Since the 1981 Act came into force in 1983, however, it has only been possible to obtain British citizenship in five ways, namely, place of birth, adoption by a British citizen, descent, registration, and naturalisation. Of these only place of birth and descent need further explanation here.

As regards place of birth, it is not enough simply to be born in the United Kingdom. In addition, one of the child's parents must either be a British citizen, or be lawfully settled in the United Kingdom (1981 Act, s. 1(1)). As regards 'descent', a child born outside the United Kingdom will obtain British citizenship if one of the child's parents is a British citizen *other than by descent* (1981 Act, s. 2). British citizenship can thus in general only be passed to one generation by descent alone (as opposed to birth in the United Kingdom combined with descent).

Turning now to the power of deportation, s. 3(5) of the Immigration Act 1971 provides that 'a person who is not a British citizen shall be liable to deportation from the United Kingdom' in certain circumstances. Note that commonwealth citizens falling within s. 2(1)(b) of the 1971 Act (above), are to be treated as British citizens for this purpose (1971 Act, s. 2(2)).

A further complication arises in relation to citizens of other member States of the European Community. Such citizens are not British citizens, and thus under s. 3(5) of the Immigration Act 1971 are liable to deportation. However, under EC law such citizens have rights of free movement between member States for certain economic purposes (such as working, or establishing a business). The power to deport is governed by Arts 48(3) of the Treaty of Rome and Council Directive 64/221, and is limited to 'public policy, public security and public health'. This must be regarded as limiting the powers contained in s. 3 of the Immigration Act 1971 (see also Immigration Act 1988, s. 7(1), and Immigration Rules 1990, paras 71 and 152). As a result, the grounds for deporting EC nationals will be considered separately in the next section.

9.3.2 Grounds for deportation

9.3.2.1 Non-EC nationals There are five grounds for deportation set out in s. 3(5) and (6) of the Immigration Act 1971. These are where:

(a) a person who has limited permission to enter breaks a condition of the permission (s. 3(5)(a)): this would apply, for example, to a student, admitted to follow a full-time course, who takes paid employment without permission; or

(b) a person who has limited permission to enter 'overstays' after the permission has expired (s. 3(5)(a)); or

(c) the Secretary of State deems the deportation of a person to be 'conducive to the public good' (s. 3(5)(b)): this ground is considered further below; or

(d) someone in the person's family (as defined in s. 5(4)) is or has been ordered to be deported (s. 3(5)(c)); or

(e) a person over the age of 17 has been convicted of an imprisonable offence, and the court recommends deportation.

The ground which has caused the most controversy is (c), i.e. that the Secretary of State deems the deportation to be conducive to the public good. This is not surprising: it is a very broadly stated power, and its exercise lies entirely at the discretion of the Secretary of State. The Immigration Rules, which give further guidance about the operation of the other grounds for deportation, in relation to this ground simply state (para. 167):

General rules about the circumstances in which deportation is justified on these grounds cannot be laid down, and each case will be considered carefully in the light of the relevant circumstances known to the Secretary of State . . .

In all cases the Secretary of State is likely to consider relevant matters such as the age of the person, length of residence in the United Kingdom, strength of connection with the United Kingdom, character, conduct and employment record, and domestic or compassionate circumstances (Immigration Rules 1990, para. 164). What matters will be regarded as contrary to the public good, however, is very unclear. All that can be done is to look at the situations where the power to deport on this ground has been used in the past. This will not necessarily provide an accurate guide to how it will be used in the future, and certainly cannot be taken as indicating the full scope of the power.

First, the 'public good' ground seems to be frequently used where a person has been convicted of an offence but no recommendation for deportation has been made by the court. In this case the guidelines set out by the Court of Appeal in R v Nazari [1980] 3 All ER 880 as regards matters a court should consider before making a recommendation for deportation will presumably also be relevant to the Secretary of State's decision. In particular the Court referred to the seriousness of the offence; whether, because of the situation in the destination country, return would be 'unduly harsh'; and the effect on the deportee's family.

Secondly, the fact that some sort of deception has been practised in order to obtain settlement in the United Kingdom may justify deportation on the 'public good' ground: Patel v IAT [1988] 2 All ER 378. This has also been accepted as an appropriate ground where the applicant is alleged to have entered into a 'marriage of convenience': R v IAT, ex parte Khan [1983] QB 790.

Thirdly, the public good ground has been used on occasions to deport people engaging in the promotion of political views which are regarded as dangerous (for example, in 1970 Rudi Dutschke, a 'student' activist, was deported on this basis), or unduly offensive to certain sections of the community (for example, members of the Ku Klux Klan could be deported on this ground). Adherents to particular religious sects may also come under this heading, as was the case in relation to members of the Church of Scientology during the 1980s.

Finally, concerns that the continued presence of the person will be detrimental to 'national security' will certainly be relevant, though this is in itself a nebulous concept (see 5.3). An example of its use is to be found in the case of R v Secretary of State for the Home Department, ex parte Hosenball [1977] 3 All ER 452. Mark Hosenball was a United States citizen who had been living on and off in the United Kingdom for over seven years. He orginally came when he was 18, as a school pupil, but by 1976 was working as a general news reporter for the Evening Standard. He had previously worked as a journalist on the magazine Time Out. During all this time he had permission to remain. In November 1976, he received a letter from the Home Office stating that the Secretary of State had decided to deport him. The reasons were given as follows ([1977] 3 All ER 452, at p. 455):

The Secretary of State has considered information that Mr Hosenball has, while resident in the United Kingdom, in consort with others, sought to obtain and has obtained for publication, information harmful to the security of the United Kingdom and that this information has included information prejudicial to the safety and servants of the Crown.

As a result, the Secretary of State had decided that 'Mr Hosenball's departure from the United Kingdom would be conducive to the public good, as being in the interests of national security . . .'. This in effect tells us that collecting, and proposing to publish, information about the security services is regarded as being contrary to national security (see Lord Denning, [1977] 3 All ER 456). No further detail, however, of the allegations against Mr Hosenball, or their source, was forthcoming, and, as will be seen below, the courts were not prepared to look behind the statement contained in the letter (see 9.3.3.2).

The national security ground was also used in 1991, at the time of the Gulf War, in relation to Iraqis and Palestinians against some of whom there was apparently information that they had links with an organisation prepared to take terrorist action in support of the Iraqi regime: *R* v *Secretary of State, ex parte Cheblak* [1991] 2 All ER 319 (see 9.3.3.1; see also, S. Bailey, D. Harris and B. Jones, *Civil Liberties Cases and Materials*, 3rd edn, London: Butterworths, pp. 677–678).

9.3.2.2 EC nationals EC nationals from other member States are not British citizens, and therefore are in general subject to the deportation powers in s. 3(5) of the Immigration Act 1971. As has been noted, above, however, in some circumstances more restricted powers apply. This will be the case if the national has entered, or wishes to enter, the United Kingdom for one of the reasons for which free movement within the Community must be ensured under European Community law. These are to work (Treaty of Rome, Arts 48–51); to establish or join a business (Treaty of Rome, Arts 52–58); or to provide or receive services (Treaty of Rome, Arts. 59–66). (For further discussion of these categories see J. Steiner, *Textbook on EEC Law*, 3rd edn, London: Blackstone Press, 1992, chapters 18 and 19.) In these circumstances the only grounds on which deportation may take place are public policy, public security, and public health (Treaty of Rome, Arts 48(3) and 56, as supplemented by Council Directive 64/221). Thus, by virtue of Art. 3(1) of the Directive, prior commission of a criminal offence will not in itself provide justification for exclusion. There must be a real possibility of re-offending, or the offence must have been sufficiently serious to arouse public revulsion, for the public policy justification to come into play: *Bonsignore* v *Oberstadtdirektor of the City of Cologne* [1975] ECR 297; *R* v *Bouchereau* [1977] ECR 1999. The question of exclusion on grounds of public policy because of membership of a particular organisation was considered in *Van Duyn* v *Home Office* [1974] 1 WLR 1107; [1974] ECR 1337. Miss Van Duyn was a member of the Church of Scientology. She was a Dutch national, but wished to enter the United Kingdom to work as a secretary at the Church's headquarters in East Grinstead. She was refused leave to enter, because of her membership of the Church, whose activities the United Kingdom considered to be not conducive to the public good. The European Court took the view that although in general a person's past associations should not restrict freedom of movement, where there was present membership of, and participation in the activities of an organisation, this could be regarded as 'personal conduct' falling within Art. 3(1). Moreover public policy 'may vary from one country to another' and national authorities therefore had an 'area of discretion within the limits imposed by the Treaty'. It followed that, if the activities of an organisation are considered socially harmful, and administrative measures have been taken to counteract them, there was no need for them to be made unlawful before the public policy ground could be relied on. As regards the fact that no similar restrictions were placed on United Kingdom nationals, it was a principle of international law that a State cannot refuse entry or residence to its own nationals, but the whole point of Art. 48 was that, while granting freedom of movement to nationals of other member States, for certain purposes, that freedom was subject to restrictions.

It follows that a member State, for reasons of public policy, can, where it deems necessary, refuse a national of another member State the benefit of the principle of freedom of movement for workers in a case where such a national proposes to take up a particular offer of employment, even though the member State does not place a similar restriction on its own nationals.

In *R* v *Bouchereau* [1977] ECR 1999, the Court emphasised, following its approach in *Rutili* v *French Minister of the Interior* [1975] ECR 1219, that reliance on public policy presupposes the existence of 'a genuine and sufficiently serious threat to the requirements of public policy affecting one of the fundamental interests of society'. The Court in *Rutili* had also expressed the view that the action taken must be justified as being 'necessary . . . in a democratic society' for the protection of the public interests concerned. The breadth of the *Van Duyn* decision was further restricted by *Adoui and Cournaille* v *Belgian State* [1982] ECR 1665, where it was held that it would be difficult to regard conduct as being sufficiently serious to justify deportation or exclusion on public policy grounds unless some action was taken against the nationals of the member State who engaged in such conduct:

. . . a member State may not . . . expel a national of another member State from its territory or refuse him access to its territory by reason of conduct which, when attributable to the former State's own nationals, does not give rise to repressive measures or other genuine and effective measures intended to combat such conduct.

It may well be, therefore, that if the *Van Duyn* case recurred, the United Kingdom would need to show that some restrictive measures (not necessarily involving the criminal law) were taken against members of the Church of Scientology who were British citizens in order to justify the deportation or exclusion of nationals of other member States on the grounds of membership of the Church.

9.3.3 Methods of challenge

Apart from a request for an internal Home Office review of the decision to deport (provided for by Immigration Rules 1990, para. 180), there are four possible methods of challenge to a decision to deport, though some of them are likely to be of limited practical use, and others are only available in relation to certain categories of decision. In so far as the challenge may involve the court issuing an order, albeit a temporary one, restraining the removal of the applicant from the jurisdiction, this will bind even the Secretary of State. In

M v *Home Office* [1993] 3 All ER 537, the applicant had been seeking asylum. A judge in chambers received an undertaking that the applicant would not be deported pending a further hearing. Nevertheless, the deportation of the applicant went ahead. The judge then ordered the Secretary of State to return the applicant to this country, but this order was not complied with. The House of Lords confirmed that this rendered the Secretary of State (in his official capacity) in contempt of court. Thus although many of the powers in this area are exercised on the basis of Ministerial discretion, there is not unlimited power in the executive. The exercise of powers may be controlled by orders from the courts, with contempt as the sanction.

9.3.3.1 *Habeas corpus* This action, which has been described in relation to extradition at 9.2.4.1, will also in theory be available in relation to a person detained pending deportation. In practice, however, it is likely to be of limited use. Since the *habeas corpus* action is concerned entirely with the issue of jurisdiction, it will only be where the Secretary of State has clearly acted *ultra vires* that the writ will issue. This might be the case, for example, if the stated ground for deportation was a recommendation of a court following conviction for an offence, where it was shown that the person concerned was below the age of 17 at the relevant time (see Immigration Act 1971, s. 3(6)). In general, however, the broad discretion given to the Secretary of State will make it unlikely that such a challenge can be mounted. In *R* v *Secretary of State, ex parte Cheblak* [1991] 2 All ER 319 (see 9.3.2.1) the Court of Appeal held that the Secretary of State did not need to give reasons for a decision to deport on grounds of national security. A notice stating simply that the applicant's deportation was deemed to be for the public good 'for reasons of national security' was perfectly valid. The applicant's detention on the basis of the notice was therefore lawful, and could not be challenged by *habeas corpus*. (See also *R* v *Governor of Brixton Prison, ex parte Soblen* [1963] 2 QB 243, discussed at 9.3.3.2.)

If the basis for challenge is not that the order is *ultra vires*, but that a discretion has been exercised improperly, then *habeas corpus* will not be available, and judicial review proceedings should be used.

9.3.3.2 Judicial review The decision to deport, and the procedures that have led to it, are clearly administrative acts that are susceptible to judicial review. This was the method of challenge used in *R* v *Secretary of State for the Home Department, ex parte Hosenball* [1977] 3 All ER 452, and was an additional argument in *R* v *Secretary of State for the Home Department, ex parte Cheblak* [1991] 2 All ER 319. The wording of the statutory powers means, however, that the applicant will generally have to establish bad faith, or *Wednesbury* unreasonableness, to have any chance of success. Moreover, where the basis for the decision to deport is stated by the Secretary of State to relate to matters of national security, the courts will not look behind that assertion: *R* v *Secretary of State for the Home Department, ex parte Hosenball* [1977] 3 All ER 452. As Lord Denning put it (at p. 461):

There is a conflict here between the interests of national security on the one hand and the freedom of the individual on the other. The balance between these two is not for a court of law. It is for the Home Secretary. He is the person entrusted by parliament with the task.

Lord Denning then went on to express perhaps surprising confidence that the Secretary of State would never use the powers improperly, asserting that successive Ministers, in using such powers, 'have never interfered with the liberty of the freedom of movement of any individual except where it is absolutely necessary for the safety of the State'. Even if the power were misused, the Minister would be answerable to parliament, rather than the courts.

It has been suggested that it may be possible to challenge a deportation order if 'the object of the exercise was simply to achieve extradition by the back door': Lord Lane in *R v Bow Street Magistrates, ex parte Mackeson* (1982) 7 Cr App R 24. There is no reported case, however, in which an order has been overturned on this ground. In *R v Governor of Brixton Prison, ex parte Soblen* [1963] 2 QB 243 (which in fact was an application for *habeas corpus* rather than judicial review) the applicant was sought by the United States in relation to espionage offences of which he had been convicted. Extradition was not at the time available for such offences, but the Home Secretary ordered Soblen's deportation to the United States. Soblen had asked to be sent to Czechoslovakia, which was prepared to accept him. He challenged the deportation order on the basis that, *inter alia*, it was being used for 'disguised extradition'. The Court of Appeal rejected this argument, because no bad faith on the part of the Home Secretary had been proved. In other words, it had not been shown that the request from the United States was the sole reason for the deportation order. The Home Secretary might well, even in the absence of this request, have ordered Soblen to be deported to the United States, on the public good ground. The order was thus upheld, but Soblen in fact committed suicide before he could be returned.

The relaxation and simplification of the procedures for extradition (see 9.2) may well mean that there will be less temptation in the future to use deportation as a substitute.

Judicial review is the usual method of challenge for those refused political asylum. (But note the new provisions relating to asylum seekers in the Asylum and Immigration Appeals Act 1993, which was not in force at the time of writing.) The current United Kingdom position on the granting of asylum is set out in para. 75 of the Immigration Rules 1990, which, after making clear that the decision will be taken by the Home Secretary in the light of the UK's international obligations under the United Nations' Convention Relating to the Status of Refugees of 1951, and the Protocol of 1966, states that:

Asylum will not be refused if the only country to which the person could be removed is one to which he is unwilling to go owing to a well-founded fear of being persecuted for reasons of race, religion, nationality, membership of a particular social group or political opinion.

This makes it clear that so-called economic refugees, who have fled their home State because of famine, or other pressing social conditions, will not qualify for asylum. There must be a fear of *persecution*. This is a strong word meaning more than simply harassment (*R* v *Secretary of State for the Home Department, ex parte Yurekli* [1990] Imm AR 334), or discrimination (*Ahmad* v *Secretary of State for the Home Department* [1990] Imm AR 61). The persecution must relate to one of the areas mentioned in para. 75, and the fear of it must be well-founded. This part of the test was considered in *R* v *Secretary of State for the Home Department, ex parte Sivakumaran* [1988] 1 All ER 193. In deciding whether it is satisfied, the burden of proof is on the applicant, on the balance of probabilities. The Home Secretary is, however, entitled to take into account all relevant information, even if this is not known to the applicant. The test is then whether there is a 'reasonable chance' or a 'real likelihood' of persecution occurring. The difficulties inherent in such a decision are shown by the fact that after the House of Lords had upheld the Home Secretary's decision in this case to refuse asylum, and return the six Tamil applicants to Sri Lanka, a immigration adjudicator upheld an appeal on the facts (see 9.3.3.3), and granted them asylum status. Given the problems of assessing at a distance exactly what treatment a person is likely to receive if returned to another country, it is an area where one would hope that the Home Secretary would err on the side of generosity, if there appears to be any substantial risk of ill-treatment.

A further problem has arisen in relation to asylum seekers who have come to this country via another, 'safe', country. The policy is to refuse asylum in the United Kingdom in such cases, and return the applicant to the safe country, to seek asylum there. In *R* v *Secretary of State for the Home Department, ex parte Ghebretatios* , *The Times*, 19 July 1993, the applicant, who originated from Ethiopia and travelled to the United Kingdom via Italy and France, sought judicial review of the Home Secretary's decision to return him to France. It was argued that this was contrary to the European Community's free movement provisions. The Court of Appeal, however, held that asylum issues were clearly intended to be treated differently from general questions of free movement, as was shown by the fact that member States had negotiated a separate convention to deal with the issue (the Dublin Convention), although this had not yet been ratified or implemented. On this basis, the Home Secretary was acting within his powers in refusing to consider asylum, and returning the applicant to France.

9.3.3.3 Appeal under the Immigration Act 1971

A right of appeal to an immigration adjudicator, or the Immigration Appeal Tribunal against certain deportation decisions is given by s. 15 of the Immigration Act 1971. No right of appeal is given where the decision to deport follows a recommendation of a court before which the deportee has been convicted of an offence (Immigration Act 1971, s. 3(6)). The correct method of challenge in such a case is to appeal against sentence under the normal procedures for appeal in criminal cases: no order to deport will be made while such an appeal is possible or pending (Immigration Rules 1990, para. 157).

Where the decision to deport is taken under s. 3(5) of the Immigration Act 1971, there will generally be an appeal to an immigration adjudicator, and thence (by either side) to the Immigration Appeal Tribunal. Adjudicators are often former immigration officers, and are appointed by the Home Office. Under the Asylum and Immigration Appeals Act 1993, s. 8, 'special adjudicators' are to be appointed by the Lord Chancellor to deal with claims that the Secretary of State's decision is contrary to the UK's obligations under the 1951 Convention (see 9.3.3.2). There must, however, have been a claim for asylum prior to the decision to deport for this to apply (Asylum and Immigration Appeals Act 1993, sch. 2, para. 2).

The Immigration Appeal Tribunal has an independent membership. The appeal process is administered by the Lord Chancellor's Department, but still has rather the look of an internal review process, rather than a properly independent appeal system. However, on appeal the adjudicator or Tribunal may review any determination of the facts, and can consider both the question of the legality of the decision, and the way in which any discretion has been exercised: Immigration Act 1971, s. 19(1). In other words the adjudicator or Tribunal is entitled to hold that the Secretary of State should have exercised a discretion differently. They are not simply limited to considering (as is the case with judicial review) whether the discretion has been exercised 'properly'. The decision of the Tribunal, or if there is no appeal, the adjudicator, is currently final, and binding on the Secretary of State. It should be noted, however, that the Asylum and Immigration Appeals Act 1993, s. 9 will, when in force, provide for an appeal on a point of law by either party from the Tribunal to the Court of Appeal. The appeal process is therefore a powerful one, and capable of providing a full reconsideration of the case, and valuable remedies. On the other hand, its scope is limited, in the sense that some of the most difficult and controversial cases are removed from it, and dealt with under a much vaguer advisory procedure, as explained below.

There is no appeal against a decision to deport on the basis that this would be conducive to the public good on grounds of national security, the interests of relations between the United Kingdom and any other country, or 'other reasons of a political nature' (s. 15(3)). In these cases the deportee must use the non-statutory advisory procedure outlined at 9.3.3.4. The same is true of a refusal to revoke a decision to deport if the Home Secretary personally (rather than through an official) refused on the basis that the deportation would be conducive to the public good (on any ground), or if the Home Secretary certifies that the exclusion would be so conducive (s. 15(4)). If a decision to deport is on the 'public good' ground, but not for one of the reasons listed above (for example, a decision to deport a person convicted of an offence where no recommendation has been made by the court), there is a right of appeal, but it goes direct to the Tribunal, rather than to an adjudicator (s. 15(7)). The same is also true where the appeal relates to a deportation order against a person as belonging to the family of another person (s. 15(7)).

9.3.3.4 The advisory procedure Where there is no statutory right of appeal, the deportee is allowed to make representations to three advisers appointed by the Home Secretary (compare the procedure which operates in relation to exclusion orders; see 9.4.3). The current chair of this panel is Lord Justice Lloyd. The other two members are likely to be senior civil servants. In 1991, following a spate of deportation decisions arising from the Gulf War, two 'reserve' advisers were apparently appointed (S. Bailey, D. Harris & B. Jones, *Civil Liberties Cases and Materials*, 3rd edn, London: Butterworths, 1991, p. 678). The procedure to be followed was set out by Reginald Maudling, the then Home Secretary, in a written answer on 15 June 1971 (*Hansard*, 819 HC Deb col 376).

The potential deportee will be given 'such particulars of allegations as will not entail disclosure of sources of evidence'. As we have seen, in the *Hosenball* case the Court of Appeal held that where national security was said by the Home Secretary to be in issue, minimal information about the allegations could be given, even though this would in ordinary circumstances be contrary to the principles of natural justice. If the applicant wishes, there will be a personal hearing before the advisers, at which a third party may also testify on behalf of the applicant. Since such representations may well have to be made without any proper knowledge of the opposing case it is hard to believe that the Home Secretary's assurance that 'the advisers will ensure that the person is able to make his points effectively' is anything more than a pious hope. Similar doubts must exist concerning the weight which the advisers will in practice give to the need to 'bear in mind' that the case against the applicant 'has not been tested by cross-examination and that the person has not had the opportunity to rebut it'. The advisers will then give their advice to the Home Secretary. It will not be made public, or disclosed to the applicant, and the Home Secretary is not obliged to follow it. It is merely 'advice' which may be accepted or rejected. Release will sometimes follow (see S. Bailey, D. Harris & B. Jones, *Civil Liberties Cases and Materials*, 3rd edn., 1991, p. 678), but because of the secrecy surrounding the procedures it is impossible to tell in what proportion of cases the Home Secretary is influenced by the advice received.

9.3.3.5 Conclusions on deportation   It is no doubt necessary that in certain circumstances the executive should have the power to deport, and that there may be situations where it is appropriate that this should be done without any judicial process being involved. This is perhaps most obviously the case with those who are in the country with knowledge that they are in breach of immigration regulations. It is less clear that the power is needed in other situations, or that, if it is, it is justifiable that there is in effect no independent review of its exercise in many cases. The use of the magic words 'national security' will emasculate the already rather weak (in this context) remedy of judicial review, and we are therefore left to trust in the good faith of the Home Secretary only to use the power where it is really necessary. Even those who are not entirely cynical about the way in which government Ministers carry out their public duties may feel that a less optimistic attitude than that taken by the courts in the *Hosenball* and *Cheblak* cases is justified.

9.4 EXCLUSION ORDERS

Exclusion orders were created by the Prevention of Terrorism (Temporary Provisions) Act 1974 as part of the measures to combat terrorism related to Northern Ireland. The relevant provisions are now contained in Part II of the Prevention of Terrorism (Temporary Provisions) Act 1989 (references to section numbers in what follows are to this Act, unless otherwise stated). There are three types of exclusion order: exclusion from Great Britain (s. 5); exclusion from Northern Ireland (s. 6); and exclusion from the United Kingdom (s. 7). The power to exclude from the United Kingdom cannot be used against a British citizen (s. 7(4)), and is thus in this way subject to the same limitation as the power to deport. The other two powers allow a British citizen to be excluded from one part of the United Kingdom, and may effectively, therefore, involve a kind of 'internal exile'. The concentration here will be on the first of these, that is exclusion from Great Britain, though the powers and procedures are to a large extent identical in relation to all three types of order.

9.4.1 Grounds for exclusion from Great Britain

The powers to exclude are available to the Home Secretary in order to *prevent* acts of terrorism 'connected with the affairs of Northern Ireland' (s. 4(1), (2)). This suggests that the order is intended to act against anticipated future behaviour, rather than to punish for what has occurred in the past. Previous involvement with terrorism, or terrorists, may of course provide a basis for believing that a person will in the future commit such acts, and as we shall see, is given as one of the grounds justifying an order. 'Terrorism' means 'the use of violence for political ends, and includes any use of violence for the purpose of putting the public or any section of the public in fear' (s. 20(1); see also, 2.4.4.1).

The grounds for making an order excluding a person from Great Britain arise where the Secretary of State is satisfied that a person either is or has been concerned in the commission, preparation, or instigation of acts of terrorism connected with Northern Ireland (s. 5(1)(a)); or, is attempting or may attempt to enter Great Britain with a view to being so concerned (s. 5(1)(b)). The power may thus be used against a person who is already in Great Britain, or is trying to enter, or may try to enter. Where the order is directed against a person who is already in Great Britain, and is ordinarily resident there, the Secretary of State must have regard to whether a person has any connection with a country or territory outside Great Britain (s. 5(3)). If the person is a British citizen, this will in effect mean whether there is any connection with Northern Ireland.

An order excluding from Great Britain may not be made against a British citizen who is at the time excluded from Northern Ireland (under s. 6 of the Act), or who is ordinarily resident in Great Britain, and has been so resident for the previous three years (s. 5(4)).

There is no power here, as there is with deportation, to exclude the family of a person who is subject to an exclusion order, and one of the problems of such orders is that they may divide families. This problem was more serious prior to 1984, when the period of ordinary residence necessary to avoid exclusion was 20 years. This was reduced following criticism of this provision by Lord Jellicoe in his *Review of the Operation of the Prevention of Terrorism (Temporary Provisions) Act 1976*, Cmnd 8803, 1983 (see also D. Bonner, 'Combating Terrorism in Great Britain: The Role of Exclusion Orders', [1982] *PL* 262, at p. 272).

9.4.2   Procedures relating to exclusion

The procedures for the operation of exclusion orders are set out in sch. 2 to the Act. A person against whom an order has been made must as soon as possible be given notice of the order (para. 2). The notice must set out the right to make representations (see 9.4.3), and how that right may be exercised. If the person consents, or if the time for representations has passed, or if the Secretary of State has rejected such representations, the person may be removed from Great Britain (paras 5 and 6).

There are in addition powers of arrest and detention in relation to people against whom directions for removal have been made (paras 7 and 8).

An order, once made, lasts for three years, unless revoked in the meantime (para. 1(2)). A further exclusion order may then be made (para. 1(3)), if the Secretary of State considers that there are still grounds for making one.

9.4.3   Challenging an exclusion order

Judicial review will clearly be available as a means of challenging an exclusion order (as will *habeas corpus* in relation to a person who is in detention pending removal). It is likely only to be of much use, however, if the person is claiming to be exempt from exclusion, for example, on the basis of three years' ordinary residence in Great Britain. In this case, the burden of proof is on the applicant (sch. 2, para. 9(1)). Otherwise, the Secretary of State's discretion is expressed in such wide terms ('is satisfied', s. 5(1)), that it is unlikely that the courts would ever be prepared to interfere with its exercise. In *R* v *Secretary of State for Home Affairs, ex parte Stitt, The Times*, 3 February 1987, review was sought on the basis that no reasons were given for the order, which made it very difficult for the applicant to challenge it, and was contrary to natural justice. The Divisional Court, following much the same line as that taken by the Court of Appeal in relation to deportation in *R* v *Secretary of State for the Home Department, ex parte Hosenball* [1977] 3 All ER 452, and *R* v *Secretary of State for the Home Department, ex parte Cheblak* [1991] 2 All ER 319, held that since the making of the order involved issues of national security, the Secretary of State could not be required to give reasons.

Judicial review is thus of limited use. The only other method of challenge is to use the review procedure provided in the Act itself (sch. 2). Under this a person who has been given notice of an order has seven days to make representations to the Secretary of State, setting out any objections to the order (para. 3(1), (2)). Alternatively, if the person is not within Great Britain at the time when the order is served, or consents to be removed from Great Britain within the seven days, the period within which representations must be made is extended to 14 days (para. 3(3), (4)). If representations are made within the required period, they are referred to an adviser, appointed for this purpose. In addition, the person making the representations is at the same time entitled to request a personal interview with this adviser (para. 3(1)(b)). This must be granted if the person is still in Great Britain. If the person is outside Great Britain, the Secretary of State should grant an interview if it appears to the Secretary to be reasonably practicable to do so (para. 3(7)), in either Northern Ireland or the Republic of Ireland (para. 3(8)).

The difficulties with this procedure for representations and interview are the same as in relation to the non-statutory appeal procedure in relation to deportation (see 9.3.3.4), in that the applicant is working in the dark. If the person has no idea why the Secretary of State has thought it appropriate to make an exclusion order, it will be very difficult to mount an effective challenge to it.

Even if no interview is sought, the Secretary of State must refer the representations to an adviser for an opinion (para. 3(5)). Once the report of any interview, and the adviser's opinion have been received, the Secretary of State must reconsider the case taking into account 'everything which appears to him to be relevant' (para. 4(1)). Thus, while the representations and advisers' report must be considered, the Secretary of State is free to take into account other matters and information, of which both the applicant, and the adviser, may be unaware. There is no obligation to accept the advice given, and the Secretary of State has complete freedom either to confirm or revoke the order.

9.4.4 Conclusions on exclusion orders

The use of exclusion orders hit the national headlines in the press, and on television and radio in July 1993 (see, for example, *The Times*, 7 and 8 July 1993). A young man from Northern Ireland had been arrested in London and interviewed by the police in connection with an attempt to place a car bomb near Downing Street. He was charged with offences related to this, but when the case came to court, the prosecution offered no evidence, and the man was acquitted. Before he could leave the court building, however, he was again arrested, and almost immediately served with an exclusion order, excluding him from Great Britain. He returned to Northern Ireland amid much publicity. A lot of the comment on the case was adverse. The man had not been convicted of any offence, and had been given no idea of the reasons for his exclusion. Moreover, the fact that he had been excluded identified him as a person who might have links with terrorism, and made him a potential target for rival paramilitary groups. The Home Secretary's counter-argument was that in such cases there was often evidence available of a kind which would not be admissible in a court, or could not be revealed without prejudicing its source, but which nevertheless strongly suggested an involvement with terrorism. Exclusion orders were specifically designed to be used in such situations.

Regular but not massive use is made of exclusion orders. In the ten years 1980–1990 the average was 20 per year. At the end of 1990, there were 97 orders in force (Lord Colville, *Report on the Operation in 1990 of the Prevention of Terrorism (Temporary Provisions) Act 1989).* Those entrusted by the government with reviewing the powers available against terrorism are divided in their views of the power. In 1983 Lord Jellicoe supported its retention, in particular as a means of stopping suspected terrorists at the point of entry into Great Britain (*Review of the Operation of the Prevention of Terrorism (Temporary Provisions) Act 1976*, Cmnd 8803, 1983, p. 69). Lord Colville, reviewing the 1984 version of the legislation concluded that, while the power might well be useful, the infringement of civil rights which it involves were such that the ends did not justify the means (*Review of the Operation of the Prevention of Terrorism (Temporary Provisions) Act 1984*, Cm 264, 1987, p. 40). The government has so far preferred the view of Lord Jellicoe to that of Lord Colville, and the events of July 1993 described above gave no suggestion that any change of policy in relation to exclusion orders is under consideration.

9.5   EUROPEAN CONVENTION AND FREEDOM OF MOVEMENT

The ECHR contains no provision guaranteeing freedom of movement. Article 2 of the Fourth Protocol (Cmnd 2309, 1963) guarantees freedom of movement within a State, and Art. 1 of the Seventh Protocol ((1984) 7 EHRR 1) deals with the rights of aliens not to be expelled, but the United Kingdom is not a party to either of these. Even if it were, both Articles contain exceptions related, amongst other things, to national security and public order, which might well be held to justify the use of deportations and exclusion orders.

It might be argued that the use of certain of the powers discussed in this chapter could infringe Art. 8, which gives a right to respect for private and family life. To the extent that extradition, deportation, or exclusion involve splitting families, or disrupting domestic arrangements they might be argued to infringe this right. The right is qualified, however, where interference is:

> in accordance with law and is necessary in a democratic society in the interests of national security, public safety or the economic well-being of the country, for the prevention of disorder or crime, for the protection of health or morals, or for the protection of the rights and freedoms of others.

It seems likely that the government would argue that the powers to extradite, deport and exclude are justified on one or more of these grounds, and would have a good chance of success.

Finally, it might be possible to challenge deportation and exclusion (but not extradition) on the basis of failure to comply with the 'due process' requirements of Arts 5 and 6. Article 5 requires judicial supervision of arrest and detention; Art. 6 requires that the determination of 'civil rights and obligations' should involve a 'fair and public hearing' before an 'independent and impartial tribunal established by law'. To the extent that deportation and exclusion depend on purely administrative procedures, and informal reviews (as with some deportations on the 'public good' ground, see 9.3.2), they would seem clearly to offend against these Articles. In relation to exclusion, the government could no doubt rely on the derogation from its obligations on the basis of the emergency situation in Northern Ireland, which has been accepted as valid by the European Court in relation to extended detention under the Prevention of Terrorism (Temporary Provisions) Act 1989 (*Brannigan and McBride* v *United Kingdom, The Times*, 28 May 1993; see 3.7). As regards deportation, however, it is unlikely that any such derogation could be relied on. Here at least there might be some possibility of challenge to the legitimacy of the procedures in those cases which are taken out of the jurisdiction of the adjudicator and the Immigration Appeal Tribunal (see 9.3.3.3).

TEN

Protection of Reputation and Privacy

10.1 INTRODUCTION

The rights considered in this chapter, and in chapter 11, are different from those considered so far, in that they generally involve a conflict between two citizens, or a citizen and a private organisation, rather than between a citizen and the State. As a result, the situations involved can be looked at from two perspectives, both involving civil liberties issues. For example, defamation can be approached from the point of view of the individual allegedly defamed, and involve consideration of the right to protect one's reputation, or from the point of view of freedom of expression, and the extent to which defamatory speech can be controlled. From the title of this chapter it will be obvious that the first approach is the one that is taken here. The primary concern is the position of those who feel that their reputation or privacy has been harmed by something which has been published about them. Freedom of expression, and the rights of a free Press, cannot, of course, be ignored in this debate, but we start from the other side of the argument. The justification for doing so is that this is consistent with the overall position taken in this book, that the rights of the private individual are of primary importance. The situations which will be under consideration are generally ones where the individual citizen is alleging an infringement of rights by a large organisation, such as a newspaper. The organisation is not the government, but may, vis-à-vis the individual, be in a position of equivalent power. There is certainly likely to be an imbalance in favour of the organisation, and therefore it is the individual that the law needs to protect. This is not universally true, of course, and there may be situations where a very wealthy or influential individual, is actually in a more powerful position than an impoverished, low-circulation, newspaper or magazine. It is submitted, however, that, despite the fact that these cases may be the ones which attract the most publicity, they are the exception rather than the rule.

With this in mind, and in particular the fact that there may well be difficult arguments about conflicting liberties to be considered, we turn to discuss first protection of reputation, and then protection of privacy.

10.2 PROTECTION OF REPUTATION

The protection of reputation is dealt with in English law primarily by the tort of defamation, which is committed by the publication of untrue, defamatory statements about another person. The law is divided into 'libel' and 'slander'. Slander covers the spoken word, whereas libel arises where the defamation is published in some permanent form, though this has been extended by statute to cover broadcasting (Defamation Act 1952, s. 1) and the theatre (Theatres Act 1968, s. 4).

The fact that the statement must be untrue to constitute the tort indicates that the protection of reputation only extends to a *justified* reputation. A person who has achieved a reputation as a person of high moral principle in relation to the use of drugs, cannot complain at being revealed as a secret cocaine user. As to whether this reputation has intrinsic worth or not, English law is equivocal. Where libel is concerned, damages are available without proof of any specific loss; in relation to slander, such a loss must in general be proved. The distinction has little by way of logic to recommend it. It is true that the publication of a libel may have a wider or longer circulation, but this is not necessarily the case. A letter published to one person can constitute a libel, and thus give rise to a claim for damages as of right, whereas a speech at a public meeting may be heard by an audience of 1,000, all of whom may repeat it widely, and yet not found an action for slander in the absence of proof of any loss. If reputation is regarded as something worthy of protection, then the distinction between libel and slander should disappear, and damages should depend simply on the degree of harm to reputation caused by a particular publication, in whatever form (see also the recommendations of the *Faulks Committee on Defamation*, Cmnd 5909, 1975, ch. 2).

10.2.1 Elements of defamation

There are three main elements of the tort which need to be considered: is the statement defamatory?; does it refer to the plaintiff, or can it be taken as so referring?; has it been published? These will now be considered in turn.

10.2.1.1 Is the statement defamatory? In answering this question the courts do not simply look at whether the plaintiff's reputation has been adversely affected, or put at risk of being so affected. This is indeed the central issue, but the courts have added various glosses to it. At one time a test of whether the libellous statement exposed a person to 'hatred, contempt or ridicule' was used: *Parmiter* v *Coupland* (1840) 6 M & W 105. More commonly nowadays the question asked is whether the statement would 'tend to lower the plaintiff in the estimation of right thinking members of society generally': *Sim* v *Stretch* (1936) 52 TLR 669. This formulation focusses specifically on a person's reputation, but it must be judged by general standards, which may not necessarily be those of the plaintiff's friends or associates. In *Byrne* v *Dean* [1937] 1 KB 818, a notice was pinned up in a golf club suggesting that Byrne (who was a member of the club) had informed the police about illegal gambling machines which had been seized from the club. It was held that this could not possibly be defamatory. Right-thinking members of society would have approved of what Byrne was alleged to have done, even though it might have adversely affected his reputation in the eyes of other members of the golf club. This also indicates the relationship between judge and jury on this issue (for libel cases are, unusually for civil actions, generally heard before a jury). It is the jury's task to decide at the end of the day whether a statement is libellous, but the judge may withdraw the issue (as in *Byrne* v *Deane*) if it is thought that as a matter of law the words are incapable of being defamatory. Moreover, the judge may apparently ignore what has actually happened following the statement in reaching this decision. Thus in *Capital and Counties Bank Ltd* v *Henty* (1882) 7 App Cas 741 the House of Lords held that a statement which had been circulated about a bank was incapable of bearing the meaning that the bank was insolvent, despite the fact that its circulation had precipitated a run on the bank.

In some circumstances a statement may only be defamatory when considered in a particular context, or together with other information. Thus to say that Mr X regularly drinks at the *Rose and Crown* is not on its face defamatory; but it will be so if Mr X is a leader of the Temperance Movement and a strict teetotaller. This is what is known as an 'innuendo', which in this context has a technical legal meaning, distinct from its popular usage. An example from the cases is *Tolley* v *Fry* [1931] AC 333. The plaintiff was an amateur golfer whose picture had been used without authorisation in an advertisement for Fry's chocolate. This was held to carry the implication that Tolley had received payment for the endorsement, and thus 'prostituted his reputation as an amateur golfer for advertising purposes'. The plaintiff does not have to show that the publisher was aware of the facts that give rise to the innuendo. In *Cassidy* v *Daily Mirror* [1929] 2 KB 331 a photograph was published of a 'Mr M Corrigan' and a woman who was stated to be his fiancée. The information had been supplied by 'Corrigan', whose real name was Cassidy. Mrs Cassidy, to whom he was still married, sued on the basis that anyone seeing the photograph would assume that she had been 'living in sin'. The Court of Appeal thought that the words were capable of bearing the alleged meaning, and that the jury's decision that they were defamatory should stand. It was irrelevant that the newspaper was unaware of the facts which gave rise to the innuendo.

If the innuendo is particularly obscure, however, the plaintiff may be required to show that the statement was published to someone who knew the relevant facts. In *Fulham* v *Newcastle Chronicle* [1977] 3 All ER 32 the plaintiff was a former Roman Catholic priest who had left the priesthood in 1962, and subsequently married, in 1964. In 1973 a local newspaper referred to his having 'gone off very suddenly' from the parish where he was a priest 'about seven years ago' (that is, by implication, in 1966). The plaintiff alleged that this carried the innuendo that he had married while still a priest. The Court of Appeal were not prepared to accept this in the absence of the plaintiff being able to specify someone who had the requisite knowledge and had drawn the inference. In effect, in this situation, potential damage to the plaintiff's reputation is insufficient; the plaintiff must prove actual damage to be able to sue, whereas in the case of more obvious libels the court will be prepared to assume an adverse effect.

There is no need in any of the above situations to prove that the defendant intended to defame. The tort is in general one of strict liability, as is shown by the decision in *Cassidy* v *Daily Mirror* [1929] 2 KB 331 (but see also 10.2.2.5 'innocent publication'). Even a professed motive of intending to benefit the plaintiff may not protect the publisher. For example, the repetition of rumours with the avowed intention of denying them, may be grounds for action, as was shown when, in 1992, the *New Statesman* published stories about an alleged relationship between the Prime Minister and a caterer. The article did not give the stories any credence, but nevertheless led to the magazine receiving a writ for libel from the Prime Minister (though the action was subsequently settled).

10.2.1.2 Does the statement refer to the plaintiff? A number of possibilities arise here. First, the defamatory statement may be made about a named person, for example, 'Richard Stone'. Very few names are unique, and anyone named 'Richard Stone' who can reasonably argue that others would have read the statement as referring to him will be able to sue. It is irrelevant whether the publisher had a particular person in mind, or not. Thus in *Hulton* v *Jones* [1910] AC 20 an article which contained the suggestion that a fictitious person called 'Artemus Jones' was an adulterer, led to a real 'Artemus Jones' (who was a respectable barrister) successfully suing for libel. In *Newstead* v *London Express* [1939] 4 All ER 319, on the other hand, the newspaper published the perfectly accurate statement that 'Harold Newstead, thirty year old Camberwell man' had been convicted of bigamy. Unfortunately for the newspaper the plaintiff, who was not a bigamist, was also named Harold Newstead, lived in Camberwell, and was about thirty. The Court of Appeal held that the words were capable of being defamatory of the plaintiff. The policy lying behind the decision is shown by the statement of Sir Wilfrid Greene, MR (at p. 325):

Persons who make statements of this character [that is, *ex facie* defamatory] may not unreasonably be expected, when describing the person of whom they are made, to identify the person so closely as to make it very unlikely that a judge would hold them to be reasonably capable of referring to someone else . . . If there is a risk of coincidence, it ought, I think, in reason to be borne, not by the innocent party to whom the words are held to refer, but by the party who puts them into circulation.

This shows that the protection of reputation is clearly being given a higher priority than Press freedom, and this is presumably the justification for the general approach to the issue of non-intentional defamation.

The second type of situation where reference to the plaintiff may be an issue is where the plaintiff is not named, but can be identified by the context. Such was the case in *Hayward* v *Thompson* [1964] AC 234, where the defamatory article simply referred to 'a wealthy benefactor of the Liberal party'. The plaintiff was able to show that he was widely identified as the 'benefactor' and was therefore able to sue. In this case, he was the person to whom the writer of the article intended to refer, but presumably, on the basis of *Hulton* v *Jones* (1910), this was irrelevant, as long as the plaintiff could show that others had identified him as the 'benefactor'.

The third situation is where a defamatory statement is made about a group, of which the plaintiff is a member. The general rule is to be found in *Knupffer* v *London Express Newspaper Ltd* [1944] AC 116. An article was published containing defamatory comments about a group called 'Young Russia'. The plaintiff was head of the British branch of this organisation, which had 24 members in this country. He was able to produce witnesses who were prepared to give evidence that they had thought of the plaintiff when reading the article. The action succeeded at trial, but an appeal was upheld by the Court of Appeal and confirmed by the House of Lords. The House emphasised that the essential test is whether the words were published 'of the plaintiff'. Statements that were in the nature of 'unfounded generalisations' or 'facetious exaggerations' (such as 'all lawyers are thieves': *Eastwood* v *Holmes* (1858) 1 F & F 347) could not, as a matter of law, be interpreted in this way, and it is irrelevant that, as a matter of fact, some people took them to refer to the plaintiff. In general, then, defamatory statements aimed at a class will not be actionable, unless they are sufficiently specific to be taken as applying to all members (for example, 'all the directors of X Ltd have been known to take bribes'), or there are circumstances which link them particularly to one or more of the class. The Court of Appeal has also suggested, *obiter*, that a specific defamatory remark about an unidentified member of a group may entitle every member of the group to sue: *Farrington* v *Leigh*, *The Times*, 10 December 1987. Thus, adapting the example given above, to publish the statement that 'one of the directors of X Ltd has been known to take bribes' would again allow all the directors to sue.

At this point it is appropriate to note the limitations on who can sue for libel or slander. In general the action is limited to living individuals: no action for defamation can be brought on behalf of the dead. This has sometimes been the subject of criticism (for example, see *Faulks Committee*, Cmnd 5909, 1975, pp. 114–116), but the *Calcutt Committee on Privacy* Cm 1102, 1990 recommended no change. It has recently been confirmed by the House of Lords in *Derbyshire County Council* v *Times Newspapers Ltd* [1993] 1 All ER 1011 that a local authority cannot sue for libel (see 1.4.2.1); nor can an unincorporated association, such as a trade union: *Electrical, Electronic, Telecommunicaton & Plumbing Union* v *Times Newspapers Ltd* [1980] QB 585. In fact the one surviving exception to the general rule that only a living individual can sue seems to be that a company can bring an action to protect its business reputation: *Metropolitan Saloon Omnibus Co.* v *Hawkins* (1859) 4 H & N 87. The action in such a case is not concerned so much with loss of reputation *per se*, but in its effect on the company's profits.

10.2.1.3 Has the statement been published? For a person to write defamatory statements about others in a private diary does not give rise to any action. Even if one of the persons defamed sees the diary, and reads the

comments, no action will arise, for the law requires publication to someone other than the plaintiff. This is, of course, in line with the objective of protecting reputation. The plaintiff cannot complain about private opinions, even if unjustly held, but is entitled to object to untrue public condemnation. 'Publication' has a wide meaning in this context. Communicating the defamatory statement to just one other individual (other than the defendant's spouse: *Wennhak* v *Morgan* (1888) 20 QBD 635) will be sufficient. There is no need for it to be intended that the statement should be widely distributed. Some difficulties may arise with the unauthorised disclosure of private material (such as letters), but this is an exceptional situation, and it is not proposed to discuss it further here (see, for example, M. A. Jones, *Textbook on Torts*, 4th edn, London: Blackstone Press, 1993, p. 366). Where a statement passes down a chain of distribution (as it will with a book, for example, from the production of the manuscript by the author, to its being sold in a bookshop), each stage in the chain will involve a separate publication. There is, however, a defence of 'innocent dissemination', which is discussed at 10.2.2.6.

10.2.2   Defences to defamation

There is a range of defences available to a libel action, in addition to the arguments that the words are not defamatory, do not apply to the plaintiff, or have not been published. These are justification, fair comment, absolute and qualified privilege, innocent publication, and innocent dissemination. In all these cases it is accepted that the plaintiff's reputation has been adversely affected, but that for some reason that infringement of rights should not provide a legal remedy.

10.2.2.1   Justification   It was pointed out at the start of this chapter that defamation was concerned with the protection of a person's *justified* reputation. If the defendant can show that a defamatory statement is true, then the plaintiff will not succeed. The law will not protect a false reputation. This is the defence of 'truth' or 'justification'.

The defendant will have to prove that the statement is substantially true. It does not matter if it is wrong in minor details which do not affect the nature of statement in lowering the plaintiff's reputation. For example, the action for defamation will not succeed if the defendant has claimed that the plaintiff has five convictions for theft, when the true figure is four. It will not help the defendant, however, if there are other equally damning facts which could have been mentioned, if the content of the statement actually published cannot be shown to be true.

If more than one defamatory statement has been made, for example that 'X is a forger and a swindler', the common law required that the truth of both must be proved in order for justification to be successful. Under the Defamation Act 1952, however, the position is slightly more favourable to the defendant. Section 5 of that Act provides that not every charge has to be proved to be true 'if the words not proved to be true do not materially injure the plaintiff's reputation having regard to the truth of the remaining charges'.

This suggests that it is the overall effect on the plaintiff's reputation that is important. On the other hand, if a publication contains two or more distinct defamatory statements not having a 'common sting', the plaintiff is entitled to select one or more, and require the defendant to try to justify those, without reference to the ones not selected: *Polly Peck (Holdings) plc v Trelford* [1986] 2 All ER 84.

English law provides one minor statutory limitation on the defence of justification, under the Rehabilitation of Offenders Act 1974. In general if the defamatory statement is that someone has committed an offence, then, by virtue of s. 13 of the Civil Evidence Act 1968, the fact that the person has been convicted of it will be conclusive proof of guilt, and automatically allow the defence of justification. This does not apply, however, when the offence is covered by the Rehabilitation of Offenders Act 1974. This Act provides that certain offences will become 'spent' after a period of time, and the person convicted will be allowed to act for many purposes as if no conviction had occurred. In relation to defamation, s. 8 of the Act nevertheless allows the defence of justification to be used in relation to spent convictions, unless the plaintiff proves that the defendant was actuated by 'malice' (this concept is discussed further at 10.2.2.2). This does therefore constitute a limitation on the defence, since the defendant's motive in making the statement is generally irrelevant, provided the statement can be shown to be true, but it is one which is unlikely to be of any significant practical importance.

It should also be noted that a plaintiff who has been acquitted of an offence cannot rely on this as a bar to a plea of justification by the plaintiff: *Loughans v Odhams Press Ltd* [1963] CLY 2007. No statutory presumption operates in relation to acquittals of the kind which applies to convictions.

10.2.2.2 Fair comment This defence indicates an acceptance that in some situations the requirements of a free press override the effect on a person's reputation. It allows considerable latitude, in particular, to reviewers of books, plays, films, etc, to state their true feelings about what they have read or seen, without needing to worry over much about the risks of a libel writ. The defence requires the defamatory statement to be 'comment', to be 'fair', to be on a matter of 'public interest', and not to actuated by 'malice'. All of these elements must be considered.

The requirement that the statement must be comment rather than fact may give rise to difficult distinctions. To say that a person is a 'bad singer' is clearly comment; to say that they are 'untrained as a singer' is fact. What of the statement that the person is 'the worst singer in England'? That has the appearance of a statement of fact, but might well be regarded as comment, because it would be impossible to prove, one way or the other. A further difficulty is that a statement cannot be a 'comment' unless it refers to some other facts. A comment cannot exist in isolation. If the statement is in the form of a comment, e.g. 'X is not fit to hold public office', it will nevertheless be treated as a statement of fact, unless it specifically refers to, or can be taken to be based on, other facts. If the statement is, for example, 'X is not fit to hold public office, because he is drunk every night', and the defendant can prove the truth of the second part of the statement, the first part will be likely to be treated as fair comment. If there are no supporting facts, however, the defendant will then have to rely on justification, rather than fair comment. This issue was considered by the House of Lords in *Telnikoff* v *Matusevitch* [1991] 4 All ER 817. The defendant had written to a newspaper attacking the views of the plaintiff, as expressed in an article previously published in the same newspaper, as racist. The majority of the House of Lords held that in deciding whether the letter was fact or comment, it should be read (by the jury) in isolation, without reference to the preceding article. This decision has been characterised by Robertson and Nicol (*Media Law*, 3rd edn, London: Penguin Books, 1992, pp. 80–81) as ignoring the realities of newspaper reading, and undermining 'the protection that the defence of fair comment has given to "free for alls" in letters' columns of local and national newspapers'.

The comment must be 'fair'. This means that the facts on which the comment is based must be true, or privileged (see 10.2.2.3–10.2.2.4). As with justification, however, there is no need to prove the truth of every fact on which comment is based, if the comment is fair having regard to the truth of those facts which are proved (Defamation Act 1952, s. 6). There is no need for all the facts which are relied on to be stated explicitly. In *Kemsley* v *Foot* [1952] AC 345 an article by Michael Foot was published in *Tribune*, under the title 'Lower than Kemsley'. It was strongly critical of newspapers owned by the Beaverbrook Press. Viscount Kemsley, who was the well-known proprietor of other newspapers sued for libel. The matter came before the House of Lords on a preliminary issue, following the judge's decision to strike out the fair comment defence. Although the article contained no specific factual allegations against the plaintiff, Lord Porter felt that a reasonable construction of the words 'Lower than Kemsley' would be 'that the allegation which is made is that the conduct of the Kemsley Press was similar to but not quite so bad as the press controlled by Lord Beaverbrook'. If it was fair comment to call the output of the Kemsley Press 'low' (which was a matter for the jury), then the defendant should succeed.

As to what is meant by 'fairness' itself, it is a matter of fact for the jury as to whether any particular comment is fair. The question is not primarily an objective one. The members of the jury are not being asked to decide whether they agree with the comment, or even whether it is reasonable. Rather, the test is whether the comment is an honest expression of the defendant's opinion (*Merivale* v *Carson* (1887) 20 QBD 275; *Turner* v *Metro-Goldwyn-Mayer Pictures Ltd* [1950] 1 All ER 449).

The comment must be on a matter of public interest. This is a question for the judge, rather than the jury, but the test is not very strict. The behaviour of people in public life (be it in politics, television, sport, the arts, etc) will be of public interest, as will anything (a book, a play, a film, etc) which is published to the public. The test is whether the matter commented on is 'of public interest', not whether the comment itself is 'in the public interest'.

The issue of 'malice' follows on from the requirement of fairness. To be fair, the comment must be made without 'malice'. This does not have here its popular meaning of 'spite' or 'ill will'. It means that the comment must not have been made for some improper motive. Lack of a genuine belief in the truth of the comment, or the facts on which it is based, will indicate malice in this sense, as will the use of abuse and insults against the plaintiff under the guise of comment.

10.2.2.3 Absolute privilege The defences looked at so far relate to the nature of the defamatory statement. The other defences concentrate on the circumstances in which the statement was made.

Parliamentary proceedings (including the proceedings of select committees) are absolutely privileged. MPs who have made defamatory statements in the course of a debate are often challenged to repeat the allegations outside the House where the privilege will be lost. The protection extends to parliamentary papers published by either House (Parliamentary Papers Act 1840). Statements by Ministers of the Crown in the course of their official duties are similarly privileged. The privilege in all these cases only attaches to the initial statement. An accurate repetition or publication of it in a non-privileged forum will not attract absolute privilege, but may be protected by qualified privilege (see 10.2.2.4).

Court proceedings are similarly privileged, and this covers not only judges and counsel, but witnesses and members of the jury. Here the absolute privilege has been extended, by s. 3 of the Law of Libel Amendment Act 1888, to fair and accurate reports in any newspaper of judicial proceedings in the United Kingdom, provided they are published contemporaneously. This privilege has subsequently been extended to reports on radio or television (Defamation Act 1952, s. 9(2); Broadcasting Act 1990, sch. 20, para. 2).

Finally, communications between solicitor and client in connection with litigation are absolutely privileged.

The justification for this type of privilege derives, as far as parliament is concerned, partly from the constitutional requirement that proceedings in parliament should not be subject to the supervision of the courts (Bill of Rights 1688). More generally, there is a wish to avoid those entrusted with public duties being restricted from speaking their minds by the fear of being sued. The risk that the privilege will be abused, and that other people's reputations will be adversely affected by unsubstantiated allegations, is thought to be worth taking. It is worth remembering, however, that because the privilege is absolute it gives protection to statements which may be made with malice, in either the legal or the popular sense. The only guard against this is that blatant abuse of the privilege might be treated by either parliament, or the courts, as a contempt. It is hard to see, however, why the protection given to Ministers for statements outside the House should be absolute, rather than qualified.

10.2.3.4 Qualified privilege This lesser type of privilege applies in a range of situations, defined by common law and statute. It is qualified, rather than absolute, because it will be lost if the plaintiff can prove that the statement was made with 'malice' (meaning for an improper purpose, or without any genuine belief in its truth; see 10.2.2.2, re fair comment).

At common law the rationale for the defence is that there may be situations where it is in the public interest that a person should be able to say what is believed to be the truth, without necessarily being able to prove that it is true. This interest will have to be sufficiently strong to override the interest in the protection of reputation. The common law recognised five such situations.

First, it will arise where the publisher is under a legal, moral or social duty to communicate the defamatory statement to the person to whom it is communicated, and that person has a corresponding interest in receiving it. The operation of this is well illustrated by *Watt* v *Longsdon* [1930] 1 KB 130. The defendant was a director of a company, and received a letter accusing the plaintiff, who was the managing director of the company overseas, of immorality, drunkenness and dishonesty. Without waiting for any corroboration, the defendant showed this letter to the chairman of the board (who was also the largest shareholder), and to the plaintiff's wife. In fact, all the allegations were false. The plaintiff sued the defendant for libel, and the defendant pleaded qualified privilege. The Court of Appeal held that the communication to the chairman was privileged. They were both employed by the same company, and the defendant had a duty to inform the chairman, who might well be asked to provide a testimonial for the plaintiff. As regards the plaintiff's wife, however, although she clearly had an interest in receiving the statement, the defendant had no *duty* to communicate it to her.

The concept of social or moral duty in this context is difficult to define, but is up to the judge to decide whether such a duty exists in the light of all the circumstances. This type of privilege clearly protects those who provide references for prospective employees, students, etc.

The second situation where the privilege may apply is the mirror image of the first. That is where the publisher has an interest to be protected, and the person to whom the statement is published has a legal, moral, or social duty to protect it. Thus, if you think that some particular individual is trying to burgle your house, or poison you, qualified privilege will attach to the communication of your suspicions to the police.

Thirdly, the publisher and the recipient may have a common interest, independent of any duty. A letter written by an auctioneer to other auctioneers in the area warning about a person who had 'purchased' goods at an auction and removed them without paying would fall in this category.

Fourthly, statements made in protection of oneself or one's property will attract the privilege. In *Osborn* v *Thomas Boulter & Son* [1930] 2 KB 226 a publican had made accusations against a firm of brewers, and they made defamatory statements in 'self-defence'. The statements were held to attract qualified privilege. Robertson and Nicol have argued that this provides the basis for a kind of 'right to reply', for example, as regards statements made with the protection of absolute privilege (*Media Law*, 3rd edn, London: Penguin Books, 1992, p. 90; see also *Adam* v *Ward* [1917] AC 309). The replies must, however, relate to the alleged defamation.

Fifthly, and finally, the communication of a public grievance to the proper authorities is privileged. In *Beech* v *Freeson* [1972] the defendant was an MP. One of his constituents wrote to him complaining about the plaintiffs, a firm of solicitors. The defendant wrote letters to the Law Society and the Lord Chancellor, passing on the complaints. The plaintiff brought an action for libel. It was held that, although the MP had no personal interest in the matter, he had a duty to pass on to the appropriate body a constituent's complaint about a professional person in practice at the service of the public.

All these types of qualified privilege apply most clearly to specific communications to particular people, and not to general publication in the press. The existence of a broad category of public interest, which would justify such press publications, was rejected by the Court of Appeal in *Blackshaw* v *Lord* [1983] 2 All ER 311. The press will gain the privilege, however, in relation to reports of parliamentary proceedings, or court proceedings, to the extent that these are not protected by absolute privilege. The reports must, of course, be fair and accurate.

Apart from the common law categories of qualified privilege, certain newspaper and broadcast reports are given this status by s. 7 of, and the schedule to, the Defamation Act 1952. This applies to various types of reports of official proceedings. Some are privileged only on the basis that the publisher must publish an explanation or contradiction if this is requested by the person defamed; others are not subject to this. The type of proceedings covered are, for example, those of foreign legislatures, trade associations, local authorities, or the general meeting of a public company. For a full list, see the schedule to the Act, or M. A. Jones, *Textbook on Torts*, 4th edn, London: Blackstone Press, 1993, pp. 380–381.

The whole area of qualified privilege shows the individual's right to reputation being made subordinate to public interests of various kinds. The argument in its favour is that people should not always have to be sure of the truth of what they are publishing, if there are strong public interests justifying running the risk of unwarranted damage to another person's reputation. For the most part the balance between these two interests seems to have been fairly struck, but the Court of Appeal was probably right in *Blackshaw* v *Lord* [1983] 2 All ER 311 to refuse to allow any more general exception.

10.2.2.5 Innocent publication We have already seen that in general a publisher cannot escape liability for defamation by pleading that there was no intention to defame. Section 4 of the Defamation Act introduced a procedure to provide a limited defence in certain situations of this kind. By virtue of s. 4(5) the publications which are defamatory of a person will be treated as innocent if:

(a) . . . the publisher did not intend to publish them of and concerning that other person, and did not know of circumstances by virtue of which they might be understood to refer to him; or

(b) . . . the words were not defamatory on the face of them, and the publisher did not know of circumstances by virtue of which they might be understood to be defamatory of that other person.

In either case, the publisher must have exercised all reasonable care in relation to the publication. As will be seen, the wording of (a) is apt to cover the situation in *Newstead* v *London Express* [1940] 1 KB 377, or *Hulton* v *Jones*

[1910] AC 29 (see 10.2.1.2), whereas (b) is designed to deal with a case like *Cassidy* v *Daily Mirror Newspapers* [1929] 2 KB 331 (see 10.2.1.1).

If the case falls within either (a) or (b) then the publisher can avoid any further liability by making an offer of 'amends', under s. 4. This means an offer to publish a correction and apology, and to take all reasonably practicable steps to notify those to whom copies of a document containing the statement have been distributed that the words are alleged to be defamatory (s. 4(3)). If the offer is accepted, then no action for defamation may be brought; if it is rejected, then it will be a defence to any subsequent action to show that the publication was innocent, that an offer of amends was made and has not been withdrawn, and that (if the defendant was not the author) the words were written by the author without malice (s. 4(1), (6)).

The offer of amends, though apparently offering the opportunity for the receipt of an apology and the publication of a correction which would satisfy many plaintiffs, has not been greatly used. This is blamed by Robertson and Nicol (*Media Law*, 3rd edn, London: Penguin Books, 1992, p. 95) on the requirement that an affidavit must be served with the offer, 'specifying the facts relied upon by the person making it to show that the words in question were published by him innocently in relation to the party aggrieved' (Defamation Act 1952, s. 4(2)). They suggest that the much simpler procedure recommended by the 1991 Supreme Court Procedure Committee would be likely to be used far more frequently.

10.2.2.6 Innocent dissemination The common law recognised one situation where the innocent publisher of a defamatory statement should be allowed to escape liability. This was in relation to so-called 'mechanical distributors' who innocently disseminate a work containing the libel. In other words, the wholesalers, newsagents, bookshops and libraries, who have no part in the production of a magazine, newspaper, or book, which contains defamation, but are nevertheless regarded as publishers for selling or supplying it to someone else. The defence will be available where the defendant can prove (a) ignorance of the fact that the work contained a libel; and (b) that such ignorance was not the result of any negligence (that is, there was no reason why the defendant *ought* to have been aware of the libel: *Vizetelly* v *Mudie's Select Library Ltd* [1900] 2 QB 170, as interpreted by Scrutton LJ in *Sun Life Assurance Co. of Canada* v *WH Smith* (1934) 150 LT 211). Where a magazine or newspaper has gained a reputation for regularly being sued for libel, this may mean that the disseminator will feel obliged to check the content of each issue, to seek a promise of an indemnity from the publisher, or to refuse to stock the publication (see, for example, *Goldsmith* v *Sperrings* [1977] 1 WLR 478).

10.2.3 Conclusions re defamation
The action for defamation clearly has a strong role in providing protection for an individual's reputation. Although there is a range of defences, in many cases the action will still lie. The problems with the law, which have led to one commentator criticising it as 'dotty' and 'susceptible to wicked abuse' (A.

Weir, *A Casebook on Tort*, 7th edn, London: Sweet & Maxwell, 1992, p. 528; see, also G. Robertson & A. Nicol, *Media Law*, 3rd edn, London: Penguin Books, 1992, chapter 2, *passim*) derive from its procedures. There are two problems in particular. One is that there is no legal aid available for libel actions. This means that in effect the ordinary private individual cannot contemplate an action for defamation, particularly against a wealthy newspaper, without facing the risk of bankruptcy. It also explains the predominance of pop stars, politicians, and businessmen amongst libel plaintiffs. Secondly, the award of damages is very erratic. It is generally in the hands of the jury, and it has not been uncommon for them to award six, or even seven, figure sums to compensate for loss of reputation, whereas much smaller sums will frequently be paid out for the victims of quite serious personal injuries. The Court of Appeal does now have a role in reviewing damages awards, which it has used to moderate excessive sums, but this ground of appeal also has the effect of tending to increase the costs of litigation. Protection of reputation would in fact be much better served by a cheaper, quicker, procedure, with a fairly low ceiling on damages, combined with a right of reply, or a right to the publication of an apology and correction. This would not carry with it the possibility of the plaintiff making a fortune, but would allow reputation a much broader protection than under the present law. Paradoxically, it might well be preferable from a freedom of expression point of view as well, since newspapers and magazines could no longer be cowed into submission by the threats of ruinous legal action, a tactic much favoured by the late Robert Maxwell.

10.2.4 Criminal libel

In certain circumstances the criminal law may be available to protect a person's reputation, by means of the offence of criminal libel. The elements of the offence are very similar to the tort of defamation. The words used must be such as would lower a person's reputation in the eyes of right-thinking members of society, or bring the person into hatred, ridicule, or contempt. The range of circumstances in which it will be appropriate for the offence to be used is, however, narrower. The current law derives from the case of *R v Wicks* (1936) 25 Cr App R 168, which was heavily relied on by Wien J in *Goldsmith v Pressdram* [1977] 2 All ER 557. In *Wicks*, the Court of Criminal Appeal recognised two situations where it is proper to use the criminal offence, these being, first, when the libel complained of is likely to disturb the peace of the community, and secondly, when it is likely *seriously* to affect the reputation of the person defamed. If the libel is so trivial that it is likely to do neither of these things, then a criminal prosecution ought not to be instituted. In *Goldsmith v Pressdram*, which involved an application for permission to prosecute under the Law of Libel Amendment Act 1888, s. 8, the defence tried to argue that proceedings ought not to be allowed except where there was a risk of a breach of the peace. Wien J, following the analysis in *Wicks*, was unable to accept that proposition, but went on to lay down three requirements which he felt should be satisfied before a judge in chambers should consent to a prosecution. First, he considered that there must be a clear *prima facie* case to answer. Secondly, the libel must be a serious one. In deciding whether it is sufficiently serious, the likelihood of a breach of the peace being caused is relevant, but not conclusive. Thirdly, it must be considered whether the public interest *requires* the institution of proceedings. Wien J did not elaborate on what he considered to be the relevant factors in answering this third question, but in the case before him, he considered (at p. 566) that:

> it can well become a matter of public importance where there is an association with the Bank of England, where his [the prosecutor's] integrity has been impugned and a criminal offence has been alleged against him and nothing has so far been made public about the matter; and where, in particular, a campaign of vilification goes on for month after month with no let-up.

It is difficult, in fact, to find any authority for this third requirement. There is no mention of it in *R* v *Wicks*, but it may arise from Wien J's more general view of the role of a judge in chambers when given the discretion to allow or disallow prosecutions. It may well be that he regarded it as being the general duty of a judge in that position only to allow those prosecutions considered to be in the public interest. If that is so, then this is not a rule that is peculiar to criminal libel, and indeed will only apply to such a libel when it is alleged against a newspaper. It is only to actions against such publications that the requirement of permission under s. 8 of the Law of Libel Amendment Act 1988 applies. In other cases a private individual may prosecute for criminal libel without seeking anyone's permission.

With the exception of fair comment, all the defences which are available in a civil action for defamation are available in respect of a prosecution for criminal libel. For a defence of justification to be successful, however, it must be shown not only that the defamatory words are true, but also that their publication is for the public benefit (Libel Act 1843, s. 6). Lord Diplock has suggested (*Gleaves* v *Deakin* [1980] AC 477 at p. 483) that this requirement might well be contrary to Art. 10 of the European Convention on Human Rights, which, as opposed to only allowing speech which can be shown to be for the public benefit:

> requires that freedom of expression shall be untrammelled by public authority except where its interference to repress a particular exercise of the freedom is necessary for the protection of the public interest.

There is no reported example of a successful prosecution for this offence in recent years. The prosecution in *Goldsmith* v *Pressdram* (1977) was dropped, following a settlement. In *Gleaves* v *Deakin*, where the statements objected to included allegations that the person had committed gross sexual offences with minors, fraud, theft, and other offences, a trial did take place, but resulted in an acquittal. In *Desmond* v *Thorne* [1982] 3 All ER 268, Taylor J, adopting the approach of Wien J in *Goldsmith* v *Pressdram*, held that there was in the light of all the information before him, doubt as to whether there was a *prima facie* case to answer, and that the case was not one where the public interest required the instititution of proceedings. In reaching this conclusion he was influenced by the fact that in *Goldsmith v Pressdram* the 'applicant's position was such as to make his integrity a matter of general public interest', and that there had been 'a campaign of vilification against the applicant'. Neither element was present in the case before him.

In conclusion, then, although the offence of criminal libel is in theory available as an additional means of protecting a person's reputation, and has the potential advantage that it can be used even where the defamatory statements are true, it is unlikely in practice to be of any great assistance.

10.2.5 Malicious falsehood

This tort is available where the plaintiff can prove that an untrue statement has been made, with malice, and that some actual loss has been suffered as a result. It is thus more limited in scope than defamation, and does not protect reputation *per se*, but only where some consequential loss can be shown. Special damage need not be alleged or proved if the statement is 'calculated to cause pecuniary damage to the plaintiff' and is 'published in writing or other permanent form' (Defamation Act 1952, s. 3(1)). Malice will be inferred if the defendant knew that the statement was false when it was published, or was reckless as to whether it was false or not (*Kaye v Robertson* [1991] FSR 62).

A recent successful use of this action occurred in *Kaye v Robertson* [1991] FSR 62. The plaintiff was a well-known actor who had suffered serious head injuries in an accident. He was recovering in hospital when a journalist and a photographer from a national newspaper entered his room without permission or authority. They obtained comments from him, and took photographs, which they intended to publish in their newspaper. The plaintiff was not in any condition to have given informed consent to any of this. It was held by the Court of Appeal that the plaintiff was entitled to an injunction to restrain publication on the basis that he had an arguable case for claiming malicious falsehood. The 'falsehood' was the suggestion that the plaintiff had consented to the proceedings. The damage was the loss of a potentially valuable right which the plaintiff had to sell his story as an 'exclusive' when he had recovered.

Although, as has been seen, the action for malicious falsehood is more limited than that for defamation, it has one big advantage for the individual citizen who has been defamed, in that legal aid is available for such an action. Thus, even though the plaintiff will face the burden of proving actual loss, and the damages awarded may well be smaller, it may still be the most practical way for people without substantial resources to try to protect their reputation, or obtain compensation where it has been adversely affected. The use of the action as an alternative to defamation for these purposes was approved by the Court of Appeal in *Joyce v Sengupta* [1993] 1 WLR 337.

10.3 PROTECTION OF PRIVACY

As Glidewell LJ stated in *Kaye v Robertson* [1991] FSR 62, 'it is well-known that in English law there is no right to privacy'. This is in contrast to many other jurisdictions where such a right is specifically recognised, and protected. In the United States, for example, there are specific torts dealing with privacy infringements of particular types, as well as a more general constitutional protection. Art. 8 of the European Convention on Human Rights states that 'Everyone has the right to respect for his private and family life, his home and his correspondence'. English law therefore appears out of line with much of the rest of the world on this issue, and it is an area where there is much pressure for reform. In July 1993 the Lord Chancellor's Department published a consultation paper proposing the introduction of a tort of invasion of privacy, and this is discussed further at 10.3.4. For the time being, however, plaintiffs in England who feel that their privacy has been infringed have to make do with a range of other causes of action, none of which was specifically designed to deal with this right. Before considering these, however, the concept of privacy itself needs some consideration.

10.3.1 The meaning of privacy

Privacy is not an easy concept to pin down. Most discussions of the subject take as their starting point the phrase 'the right to be let alone' coined by Cooley (*Torts*, 2nd edn, 1888) and adopted by Warren and Brandeis in a seminal Harvard Law Review article ((1890) 4 Harv Law Rev 193), which is credited with having provided the basis for the development of the law in this area in the United States. Unfortunately the phrase is, as Wacks has commented, 'a sweeping phrase which is as comprehensive as it is vague' (*The Protection of Privacy*, London: Sweet & Maxwell, 1980). On its back, 'privacy' has been used as the focus for discussion of a wide range of issues, from abortion rights to the unauthorised taking of photographs, from unreasonable searches of premises to disclosure of secret documents. For our purposes, a narrower definition is required. The Calcutt Committee used as its working defintion (*Report of the Committee on Privacy and Related Matters* Cm 1102, 1990, p. 7):

> The right of the individual to be protected against intrusion into his personal life or affairs, or those of his family, by direct physical means or by publication of information.

This is narrower, but still threatens to encompass matters which, it is submitted, are not appropriate subject matter for discussion, in this context. Would, for example, it be right to include the issue of what to do about a person who gatecrashes a private party, or the common burglar in this debate? It is behaviour which clearly comes within the Calcutt definition. Although any entry on to private property, however, can be discussed in privacy terms, as was recognised in chapter 4 in the discussion of police powers of entry, search and seizure, it is not what people are generally concerned about when privacy is raised as an issue. It is submitted that it is the acquisition and publication of information which is in fact the central concern. The following working definition is therefore adopted, to indicate the scope of what is to follow, and the approach to the discussion. The right to privacy will here be treated as:

The right to prevent, or to be compensated for, the unauthorised acquisition
or publication of secret personal information.

With this narrow definition to work with, we must now turn to the issue of why
this right is thought to need protecting. Leaving aside the question of physical
intrusions, which are objectionable in their own right, why do people object to
the 'unauthorised acquisition or publication of secret personal information'?
Publication of personal secrets may, of course, cause embarrassment, or even
financial loss, if it results in damage to a business, for example (as might be the
case if the information concerned relates to previous criminal convictions, of
failure to pay debts). It does not necessarily do so. Many people are sensitive
about their salary, yet publication of the details of it will in most cases cause
them no measurable harm. We would still, no doubt, wish to include this
within our definition of an infringement of privacy. When we turn to the
acquisition of information, without publication, the problem becomes if
anything more difficult. Of course, if the acquirer intends to benefit from the
information, or to use it against the person to whom it refers, then there are
clear grounds for objection. What about simple acquisition, however, where
no further use is made of the information: is this still an invasion of privacy?
We would no doubt wish so to categorise the behaviour of the person who
deliberately, secretly, and undetected, watches a neighbour undressing, or the
deliberate eavesdropper, who secretly listens in to a private conversation
simply out of nosiness. What of the unintentional eavesdropper, however, who
happens to overhear a conversation on private premises; or the person who just
happens to look out of the window at the time the neighbour is undressing? In
the latter two cases the effect on the people observed or overheard is exactly the
same as in the first two, and yet the first two seem much more serious, even
though the victim's privacy has not been invaded to any greater extent than by
the unintentional overhearing or observation. Even the latter two situations
will become more serious, however, if the person who has innocently intruded
then makes use of the information so acquired.

It is suggested that the answers to the questions posed in the previous
paragraph are as follows. *All* the situations outlined involve an invasion of
privacy, since that concept must be defined from the point of view of the
'victim' rather than the 'invader'. We will only regard infringement of privacy
as needing the protection of the law, however, if the invasion is deliberate (or
perhaps reckless, or even negligent), or if the invader makes use of any
information acquired as a result of the infringement. Even then, there will be
a need to provide for defences, so that, for example, the disclosure of
wrongdoing which can only be achieved by an invasion of the privacy of the
wrongdoer is not prevented. There is also the problem of whether the
development of a 'public interest' defence should mean that those who are in
the 'public eye' should be entitled to less protection in relation to their privacy,
than the ordinary private individual. If the answer is yes, as it is in the United
States (see *New York Times* v *Sullivan* (1964) 376 US 254), then the question
arises as to how you indentify a 'public person'. Should it mean anyone who
attracts media attention (including, for example, the victims of crimes or

natural disasters), or only those who choose to put themselves in the public eye, such as politicians, and entertainers?

With these general issues in mind, we now turn to the ways in which privacy may be protected under current English law. The word 'privacy' will, of course, be used throughout in the sense given in the working definition set out above, unless otherwise indicated.

10.3.2 Existing means of protection
Although the English courts have refused to recognise a separate action to deal with privacy, some other types of action can be used to protect the concept, and the fact that privacy has been invaded may in some situations be taken into account in assessing damages. A number of possibilities need to be considered.

10.3.2.1 Defamation The action for defamation has been fully considered above. As we have seen it is concerned with the disclosure of *false* information, whereas privacy concerns *true* information. Nevertheless, there is no doubt that the rich and powerful have in recent years used, or attempted to use, writs for defamation as a means of keeping guilty secrets quiet. The potential publisher, if brave enough, can resist any attempt to 'gag' by means of such writ, by indicating an intention to plead justification. The courts will not then issue an injunction restraining publication pending the trial. The danger of this course of action is, however, that if the defendant fails to prove justification, the damages may be increased. See, for example, *Maxwell* v *Pressdram* [1987] 1 All ER 656 at 6.2.7. The action for defamation can, therefore, in this rather disreputable way, be used as a means of protecting privacy. It is not a use which anyone would wish to extend, however.

10.3.2.2 Trespass The tortious action for trespass to land protects one aspect of privacy, that is the acquisition of private information through the intrusion into private premises. The person who infringes privacy by entering premises to photograph documents, or to place a listening device, can thus be dealt with by means of this tort. Its limitation, however, is that it requires a physical intrusion. Thus the taking of photographs from outside the victim's land will not constitute a trespass, even if taken from an aeroplane flying overhead: *Bernstein* v *Skyviews* [1978] 1 QB 479. With the vast increase in electronic surveillance devices which can enable a person to monitor what people are doing or saying from a considerable distance, the action for trespass becomes correspondingly of decreasing importance as a means of protecting privacy. In any case, it was never of any use in relation to preventing the *publication* of information which had been acquired, even if this was as a result of a trespass.

10.3.2.3 Nuisance The action for private nuisance protects an occupier's quiet enjoyment of land. As a result, like trespass, it has the potential for protecting against the acquisition (though not the publication) of private information. The possibility of its use to protect privacy was recognised by Griffiths J, in *Bernstein* v *Skyviews* [1978] 1 QB 479 at p. 489:

[I]f the circumstances were such that a plaintiff was subjected to the harrassment of constant surveillance of his house from the air, accompanied by the photographing of his every activity, I am far from saying that the court would not regard such a monstrous invasion of his privacy as an actionable nuisance, for which they would give relief.

This quotation indicates, however, the limitation of nuisance, in that it requires some degree of repetition and persistence. That is why in *Bernstein* v *Skyviews*, which concerned just one flight, nuisance was not relevant. The action will also not be of any use in relation to surreptitious surveillance, of which the occupier is unaware.

In *Khorasandjian* v *Bush* (1993) 143 New LJ 329, the Court of Appeal showed a willingness to be flexible in relation to the development of the law, and in a case where the defendant had been pestering the plaintiff with telephone calls, allowed it to be applied for the protection of any lawful occupant of premises, not simply someone with a proprietary interest. At the same time the Court confirmed that harassment by means of unwanted telephone calls could constitute a private nuisance. It seems unlikely, however, that the tort could be developed in a way which will ever provide more than a marginal contribution to the protection of privacy.

10.3.2.4 Copyright

In *Williams* v *Settle* [1960] 1 WLR 1072 the defendant was a photographer who was commissioned to take photographs at the plaintiff's wedding. Two years later the plaintiff's father-in-law was murdered. The defendant sold photographs of the wedding, some of which showed the deceased, to national newspapers, which published one of them. The plaintiff had retained the copyright in the photographs. He succeeded in an action against the defendant for breach of copyright, and the Court of Appeal upheld the judge's award of 'vindictive' (rather than compensatory) damages of £1,000. There had been an intrusion into the plaintiff's life 'deeper and graver than an intrusion into a man's property' (p. 1082).

This case indicates that where the victim retains the copyright in documents or photographs, the publication of which may amount to an infringement of privacy, not only can such publication be stopped, but if it occurs, the damages may take into account the non-pecuniary loss caused by the infringement. Because English law requires no formality as regards the creation of copyright, documents such as private diaries, or personal photographs, or videos, will be protected against exploitation in this way. The limitation is that if the victim did not create the relevant document, or take the photograph, someone else will own the copyright, and the victim will be powerless to prevent its use.

An exception to the supremacy of the copyright holder is to be found in the current position as regards commissioned photographs and films, as set out in s. 85 of the Copyright, Designs and Patents Act 1988. Where a person has commissioned a photograph or a film for 'private and domestic purposes', the person who takes the photograph or makes the film will normally retain copyright (unlike the position in *Williams* v *Settle*). The commissioner, however, will have the right not to have:

(a)   copies of the work issued to the public,
(b)   the work exhibited or shown in public, or
(c)   the work broadcast or included in a cable programme service.

The side note to the section describes this as a 'right to privacy', which indeed it is, to a limited extent, and one which overrides the normal rights of the holder of copyright.

10.3.2.5 Data Protection Act 1984 This piece of legislation provides limited protection for privacy in relation to personal information which is stored electronically (as is increasingly the case). All those who hold such data ('data users') are obliged to comply with the 'data protection principles' set out in sch. 1 to the Act. The most important for the purposes of the present discussion are the first three:

(a)   The information to be contained in personal data shall be obtained, and personal data shall be processed, fairly and lawfully.
(b)   Personal data shall be held only for one or more specified and lawful purposes.
(c)   Personal data held for any purpose or purposes shall not be used or disclosed in any manner incompatible with that purpose or those purposes.

'Personal data' means 'data consisting of information which relates to a living individual who can be identified from that information . . . including any expression of opinion about the individual . . .' (s. 1(3)).

The first principle relates to the acquisition of personal information by a data user, and requires that this should be done 'fairly and lawfully'. This aspect of privacy is thus protected. More importantly, perhaps, the second and third principles taken together, restrict the use to which personal information may be put. The idea is that the person on whom information is held (the 'data subject') should know the purpose for which it is being held, and should be able to object to its use for any other purpose.

The primary methods for ensuring compliance with the Act lie with the Data Protection Registrar, whose powers of registration, investigation and supervision are backed up by criminal sanctions. There are also, however, rights for a data subject to seek compensation through the courts in relation to losses caused by inaccurate data (s. 22) or the improper use of data (s. 23). The action requires, however, that actual loss be proved, so that the breach of privacy involved in the unauthorised disclosure of personal information is not *per se* actionable.

Sir David Calcutt has suggested that the increased use by newspapers of electronic means of storing information means that there is potential for use of the Data Protection Act in this context (*Review of Press Self-Regulation*, Cm 2135, 1993, para. 7.46). He has recommended that the government should give:

further consideration to the extent to which the Data Protection Act may contain provisions which are relevant for purposes of misrepresentation or intrusion into personal privacy by the press.

10.3.2.6 Breach of confidence This developing action has been the strongest candidate in recent years for increasing the protection of privacy under English law. Its use for the rather different purpose of protecting government secrets has already been discussed at 5.6. It use in the context of the privacy of the individual can be traced back to *Prince Albert* v *Strange* (1849) 1 Mac and G 25. Queen Victoria and Prince Albert had occasionally, for their amusement, made drawings and etchings of subjects of private and domestic interest to themselves, and not intended for publication. Although the precise course of events is obscure, it seems that unauthorised copies from some of the etchings were made by an employee of a printer to whom the etchings had been entrusted by the plaintiff. These copies had found their way into the hands of the defendant, who proposed to exhibit them. The Court of Chancery held that the plaintiff was entitled to an injunction to restrain the publication, since the defendant must have obtained them as a result of a breach of confidence. Similarly in *Argyll* v *Argyll* [1967] Ch 302 it was held that the Duke of Argyll could obtain an injunction to prevent newspapers from revealing the secrets of his marriage, which had been disclosed to them by the Duchess. The Duchess had broken the confidence that exists between marriage partners, and her husband was entitled to take action to restrain any further disclosure. The case confirmed that the breach of confidence action can arise independently of any rights derived from property and contract, and is therefore a separate cause of action.

Secrets of sexual relationships may be confidential even if they take place outside marriage. This was confirmed by *Stephens* v *Avery* [1988] 2 All ER 477, where the disclosure related to a lesbian relationship in which the plaintiff had been involved. This case also discussed the limitations of the right to restrain breaches of confidence. It is well-established that disclosures which are in the 'public interest' will not be restrained, even if they breach a confidence. The person who is told 'in confidence' about criminal activities need have no hesitation in disclosing them (at least to the proper authorities). In *Stephens* v *Avery* it was suggested by the defence that this should also apply to the disclosure of 'immoral' activities. The court accepted that a duty of confidence would not apply to 'matters which have a grossly immoral tendency' (at p. 480), but it refused to categorise a lesbian relationship, or indeed any sexual conduct between consenting adults, as falling into that category.

The public interest defence goes wider than the disclosure of 'iniquity'. In *Lion Laboratories* v *Evans* [1985] QB 526 it was held to legitimise disclosure of information about the problems with the operation of a machine used for carrying out breath tests on motorists. In *X* v *Y* [1988] 2 All ER 648, however, it was held not to justify the disclosure of the names of doctors who were suffering from AIDS, this information having been obtained from confidential medical records. The doctors' privacy was thus protected, but this was as much on the basis of the public interest in maintaing the confidentiality of hospital records, as the doctors' individual rights.

The breach of confidence action may also be of use in cases involving the interception of telephone conversations, but this area is discussed further at 10.3.3.

As will be seen from the above, the action for breach of confidence meets many of the requirements of the protection of privacy. It provides compensation for the publication of secret personal information in many circumstances, and, perhaps more importantly, the courts are quite willing to allow injunctions to be used to restrain publications in this context, in contrast to the situation in relation to defamation. The limitations of the action are first, that it requires there to be a breach of confidence at some point. If the information is acquired without such a breach, for example by covert surveillance, then the action may well fail. Secondly, the action is not useful for attacking the *acquisition* of information as opposed to its publication. Thus, in *Kaye* v *Robertson* [1991] FSR 62 the intrusion into the plaintiff's hospital room in order to acquire information (the 'interview' and photographs) could not be dealt with as a breach of confidence, even though it involved a clear infringement of privacy. Widening the scope of breach of confidence may be regarded as a useful staging post in the development of the English law relating to privacy, but it certainly cannot be regarded as providing the whole answer.

10.3.3 Interception of communications

This has been an area of increasing concern. The growth in the use of various types of 'mobile phone' and the increased opportunity (because such telephones operate by means of wireless rather than wired connections) for electronic eavesdropping, has raised issues concerning the adequacy of the present law, which is contained primarily in the Interception of Communications Act 1985. This Act was introduced primarily in response to a decision by the European Court of Human Rights in *Malone* v *United Kingdom* (1985) 7 EHRR 14 that the United Kingdom was in breach of Art. 8 of the ECHR. Malone had brought an action in the High Court challenging the legality of a police telephone tap: *Malone* v *Metropolitan Police Commissioner* [1979] Ch 344. Sir Robert Megarry held that Malone had no cause of action. There was no general right to privacy under English law. The tapping procedure involved no trespass or other interference with Malone's property. Moreover, telephone conversations did not automatically attract breach of confidence (at p. 376):

> No doubt a person who uses a telephone to give confidential information to another may do so in such a way as to impose an obligation of confidence on that other: but I do not see how it could be said that any such obligation is imposed on those who overhear the conversation, whether by means of tapping or otherwise.

Sir Robert came to this conclusion on the basis of a more general view that confidential information which is obtained without a breach by one of the parties to the confidence is not protected by the law. A different view of this issue was taken by the Court of Appeal in *Francome* v *Mirror Group Newspapers* [1984] 2 All ER 408, which concerned an action to prevent the *Mirror* from publishing secretly obtained tapes of telephone conversations, alleged to reveal breaches of Jockey Club regulations, and possibly criminal offences. Although only dealing with the matter at the interlocutory stage, and therefore not needing to reach a final decision, they regarded the issue of the confidentiality of telephone conversations as 'live', particularly when the eavesdropping occurred by means of an illegal tap.

The situation is now largely covered by the Interception of Communications Act 1985, though it does not exclude the possibility of the use of other remedies, such as breach of confidence, or trespass, in appropriate cases. Much of the Act is concerned with setting up a statutory scheme for the control of telephone tapping, and other interception of communications, carried out by the police or security services. This is to be regulated by means of warrants issued by the Home Secretary (ss. 2–6), and supervised by an independent Commissioner (s. 8). The only grounds on which such a warrant may be issued are that it is in the interests of national security; for the purpose of preventing or detecting serious crime (as defined in s. 10(3)); or for the purpose of safeguarding the economic well-being of the United Kingdom (s. 2(2)).

The Act tackles the problem of unauthorised interceptions in s. 1, which makes any such intentional interception of a communication in the course of transmission by post, or by a public telecommunication system, a criminal offence. The method of interception is irrelevant. Proceedings may not be brought without the consent of the Director of Public Prosecutions (s. 1(4)). This means that the section provides little help for the individual citizen whose privacy has been infringed by an unlawful interception. There is a procedure for complaint to a tribunal (s. 7, and sch. 1), but its role is primarily to ensure that the proper procedures have been followed by the public authorities in carrying out an interception. It does not really deal with the problem of interceptions by the press, or other private individuals. There is no provision for a civil remedy in such cases.

The 1985 Act, then, while providing a statutory framework for interceptions, and providing for criminal penalties, provides little assistance for the individual whose privacy has been infringed. Where such an infringement is thought to have occurred, the individual is left with the action for breach of confidence as probably the best way of trying to prevent disclosure, or recovering compensation following disclosure.

10.3.4   Proposals for reform
The area of privacy has probably seen more proposals for reform than any other area of law over the past twenty years. The chronology is as follows:

1970 Justice Report, *Privacy and the Law*
1972 Younger Committee, *Report of the Committee on Privacy*, Cmnd 5012
1981 Law Commission, *Breach of Confidence*, Law Com No 110, Cmnd 8388
1990 Calcutt Committee, *Report of the Committee on Privacy and Related Matters*, Cm 1102
1993 Sir David Calcutt, *Review of Press Self-Regulation*, Cm 2135
1993 National Heritage Select Committee, Fourth Report, 294-I
1993 Lord Chancellor's Department, *Infringement of Privacy*, consultation paper

In addition, various private members' Bills have been brought forward at different times to address the problems. The concentration here will be on the two Calcutt reports (the 1990 one will be referred to as the *Report*, and the 1993 one as the *Review*) and the Lord Chancellor's Department's consultation paper (referred to here as the *Paper*).

A major concern of the Calcutt Committee was the question of Press self-regulation. There had been a 'Press Council' in operation since 1953, with the role of supervising Press conduct, *inter alia*, in relation to privacy issues. The history of this body is clearly outlined by Robertson and Nicol in *Media Law* (3rd edn, London: Penguin Books, 1992, pp. 521-524). By 1990 it had become to be seen as a largely toothless body, whose adjudications the Press felt able to treat with contempt. Nevertheless the Calcutt Committee preferred self-regulation to statutory control and therefore the first main recommendation of its *Report* was that a reformed Press Complaints Commission should be established. This would mirror the work of the Broadcasting Complaints Commission which has been in operation since 1981 in relation to radio and television, and has been the cause of little controversy or concern. The new Press Complaints Commission ('PCC')was to be a smaller body than the Press Council with the membership not representing any particular interest. It should concentrate on handling complaints (including complaints of unfairness or intrusion into privacy). The Committee also put forward a draft Code of Practice which the Press would be expected to follow, and the operation of which the PCC should monitor. This was to be the 'last chance' for the Press to put its own house in order, and, if it failed, then a statutory supervisory body should be introduced.

The second main recommendation of the *Report* was that certain forms of physical intrusion into private property should become a criminal offence. This would cover, for example, entry to obtain personal information with a view to its publication, or to place bugging devices, or the taking of photographs with long-range cameras, again with a view to publishing the results. The criminal offences would be further backed up by a civil action which would be available to prevent, or obtain compensation for, the publication of material obtained as a result of the commission of such a criminal offence.

The *Report* also recommended the extension of the statutory prohibition on identifying rape victims to the victims of other sexual assaults.

The Committee considered but rejected the introduction of a statutory tort of invasion of privacy as not being the appropriate response at the time, in the context of the other proposals being put forward.

The recommendations of the Committee contained in the *Report* were accepted, and the government indicated that the Press would have 18 months to show that self-regulation could work. The Press Complaints Commission was formed, under the chairmanship of Lord McGregor, though with not quite the level of independent membership intended (see *Review*, paras 3.34-3.35). The Sexual Offences (Amendment) Act 1992 gave effect to the recommendation for the protection of the identity of victims of sexual assaults. However, no action was taken by the government to enact the proposed new criminal offences relating to physical intrusion.

In 1992 Sir David Calcutt was asked to consider what had happened since 1990, and his *Review* was published in January 1993. He found that there had been a spate of cases attracting much publicity, and involving infringements of privacy in relation to members of the Royal Family, and members of parliament (*Review*, paras. 4.41–4.69). He found that the PCC had proved inadequate to deal properly with these incidents. Furthermore, the Code of Practice recommended by the 1990 Committee had been significantly watered-down, in favour of the Press (*Review*, para. 3.62), and many private individuals who had complained to the PCC were unhappy about with the Commission's performance in handling their complaints (*Review*, para. 4.22). Sir David Calcutt's overall assessment was that the PCC is not 'an effective regulator of the Press' (*Review*, para. 5.26). It does not hold the balance fairly between the Press and the individual, and is not the independent body which it should be. He stated:

> The Commission, as constituted, is, in essence, a body set up by the industry, financed by the industry, dominated by the industry, operating a Code of Practice devised by the industry and which is over-favourable to the industry.

As a result, Sir David concluded that the 'last-chance' had gone, and recommended that there should now be created a statutory Press complaints tribunal, operating a statutory Code of Practice, and with the power, amongst other things, to investigate complaints, and to initiate its own investigations; to hold hearings; to require the printing of apologies and corrections; to award compensation and to impose fines (*Review*, para. 6.5).

He also repeated the earlier recommendation in relation to making certain physical intrusions criminal, and recommended that further consideration should be given to the introduction of a tort of infringement of privacy.

As noted at 10.3.2.5 he considered that there was increased scope for using the Data Protection Act 1984 in relation to the Press. He also recommended increased powers to restrict the reporting of the identity of defendants in criminal proceedings. Finally, as a result of concern about the use of unauthorised recordings of telephone conversations in two of the cases which had arisen during the course of the review, one involving the Royal Family, and the other an MP, he recommended that consideration be given to identifying any gaps in the current legislation on the interception of communications (see 10.3.3), and how these might be filled.

The two recommendations which appear to have some chance of being acted upon, are the proposal for new criminal offences to deal with intrusion, and the recommendation for a statutory tort to deal more generally with infringements of privacy. In both cases it is recognised by the *Review* that some sort of defence of public interest would be necessary. In relation to the criminal offences, draft clauses for which are contained in Appendix D to the *Review*, it would be a defence to show that the act was done:

(a) for the purpose of preventing, detecting or exposing crime, or other seriously anti-social conduct; or

(b)   for the purpose of preventing the public from being misled by some public statement or action of the individual concerned; or

(c)   for the purpose of informing the public about matters directly affecting the discharge of any public function of the individual concerned; or

(d)   for the protection of public health or safety; or

(e)   under any lawful authority.

Thus the approach is one of closely defining the situations covered, rather than enacting a general defence of 'public interest'. However, certain aspects of these defences would be likely to cause problems, such as the definition of 'anti-social conduct', as is indeed recognised in para. 7.21 of the *Review*. The defences in (b) and (c) were added to deal with the position of public figures, who, it is accepted in the *Review*, might have to accept more limited protection than the general public (para. 4.38):

> I conclude that while, *prima facie*, everyone is entitled to protection of their privacy, those persons discharging public functions must be prepared to expect the level of that protection to be reduced to the extent, but only to the extent, that it is necessary for the public to be informed about matters directly affecting the discharge of their public functions.

The *Review* contrasts this very limited scope for public interest to restrict privacy, with the view of the PCC that 'In the case of politicians, the public has a right to be informed about private behaviour which affects or may affect the conduct of public business'.

As regards the issue of the general tort of infringement of privacy, the *Review* carries no specific recommendations, on the basis that this is a matter for further discussion. That has now been picked up by the Lord Chancellor's Department's consultative paper ('the *Paper*'), published in July 1993. The one firm proposal contained in the *Paper* is that there should be a new tort with the following characteristics (*Paper*, para. 5.22).

First, the tort should be available to a 'natural person' (that is, not a company, local authority, etc), in respect of conduct which constitutes an infringement of privacy, and which causes the person 'substantial distress', and would have caused such distress to a 'person of ordinary sensibilities in the circumstances of the complainant'.

Secondly, 'privacy' is to be taken to include matters pertaining to the person's health, personal communications, and family and personal relationships, and a right to be free from harassment and molestation.

Thirdly, defences of consent, lawful authority, absolute or qualified privilege, and public interest, should all be available.

Many of these issues are ones on which the *Paper* seeks further discussion. Taking the broad outlines of what it proposed, however, together with the criminal offences proposed in the *Review*, would this be likely to lead to a satisfactory law protecting privacy, bearing in mind the definition of the concept adopted at the start of this section (see 10.3.1) as:

The right to prevent, or to be compensated for, the unauthorised acquisition or publication of secret personal information.

The criminal offences clearly deal directly with the question of acquisition of information, but link it to an intention to publish. The 'peeping tom' type of offender, therefore, who acquires information by intrusive means simply from nosiness, or the person who seeks the information for private gain, or to obtain an advantage over the victim, would not be covered. The private detective gathering information in a marital dispute, for example, would fall outside these provisions, assuming that publication means more than 'pass to another person'. To that extent, it may be argued that the offence is too narrowly defined. The list of defences is also now quite long. It may well be that in the end there would be very few situations where the criminal offences would be likely to succeed with any degree of certainty.

It is difficult to assess the tort of infringement of privacy, because so many aspects of it are left open for further debate. It covers both acquisition and publication of personal information, and so deals with the two aspects of privacy as defined here (the *Paper* adds to these 'physical seclusion'). Is it really necessary, however, to limit the tort to cases of 'substantial distress'? The justification for this is the wish to avoid frivolous claims (for example, about telephone calls in the middle of dinner, *Paper*, para. 5.11). Even if it is necessary to guard against this, it is submitted that a requirement of 'distress', which is stronger that 'annoyance' or 'emabarrassment' (see *Paper*, para. 5.14), would be sufficient.

The recommendations in the *Review* and in the *Paper* are steps in the right direction towards providing a more rational protection for privacy rights than is the case under current English law. Further thought is needed, however, about the precise definitions to be used, and also what exactly should be the relationship between the criminal and civil law. There does, however, now seem to be a fairly general acceptance that some change in the law is needed. If the tort, and the new offences, were to be enacted it may well be that there would then be much less need for the statutory supervisory body recommended in the *Review*. The avoidance of the setting up of such a body might also in the end be of more benefit to the Press than holding out against the enactment of a statutory right of privacy, provided that appropriate public interest defences are included.

10.4 EUROPEAN CONVENTION AND REPUTATION AND PRIVACY

The issues of the protection of reputation, and privacy, will be dealt with separately, since they are treated differently within the ECHR.

10.4.1 Protection of reputation

The ECHR does not include a person's 'right to reputation' as one of the positive rights to which protection is given. Within Art. 10(2), however, one of the justifiable reasons for restricting freedom of expression is stated to be 'the protection of the reputation or rights of others'. This appears to make acceptable legal restrictions such as the English law of defamation which are designed to protect a person's reputation from false allegations. As with all the qualifications to Art. 10, however, they are only justifiable to the extent that they are 'necessary in a democratic society'. Two cases from Austria (*Lingens v Austria* (1986) 8 EHRR 103, and *Oberschlick v Austria* (1981) (Case 6/1990/197/257)) indicate some of the limits which the Court will place in this area. In both cases a politician had been criticised in the media for alleged support for Nazi views or sympathies. This had resulted in private criminal prosecutions for defamation being successfully taken by the politicians. In both cases the Court found the prosecutions to constitute a breach of Art. 10, in that the restrictions on freedom of expression went beyond what was necessary in a democratic society for the protection of a person's reputation. Two points which contributed to the decision are of particular importance. First, the Court had no doubt that the position of a politician is different from that of a private individual:

> Freedom of political debate is at the very core of the concept of a democratic society . . . The limits of acceptable criticism are accordingly wider as regards a politician as such than as regards a private individual (*Lingens*, para. 42; *Oberschlick*, para. 59).
>
> A politician is certainly entitled to have his reputation protected, even when he is not acting in his private capacity, but the requirements of that protection have to be weighed against the interests of the open discussion of political issues. (*Oberschlick*, para. 59).

Secondly, the Court was at pains to emphasise that a distinction needs to be drawn in this area between facts on the one hand, and opinion, or 'value-judgments' on the other (*Lingens*, para. 46; *Oberschlick*, para. 63). Whereas it was reasonable to expect a person to be able to establish the truth of defamatory facts, to require the same in relation to value-judgments (as the Austrian court had done) was 'impossible of fulfilment and . . . itself an infringement of freedom of opinion' (*Oberschlick*, para. 63).

What relevance, if any, do these points have in relation to the English law on defamation? The first requirement, that politicians are treated differently from others, has gained no recognition in English law. It is possible, then, that English law might be regarded as going too far in the restriction of freedom of expression on this point. It may be, for example, that the European Court would regard it as too restrictive that the burden of proof in relation to the defence of justification is on the defendant when the plaintiff is a politician. Perhaps in that situation it should be up to the plaintiff to prove that the statements were untrue? There is no direct suggestion of that kind in the Court's decisions, but it would be one way in which the general policy of treating politicians differently could be given effect.

As to the second point, dealing with the question of 'value-judgments', English law does meet this *via* the defence of 'fair comment' (see 10.2.2.2). This is clearly based on the need to distinguish facts from opinions, and would seem to fulfil the requirements of the European Court in this area.

10.4.2   Privacy
Privacy is dealt with by Art. 8 of the ECHR: 'Everyone has the right to respect for his private and family life, his home and his correspondence'. This broad phraseology has led to the Article being used in situations far beyond the scope of privacy as defined in this chapter, such as sexual orientation (*Dudgeon* v *United Kingdom* (1981) 4 EHRR 149) or the treatment of illegitimacy (*Marckx* v *Belgium* (1979–80) 2 EHRR 330). Two cases, however, have dealt with the question of telephone tapping: (*Klass* v *Federal Republic of Germany* (1978) 2 EHRR 214; *Malone* v *United Kingdom* (1985) 7 EHRR 14). Both cases concerned telephone tapping by government agencies. In *Klass* the Court accepted that such activities involved an infringement of privacy. Indeed it considered that (para. 41):

in the mere existence of the legislation, there is involved, for all those to whom the legislation could be applied, a menace of surveillance; this . . . strikes at freedom of communication . . . and thereby constitutes an 'interference by a public authority' with the exercise of the . . . right to respect for private and family life and for correspondence.

Nevertheless, in the particular case before it, the measures taken were sufficiently 'in accordance with the law' and 'necessary in a democratic society for the prevention of disorder or crime' to fall within the qualifying provisions of Art. 8(2).

In *Malone*, however, the Court found that at the relevant time, the English law governing interceptions of post or telephone communications was not laid down with any precision in accessible legal rules (para. 70). In fact, the Court found that, on the evidence before it (para. 87):

there would appear to be no legal rules concerning the scope and manner of exercise of the discretion enjoyed by the public authorities.

This meant that the provisions as to inteceptions could not be said to meet the requirement of being 'in accordance with the law'. There was therefore, on that basis, a breach of Art. 8, without there being any need to consider whether the tapping was justified on substantive grounds.

The response of the United Kingdom was to enact the Interception of Communications Act 1985 (see 10.3.3) which probably now brings English law in this area into line with the requirements of the ECHR.

More generally, however, it could be argued that the lack of any specific legal recognition of privacy rights as such by English law amounts to a failure under Art. 1 of the ECHR to 'secure' the right of privacy embedded in Art. 8. It might be possible, therefore, in a case such as *Kaye* v *Robertson* [1991] FSR 62 (10.2.5) that a challenge could be mounted on this basis. The possibility of this happening should act as a spur to the government to deal speedily with the various recommendations that have now come forward (see 10.3.4) for legislative reform and development in this area.

ELEVEN

Freedom from Discrimination

11.1 GENERAL ISSUES

11.1.1 The meaning of discrimination

The word 'discrimination' is not in itself a 'dirty word'. To say of a person that she is discriminating in her choice of boyfriends would probably be taken as a compliment. In this sense, to show discrimination is a virtue, not a vice. Similarly, to discriminate against blind people in relation to the issue of driving licences, against unqualified people in appointing doctors, or against rich people in imposing taxes, is not seen as being something which should be criticised. Discrimination only becomes objectionable where it is arbitrary, or where the basis of the discrimination has no connection with the decision being taken. In other words, it is only *unjustifiable* discrimination that is thought to be wrong. Even here there are different levels of discrimination which will provoke different responses. To refuse to sell your house because the prospective purchaser has dyed hair, or blue eyes, might be seen as strange, but not particularly heinous. On the other hand, for an employer to decide as between a number of female applicants for a job to employ the one who wears the shortest skirts, would be seen as objectionable (though probably not unlawful), particularly if the employer is male.

English law has intervened to control unjustifiable discrimination in only a very limited way. It only applies to certain types of discrimination, and only in relation to discrimination for certain purposes. The types of discrimination covered are discrimination on the basis of race or sex; the purposes for which discrimination may not lawfully be based on these grounds are, broadly speaking, employment, education, housing, and the provision of goods and services.

11.1.2 The problems of race and sex

Why has English law focused on race and sex as areas of unacceptable discrimination, which require a legislative response? It is not simply that these are features of a person over which the individual has virtually no control. It is not unlawful to discriminate against people on the basis of the size of their feet, or their height. It is the social context which is important. In terms of race, it was the immigration of the 1950s and 1960s which brought the problem of discrimination to the surface. Although it is discussed in terms of race, in practice it is colour of skin which has been the basis for most discrimination on racial grounds. Immigrants from the West Indies, from Kenya, and from India and Pakistan, were clearly identifiable from their skin colour, and therefore easy targets for those who felt that they were responsible for taking jobs from the indigenous workforce, or for bringing about increases in crime, or the lowering of social standards. By the mid-1960s the problem was sufficiently widespread to require a legislative response, which came initially in the Race Relations Acts of 1965 and 1968, and which is discussed further below.

As regards sex, it was again in the 1960s that the women's movement began to develop, first in the United States, and then here. Many would point to the growth in use of the contraceptive pill, and the consequent freedom that this gave to women to decide whether to become pregnant, and so to control their own lives, as one of the most significant developments. Whatever the reason, it came to be recognised that women were being disadvantaged in many areas of life, and that there was little chance of any significant improvement without government intervention. The problem here was not that of an oppressed and easily targeted minority, as in the case of racial discrimination; rather the problem lay in long-established societal attitudes as to the proper role of women within an essentially patriarchal society. These attitudes were too firmly entrenched to expect them to change without some direction from the government and the legal system. It was in this context that the Equal Pay Act 1970 and the Sex Discrimination Act 1975 came to be passed.

11.1.3   The legislative response

The English common law could provide no remedy against unjustifiable discrimination, except as an incident of a legal action based on some other grounds (as, for example in *Constantine* v *Imperial Hotels Ltd* [1944] KB 693: refusal of innkeeper to serve a *bona fide* customer). If racial or sexual discrimination was to be tackled, therefore, legislation was inevitable. The first, rather limited, attempt in relation to race was the Race Relations Act 1965. This dealt with discrimination in the provision of certain types of services to the public, for example in public houses, and also created an offence of 'incitement to racial hatred'. It was followed in 1968 by the wider Race Relations Act 1968, which extended the scope of the law into the areas of employment and housing. As far as sex discrimination was concerned, the first step was the Equal Pay Act 1970. This did not come into force, however, until 1975, at the same time as the more broadly based Sex Discrimination Act 1975 ('SDA') (reproducing the 1970 Act as amended in sch. 1), which established the current legislative framework. This model was then followed in the Race Relations Act 1976 ('RRA').

The approach in the SDA and the RRA is to use not the criminal law, but civil remedies. Unlawful discrimination becomes a statutory tort, giving a right to damages and injunctions. The civil nature of the action means that the onus is put on the private citizen who has suffered from discrimination to bring an action. The unlawful act is thus categorised as a dispute between individuals, rather than a conflict between the wrongdoer and the State. Some support for the citizen is provided, however, by the creation of two statutory bodies, the Equal Opportunities Commission (SDA, s. 53), and the Commission for Racial Equality (RRA, s. 43), with the responsibility of furthering the aims of the legislation, conducting investigations, and in some circumstances, providing support for the individual complainant. The success of the legislation in achieving its objectives nevertheless depends to a large extent on the willingness of the victim of unlawful discrimination to take advantage of its provisions.

The Acts define three basic types of discrimination, direct discrimination, indirect discrimination, and victimisation.

11.1.4 Direct discrimination

Direct discrimination occurs when a person is treated less favourably than someone of the opposite sex, or not of that person's racial group, would be in the same circumstances (SDA, s. 1(1)(a); RRA, s. 1(1)(a)). To deny person a job because of their colour, or to refuse promotion on the grounds of sex, is clearly direct discrimination. The motive is irrelevant. It would not be a justification to prefer a female to a male employee because it was thought that male employees were more likely to drink, and so perform their work less competently. It would have to be shown that this fear applied to the particular individual concerned (compare *Hurley* v *Mustoe* [1981] ICR 490: all married women with small children thought to be unreliable). Even if the motive is protective towards the individual, as for example in *Greig* v *Community Industry* [1979] ICR 356, where a girl was refused a place on a training scheme because of fears of the way in which she would be treated by her all-male fellow trainees, the action is still discriminatory. It follows that it is not necessary to show an intention to discriminate on grounds of race or sex, if that is the effect of a decision. The test is a 'but for' one. That is, would the treatment have been different but for the person's race or sex? As Lord Goff Stated in *James* v *Eastleigh Borough Council* [1990] 2 AC 751:

> . . . cases of direct discrimination under s. 1(1)(a) can be considered by asking the simple question: would the complainant have received the same treatment from the defendant but for his or her sex?

As Lord Goff went on to point out, this simple test:

> . . . avoids, in most cases at least, complicated questions relating to concepts such as intention, motive, reason, or purpose, and the danger of confusion resulting from the misuse of these elusive terms.

The case concerned the free admission to public swimming baths of people of retirement age. Since at the moment (though the position will change in the near future) the statutory retirement ages are different for men (65) and

women (60), any distinction using this as a criterion is potentially discriminatory. The House of Lords in using the 'but for' test, followed its earlier
decision in *Equal Opportunities Commission* v *Birmingham City Council* [1989]
1 All ER 769, which was concerned with differing admissions procedures as
between boys and girls seeking entry to grammar schools, applied because
there were fewer places available to girls.

As regards racial discrimination, there are two further aspects of direct
discrimination which need to be noted. First, s. 1(2) of the RRA states that
segregation on racial grounds is to be regarded as less favourable treatment.
Thus even if facilities provided to two racial groups are exactly equal in
quality, there will still be discrimination. Secondly, discrimination does not
necessarily have to be on the basis of the *victim's* race, as long as it is based on
racial grounds. Thus in *Zarcynska* v *Levy* [1979] 1 All ER 814, a white barmaid
was dismissed after she had refused to obey an instruction not to serve black
customers. It was held that she had been discriminated against on racial
grounds. The same view was taken in *Showboat Entertainment Centre* v *Owens*
[1984] 1 WLR 384. This approach does not, however, apply to sex discrimination, since the wording of s. 1(1)(a) specifically refers to a person being less
favourably treated 'on the ground of *her* sex'.

11.1.4.1 Racial grounds The wording of s. 1(1)(a) refers to less favourable treatment on 'racial grounds'. This concept is then further defined in
s. 3(1), which states that racial grounds means: 'colour, race, nationality or ethnic
or national origins'. It is made clear by s. 3(2) that a racial group can itself be made
up of other racial groups. It follows that a person can be a member of several
racial groups at the same time. A Sikh, for example, will be in at least three racial
groups on the basis of colour of skin, nationality (for example British, or Indian),
and ethnic origins (see *Mandla* v *Dowell Lee* [1983] 2 AC 548, discussed below).

The problem of deciding what is covered by the concept of 'ethnic origins'
has been considered in a number of recent cases. The starting point is *Mandla*
v *Dowell Lee* [1983] 2 AC 548, where the House of Lords had to decide
whether Sikhs constituted a racial group. Lord Fraser set out what he
considered to be eight relevant criteria for identifying a group on the basis of
ethnic origins. The first two he considered to be essential, namely:

(1)   a long shared history, of which the group is conscious as distinguishing it from other groups, and the memory of which it keeps alive;
(2)   a cultural tradition of its own, including family and social customs
and manners, often but not necessarily associated with religious observance.

The other six criteria were, in his view, relevant, but not essential. They were:

(3)   either a common geographical origin, or descent from a small
number of common ancestors;
(4)   a common language, not necessarily peculiar to the group;
(5)   a common literature peculiar to the group;
(6)   a common religion different from that of neighbouring groups or
from the general community surrounding it;

(7)   being a minority or being an oppressed or dominant group within a larger community . . .

Lord Templeman, while agreeing with Lord Fraser's conclusion that Sikhs did constitute a racial group, put the emphasis simply on the fact that a racial group must have some of the characteristics of a race, namely 'group descent, a group of geographical origin and a group history'.

As well as bringing Sikhs within the scope of a racial group defined by ethnic origins, the case confirmed that Jews similarly constitute a racial group. In *Commission for Racial Equality* v *Dutton* [1989] 1 All ER 306, the Court of Appeal applied the same approach discussing the status of 'gypsies'. In the narrow sense of this word, meaning those originally descended from a people who originated in the Punjab and migrated to Europe via Persia (Iran) in medieval times, the Court found that in the light of their shared customs, distinctive dress and furnishings, particular dialect, and repertoire of folk-tales and music passed on from one generation to another, they did constitute a racial group. To the extent, however, that the word 'gypsies' is applied to all travelling people who move around the country in caravans, this wider group did not constitute a racial group.

On the other hand, the Employment Appeal Tribunal has refused to recognise rastafarians as a racial group, primarily because it was felt that a group that has existed for only 60 years cannot be said to have a 'long shared history': *Crown Suppliers (PSA)* v *Dawkins* [1991] 22 LS Gaz R 36.

Muslims have also been denied the status of a racial group. This emphasises the fact that the RRA does not cover discrimination on religious grounds. A religious movement, such as Sikhism, will not be protected unless its adherents also satisfy the other criteria laid down in *Mandla*. Islam is too broadly based as a world-wide religion for it to be able to claim to do so, any more than could Christianity. Thus the protection given to Jews does not relate primarily to the religion of Judaism, but to the shared cultural traditions of those of Jewish descent.

11.1.4.2   Marital status   For the most part 'sex' in the SDA simply means whether a person is male or female. The Act does not protect against prejudice based on sexual orientation, or sexual practices. The homosexual, the transvestite, and the transsexual receive no protection under this legislation. In one respect, however, the scope is broadened, in that the SDA brings marital status within the scope of direct discrimination by virtue of s. 3(1)(a). This provides that a person discriminates by treating a married person, by reason of that marital status, less favourably than an unmarried person of the same sex would be treated. An obvious example might be the reluctance of an employer to employ a young married woman on the basis that she might leave to have children, whereas no such qualms would be felt about employing a single woman of the same age. This would clearly be discrimination on the basis of s. 3(1)(a). Note, however, that if the basis of the discrimination was that a young married man of the same age would be employed, it would fall within s. 1(1)(a) as being discrimination on the basis of sex. Note also that the protection only extends to the married. To treat a single person, simply on the basis of that status, less favourably than a married person is outside the scope of the Act.

11.1.5 Indirect discrimination
Some of the most insidious types of discrimination, and therefore the most difficult to tackle, arise not through the direct imposition of discriminatory conditions, such as 'only whites need apply', but through the imposition of requirements that appear on their face to be neutral, but which have the effect of prejudicing members of a particular racial group or sex. For example, a club which has all white members might require all new members to be proposed by an existing member, which may well make it more difficult for non-whites to join; or an employer might require all applicants to have attended school in this country, or to have been baptised into the Church of England. Again these conditions will have an indirectly discriminatory effect. The statutes deal with this type of discrimination in ss. 1(1)(b) of the RRA and SDA, and s. 3(1)(b) of the SDA (dealing with marital status).

The wording of s. 1(1)(b) of the RRA will act as an example of all three provisions. It provides that a person discriminates against another person when:

he applies to that other a requirement or condition which he applies or would apply equally to persons not of the same racial group as that other but —

    (i)   which is such that the proportion of persons of the same racial group as that other who can comply with it is considerably smaller than the proportion of persons not of that racial group who can comply with it; and

    (ii)   which he cannot show to be justifiable irrespective of the colour, race, nationality or ethnic or national origins of the person to whom it is applied; and

    (iii)   which is to the detriment of that other because he cannot comply with it.

Sections 1(1)(b) and 3(1)(b) of the SDA are in exactly the same form, subject to the necessary amendments to relate them to sex, and marital status. In effect, then, the concept of indirect discrimination arises where a condition is applied which places a disproportionate obstacle in the way of people who are married, or who are of a particular racial group, or sex, as opposed to people who are unmarried, or not of that racial group or sex.

The concept of the 'racial group' is to be approached in exactly the same way as described at 11.1.4.1 in relation to direct discrimination. Indeed, as we shall see, *Mandla* v *Dowell Lee* [1983] 2 AC 548, was in fact a case on indirect discrimination.

There are four elements to indirect discrimination:

(a)   the imposition of a requirement or condition;
(b)   the proportionality issue;

(c)   the lack of independent justification;
(d)   detriment to the victim.

These will now be considered in turn.

11.1.5.1   Requirement or condition   This element means that what is imposed must be something which *has* to be complied with: *Perera* v *Civil Service Commission (No. 2)* [1983] ICR 428. A statement that applicants without children are 'preferred', which would probably disproportionately affect married people, would not fall within the definition. Similarly, factors which are simply to be taken into account (as in *Perera*, command of English and experience in the UK), but are not in themselves conclusive, are not requirements or conditions. This approach considerably limits the scope of the concept of indirect discrimination, and later courts have followed the Court of Appeal's ruling in *Perera* with some reluctance (see, for example, *Meer* v *London Borough of Tower Hamlets* [1988] IRLR 399).

11.1.5.2   The proportionality issue   The number of people falling into the victim's group who can comply with the requirement or condition must be 'considerably smaller' than those not of that group who can do so. There are several issues here. First, what does 'considerably smaller' mean? There is no case law on this, but it is submitted that a court, if considering statistical information, would probably look for at least a 10 per cent difference. The Commission for Racial Equality (CRE) in its recommendations for the reform of the concept of indirect discrimination has referred to a 20 per cent difference. There is authority, however, that if none of the victim's group can comply, then there will be no indirect discrimination, because it cannot be said that 'none' is any proportion of the group at all: *Wong* v *GLC* (1979) (EAT 524/79, unreported). That has subsequently been doubted, also by the Employment Appeal Tribunal, in *Greencroft Social Club and Institute* v *Mullen* [1985] ICR 796, and it is submitted that this is the better line to follow, despite the fact that if none of a group can comply there may well be a claim for direct discrimination.

The next issue is to decide on the groups between which the comparison is to be made. This is relatively easy in relation to sex and marital status, in that the other group will be people of the opposite sex, or who are unmarried. Even here, however, the provision of s. 5(3) of the SDA must be noted. This states that where a comparison of cases is made, it 'must be such that the relevant circumstances in the one case are the same, or not materially different, in the other'. Thus, if the complainant is a university lecturer who is claiming that a requirement of 10 years' continuous service before promotion to senior lecturer is indirectly discriminatory against women, the comparison which should be made is with male university lecturers, rather than any other group.

The same provision applies to indirect racial discrimination by virtue of s. 3(4). The comparison between groups, however, is further complicated in this context by the fact that every person belongs to at least two racial groupings (colour, nationality), and, as we have seen, may well belong to more. It seems that is up to the complainant to decide which racial group is the significant one in relation to a claim. The comparison is then with similar people not of that racial group. The court or tribunal will decide exactly what are the appropriate 'pools' for comparison, and the complainant may well be expected to provide statistics to back up the claim of disproportionality on the basis of these 'pools'. In *Perera* v *Civil Service Commission (No. 2)* [1983] ICR 428, for example, Stephenson LJ said that the two relevant groups were people of Sri Lankan nationality who had passed the English bar or solicitors examinations, as compared with people not of that nationality who had passed these examinations. If the court takes an unexpected view as to the relevant pools, this may cause difficulties to the complainant in providing the evidence necessary.

The final issue to consider in relation to proportionality is the meaning of the phrase 'can comply'. This was considered by the House of Lords in *Mandla* v *Dowell Lee* [1983] 2 AC 548, where the alleged indirect discrimination arose out of the refusal to admit a Sikh boy to a school, on the grounds that since his religious obligations involved the wearing of a turban, he would not be able to comply with the school uniform requirements which involved the wearing of a cap. It was clear that a Sikh could *physically* have complied with the uniform requirements by removing his turban and having his hair cut. The House of Lords, however, interpreted the phrase 'can comply' in s. 1(1)(b) of the RRA as meaning 'can in practice' or 'can consistently with the customs and cultural traditions of the racial group'. The proportion of Sikhs who could, in that sense, comply with the uniform requirement, was clearly considerably smaller than the proportion of non-Sikhs, and this element of the test of indirect discrimination was therefore made out.

11.1.5.3 Lack of independent justification The burden of proof shifts here. Whereas in relation to the requirement and condition, and the proportionality issue, it lies on the complainant, it is up to the alleged discriminator to try to show that there was a justification for what was done irrespective of sex or race. For example, a requirement that applicants for a university place to study law have a pass in English Language at GCSE grade C, or its equivalent, almost certainly disproportionately disadvantages people not of British nationality. It is nevertheless justifiable, in that people studying the course, for which the teaching, and probably all the reading material, will be in English, will need a certain level of proficiency in order to be able to cope. The same requirement, however, applied to people applying for work in a non-skilled job which does not require contact with the general public, would almost certainly be unjustifiable.

In this type of case it is fairly easy to see on which side of the line the decision as to justification should fall. The precise scope of the word 'justifiable' has, however, given rise to considerable difficulties. The most stringent definition was applied in *Steel* v *Union of Post Office Workers* [1978] ICR 181, where the Employment Appeal Tribunal said the test was one of 'necessity'. Subsequent case law has, however, weakened this early ruling. In *Ojutiku* v *Manpower Services Commission* [1982] ACR 661, the Court of Appeal considered that a requirement that a person have managerial experience before being sponsored for a management course was justifiable on the grounds that people without such experience would be unlikely to obtain employment after taking the course. In reaching this conclusion the Court did not apply a test of necessity (which would clearly not have been satisfied on the facts) but one of whether the employer had 'adduced adequate grounds'; in other words, as Eveleigh LJ put it (at pp. 667–8):

> . . . if a person produces reasons for doing something which would be acceptable to right-thinking people as sound and tolerable reasons for so doing, then he has justified his conduct.

This approach, which seems to equate 'justifiable' with 'reasonable', was not followed by the House of Lords in *Mandla* v *Dowell Lee* [1983] 2 AC 548. Some of the reasons for having a school uniform, and therefore a 'no-turban' rule, were said to be:

> . . . to minimise external differences between races and social classes, to discourage the 'competitive fashions' which . . . tend to exist in a teenage community, and to present a Christian image of the school to outsiders, including prospective parents.

No doubt many 'right-thinking' people would regard these objectives as 'reasonable', but the House was clear that they were insufficient to justify the indirect discrimination involved. Unfortunately, the House did not make it clear at what point between 'reasonableness' and 'necessity' the concept of justification should operate, though Lord Fraser stated, *obiter*, that in some circumstances prohibitive cost might justify a discriminatory procedure.

The most recent consideration of this issue was by the Court of Appeal in *Hampson* v *Department of Education* [1990] 2 All ER 25. (The House of Lords did not consider the point when reversing the Court of Appeal on other grounds: [1990] 2 All ER 513.) Balcombe LJ cited with approval the judgment of Stephenson LJ in *Ojutiku* v *Manpower Services Commission*, in which he referred to the need to balance the discriminatory effect of a condition against the discriminator's need for it. Balcombe LJ concluded (at p. 34):

> In my judgment 'justifiable' requires an objective balance between the discriminatory effect of the condition and the reasonable needs of the party who applies the condition.

This statement was approved by the House of Lords in *Webb* v *EMO Air Cargo* [1992] 4 All ER 929 as setting out the appropriate test to apply, and to be regarded as superseding that of Eveleigh LJ in *Ojutiku*. The test is thus clearly objective, and presumably means that the greater the discriminatory effect, the stronger the justification must be.

Balcombe LJ had found support for his approach in the decision of the House of Lords in *Rainey* v *Greater Glasgow Health Board* [1987] ICR 129, which was a case on s. 1(3) of the Equal Pay Act 1970, concerning the way in which a variation in terms between a woman's contract and a man's may be justified by a 'material difference' in their cases. The House had applied the ruling of the European Court of Justice in *Bilka-Kaufhaus GmbH* v *Weber von Hartz* (Case 170/84) [1987] ICR 110, and held that:

> to justify a material difference . . . the employer had to show a real need on the part of the undertaking, objectively justified, although that need was not confined to economic grounds; it might, for instance, include administrative efficiency in a concern not engaged in business or commerce.

Balcombe LJ found this entirely consistent with Stephenson LJ's approach in *Ojutiku*.

The current test of 'justifiability' is thus based on an objective balancing of 'reasonableness'. It is not at all easy, however, to predict how the test will apply in a particular case, and it therefore leaves a considerable degree of uncertainty around this issue.

11.1.5.4   The requirement of detriment   The complainant must be able to show detriment resulting from the inability to comply with the requirement or condition. If, for example, there is an unjustifiable language provision attached to a job, but the reason that the complainant was rejected was failure to meet some other, justifiable condition, then it would seem that there has been no detriment. The complainant will be unable to bring an action for indirect discrimination, but the Commission for Racial Equality may be able to investigate the possibility that the employer is engaging in a discriminatory practice (see 11.4.2).

'Detriment' has been interpreted broadly under both the SDA (*Ministry of Defence* v *Jeremiah* [1980] ICR 13 at p. 26) and the RRA (*BL Cars Ltd* v *Brown* [1983] ICR 143 at p. 146) as meaning simply 'put under a disadvantage'. It is not necessary for any material loss to have been suffered.

11.1.6   Victimisation
In relation to both racial and sexual discrimination there is always going to be a fear on the part of victims that if they make trouble by complaining, or taking legal action, they will simply end up suffering worse discrimination. Both the SDA (in s. 4) and the RRA (in s. 2) go some way to meeting this fear by treating 'victimisation' itself as a form of discrimination. It will amount to such where a person is treated less favourably because that person has done, or is suspected of having done, one of four things, or is known or suspected to be intending to do one of them. The four things are:

(a)   bringing proceedings against the discriminator under the relevant Act; or
(b)   giving evidence or information in connection with proceedings brought by any person under the relevant Act; or
(c)   otherwise doing anything under or by reference to the relevant Act in relation to the discriminator or any other person; or

(d)   alleging that the discriminator or any other person has committed an act which (whether the allegation so states or not) would amount to a contravention of the relevant Act.

The relevant Act includes, under s. 4 of the SDA, the Equal Pay Act 1970.

The victimisation provisions do not seem to have been greatly used, though perhaps this is because their existence operates as a deterrent to such behaviour. Two cases, however, illustrate a difficulty with trying to use the provisions. In *Cornelius* v *University College of Swansea* [1987] IRLR 147, the complainant alleged victimisation when she was refused a job transfer on the grounds that this might prejudge proceedings based on sexual harassment which she was bringing. In *Aziz* v *Trinity Street Taxis Ltd* [1988] IRLR 204 a taxi-driver was expelled from a company after making secret tape-recordings of conversations with other members in connection with a prospective action for racial discrimination. In both cases the Court of Appeal found that there had been 'less favourable' treatment, but that it was not related to an act protected by the statutes. In *Cornelius* the same refusal of transfer would have occurred whatever the nature of the legal proceedings; it was irrelevant for this purpose that they were proceedings under the SDA. Similarly in *Aziz*, it was held that it was the breach of trust involved in the secret recordings which led to the expulsion, and that the same action would have been taken whatever the purpose of the recordings. Once again, the fact that they were made with a view to an action under the RRA was irrelevant.

These decisions seem to open a large loophole in the victimisation provisions. Provided that the alleged victimiser can convincingly argue that the same action would be taken against any person behaving in a similar way, and that the fact that their behaviour happens to be concerned with allegations of discrimination is irrelevant, it seems that the victimisation will fall outside the scope of the Acts.

11.1.7   Definitions
Both the RRA and the SDA use certain phrases to designate particular types of discrimination. 'Racial' or 'sex' discrimination, for example, refer simply to direct or indirect discrimination (RRA, s. 3(3); SDA, s. 5(1)). 'Sex discrimination' excludes discrimination on the grounds of marital status. The word 'discrimination' on its own, however, covers all types of discrimination, including victimisation, and in the SDA, discrimination on the basis of marital status.

11.2   AREAS OF UNLAWFUL DISCRIMINATION

Just because behaviour fits within one of the definitions of direct discrimination, indirect discrimination, or victimisation, does not mean that it is necessarily unlawful. For a man to decide to hold a 'stag' party on the night before his wedding, and not to invite any female friends, is clearly an act of sex discrimination, but there is no legal remedy. Discriminatory actions only become unlawful if they relate to the specific areas set out in Parts II to IV of the RRA and the SDA. The following broad headings are looked at here: employment, education, housing, provision of goods and services, and advertising. In most cases the discussion is based on examples, rather than a comprehensive description of all the aspects of each area.

11.2.1 Employment

There are two main ways in which an employer may discriminate: first, in relation to recruitment; secondly, in relation to the treatment of existing employees. In the context of sex discrimination, the provisions of the Equal Pay Act 1970 and of EC law are very important. Their complexity means that there is not space to discuss them in detail here, but some reference to EC law is made at 11.5. The Equal Pay Act operates by implying into the contract of employment an 'equality clause' which has the effect of ensuring that as between men and women employed on 'like work' there is equal treatment in relation to all terms of their contracts. (For a full discussion see Bourn, C.J. and Whitmore, J., *Race and Sex Discrimination*, 2nd edn, London: Sweet & Maxwell, 1993, ch. 7.)

Where an employer is seeking to fill a post, it is unlawful, as one would expect, to discriminate by refusing to offer the job to a person because that person is of a particular racial group or sex (RRA, s. 4(1)(c); SDA s. 6(1)(c)). The main difficulty here may be the problem of proof. This may be possible where there is either a clear discrepancy between the level of qualification of the person appointed and the complainant, or the employer can be shown to have made comments indicating an intention to discriminate. If the decision takes place at an early stage of the application process, however, for example at the point of deciding who to interview, it may be very difficult to show that it was based on discriminatory grounds. The problems of enforcement are considered further at 11.4.

The Acts also make it unlawful for the employer to discriminate 'in the arrangements he makes for the purpose of determining who should be offered' employment. This is wide enough to cover the whole recruitment process from advertisement to interview. In terms of advertising the biggest danger nowadays is probably indirect discrimination. The provisions of s. 29 of the RRA, and s. 38 of the SDA (see 11.2.5.1), and the activities of the CRE and the Equal Opportunities Commission (EOC) mean that advertisements which overtly indicate an intention to discriminate ('whites only need apply', 'barman wanted') are rarely seen. More insidious are recruitment processes which rely on word of mouth, or the recommendation of the existing workforce. These may well, whether intentionally or not, disadvantage particular groups. Qualification requirements which are unnecessary and potentially discriminatory may have the same effect. In interview, questioning female applicants about child care arrangements or other domestic responsibilities is fraught with danger, unless it can convincingly be shown that male applicants would be treated in the same way, or possibly, that the questioning relates to a particular problem with the individual applicant, rather than being a general issue relating to all women (see, e.g. *Hurley* v *Mustoe* [1981] IRLR 208 at 11.1.4; *Saunders* v *Richmond Borough Council* [1978] ICR 75).

Both the CRE and the EOC produce Codes of Practice in relation to recruitment which the wise employer will be careful to follow.

The final requirement in relation to recruitment is that there must be no discrimination in the terms on which employment is offered (RRA, s. 4(1)(b); SDA, s. 6(1)(b)).

Turning to existing employees, it is unlawful to discriminate in relation to the terms of employment (RRA, s. 4(2)(a); as regards sex discrimination, this is governed by the Equal Pay Act 1970, s. 1(2)), access to opportunities for promotion, transfer, training, or other benefits, etc (RRA, s. 4(2)(b); SDA, s. 6(2)(a)), or in relation to dismissal or subjection to 'any other detriment'. Differences in rates of payment, opportunities for overtime, or availability of employee discounts, are all examples of matters on which discrimination is unlawful. Selection for dismissal, or for short-time working, on the basis of race or sex will also give rise to possible action against the employer.

In recent years, racial, and more especially sexual, 'harassment' in employment, has been a matter of particular concern. Both types of harassment have been regarded as falling within subjecting the employee victim to a 'detriment' within the RRA, s. 4(2)(c) (see, for example, *De Souza* v *Automobile Association* [1986] IRLR 103), or the SDA, s. 6(2)(c) (see, for example, *Wilemen* v *Minilec Engineering Ltd* [1988] IRLR 145). The harassment will be regarded as sexually or racially based, provided that sex or race is the 'weapon' that is being used against the employee, even though the motive may be to get rid of the employee for other reasons: *Strathclyde Regional Council* v *Porcelli* [1986] IRLR 134. The *effect* of the behaviour will be viewed through the eyes of the victim, not the 'harasser'. The starting point is, as was stated in *De Souza* v *Automobile Association* [1986] IRLR 103 at p. 107, whether:

a reasonable worker would or might take the view that he had thereby been disadvantaged in the circumstances in which he had thereafter had to work.

Once this is established, then it is a question of the reaction of the individual employee, and the fact that others might not have felt harassed by the behaviour is irrelevant: *Wilemen* v *Minilec Engineering Ltd* [1988] IRLR 145.

In *Wadman* v *Carpenter Farrer Partnership, The Times*, 31 May 1993, the Employment Appeal Tribunal recommended to tribunals the definition of sexual harassment put forward by the European Commission in its recommendations on the protection of the dignity of women and men at work, 27 November 1991. This provided that:

Sexual harassment means 'unwanted conduct of a sexual nature, or other conduct based on sex affecting the dignity of women and men at work'. This can include unwelcome physical, verbal, or non-verbal conduct.

There are certain exemptions available to employers in connection with either race or sex discrimination, and these must now be considered.

11.2.1.1 Genuine occupational qualification Both the RRA (in s. 5) and the SDA (in s. 7) recognise that in certain circumstances there may be a genuine need to restrict certain jobs to people of a particular race or sex. In relation to race, the principal reason is that of authenticity. A person may be required to 'look' right in a particular job. Thus in relation to the casting of plays (s. 5(2)(a)), the engagement of artistic or photographic models (s. 5(2)(b)), or the employment of waiters or waitresses (s. 5(2)(c)), it may be justifiable to discriminate in favour of a particular racial group or groups. The Act states that a person of the particular group must be 'required' for reasons of authenticity. It is not clear how strict this test is. If, for example, a director casting Shakespeare's *Othello* decides only to consider black actors for the lead role, does the fact that the part has been frequently played by white actors mean that it cannot be said that authenticity 'requires' a black actor? It is to be hoped that 'necessity' will be tempered by 'reasonableness' in this context, so that the test becomes whether the requirement is one that may reasonably be imposed in the interests of authenticity, even if not every employer would impose it in filling a particular post.

The final genuine occupational qualification in the racial context is where the job involves the provision of personal services promoting welfare to a particular racial group and 'those services can most effectively be provided by a person of that racial group'(RRA, s. 5(2)(d)). The employer's opinion will apparently be given considerable weight in deciding whether a person from the racial group will be the most effective: *Tottenham Green Under Fives Centre* v *Marshall* [1989] IRLR 126.

The genuine occupational qualifications in the SDA have a rather different emphasis. There is some overlap, in that s. 7(2)(a) refers to authenticity in dramatic performances and other entertainment, and s. 7(2)(e) deals with personal services (though it includes education as well as welfare), but the remainder of the provisions are mainly concerned with decency or privacy, or related issues. So where the job is likely to involve physical contact with men 'in circumstances where they might reasonably object to it being carried out by a woman', or the work will be likely to be done in circumstances 'where men might reasonably object to the presence of a woman because they are in a state of undress or are using sanitary facilities', being a man may become a genuine occupational qualification (s. 7(2)(b)). The same will apply where the work involves sharing living accommodation (s. 7(2)(c)), or is at a 'single-sex' establishment involving supervision or special care, such as a prison or hospital (s. 7(2)(d)). A further provision of this kind (s. 7(2)(ba)) was added by the Sex Discrimination Act 1986, where the job involves living or working in a private home, and:

objection might reasonably be taken to allowing a woman —
 (i)   the degree of personal or physical contact with a person living in the home, or
 (ii) the knowledge of intimate details of of such a person's life,
which is likely . . . to be allowed to, or available to, the holder of the job.

This was added in response to a ruling by the European Court that there was no justification for the previous more general exclusion of private households and small businesses from the scope of the SDA, by virtue of s. 6(3) (now repealed): *EC Commission* v *UK* [1984] ICR 192.

Further miscellaneous genuine occupational qualifications may arise from reasons of 'phsyiology' (but excluding strength or stamina) (s. 7(2)(a)), the fact that the job is likely to involve working in a country outside the UK where the laws or customs mean that 'the duties could not, or could not effectively, be performed by a woman' (s. 7(2)(g)), or where the job is one of two to be held by a married couple (s. 7(2)(h)).

In relation to the provisions of both the RRA and the SDA, the employer will not be able to rely on them if there are other existing employees who could carry out the duties which give rise to the claim for the genuine occupational qualification (RRA, s. 5(4); SDA, s. 7(4)).

11.2.1.2 Other exemptions As far as racial discrimination is concerned (but not victimisation or sex discrimination), employment in a private household is excluded from the provisions of s. 4(1) and (2). This may seem reasonable in relation to recruitment and the offer of employment, but there seems less justification in allowing racial discrimination between existing employees, even within a private household.

Other exemptions under the RRA apply to training in skills to be exercised outside Great Britain (s. 6), and seamen recruited abroad (s. 9). Under the SDA there are exclusions for height requirements in relation to prison officers (s. 18), and for the employment of ministers of religion (s. 19) where:

the employment is limited to one sex so as to comply with the doctrines of the religion or avoid offending the religious susceptibilities of a significant number of its followers.

11.2.1.3 Activities related to employment The Acts extend the scope of protection to various situations related to employment, but which are not covered by the ordinary employment contract. Thus they make unlawful discrimination in relation to contract workers (that is workers employed by a third party who supplies them to the discriminator under a contract) (RRA, s. 7; SDA, s. 9); or in relation to potential or actual partners in a firm of six or more partners (RRA, s. 10; SDA, s. 11); or by trade unions in relation to membership, etc (RRA, s. 11; SDA, s. 12); or by 'qualifying bodies', vocational training bodies, or employment agencies (RRA, ss. 12–15; SDA, ss. 13–16). There are also special provisions applying to the police (RRA, s. 16; SDA, s. 17).

11.2.2 Education
The basic provisions relating to unlawful discrimination in the sphere of education are contained in RRA, s. 17, and SDA, s. 22. They apply to virtually all educational establishments, publicly or privately funded, from primary schools to universities. In the same way as the employment provisions apply to both potential and actual employees, so discrimination in education may occur in relation to both prospective and actual pupils. Thus refusal of

admission, the terms on which admission is offered, the degree of access to benefits, facilities or services, and exclusion or subjection to some other detriment, can all amount to unlawful discrimination. We have already considered one example of discrimination in this area, that is *Mandla* v *Dowell Lee* [1983] 2 AC 548 (see 11.1.5.2), where the discrimination consisted of a refusal to admit, which was based on indirectly discriminatory racial grounds arising from uniform requirements.

Problems may also arise from actions taken for apparently benevolent motives. For example, in one case it was thought that the best way of dealing with the problems of pupils who used English as a second language was to teach them in separate units. This was found by the CRE to amount to unlawful indirect discrimination. It clearly affected some racial groups disproportionately, and was a detriment because it might involve the pupils in being 'bussed' to schools away from their home area, and would require them to follow a restricted curriculum. It was not justifiable because current educational research no longer supported the idea of separate teaching for English as a second language, as opposed to the integration of support into the normal classroom (*Teaching of English as a Second Language*, Formal Investigation Report, 1986).

There is a general exception in the SDA, s. 26, for 'single-sex establishments'. This applies to schools which generally only admit pupils of one sex (though there may be some minor exceptions (s. 26(1)(a), (b)), or, where some of the pupils are boarders, only admits boarders of one sex. There are also special transitional provisions for single-sex schools wishing to become co-educational: SDA, s. 27.

11.2.3 Housing

The pattern of protection in relation to housing is similar to that which applies to employment or education. In other words, it applies both to those who are seeking housing (either to rent or purchase), and those who are living in premises managed by somebody else. The controls are set out in s. 21 of the RRA, and s. 30 of the SDA. The most significant area is probably that of racial discrimination in relation to the disposal of premises. It is common for those selling houses in an area dominated by one racial group to feel, or actually to be put, under pressure not to sell outside that group. It is, however, only lawful to discriminate in this way in selling your house if you do not use an estate agent, and do not advertise it for sale in any other way. If, however, an advertisement has been displayed in the window of the house indicating that a purchaser is being sought, then any discrimination on the grounds of race, or sex, will be unlawful. Moreover, the exception allowing discrimination only applies where the discriminator wholly occupies the premises. It does not, therefore, apply to the letting of premises. If, for example, a landlord asks a departing tenant to try to find a replacement, and two possible new tenants are put forward, one black and one white, the landlord will be acting unlawfully in choosing on racial grounds, despite the fact that the tenancy has not been advertised in any way. In this context, however, the 'small dwellings' exception should be noted (RRA, s. 22; SDA, s. 32). This applies where the discriminator, or a near relative (as defined in RRA s. 78(5); SDA, s. 82(5)), is living on the premises, some of the accommodation is shared, and the premises are 'small'. This is defined (RRA, s. 22(2); SDA, s. 32(2)) as premises with accommodation for two households, or six persons in addition to the household of the discriminator (or near relative).

Local authority housing lists have been investigated on a number of occasions by the CRE, and its predecessor under the 1968 Act, the Race Relations Board. Such lists are specifically covered by the wording of s. 21(1)(c) of the RRA, and s. 31(1)(c) of the SDA, which refer to treatment 'in relation to any list of persons in need of premises'. A particular significant investigation was that into Hackney Council (*Hackney Council Housing* case, Formal Investigation Report, January 1984). Working for the first time simply from statistical information, rather than in response to complaints, the CRE found breaches of s. 21 of the RRA, in that officials had discriminated on the basis of colour in allocating council houses and flats. The best houses and flats went to whites, the poorer ones to blacks. The CRE issued a non-discrimination notice (see 11.4.2.3).

11.2.4 Goods, facilities or services
The broadest area of unlawful discrimination is identified in s. 20 of the RRA and s. 29 of the SDA. These sections make it unlawful to discriminate in the provision (whether for payment or not) of goods, facilities or services to the public, or a section of the public. The discrimination may take the form of a refusal to supply at all, or refusal or omission to supply goods, etc, of equal quality, in the same manner, and on the same terms, as those which the discriminator supplies to others. This covers almost all everyday activities. Examples are given in RRA, s. 20(2), and SDA, s. 29(2). This confirms that the sections apply to shops, theatres, pubs, restaurants, hotels, banks, and transport. They also apply to professionals (such as solicitors), tradespeople (such as plumbers), or any other businesses which offer their services to the public. The scope of the provisions makes them very important in connection with the objective of changing attitudes. They have the effect of requiring people to avoid discrimination in all their working dealings with others.

One area which has caused problems is the statement in s. 20(2)(g) of the RRA, that s. 20(1) applies to the services of 'any local or other public authority' (though the equivalent provision in the SDA does not seem in practice to have given rise to the same difficulties). To what extent are activities such as the granting of planning permission, or the issue of a licence, or the processing of a tax return to be regarded as the provision of a facility or service? Some local authority responsibilities, such as the obligation to provide accommodation for the homeless, have been accepted as falling within s. 20: *Hillingdon London Borough Council* v *Commission for Racial Equality* [1982] AC 779. The position as regards planning permission, however, was so uncertain that a new section was added to the RRA to make it clear that it is covered: s. 19A (added by the Housing and Planning Act 1986). The case which gave rise to the difficulties was *R* v *Entry Clearance Officer, ex parte Amin* [1983] 2 AC 818. In this case the majority of the House of Lords ruled that the decision of an entry clearance officer as to whether or not to issue a person with a special entry voucher for admission to the UK was not the provision of a service within s. 20. It was, rather, simply the exercise of a duty in connection with the control of immigration. In reaching this conclusion the majority approved the decision in *R* v *Immigration Appeal Tribunal, ex parte Kassam* [1980] 2 All ER 330, in which the Court of Appeal, in interpreting the equivalent provision in s. 29 of the the SDA, held that the Secretary of State was not providing a 'facility' in exercising powers given by the Immigration Act 1971. The House in Amin also approved, however, the later Court of Appeal decision in *Savjani* v *IRC* [1981] QB 458, in which it was held that the Inland Revenue performed both duties (which were outside the scope of s. 20), and services (which were within it). As Templeman LJ put it (at p. 467):

> The duty is to collect the right amount of revenue; but, in my judgment, there is a service to the taxpayer provided by the board and the inspector by the provision, dissemination and implementation of regulations which will enable the taxpayer to know that he is entitled to a deduction or a repayment, which will entitle him to know how he is to satisfy the inspector or the board if he is so entitled, and which will enable him to obtain the actual deduction or repayment which parliament said he is to have.

Racially discriminatory requirements as to provision of birth certificates in connection with a claim for tax relief for a child were held to fall within the scope of s. 20.

The line between a 'duty' and a 'service' may be a difficult one to draw, but it remains crucial in deciding whether the actions of a public official come within the scope of s. 20 of the RRA, or s. 29 of the SDA. As Bourn and Whitmore point out (*Race and Sex Discrimination*, 2nd ed., London: Sweet & Maxwell, 1993, p. 250), if the distinction which Lord Fraser drew in *Amin* ([1983] 2 AC 818 at p. 834) between the direct provision of facilities and the mere grant of permission to use facilities is right:

> it is difficult to see why issuing somebody a ticket to enter a swimming bath should not equally be regarded as the mere grant of a permission to use a facility, yet nobody could really doubt that it was intended that the Act cover discrimination by refusing somebody such a ticket.

Because of the fact that in many situations it will be possible to regard the exercise of a particular power by a public official as either the provision of a facility or a mere grant of permission, this allows great scope for the courts to decide, presumably on the basis of an ill-defined 'public policy', into which category each example will fall. Moreover, the uncertainty surrounding the area will almost certainly discourage complainants from taking action against what they may see as discriminatory behaviour on the part of public officials.

11.2.4.1 Exceptions There are several exceptions to the provisions of s. 29 of the SDA recognised in the statute.

Section 29(2), for example, makes it clear that where a particular skill is commonly exercised in a different way for men and women, there is no breach of s. 29(1) where a practitioner of this skill insists on offering a service appropriate to one sex only. An obvious example of this would be hairdressing, in relation to which there is thus no obligation for all salons to become 'unisex'. A woman seeking a haircut in a gentlemen's 'barbers' would have to put up with the hairdresser's standard approach to cutting male hair, or could, if the hairdresser considers it impracticable to supply the service at all, be refused a cut altogether.

There are further exceptions in relation to political parties (s. 33), thus making 'women's' sections lawful, or for voluntary bodies (s. 34), such as the Women's Institute.

Finally, s. 35 contains a further group of exceptions covering the provision of facilities or services:

(a)   at establishments for persons requiring special care, supervision or attention, such as hospitals;

(b)   at places used for an organised religion, where its doctrines, or the religious susceptibilities of its followers, require single-sex provision;

(c)   where the facilities or services are provided for, or are likely to be used by, two or more persons at the same time, and their nature is such that either people are likely to be seriously embarrassed at the presence of others of the opposite sex, or people are likely to be in a state of undress and reasonably object to the others' presence;

(d)   where the services or facilities are such that physical contact is likely between the user and some other person, and that other person might reasonably object if the user were of the opposite sex.

Note also the provisions of s. 43 (charities), s. 44 (sporting activities), and s. 46 (communal accommodation).

11.2.4.2   The problem of clubs   Clubs which openly operated a 'colour bar' were a considerable problem in the 1960s, and there were several cases under the Race Relations Act 1968 dealing with this, brought under the equivalent to s. 20 of the RRA. The problem which arose was whether a 'private' club could be said to be offering its facilities to 'the public or a section of the public'. In *Charter* v *Race Relations Board* [1973] AC 868, the House of Lords held that a Conservative club, which operated a membership selection process was not offering its facilities to the public or a section of the public. The same conclusion was reached in *Dockers' Labour Club and Institute Ltd* v *Race Relations Board* [1976] AC 285, where the issue was the refusal of a club to provide facilities to a member of an associate club. There must be a genuine selection process, so that a sports club which simply requires the payment of a membership fee, whereupon access to the facilities is allowed, would not count (see, for example, in another context, *Panama (Piccadilly) Ltd* v *Newberry* [1962] 1 WLR 610). Provided, however, that there is something like, for example, a nomination process, and then a decision by a membership committee, the club will be outside the scope of s. 20 of the RRA, and s. 29 of the SDA.

As far as racial discrimination is concerned, the problem is addressed by s. 25 of the RRA, which makes discrimination in relation to offers of membership, or provision of facilities to members or associate members, unlawful as regards clubs with 25 or more members, which have a constitution regulating membership. The only clubs which can now take advantage of the *Charter,* and *Dockers' Labour Club* decisions are thus those which have less than 25 members, plus a genuine system of selection. There is, however, a large exception to s. 25 provided by s. 26. This makes it clear that the target of s. 25 is primarily discrimination on the grounds of colour. Section 26 excludes from the provisions of s. 25 associations of which:

> the main object is to enable the benefits of membership . . . to be enjoyed by persons of a particular racial group defined otherwise than by reference to colour.

This legitimises, therefore, ethnic or national clubs, such as the London Welsh rugby club, or an Indian cultural society, provided that they are not offering their facilities or services to the public or a section of the public, within the meaning of s. 20.

No comparable provision to s. 25 of the RRA was included in the SDA. Single-sex private clubs are therefore perfectly lawful, provided that they meet the tests in *Charter,* etc, in order to be regarded as not offering their facilities to the public. This must be regarded as having been a deliberate omission, perhaps on the basis that organisations such as the traditional London 'gentlemen's club' (to which, no doubt, many members of parliament belong), were institutions too deeply entrenched in national culture to be legislated out of existence.

11.2.5 Other unlawful acts
Part IV of both the RRA and the SDA contain a number of sections making certain other miscellaneous activities unlawful. They start with 'discriminatory practices' (RRA, s. 28; SDA. s. 37), but these will be considered at 11.4.2 in relation to the powers of the CRE and EOC.

11.2.5.1 Advertisements Discriminatory advertisements are made unlawful by RRA, s. 29, and SDA, s. 38. An advertisement which indicates an intention, or might reasonably be understood as indicating an intention, to do an unlawful act of discrimination will potentially render both the author and the publisher of the advert liable. Under the RRA, advertising to do lawful acts which are racially discriminatory will also be unlawful, unless the acts are lawful by virtue of s. 5 (genuine occupational qualification), s. 6 (employment for training in skills to be exercised outside Great Britain), s. 7(3) and (4) (contract workers), s. 10(3) (partnerships), s. 26 (national associations), s. 34(2)(b) (charities), ss. 35–39 (training and welfare), or s. 41(statutory authority). Thus an advertisement seeking a waiter or waitress of Chinese extraction for a Chinese restaurant will be lawful; an advertisement in a newspaper's 'lonely-hearts' column, on the other hand, indicating that only respondents of a particular ethnic group will be considered, will be unlawful, even though choosing a partner on racial grounds is a lawful action. The reason for the difference between the RRA and the SDA on this point is presumably that the public display of racial prejudice, through the means of an advertisement, is considered more pernicious than the equivalent in relation to sexual prejudice. Why this should be thought to be so is not clear.

The SDA on the other hand makes it clear, in a way that the RRA does not, that care must be taken in the particular words that are used in an advertisement. Section 38(3) provides that job descriptions with a sexual connotation (for example, 'waiter', 'salesgirl', 'postman', or 'stewardess') will be taken as an indication of an intention to discriminate, unless the advertisement itself contains an indication to the contrary.

11.2.5.2 Instructions Instructions to discriminate issued by a person with actual or customary authority to tell another how to act, and putting pressure on a person to discriminate, are unlawful by virtue of the RRA, ss. 30 and 31, and the SDA, ss. 39 and 40.

11.2.5.3 Vicarious liability Principals are liable for the expressly or impliedly authorised acts of agents, and employers are liable for employees acting in the course of employment, unless the employer had taken reasonable steps to prevent the employee discriminating (RRA, s. 32; SDA, s. 41).

11.2.5.4 Aiding unlawful acts Knowingly to aid another to do an unlawful act of discrimination, renders the aider liable for the discrimination, in the same way as the principal offender (RRA, s. 42; SDA, s. 33).

11.3 POSITIVE DISCRIMINATION

Both the RRA and the SDA attack discrimination regardless of the motive of the discriminator, or the target for the discrimination. Thus the legislation can be, and has been, used by white against black, and by men against women. The need for legislation of this kind, as has been noted at 11.1.2, stems from a background of prejudice and inequality in relation to a particular section of the community. The legislation itself, however, is almost exclusively based on the premise of equal treatment as of now, without paying attention to past inequalities. Some may see this as a serious defect (see, for example, the comments of Lord Scarman in his *Report on the Brixton Disorders 10–12 April 1981*, Cmnd 8427, para. 6.32). There may well be scope for what is sometimes called 'positive discrimination', or 'affirmative action', to favour a particular group or groups, and provide much more direct help, much more quickly, than can be achieved by a strict policy of equal treatment. The danger, however, is that such an approach may be counterproductive in terms of changing attitudes. The white worker who sees a job going to a person from an ethnic minority under an affirmative action programme is unlikely to become less prejudiced as a result. Moreover, the members of the favoured group may themselves find such programmes patronising. Fears of this kind have led to the current legislation containing only very limited provision for positive discrimination, as was recognised by the Court of Appeal in *Lambeth Borough Council* v *Commission for Racial Equality* [1990] IRLR 231. The Council had advertised two jobs within the housing benefits department as open to Afro-Caribbean or Asian applicants only. The Court of Appeal said that it was not possible to use the 'genuine occupational qualification' exception under the RRA, s. 5(2)(d) (see 11.2.1.1) to achieve positive discrimination. As Balcombe LJ commented (at p. 234):

> I am wholly unpersuaded that one of the two main purposes of the Act is to promote positive action to benefit racial groups . . . It is true that ss. 35, 37 and 38 do allow for limited acts of positive discrimination which would otherwise be unlawful, but that does not constrain us to give s. 5(2)(d) a meaning which its words do not naturally bear.

In both Acts, the relevant provisions which do allow positive discrimination are to be found in Part VI.

11.3.1 Provision for special needs

The RRA contains a general provision, s. 35, for which there is no equivalent in the SDA. This states that nothing in Parts II to IV of the Act:

> shall render unlawful any act done in affording persons of a particular racial group access to facilities or services to meet the special needs of persons of that group in regard to their education, training or welfare, or any ancillary benefits.

A particular example of the kind of provision which would fall within this would be language training, which by virtue of s. 35 can lawfully be made available exclusively to particular racial groups, but it clearly has the potential for a much wider scope, and one that goes beyond positive discrimination. It might be used to justify, for example, the provision of schools where teaching is centred around the religious beliefs associated with a particular ethnic community, and to which access is restricted to members of that community.

11.3.2 Discriminatory training

Both Acts contain provisions allowing for discrimination in training where a particular racial group or sex is under-represented in a particular type of work, either in the country as a whole, or in a particular area, or at a particular place of work. Provisions of this kind apply to training bodies (RRA, s. 37), to employers (RRA, s. 38; SDA, s. 48), or, in relation to sex discrimination, to 'any person' (Sex Discrimination Act 1986, s. 4, amending SDA, s. 47). They permit, for example, allowing access to training to the under-represented group only, or encouraging only that group 'to take advantage of opportunities for doing that work'. This might legalise, for example, advertising or other recruitment procedures which might otherwise be indirectly discriminatory. Publication of advertisements only in a particular language, or in particular areas of a town, might fall within this. What the sections do not legitimise is direct discrimination in the recruitment process, or in the selection of existing employees to do particular work. An employer cannot consider applications only from the under-represented group, nor prefer a minority applicant over a better-qualified representative of the majority. Internal promotions, or other allocation of work, must similarly be carried out without discrimination on grounds of race or sex. As can be seen from this, affirmative action has yet to receive any significant recognition in English law.

11.4 ENFORCEMENT AND REMEDIES

11.4.1 Right of individual action

The primary means of enforcement of the rights to equal treatment contained in the RRA and the SDA is through individual legal action taken by the victim of discrimination.

Claims in relation to a breach of Part II of either Act (that is, a complaint concerning employment), must be brought before an industrial tribunal (RRA, s. 54; SDA s. 62). Claims in relation to breaches of Part III (education, housing, goods, facilities and services) are treated as a statutory tort, and dealt with in the County Court (RRA, s. 57; SDA, s. 66). Where the claim is for unlawful discrimination under Part III of the RRA, it must be brought before a 'designated' county court, that is one where the judge sits with two specialist lay assessors (RRA, s. 67). Under both Acts, claims in relation to education must generally first be referred to the Secretary of State (RRA, s. 57(5); SDA, s. 66(5)). The legal aid position for discrimination cases is the same as for most other types of action, that is, that it will be available in relation to county court proceedings, but not those before an industrial tribunal.

In order to assist a potential claimant, both Acts provide for a form of 'questionnaire' to be produced by the Secretary of State, by which the claimant can seek answers from the respondent 'on his reasons for doing any relevant act, or on any other matter which is or may be relevant' (RRA, s. 65(1)(a); SDA, s. 74(1)(a)). Any answers provided will generally be admissible in evidence, and a failure to answer may lead to the court or tribunal drawing an inference, including an inference that the respondent has committed an unlawful act (RRA, s. 65(2); SDA, s. 74(2)).

A full range of remedies is available in the industrial tribunal or the county court, corresponding to those that would be available in any other action brought in those fora. Most claimants will be seeking damages. It is specifically provided that damages may be awarded for injury to feelings (RRA, s. 57(4); SDA, s. 66(4)). In *Bradford City Metropolitan Council* v *Arora* [1991] 2 WLR 1377, the Court of Appeal accepted that exemplary damages might be available in discrimination cases. In *AB* v *South West Water Services Ltd* [1993] 1 All ER 609, however, a different Court of Appeal ruled that the House of Lords decision in *Cassell* v *Broome* [1972] AC 1027 had restricted the availability of exemplary damages to those torts which were in existence in 1964, at the time of the earlier House of Lords decision in *Rookes* v *Barnard* [1964] AC 1129. Since this issue had not been argued in *Bradford* v *Arora* the Court of Appeal in *AB* v *South West Water Services* refused to be bound by its earlier decision, and held that exemplary damages were not available in relation to statutory torts, such as those created by the SDA and RRA, which were not in existence in 1964. It seems, then, that only compensatory damages are available.

Where the claim is for indirect discrimination, no damages will be awarded if the discriminator proves that the requirement or condition was not applied with the intention of treating the claimant unfavourably on grounds of race or sex (RRA, s. 57(3); SDA, s. 66(3)). Although the burden of proof is on the respondent, the prospect that even a successful claim may not result in any compensation is likely to be a considerable disincentive to bringing an action purely on the basis of indirect discrimination.

11.4.2   Role of the CRE and EOC
The two Commissions are independent bodies created by statute (RRA, s. 43 and sch. 1; SDA, s. 53 and sch. 3). Their members are appointed by the Secretary of State, but they are not part of the Civil Service. Their duties are:

(a)   to work towards the elimination of discrimination;
(b)   to promote equality of opportunity, and, in the case of the CRE, to promote good relations between people of different racial groups;
(c)   to keep under review the working of the Acts (including for the EOC the Equal Pay Act 1970), and at the request of the Secretary of State, or on their own initiative, to draw up proposals for amendment.

As will be seen, the activities of the Commissions are wide-ranging. The concentration here will be on their powers in relation to enforcement. These take the form of assisting individual claimants; taking action against certain breaches of the Acts where the Commissions have exclusive rights to act; and carrying out formal investigations.

11.4.2.1   Assisting individual claimants   The power of the Commissions
to assist individual claimants is specifically recognised in RRA, s. 66, and SDA, s. 75. The claimant must make an application for assistance, which the Commissions may give if 'they think it fit to do so' on one of three grounds. These are, first, that the case raises a question of principle; secondly, that it is unreasonable for the claimant to deal with the case unaided, because of, for example, the complexity of the case, or the claimant's position in relation to the respondent or another person involved; or, thirdly, 'by reason of any other special consideration'. The discretion is thus very wide. There is no obligation on a Commission to assist even if one of the above criteria is satisfied, and those criteria are so broadly stated, that they impose very few limitations on the Commissions. If a Commission decides that it wishes to become involved, it will generally be possible to fit the case into one of the specified categories. The Commissions will also need to keep in mind their overall duties under the legislation, as set out above.

The type of help which can be given is set out in RRA, s. 66(2), and SDA, s. 75(2). It may include giving advice, negotiating a settlement, arranging legal advice or representation, or 'any other form of assistance which the Commission may consider appropriate'. The Commissions thus have a broad discretion as to what assistance should be given. They may recover their expenses from any costs awarded to the claimant in an action, or under a settlement (RRA, s. 66(3); SDA, s. 75(3)).

In 1992 the CRE received 1,557 applications for assistance, of which the vast majority (1,105) were concerned with employment. Representation was granted in 353 cases, and other advice and assistance in 907 (CRE *Annual Report for 1992*). The figures for the EOC are much smaller. In 1991 448 applications were received, with legal assistance being given in 150, and advice in 11 (EOC *Annual Report for 1991*).

11.4.2.2 The Commissions' power to take proceedings In relation to certain types of proceedings only the Commissions have status under the legislation to bring an action. These are actions in relation to discriminatory advertisements (RRA, s. 29; SDA, s. 38), instructions to discriminate (RRA, s. 30; SDA, s. 39), and pressure to discriminate (RRA, s. 31; SDA, s. 40). In relation to such actions it may be difficult to identify an individual victim of discrimination, though as regards instructions or pressure to discriminate on racial grounds, the cases of *Zarcynska* v *Levy* [1979] 1 All ER 814, and *Showboat Entertainment Centre* v *Owens* [1984] 1 WLR 384, show that it may be possible to bring an action on the basis of direct discrimination (see 11.1.4).

Proceedings in respect of these three types of unlawful act will be brought by the relevant Commission in an industrial tribunal (for employment matters), or county court (for other matters). The Commission may ask the tribunal or court to decide whether there has been a contravention of the relevant Act (RRA, s. 63(2)(a); SDA, s. 72(2)(a)). In addition, where the Commission considers that the person who is alleged to be in breach may commit further unlawful acts of the same type, the Commission may seek an injunction from a county court (RRA, s. 63(4); SDA, s. 72(4)). The application for an injunction must be to a county court even if the breach relates to employment, but in such a case the county court will not issue an injunction unless an industrial tribunal has already held that an unlawful act has taken place (RRA, s. 63(5); SDA, s. 72(5)). To obtain an injunction in an employment matter, therefore, two sets of proceedings will be necessary, the first in the tribunal, the second in the county court. In other matters, the action for a declaration of a contravention, and the application for an injunction may be combined.

In addition to these three areas, the Commissions also have a role in relation to 'persistent discrimination' (RRA, s. 62; SDA, s. 71). Where there has been a finding by a court or tribunal, as a result of an individual claim, that a person has committed an unlawful discriminatory act, and it appears to the Commission that unless restrained the person is likely to commit more such acts, the Commission may apply to a county court for an injunction. The power to seek such an order lasts for five years from the original finding of unlawful discrimination.

11.4.2.3 Formal investigations The powers of the Commissions to conduct investigations are contained in RRA, ss. 48–52, and SDA, ss. 57–61.

They are a very important part of the Commissions' powers, enabling them to investigate people, organisations, or general areas of activity, in the pursuit of their overall duties under the legislation (see 11.4.2). The decision in *Home Office* v *Commission for Racial Equality* [1982] QB 385 indicates that the general duties of the Commissions to promote equality of opportunity, or, in the CRE's case, good relations between racial groups, may entitle a Commission to investigate an activity which would not involve unlawful discrimination under the Act. In this case it was the operation of the immigration controls, which, as we have seen (*R* v *Immigration Appeal Tribunal, ex parte Kassam* [1980] 2 All ER 330, see 11.2.4), had been found not to involve the provision of a 'service'.

The powers to investigate are also strong in that they can involve the Commissions in *requiring* information or documentary evidence to be given, with the possibility of court orders being used to back this up: RRA, s. 50; SDA, s. 59. It is this aspect of the Commissions' powers which provides the strongest justification of the restrictive, and controversial, interpretation of ss. 48–50 of RRA (which must be taken to apply equally to ss. 57–59 of the SDA) adopted by the House of Lords in *R* v *Commission for Racial Equality, ex parte London Borough of Hillingdon* [1982] AC 779, and *Re Prestige Group plc, Commission for Racial Equality* v *Prestige Group plc* [1984] 1 WLR 335. As a result of these decisions the Commissions can undertake only two types of investigation: a general investigation, or a 'named-person' investigation. A named-person investigation is sometimes also called an 'accusatory' investigation. The importance of the difference lies in the basis on which the Commissions may act, the notice which has to be given, and the procedures to be followed. A general investigation will look at a broad area of activity, rather than what is being done by a particular organisation or individual. Patterns of ethnic employment in the hosiery industry in Leicester, might be investigated, for example. There is no need for there to be any suspicion or belief that unlawful discrimination is taking place. 'General notice' of the intention to hold the investigation must be given. This means (RRA, s. 78(1); SDA, s. 82(1)):

> a notice published by [the Commission] at a time and in a manner appearing to [the Commission] suitable for securing that the notice is seen within a reasonable time by persons likely to be affected by it.

The Commission must draw up terms of reference for the investigation, but (as held in the *Hillingdon* and *Prestige* cases) these may not name any individual or organisation, and there will be no powers for the Commission to require evidence, unless the Secretary of State authorises this (RRA, s. 50(1); SDA, s. 59(1)). Once the investigation is complete, the Commission will be expected to issue a report, and, if appropriate, recommendations (RRA, s. 51; SDA, s. 60).

More frequently the Commissions carry out 'named-person' investigations. As Lord Diplock pointed out in the *Prestige* case ([1984] 1 WLR 335 at p. 345) to be made the subject of a named-person investigation is not a trivial matter. An announcement of such an investigation by the CRE, for example:

is likely to be understood by many of those to whose attention it may come as pointing the finger of suspicion of racial bias at the persons who are named in it, and by doing so, it may well damage or put at risk harmonious race relations that presently exist in the employer's undertakings.

Moreover, the actual conduct of the investigation is likely to involve those subject to it in considerable 'inconvenience, expense and dislocation', which may extend over a number of years (more than four years in the *Prestige* case). For these reasons, as well as the fact that persons subject to the investigation can be virtually compelled to provide information and documents, the House of Lords emphasised two important restrictions. First, a named-person investigation may not be launched unless the Commission has at least some belief that the person concerned has engaged in unlawful discrimination. The test is not particularly high. There is no need for anything in the nature of a *prima facie* case, but there must be some basis for the suspicion, even though the grounds for such suspicion may be 'no more than tenuous' (*Prestige* case, at p. 342). As Lord Diplock put it in the *Hillingdon* case (at p. 791):

> To entitle the Commission to embark upon the full investigation it is enough that there should be material before the Commission sufficient to raise in the minds of reasonable men, possessed of the experience of covert racial discrimination that has been acquired by the Commission, a suspicion that there may have been acts by the person named of racial discrimination of the kind which it is proposed to investigate.

The last sentence indicates that care must be taken in drawing up the terms of reference to ensure that they do not go further than is justifed by the Commission's belief. Furthermore the 'acts' referred to are limited by RRA, s. 50(2)(b) and SDA, s. 59(2)(b) to 'unlawful discriminatory acts' or acts in relation to which only the Commission has enforcement powers (see 11.4.2.2).

Secondly, when embarking on a named-person investigation, the Commission must give the person the opportunity to make oral or written representations (RRA, s. 49(4); SDA, s. 58(3A)). If oral representations are made the person may be represented by a barrister, solicitor, or 'some other person' not being a person to whom the Commission objects on grounds of unsuitability. The object of this right to be heard is to fulfil the natural justice requirement of *audi alteram partem*. As Lord Diplock put it in the *Hillingdon* case (at p. 787):

> before deciding to embark on a full investigation the Commission should hear what any person whom it suspects of unlawful discriminatory acts has got to say as to why and to what extent the Commission's suspicions are unjustified.

Lord Diplock went on to rule that the right to be heard also implies that the terms of reference must be reasonably specific as to the acts which are to be investigated. These must be related to the particular belief which the Commission has as to the person's unlawful behaviour. In the light of any representations made by or on behalf of the person, the Commission may decide to amend the terms of reference, or even to abandon the investigation.

Once a named-person investigation is underway, the Commission has the power to serve a notice requiring a person to supply written information, or attend an oral hearing, at which documents may be required to be produced (RRA, s. 50(1); SDA, s. 59(1)). This will not apply to information or documents which could not be required to be given in evidence or produced in civil proceedings, and travel expenses can be claimed for the cost of attending any hearing (RRA, s. 50(3); SDA, s. 59(3)). Failure to comply with the notice can be backed up by court orders, and may in some circumstances amount to a criminal offence (RRA, s. 50(4)-(7); SDA, s. 59(4)-(7)). There are restrictions on the purposes for which information disclosed in compliance with a notice may be used (RRA, s. 52; SDA, s. 61).

A named-person investigation will result in a report and, possibly, recommendations, in the same way as a general investigation. If, however, the Commission is satisfied that a person is committing, or has committed, an unlawful discriminatory act, or any of the acts against which the Commission alone can take enforcement proceedings (see 11.4.2.2), the Commission may issue a 'non-discrimination notice' (RRA, s. 58; SDA, s. 67). Before doing so, however, the Commission must inform the person that they have it in mind to issue such a notice, and allow the person the opportunity to make oral or written representations (RRA, s. 58(5); SDA, s. 67(5)). Any such representations must be taken into account before a notice is issued.

A non-discrimination notice may require a person not to commit any of the acts to which it relates, and, if it requires changes in practice, to inform the Commission and 'other persons concerned' as to when and how those changes have been made (RRA, s. 58(2); SDA, s. 67(2)). It thus has some similarity with an injunction. If the notice is not complied with, however, there is no direct sanction which the Commission can impose. It may, however, seek an injunction from a county court, in the same way as for persistent discrimination (RRA, s. 62; SDA, s. 71).

There is a right of appeal against any requirement contained in a non-discrimination notice, which must be brought within six weeks to an industrial tribunal (in employment matters), or county court (RRA, s. 59; SDA, s. 68). The challenge need not, therefore, be to the notice as a whole, but may relate to just one part of it. It seems that judicial review proceedings may also be possible (*R v CRE, ex parte Westminster City Council* [1984] ICR 827), though Bourn and Whitmore query whether 'it is sensible to add in this way to an already cumbersome procedure' (C. J. Bourn, and J. Whitmore, *Race and Sex Discrimination*, 2nd edn, London: Sweet & Maxwell, 1993, p. 282).

Despite the limitations on the power to conduct 'exploratory' investigations into typical businesses or organisations which have resulted from the *Hillingdon* and *Prestige* decisions, formal investigations remain one of the most powerful ways in which the development of equal treatment on grounds of race or sex can be promoted. It will be suggested at 12.3.2, that these powers could well be used as a model for a more general 'Commission for Rights and Liberties', having a much broader remit.

11.5 EUROPEAN APPROACHES TO DISCRIMINATION

There are two areas that need to be considered here. First, the position as regards sex discrimination under EC law; secondly, the principle of freedom from discrimination under Art. 14 of the ECHR.

11.5.1 European Community law

It is important to note two limitations on the scope of EC law in relation to discrimination: it is only concerned with discrimination on the grounds of sex, and, moreover, only with such discrimination in relation to employment. In these areas, however, EC law has had a significant impact. There have been a number of decisions by the European Court of Justice ('ECJ'), that English law is not in line with the requirements of EC law, and which have therefore led to amending legislation. There is only space here to give the broadest outline of the provisions. For further discussion see, for example, J. Steiner, *Textbook on EEC Law*, 3rd edn, London: Blackstone Press, 1992, chapter 22 (*'Steiner'*), or C. J. Bourn, and J. A. T. Whitmore, *Race and Sex Discrimination*, 2nd edn, London: Sweet & Maxwell, 1993 (*'Bourn & Whitmore'*).

The ECJ has recognised that the 'elimination of discrimination based on sex' is one of the fundamental human rights within EC law, the observance of which the Court has a duty to ensure: *Defrenne* v *SABENA (No 3)* (case 149/77) [1979] ECR 1365. Of much more practical significance, however, are the specific rights contained in the Treaty of Rome, and in various Directives.

Article 119 of the Treaty of Rome sets out the general principle that 'men and women should receive equal pay for equal work'. The ECJ has held that this applies to indirect discrimination as well as direct discrimination: *Bilka-Kaufhaus GmbH* v *Weber von Harz* (case 170/84) [1986] ECR 1607. The Article is supplemented by Directive 75/117, which specifically includes within the concept of 'equal pay', the absence of discrimination on grounds of sex in respect of work of 'equal value'. Freedom from discrimination was extended beyond the area of 'pay' by the 'equal treatment' Directive (76/207), and this has subsequently been applied by other Directives to matters such as social security (79/7), pension schemes (86/378), and self-employment (86/613). For further detail see *Steiner*, chapter 22.

Article 119 has been held to have (in the terminology of EC law) both 'vertical' and 'horizontal' direct effect in the law of member States: *Defrenne* v *SABENA (No 2)* (case 43/75) [1976] ECR 455. This means that it can be relied on in domestic courts for claims against the State (that is, vertical direct effect), and also in claims between individuals (horizontal direct effect), without any need to rely on municipal law. In other words, EC law itself provides the basis for a legal action in the courts of each member State. In the United Kingdom, the Equal Pay Act 1970, and the Sex Discrimination Acts of 1975 and 1986, provide relevant rights and remedies, but it is still possible for an individual to base a claim on the Article itself, if it is thought that English law does not provide the protection required under EC law.

The Directives, however, can have only *vertical* direct effect: *Marshall* v *Southampton & South West Hampshire Water Authority* (case 152/84) [1986] 2

All ER 584. So an individual cannot bring an action against another individual, or a private organisation, in the English courts, as a result of an alleged breach of one of the Directives. Organs of the State, can, however, be made the subject of an action. Thus, the British Gas Corporation, prior to privatisation, was held to be an organ of the State, and bound by the Equal Treatment Directive: *Foster* v *British Gas* [1990] IRLR 353 (ECJ), [1991] IRLR 268 (HL). The scope for such actions is likely to be reduced by the current trend in the United Kingdom towards privatisation, and the reduction in the role of the State. The government, of course, may be liable under EC law if it fails to give effect to a Directive and enact appropriate remedies in English law. See, for example, *EC Commission* v *UK* (Case 61/81) [1982] ECR 2061, concerning the inadequacy of the Equal Pay Act 1970 (as originally drafted) in situations where no job evaluation scheme was in operation. This led to amendment of the legislation (Equal Pay Act (Amendment) Regulations 1983 (SI 1983 No 1794)).

It is not entirely clear whether in relation to English legislation passed prior to a Directive, English courts should, in an action between individuals rather than against the State, have regard to the Directive in interpreting the legislation. The ECJ decision in *Marleasing SA* v *Commercial International de Alimentacion SA* (Case 106/89) indicates that they should. The English appeal courts have shown a reluctance to follow this, however. See, for example, the Court of Appeal's approach in *Webb* v *EMO Air Cargo Ltd* [1992] IRLR 116. This case has now been referred to the ECJ by the House of Lords: [1992] 4 All ER 929. (For further discussion of this issue in the discrimination context, see *Bourn & Whitmore*, pp. 24–39.)

It will be clear from the above that any consideration of the operation of the Equal Pay Act 1970, or the employment provisions of the Sex Discrimination Act 1975, must take account of the impact of EC law. Although it may be that in some situations the domestic legislation goes further in protecting against discrimination than is required by Art. 119, or the Directives, these EC documents, as interpreted by the ECJ, provide a minimum standard below which English law must not fall. They may therefore provide not only a valuable point of reference, but also a basis for action, for individuals who consider that their rights have been infringed in this context.

11.5.2 European Convention on Human Rights
Article 14 of the ECHR states that:

> The enjoyment of the rights and freedoms set forth in this Convention shall be secured without discrimination on any ground such as sex, race, colour, language, religion, political or other opinion, national or social origin, association with a national minority, property, birth, or other status.

The scope of this article is in one way rather narrow, but in another way quite broad. The broad aspect is in the list of illegitimate grounds for discrimination, which goes far beyond the categories recognised by English law, and is even then (as indicated by the use of the phrase 'such as') apparently not exclusive. The narrow aspect is that the principle of non-discrimination is stated not as a general right, but as existing only in relation to the other rights and freedoms set out in the ECHR (including, however, those contained in the Protocols). It is thus parasitic on these other rights. If, therefore, the ECHR has nothing to say on a particular issue, such as employment, or housing, then Art. 14 will be of no relevance or use to an individual who has suffered from discrimination in this context. The Court has, however, interpreted Art. 14 as providing a remedy providing that the discrimination occurs within a general area covered by the Convention, even if it relates to a right which is not specifically spelt out. In the *Belgian Linguistic case* (1968) 1 EHRR 578, the Court gave two examples of how this might operate. First, although Art. 2 of the First Protocol (see 1.5.3) does not provide a right to the establishment of a particular type of school, nevertheless 'a State which had set up such an establishment could not, in laying down entrance requirements, take discriminatory measures within the meaning of Article 14' (para. 9). Secondly, Art. 6, which deals with the right to a fair trial, does not compel States to institute a system of appeal courts. If such a system is put in place, however, it would infringe Art. 14 to discriminate on illegitimate grounds in allowing access to the system (para. 9).

The freedom as stated in Art. 14 is unqualified, unlike, for example, freedom of expression under Art. 10. There is here no list of grounds on which discrimination will be regarded as permissible. Nevertheless, the Court held in the *Belgian Linguistic* case, that the Article did not imply a right to complete equality of treatment in every situation. Drawing on the common approach to be found in many democratic States, the Court stated that the principle of equality of treatment is violated if a distinction is drawn which has 'no objective and reasonable justification'. Such a justification will require first that the differential treatment has a legitimate aim, and secondly that there is a reasonable relationship of 'proportionality' between the means employed, and the aim being pursued (para. 10). Thus, in a subsequent case concerning United Kingdom immigration procedures (*Abdulaziz, Cabales and Balkandali v United Kingdom* (1985) 7 EHRR 471), the Court held that a procedure for the admission of spouses of those with a right of abode in the United Kingdom, which operated more harshly in relation to husbands than wives, was pursuing a legitimate aim, that is the protection of the labour market. It also held, however, that it was not reasonable to pursue this aim by means of such a sexually discriminatory policy. In reaching this conclusion the Court pointed out that (para. 78):

> the advancement of the equality of the sexes is . . . a major goal in the member States of the Coucil of Europe. This means that very weighty reasons would have to be advanced before a difference of treatment on the ground of sex could be regarded as compatible with the Convention.

The avoidance of sex discrimination is thus given a particularly high status, and the margin of appreciation allowed to States to formulate laws appropriate to local circumstances is likely to be much narrower in relation to this than to other types of discrimination. As Bailey, Harris and Jones comment (*Civil Liberties Cases and Materials*, 3rd edn, London: Butterworths, 1991, p. 840), it is surprising that freedom from racial discrimination has not been given a similar status. This is particularly so given that in the *East African Asians* cases (1981) 3 EHRR 76 the Commission held that racially discriminatory immigration procedures could amount to degrading treatment contrary to Art. 3 of the ECHR (for which, in a different context, see 1.5.4). These cases were not referred to the Court, and by the time they were considered by the Committee of Ministers, all the applicants had been admitted to the United Kingdom, so that there was no final ruling on this issue.

In conclusion, Art. 14 has the potential to provide a remedy in two situations where none is available under English law. First, it may do so as regards racial or sexual discrimination which is authorised by statute or statutory instrument, and therefore not susceptible to challenge under the RRA (by virtue of s. 41), or SDA (by virtue of s. 51; though in employment cases EC law may, as we have seen, provide a means of challenge). Secondly, Art. 14 may be of use as regards discrimination on grounds other than race or sex, where English law provides no remedy. Provided that the discriminatory act relates to one of the rights protected under the ECHR, and it may reasonably be argued that the discrimination does not reasonably protect some legitimate aim, then there seems no reason why a challenge should not be made. If, for example, a person has been discriminated against in an employment context on the basis of religion, it would be possible to claim under the ECHR that the United Kingdom government is in breach of its obligation under Art. 1 to provide a remedy for illegitimate discrimination falling within Art. 14, in relation to a right recognised by Art. 9 (freedom of religion) (cf *Hoffmann* v *Austria* (Case No. 15/1992/360/434), where the Court held that the refusal of parental rights on religious grounds, the mother being a Jehovah's Witness, constituted a violation of Art. 8, taken in conjunction with Art. 14).

TWELVE

A Bill of Rights?

12.1 INTRODUCTION — THE ISSUES

We are now in a position, in the light of the material dealt with in chapters 1 to 11, to consider the issue of the possible introduction of a British 'Bill of Rights', giving a constitutional guarantee to certain freedoms. The issues which need to be considered under this heading are, first, whether there is a need for such a Bill at all (see 12.2). Secondly, if the answer to the first question is yes, there is the question of how it should fit in with our existing constitution. What should the relationship be between the powers of parliament and the courts, and the Bill itself (12.3.1)? Who would have the power to amend the Bill? Related to this are the problems of enforcement and adjudication. Would there need to be new organisations or tribunals to deal with issues arising out of alleged infringements of the Bill, or would existing structures be adequate (see 12.3.2)? The answer to this question may well depend on the precise role that the Bill is supposed to play in the protection of civil liberties. Finally, what should the content of the Bill be? Who should decide which rights should be included, and how should it be drafted? Would the European Convention on Human Rights ('ECHR') be the best model, or not (see 12.4)?

These issues are complex, and to some extent interrelated. It is necessary, however, to try to divide them for the purposes of exposition and ease of discussion. The rest of this chapter is devoted to considering them each in turn. The final section (12.5) will attempt to draw the threads together, and reach some conclusions. We start, however, with the central issue, on which all else depends, that of whether we need a Bill of Rights at all.

12.2 DO WE NEED A BILL OF RIGHTS?

A useful starting point on this issue is the conclusion which Professor Zander reached in his survey of the issues relating to the possible introduction of a British Bill of Rights (M. Zander, *A Bill of Rights*, 3rd edn, London: Sweet & Maxwell, 1985, p. 90):

In my view a Bill of Rights is desirable not because human rights are grossly abused in Britain, nor to provide against the danger of future tyranny. The former is untrue: the latter unlikely. The case for a Bill of Rights rests rather on the belief that it would make a distinct and valuable contribution to the *better* protection of human rights.

The implication of this eminently sensible conclusion is that the present means of protection of civil liberties in Britain are in some way inadequate, or, at least, capable of being improved. It was argued in chapter 1 that neither Parliament, nor the courts as they presently operate, are effective guardians of our liberties. parliament is too easily led by an executive which commands a large majority, or by 'moral panics' which preclude rational discussion of civil liberties' issues (see 1.4.1). The courts, though prepared to take civil liberties into account in appropriate circumstances, have not evolved any clear jurisprudence as to the way in which this should be done, and in any case, cannot act in contravention of the clear and unambiguous directions of parliamentary legislation, even where this involves significant limitations on individual freedom (see 1.4.2). This suggests that there is room for improvement, which might be provided by a Bill of Rights.

It might well be objected at this point that the ECHR already fulfils the role that a Bill of Rights might play. It is undoubtedly true that the existence of the ECHR, and the fact or threat of cases being brought against the United Kingdom, has led to improvements in liberties. The abolition of corporal punishment in schools (see 1.5.4), the reform of the law of contempt (6.4), and the placing of the law relating to interception of communications by the police or security services on a statutory basis (10.4.2), can all be said to derive from the influence of the ECHR. There are significant limitations to it, however. First there is the question of time. The combination of the 'exhaustion of local remedies' rule (see 1.5.2.1), and the inherent slowness in its procedures, means that it takes a long time before an issue is ruled on by the Court. A period of five to six years may well have elapsed after the event which involved the alleged infringement before the final decision is given. There may then need to be a delay while the government finds time to enact amending legislation. The *Sunday Times* 'thalidomide' case, for example (see 6.4), was initially decided by the High Court in 1972, and the House of Lords in 1973. The European Court of Human Rights gave its ruling in 1979, and parliament enacted the Contempt of Court Act in 1981. Thus nearly ten years had elapsed between the events giving rise to the action, and the enactment of an appropriate amendment to the law. This speed of progress does not lend itself to the dynamic development of protection for civil liberties.

A further problem with the ECHR is that, because it relies on individual complaints, but is at the same time concerned with the activities of governments, it does not fulfil very satisfactorily either of the roles which a Bill of Rights might be expected to play. First, because of the delays, and the rather unpredictable way in which compensation may be awarded (see 1.5.2), the ECHR does not provide a satisfactory mechanism for compensating the individual whose civil liberties have been infringed. Secondly, because it is dependent on individual claims, and only decides the issue raised by the case before it, the ECHR does not operate as a satisfactory means of reviewing a general area of activity, and measuring it against the standards set by the Convention. A clear example of the problems which this can raise is shown by the corporal punishment case of *Y* v *UK* (1992) (Series A no. 247-A) (see 1.5.4). The Commission were clearly of the view that this was a good case for testing the limits of permissible corporal punishment, but were unable to bring it before the Court, because the applicant decided to accept a settlement. This meant that only the much weaker *Costello-Roberts* case (1.5.4), was considered, in which it was found that the punishment did not to reach the minimum level necessary for degrading treatment. It would have been far more satisfactory in terms of dealing with the issues, and indicating what reforms, if any, were necessary in English law, if the Commission had been able to bring certain example cases before the Court, and obtained a ruling as to which involved, or did not involve a breach of the Convention.

Finally, the ECHR has limitations in terms of its content. The rights contained in it are virtually all 'political', and represent a consensus view among a fairly disparate group of States. It may therefore be regarded as representing the 'lowest common denominator' in some areas, rather than setting a standard to which we should wish to aspire. As a result, it does not necessarily include all the rights which might be thought appropriate for inclusion in a British Bill of Rights. For example, it is probable that we should wish to include a much wider ranging (in terms of the activities covered) discrimination provision than is to be found in Art. 14 (see 11.5.2). Moreover, it may be that we would not wish to include all the qualifications which exist in relation to many of the rights which are included. The issue of the content of a Bill of Rights is discussed further at 12.4.

For all these reasons it is possible to argue that the individual application procedure under the ECHR does not provide a satisfactory substitute for a domestic Bill of Rights.

Finally, in considering whether a Bill of Rights is needed, it may be instructive to consider the position as regards trends in the protection or restriction of civil liberties over the past 10–15 years. This is an issue which was examined fully by Ewing and Gearty in 1990 (K. D. Ewing, and C. A. Gearty, *Freedom under Thatcher*, Oxford: Clarendon Press, 1990). Their conclusion was that 'civil liberties in Britain are in a state of crisis' (p. 255). They saw legislation such as the Police and Criminal Evidence Act 1984, the Interception of Communications Act 1985, the Public Order Act 1986, and the Official Secrets Act 1989, as all being balanced in favour of the State and restriction, as against the individual and freedom. It is certainly true that, going back to 1978, it is hard to find any legislation which is unequivocally civil libertarian in its approach, that is, which left people with significantly more freedom than before it was passed. There is nothing, for example, to match the extended freedom of expression given in 1959 by the Obscene Publications Act, or in 1968 by the Theatres Act. The Contempt of Court Act 1981, and the Official Secrets Act 1989, might be argued to have had such an effect, but, as has been seen in chapters 5 and 6, the increased freedom has been marginal, and has been balanced by increased restriction in some areas. In terms of personal freedom, the extended police powers given by PACE have been shown to be inadequately balanced by the recording and notification procedures. Section 78 has allowed the courts to operate some check on police malpractice (see 3.6.3.3), but only in a limited area. The police powers to obtain information and property have increased significantly. In those areas where individual rights may have increased, for example, in relation to sexual discrimination, this may well be said to be mainly due to an external influence, that is EC law.

Overall, although it may be that the picture is not quite so bleak as that painted by Ewing and Gearty, there is no doubt that there is room for improvement. It may well be that the enactment of a Bill of Rights could prove a spur to a change of direction, or at least put a brake on the increasing restrictions.

If, then, the conclusion is that a Bill of Rights has some role to play in improving the protection of civil liberties, why has one not been put in place? This brings us to a consideration of the problems that such a development would involve.

12.3   THE PROBLEMS

The problems surrounding the introduction of a Bill of Rights are both constitutional, and practical, though there are some links between them. We shall consider the constitutional problems first.

12.3.1   Constitutional problems

The constitutional problems connected with a Bill of Rights involve the interconnected issues of parliamentary sovereignty, entrenchment, and implied repeal. British constitutional law has as one of its fundamental principles the rule that parliament can do what it likes. As classically stated by Dicey (A. V. Dicey, *An Introduction to the Study of the Law of the Constitution*, 10th edn, London: Macmillan & Co., 1965, pp. 39–40):

> The principle of parliamentary sovereignty means neither more nor less than this, namely, that parliament [defined as the 'Queen in parliament'] has, under the English constitution, the right to make or unmake any law whatever; and, further, that no person or body is recognised by the law of England as having a right to override or set aside the legislation of parliament.

There are, in theory, no restrictions on what parliament can enact, and the courts will give effect to any legislation that is properly passed, without regard to its content. This raises a problem for the proponents of a Bill of Rights. If such a Bill were to be enacted simply as an ordinary Act of Parliament, there would be nothing, under the Diceyan view, to stop parliament in the future from enacting legislation which conflicted with the Bill, and the courts would be obliged to give effect to such legislation. This would significantly reduce, if not destroy altogether, the function of a Bill of Rights as a *guarantee* of the freedoms contained in it. Thus, if freedom of expression were one of the freedoms recognised, there would still be nothing to stop parliament enacting a restrictive piece of legislation such as the Video Recordings Act 1984 (see 7.5.2). Is it not possible somehow to 'entrench' the Bill, so that later legislation would not have this effect?

One answer which might be proposed is that the legislation enacting the Bill should indicate that subsequent legislation must be interpreted as complying with the Bill, at least unless parliament specifically indicates otherwise (see, for an example of this approach, s. 33(1) of the Canadian Charter of Rights and Freedoms). This would retain parliamentary sovereignty, but require it to be exercised deliberately in certain fields. Alternatively, the Bill could state that no derogation from its provisions would be possible without a specific majority of both Houses of Parliament (see, for example, *Harris* v *Minister of the Interior* [1952] 1 TLR 1245). The difficulty with both these approaches is the so-called doctrine of 'implied repeal', most clearly stated by Maugham LJ in *Ellen Street Estates Ltd* v *Minister of Health* [1934] 1 KB 590, at p. 597:

> The Legislature cannot, according to our constitution, bind itself as to the form of subsequent legislation, and it is impossible for Parliament to enact that in a subsequent statute dealing with the same subject-matter there can be no implied repeal.

This approach requires that if two Acts of Parliament are in conflict, the courts should treat the latter as having impliedly repealed the former. Thus, whatever procedural or substantive requirements were included in a Bill of Rights contained in an ordinary Act of Parliament, they would not be able to withstand expressly or impliedly contradictory provisions in any subsequent legislation. If this view of parliamentary sovereignty stands, then some other answer will have to be found to giving a Bill of Rights the special status it needs to have any significant effect.

The most radical solution would be to decide that the whole British Constitution requires revision and re-statement. A new constitutional document could be produced setting out the powers of the executive, the courts, and the legislature. In that context it might be possible to include a Bill of Rights as part of the new constitution, and thus to give it a status distinct from an ordinary piece of legislation. The difficulty with such an approach would be finding the political will and consensus to embark on such an enterprise. New constitutions are usually the result of conquest, revolution, achieving independence, or, at least, severe internal political pressure for change. None of these seems likely to be relevant in the United Kingdom in the foreseeable future. The new constitution, while probably the most satisfactory solution to the problem of entrenching a Bill of Rights, does not seem a very realistic possibility.

An alternative is to question the solidity of the doctrine of parliamentary sovereignty. It may be argued that a crack has appeared deriving from the United Kingdom's membership of the European Community. As far as international law is concerned it is clear that the British government, as a result of our membership of the Community, is obliged to bring English law in line with the requirements of Community law. The British government accepts the jurisdiction of the European Court of Justice to give definitive rulings on European law. At the domestic level, s. 2(1) of the European Communities Act 1972 acknowledged the direct effect of Community law, without the need for enactment by parliament (see, for example, 11.5.1). The English courts likewise have accepted this, and regularly refer questions of law to the European Court of Justice, accepting as binding the rulings of that Court. The final question arises as to what the courts should do if the United Kingdom parliament enacts legislation that is in conflict with European law. The doctrine of parliamentary sovereignty and implied repeal would suggest that the British Act of parliament should take precedence over the requirements of European law. In *R v Secretary of State for Transport, ex parte Factortame Ltd* (No 2) [1991] 1 AC 603, however, the House of Lords accepted a ruling from the European Court of Justice that it could provide interim relief restraining the Secretary of State for Transport from withholding or withdrawing registration of fishing vessels under regulations made under the Merchant Shipping Act 1988, pending consideration of the validity of that legislation by the European Court. In effect, therefore, European law was being regarded as overriding the provisions of duly enacted legislation. In this area, at least, then, the doctrine of parliamentary sovereignty has been severely weakened. Of course parliament could change the position by repealing the European Communities Act 1972, and withdrawing from the Community, but while the United Kingdom remains a member, it seems that the English courts will give effect to European law, even where this is in conflict with subsequent enactments of the United Kingdom parliament. Since this breach has been made in the edifice, it is not impossible that other breaches could follow, including the recognition of a Bill of Rights as superior to other legislation. For the courts to accept this, however, it would probably be necessary for the enactment of the Bill to be the result of a broadly based political consensus (so that the courts could not be accused of being partisan), and for the Bill to be specifically stated to have a special status within the constitution.

The constitutional obstacles to an effective Bill of Rights are therefore serious, but not insuperable.

12.3.2 Practical problems

Once it is established that it may be possible to enact a Bill of Rights which will override other laws, some practical problems arise, in relation to enforcement and adjudication.

Consideration of methods of enforcement raises a number of questions. What remedies should be available under a Bill of Rights? Should it be treated as simply giving rise to a civil right of action, in the form of a kind of statutory tort, with remedies in the form of damages or injunctions? Should the model be that of judicial review, empowering the court to issue orders and declarations? Should a right of action be available against private individuals or organisations, or only against organs of the State? Should there be a power to scrutinise legislation prior to its enactment for compliance with the Bill? In any of the above situations, who should have status to bring an action? Should it be limited to an individual who has suffered loss? Should organisations be able to challenge legislation on the basis of potential infringement? Would there be a role for a 'Rights Commission', as under the existing discrimination legislation (see 11.4.2)?

The answers to be given to these questions will depend on the exact role that is envisaged for the Bill of Rights. It has been argued at 12.2 that one of the deficiencies of the ECHR is that it does not operate satisfactorily either in providing remedies for individuals, or in scrutinising more generally the protection of rights. From this it may be inferred that these are the two roles which will be regarded here as being the function of a Bill of Rights. In other words, it should provide a mechanism whereby an individual whose freedom has been infringed can achieve compensation. It should, however, also provide a basis for a more general challenge to laws, or activities, which appear to be in conflict with the Bill, without the need to identify specific victims. If these are accepted as the appropriate objectives for a Bill of Rights, then the answer to the questions posed above should be as follows. Individuals whose rights under the Bill have been infringed should be able to obtain a full range of remedies (damages, injunctions, declarations) against whoever has caused the infringement. Thus the potential defendants should include other private individuals and organisations, as well as emanations of the State. The basis of the action would be civil, rather than criminal, since its objective would be compensation rather than punishment. As regards the more general supervision, the most efficient way to handle this, though it might be controversial politically, would be via an independent 'Commission for Rights and Liberties' ('CRL'), which might well also take over the functions of the existing Equal Opportunities Commission ('EOC'), and Commission for Racial Equality ('CRE') (see 11.4.2). Again, in the interests of efficiency, it would make sense to allow the CRL to scrutinise legislation *before* it has been enacted, and to seek a ruling as to whether, if enacted, it would infringe the Bill of Rights. If this could operate effectively it might greatly reduce the need for individual actions. Where these are brought, however, the CRL could have a role in assisting individual applicants, as do the EOC and the CRE (see 11.4.2.1).

The above discussion of enforcement contains the implicit assumption that cases would be brought before the ordinary courts, but this is not an uncontroversial issue. Some have argued that our existing judges are not appropriately trained, and do not have the right background, to deal with the broad political or quasi-political, issues which would inevitably arise in attempting to construe and apply a generally worded Bill of Rights. English judges are used to dealing with narrowly specific issues raised by particular cases, applying or distinguishing precedents, or interpreting closely worded statutes. Furthermore, there is another school of thought, represented most powerfully by Professor J. A. G. Griffith in *The Politics of the Judiciary* (4th edn, London: Fontana Press, 1991), which argues that judges in the United Kingdom when required, as they inevitably are, to make political choices, do

so in a way which is, as a result of their backgrounds, and the position they hold
in society, 'necessarily conservative and illiberal' (p. 319). Judges are part of
the establishment, and will therefore tend to support the established order,
which in many cases will mean supporting the government. For this reason
Professor Griffith expresses the hope (in the *Preface* to the 4th edition) that:

> the liberals will not succeed in persuading political leaders that, by enacting
> a Bill of Rights, judges should have even greater scope for their political
> adventures.

It is no doubt true that, looking back on the earlier chapters of this book, it is
difficult to find examples of judges taking a clear stand in favour of individual
freedom, and against the government. Nevertheless there are occasions where
a judge will speak out strongly against unnecessary restriction. A good
example is Lord Bridge's dissenting speech in the House of Lords' hearing in
relation to the interlocutory injunctions in the *Spycatcher* case (see 5.6.2)
(*Attorney-General* v *Guardian Newspapers* [1987] 3 All ER 316 at p. 346):

> Freedom of speech is always the first casualty under a totalitarian regime.
> Such a regime cannot afford to allow the free circulation of information and
> ideas among its citizens. Censorship is the indispensable tool to regulate
> what the public may and what they may not know. The present attempt to
> insulate the public in this country from information which is freely available
> elsewhere is a significant step down that very dangerous road . . . If the
> government are determined to fight to maintain the ban to the end, they will
> face inevitable condemnation and humiliation by the European Court of
> Human Rights in Strasbourg. Long before that they will have been
> condemned at the bar of public opinion in the free world.

This is strong stuff, but Lord Bridge was, of course, in the minority (and so
disillusioned with his fellow judges that he was moved to think seriously about
the advantages of incorporating the ECHR into English law). Looked at
overall, the *Spycatcher* litigation supports Professor Griffith's thesis, since in
this case the judges were not constrained by statute, but were nevertheless
prepared to interpret and develop the common law in a way which helped the
government and restricted freedom of expression.

If then there are doubts about the judges' approach to the interpretation of
a Bill of Rights, what is the alternative? One option, of course, is to follow
Professor Griffith, and say that because the judges cannot be trusted it would
be better not to have a Bill of Rights at all. If, however, it is felt that there is a
genuine need for a Bill, for the reasons outlined earlier in this chapter, is there
any alternative to using the courts as a means of enforcement? One possibility
would be to set up a separate system, outside the normal court structure, for
dealing with issues arising under a Bill of Rights. There could be a special
Rights Tribunal, to which relevant issues could be referred. It could be staffed
by people other than lawyers, and could even be an elected body. There would
be difficult decisions to be taken as to what precisely the membership should

be, and how it should be selected. Would it be right to have a membership that was drawn from people active in dealing with 'rights' issues; should it be the 'great and good' (though ignoring any lawyers falling into that category); or should it attempt to be representative of the population as a whole? All of these possibilities give rise to difficulties. None of them can escape the fact that the enforcement of, and adjudication on, issues arising out of a Bill of Rights will be a political process, and will therefore be affected by the political perspective of those charged with these tasks. Moreover, once the Rights Tribunal has given a ruling on an issue, what happens then? Suppose, for example, that the Tribunal rules that a power of arrest given to the police offends against a provision in the Bill of Rights guaranteeing freedom from arbitrary detention. If the person has been charged with, for example, the offence of obstructing a police officer, that will have to be dealt with, presumably, by the ordinary criminal courts. It will be necessary, therefore, for the civil and criminal courts to be prepared to accept rulings from the Tribunal as giving binding interpretations of the scope of the Bill of Rights. Would they be prepared to do this, given the general reluctance of the courts to abdicate responsibility for determining issues of law? There is clearly a possibility that a conflict could result between the Tribunal and the House of Lords, which would only be likely to be resolved by a thorough restructuring of the constitution, to make it clear where the relevant power lies.

For these reasons, it is hard to view the creation of a separate Rights Tribunal as operating satisfactorily or efficiently as the enforcement and adjudication agency under a Bill of Rights. It is suggested, therefore, that there are only two realistic options. One is to abandon the idea of a domestic Bill of Rights, and leave it to the ECHR, with all its deficiencies, to continue to operate as a 'long-stop' protection at the international level. The second is to introduce a Bill of Rights, and to trust the judges. That is to leave the adjudication of Bill of Rights' issues within the jurisdiction of the ordinary courts, in the hope that British judges may be inclined to adopt a different approach to its interpretation than that which they normally use in dealing with other areas of law. Some encouragement towards the view that such a change of attitude may be possible may be drawn from the experience in Canada.

From 1960 to 1982 Canada had a Bill of Rights which was widely regarded as being ineffective. It was contained in an ordinary Act of Parliament, and was not regarded by the courts as having any special status. In 1982, however, as part of a new constitution, the Canadian Charter of Rights and Freedoms was introduced. To many people's surprise, the approach of the Canadian Supreme Court to this document was significantly different, as was shown by one of the first cases to be decided under it, *Hunter* v *Southam* (1984) 11 DLR (4th) 641. The Court was here concerned with a power of entry to premises given by s. 10 of the Combines Investigation Act, RSC 1970, c. C–23. The relevant provision of the Charter was s. 8, which states that 'Everyone has a right to be secure against unreasonable search or seizure'. The issue before the Court was, therefore, whether the search power was 'reasonable'. A possible approach to this issue would have been to hold that if a power was part of formally unimpeachable legislation, it could not be regarded as unreasonable. This would have been in line with the common law approach in *Entick* v *Carrington* (1765) 19 State Tr 1029; 95 ER 807 (see 4.2.5). Dickson J, however, took the view that the interpretation of the Charter required a 'purposive' approach. In other words, it was necessary to investigate the purpose underlying s. 8 to determine what interests it protects, and thus what searches are 'unreasonable'. On this basis it was held that s. 8 was intended to protect a reasonable expectation of privacy. This meant that an assessment as to whether a search of private premises is necessary should made by an *impartial arbiter*, on the basis of reasonable grounds for suspicion that relevant evidence *will* (as opposed to 'may') be found. On both these points s. 10 of the legislation was defective, and was therefore struck down.

This much broader-based approach to the interpretation of the Charter is perhaps an encouraging sign for proponents of a Bill of Rights for the United Kingdom. If the Canadian courts which, prior to 1982, were regarded as having much the same traditions and attitudes to statutory interpretation as the English courts, have been able to adapt, and take a different view of the Charter, why should English judges not be capable of a similar change? Moreover, as was pointed out in chapter 1, some judges have already shown a preparedness to take on board the requirements of the ECHR in interpreting English law (see 1.4.2.1). This in itself may be taken as an encouraging sign.

Even if it is decided, however, to 'trust the judges', this does not necessarily answer all issues related to adjudication. Questions may also be raised as to whether issues involving the Bill of Rights should be determinable by all courts, or, for example, only by the House of Lords. The problem with allowing jurisdiction to all courts is that it may well mean that the issue of the interpretation of the Bill in a particular case has to be dealt with as a preliminary issue through the whole appeal process, which will add considerably to the length of litigation. An alternative would be to adopt the referral procedure which operates under Art. 177 of the Treaty of Rome in relation to issues of EC law, whereby any court can refer a point direct to the European Court of Justice for a legal ruling, prior to dealing with the merits of the case. It is suggested that it might be desirable to have a system whereby any English court which decides that there is an issue before it which involves an interpretation or application of the Bill of Rights, should have the power to refer the issue direct to the House of Lords. Once the House had ruled on this point, the court which referred the issue would resume jurisdiction, and decide the case in the light of the ruling. The only danger with this is that it might, particularly in the early years, produce a flood of referrals, and therefore an overburdening of the House of Lords. If that was thought likely to be the case, the best solution might be to say that it is only on appeal to the House of Lords that Bill of Rights issues can be raised. This would reduce the number of cases, but might be thought unduly restrictive, in that only those litigants who had the time and money to take the case all the way would have any chance of having the Bill of Rights issue raised. This would not matter so much if the suggestion raised earlier of a Commission for Rights and Liberties, with *locus standi* to raise issues directly before the courts, was adopted.

These issues of the detail of enforcement and adjudication are, of course, subsidiary to the more general question of whether we want a Bill of Rights in the first place. They are, however, important, in that the decisions taken in relation to them may determine whether the Bill does in fact achieve the objectives to which it is directed.

12.4   THE CONTENTS OF A BILL OF RIGHTS

What rights and freedoms should be included within a Bill of Rights for Britain? Much care needs to be taken over this issue, not least because the expectation will be that the Bill will be difficult to amend, and that therefore, the rights which it contains should be ones which it is reasonably certain will still be thought worthy of protection in 10, 20, 50 years time. The United States Bill of Rights contains a reminder of the need to take care, in that the right to bear arms contained in the Second Amendment is one that many would now prefer not to have been included. It was an understandable provision at the time when it was drafted, but one that has in recent years proved a frustrating obstacle to effective gun control.

In trying to decide what rights to include, it is difficult, once one has enumerated such basic rights as the right to life, or the right to a fair trial, to avoid the fact that the decision as to what include or exclude is very much a political one. Even in relation to the right to life, there may be problems over the wording because of the opposing views of the pro and anti-abortion lobbies. An inclusion of a 'right to life' which was clearly drafted to include or exclude the human foetus would inevitably raise considerable political controversy.

There are a number of possible responses to this type of difficulty. One would be to try to narrow the scope of the Bill to those areas where there could be said to be a widespread consensus as to the rights which should receive constitutional protection. Such an approach runs the risk of producing a document which is bland and ineffective. As indicated at the beginning of this chapter, the reason for seeking a Bill of Rights is not primarily to protect us from tyranny, but to try to *improve* the current situation. A Bill which is little more than the equivalent of a political speech in favour of motherhood is unlikely to have any such dynamic effect.

Another way of tackling the issue would be to give the job of drafting the Bill to a specially constituted working group, with a membership drawn from all shades of the political spectrum. Such a body might be able to produce a Bill which was widely supported, without being totally ineffective. There is no guarantee that such would be the result, however, and it is just as possible that the group would either end in deadlock, or produce a document just as bland as the procedure suggested in the previous paragraph.

A third possibility, and one which many have favoured, is to look for a 'ready-made' Bill from elsewhere, which could be incorporated into English law. The principal candidate for this has been the ECHR. The reasons for this are obvious. The ECHR has been accepted for 30 years as setting an appropriate standard for United Kingdom laws, and is well recognised as providing a route by which alleged infringements of civil liberties can be challenged. Some of the difficulties with the ECHR in terms of content have been indicated at 12.2, however. In particular, the qualifications allowed in relation to many of the rights seem unnecessarily wide. Straightforward incorporation of the ECHR is thus less than satisfactory. What might be preferable, is to accept the general headings contained in Arts 1 to 14 as delimiting the scope of the Bill, but re-drafting the rights as stated in a way more appropriate for the needs of the United Kingdom in the twentyfirst century. Article 14, for example, could be amended to provide a more general protection against discrimination, as opposed to relating it solely to non-discrimination in relation to the other rights contained in the Convention (see 11.5.2). This process, if adopted, would require a decision as to whether to include any limitations on the rights, or to state them all as absolute. The experience in the United States is that the absolute statement protecting freedom of speech in the First Amendment has been found unacceptable by most members of the Supreme Court (with some notable exceptions; see for example the judgment of Black J in *Miller* v *California* (1973) 413 US 15, 37 L Ed 2d 419). The Court has therefore had to find ways of interpreting the Amendment so as to exclude from its scope speech which is thought not to be worthy of protection (for example, some types of pornography). This suggests that it may well be better to follow the model of the ECHR, and allow qualifications to be stated in the Bill itself, but to be careful that these do not go further than is regarded as absolutely necessary for the avoidance of harm to others, or, perhaps, to the State itself (for example, in the area of national security).

Whatever approach is taken to the issue of determining the content of a Bill of Rights, it seems clear that it is unlikely to be possible to extend the scope of the Bill beyond 'political rights' (see 1.3.2). There is no political consensus at the moment as to the value to be placed on social and economic rights. The Conservative government's hostility to the Social Chapter of the Maastricht treaty, and its general resistance to pressures from Europe in the field of social legislation, makes it extremely unlikely that it would be prepared to accept a Bill of Rights which entrenched obligations in this field. The best that can realistically be hoped for is therefore a somewhat strengthened version of the ECHR.

12.5 CONCLUSIONS

This section will serve as a conclusion not only to the Bill of Rights issue, but to the book as a whole.

Looking first at the Bill of Rights, however, it is clear that there are considerable hurdles to be overcome if such a document is to become part of the British Constitution. Not only are there important issues relating to the constitutional status of a Bill, and how the courts would react to it, but also many practical problems concerning its operation and enforcement, to many of which there is no easy or obvious answer. Such difficulties are only likely to be overcome where there is a clear political consensus in favour of the general principle which will provide the impetus to solve the practical difficulties. Unfortunately it cannot be said that that is the position at the moment. The Conservative Party has gone down the route of setting standards for the operation of government departments and public services which are not enforceable at law: in other words the 'Citizens' Charter'. It has rejected the introduction of a Bill of Rights. The Labour Party accepts the need for improvement in civil liberties, but currently proposes to achieve this through the enactment of specific statutes dealing with particular areas, rather than through an entrenched Bill of Rights. Of the mainstream parties, only the Liberal Democrats currently favour a Bill of Rights.

In this context it seems unlikely that the political will to introduce a Bill of Rights will be found in the near future. The most likely scenario might be a hung parliament following a general election, where the Liberal Democrats made the introduction of a Bill of Rights a condition of coalition or cooperation. In that situation, a Bill involving the incorporation or adaptation of the ECHR would probably be the result, but, as has been shown above, this would still leave a number of questions as to the operation of the Bill in practice to be resolved. This is in many ways a disappointing conclusion for those who see considerable advantages for the protection of civil liberties in the introduction of a Bill of Rights, but it is the only realistic one that can be drawn at the present.

Turning to the broader issues of the protection of civil liberties, what conclusions may be drawn from the areas surveyed in this book? As pointed out at the beginning of chapter 1, the focus has been on the legal rules. Inevitably, the concentration is on rules which restrict freedom since, in the absence of a Bill of Rights, that is the role which the law primarily plays. Moreover, as was pointed out earlier in this chapter at 12.2, it cannot be denied that the current trends are towards greater restriction of individual freedom. There are significant areas of concern in relation to police powers to stop and search, to detain and question, and to gain access to property or information. It is not clear that the balance between the need to control crime, and the claims of personal freedom has been struck correctly. Freedom of speech is the subject of controls which may well be regarded as excessive in relation to the disclosure of government information, and the censorship of films and videos. The freedom to engage in public protest operates within a framework which is the subject of close supervision by the police, and may be the subject of somewhat haphazard control as a result of the ill-defined common law power to control breaches of the peace. Extradition has become more difficult to challenge, and deportation and exclusion orders operate with unsatisfactory appeal procedures. The right to privacy receives no proper recognition.

There are, however, a few positive areas. Freedom from discrimination in the areas of race and sex is fully recognised by the law, and the position in relation to this, while by no means perfect, does provide significant protection for individual rights. There are a number of positive aspects to the contempt law, though the 1981 Act has not proved to be quite the liberalising measure that might have been hoped for. Perhaps most importantly, political speech, in the sense of the freedom to criticise the government, and to put forward controversial or unpopular ideas, is the subject of very little control, provided that the language does not become 'threatening, abusive or insulting'.

On balance, however, the verdict must be that there is substantial room for improvement. This is not to say that we do not live in a free society; that would be to overstate the case. We live, however, in a society which is less free than it could be (without threatening its stability), and where the current trend is for existing freedoms to be further restricted. It is important for those who study the law to be aware of this and to be prepared to argue against any further encroachment on our liberties. For it is through the law, rather than through tyranny, that our freedom is restricted, just as it is through the law, rather than political action, that our rights can be best protected. Those who study and work with the law have a responsibility to try to ensure that the balance is properly kept between such restriction and protection.

Index